Google Anthos in Action

Google Anthos
in Action

MANAGE HYBRID AND
MULTICLOUD KUBERNETES CLUSTERS

ANTONIO GULLI
MICHAEL MADISON
SCOTT SUROVICH

MANNING
SHELTER ISLAND

For online information and ordering of this and other Manning books, please visit
www.manning.com. The publisher offers discounts on this book when ordered in quantity.
For more information, please contact

Special Sales Department
Manning Publications Co.
20 Baldwin Road
PO Box 761
Shelter Island, NY 11964
Email: orders@manning.com

 Manning Publications Co.   Development editor: Doug Rudder
20 Baldwin Road   Review editor: Adriana Sabo
PO Box 761   Production editor: Andy Marinkovich
Shelter Island, NY 11964   Copy editor: Pamela Hunt
                                    Proofreader: Katie Tennant
                          Technical proofreader: Paul Jones
                                     Typesetter: Dennis Dalinnik
                                 Cover designer: Marija Tudor

ISBN: 9781633439573
Printed in the United States of America

brief contents

contents

The following bonus appendixes are available in the ePub and Kindle versions of this book, and you can read them online in liveBook:

preface

The idea to write *Google Anthos in Action* came after discussions with hundreds of customers interested in managing applications anywhere, delivering software faster, and protecting applications and the software supply chain. Customers wanted to better understand how Anthos can help them manage their application deployments in traditional on-prem setups, at the edge, and in cloud native and multicloud environments. They were interested in achieving the benefits of containers, serverless, infrastructure as code, and service meshes to improve productivity and velocity. They wanted to understand how to guarantee and increase security in each stage of the application life cycle with automatization and transparent policy management.

Google Anthos in Action brings together the collective expertise of Googlers passionate about Kubernetes, serverless, and Anthos, as well as Google Cloud Certified Fellows, an elite group of cloud architects and technical leaders who are experts in designing enterprise solutions.

acknowledgments

Google Anthos in Action would not be possible without the work of countless fellow travelers (https://en.wikipedia.org/wiki/Fellow_traveller).

The lead authors would like to thank the other authors for their contributions; in alphabetical order, we thank Ameer Abbas, Amita Kapoor, Aparna Sinha, Eric Brewer, Giovanni Galloro, Jarosław Gajewski, Jason Quek, Kaslin Fields, Konrad Cłapa, Kyle Bassett, Melika Golkaram, Onofrio Petragallo, Patricia Florissi, and Phil Taylor. Some of the authors were selected for the book's preview edition published at Google Cloud Next in 2021. In this full-edition publication, all of the authors are included in the 17 chapters in this book and the six additional chapters available in the eBook and online in liveBook.

The authors would like to thank all of the reviewers for their thoughtful input, discussion, and review. In alphabetical order, we thank Ady Degany, Alex Mattson, Alon Pildus, Amina Mansur, Amr Abdelrazik, Anil Dhawan, Ankur Jain, Anna Beremberg, Antoine Larmanjat, Ashwin Perti, Barbara Stanley, Ben Good, Bhagvan Kommadi, Brian Grant, Brian Kaufman, Chen Goldberg, Christoph Bussler, Clifford Thurber, Conor Redmond, Eric Johnson, Fabrizio Pezzella, Gabriele Di Piazza, Ganesh Swaminathan, Gil Fidel, Glen Yu, Guy Ndjeng, Harish Yakumar, Haroon Chaudhry, Hugo Figueiredo, Issy Ben-Shaul, Jamie Duncan, Jason Polites, Jeff Reed, Jeffrey Chu, Jennifer Lin, Jerome Simms, John Abel, Jonathan Donaldson, Jose San Leandro, Kamesh Ganesan, Karthikeyarajan Rajendran, Kavitha Radhakrishnan, Kevin Shatzkamer, Krzysztof Kamyczek, Laura Cellerini, Leonid Vasetsky, Louis Ryan, Luke Kupka, Maluin Patel, Manu Batra, Marco Ferrari, Marcus Johansonn, Massimo Mascaro, Maulin

Patel, Micah Baker, Michael Abd-El-Malek, Michael Bright, Michelle Au, Miguel de Luna, Mike Columbus, Mike Ensor, Nima Badiey, Nina Kozinska, Norman Johnson, Purvi Desai, Quan To, Raghu Nandan, Raja Jadeja, Rambabu Posa, Rich Rose, Roman Zhuzha, Ron Avnur, Scott Penberthy, Simone Sguazza, Sri Thuraisamy, Stanley Anozie, Stephen Muss, Steren Giannini, Sudeep Batra, Tariq Islam, Tim Hockin, Tony Savor, Vanna Stano, Vinay Anand, Yoav Reich, Zach Casper, and Zach Seils.

This book would not have been possible without a massive collaboration among the authors, reviewers, editors, and marketing. We are particularly thankful to Arun Ananthampalayam, J. P. Schaengold, Maria Bledsoe, Richard Seroter, Eyal Manor, and Yash Kamath from Google; and Doug Rudder, Aleksandar Dragosavljević, and Gloria Lukos from Manning. Thanks for your continuous support and inspiration.

A special thanks goes to Will Grannis, founder and managing director of Google Cloud's Office of the CTO, for being a servant leader, always inspiring others. In addition, special gratitude goes to Eric Brewer, professor emeritus of computer science at the University of California, Berkeley, and vice president of infrastructure at Google. This book could not have been written without his support and encouragement.

All the authors' royalties will be donated to charities.

Authors

- **Ameer Abbas,** senior product manager at Google, focused on modern applications and platforms
- **Amita Kapoor,** former associate professor, University of Delhi, now founder of NePeur, passionate about using AI for good
- **Antonio Gulli,** director of engineering at Google, worked all his life on search and Cloud, proud father of three angels
- **Aparna Sinha,** senior director, product management and DevRel, built and led Kubernetes and developed PM teams, growing the P&L 100 times
- **Eric Brewer,** professor emeritus of computer science at the University of California, Berkeley, and vice president of infrastructure at Google
- **Giovanni Galloro**, customer engineer at Google focused on Kubernetes, cloud-native tooling, and developer productivity
- **Jarosław Gajewski,** global lead architect and Distinguished Expert in Atos, Google Cloud Certified Fellow, passionate about Cloud, Kubernetes, and the entire CNCF framework
- **Jason Quek,** global CTO Devoteam, G Cloud, started as a programmer, now building on Google Cloud, passionate about Kubernetes and Anthos
- **Kaslin Fields**, GKE and open source Kubernetes developer advocate at Google Cloud, CNCF ambassador
- **Konrad Cłapa,** Google Cloud Certified Fellow #5 and a lead Cloud architect responsible for the design of managed GCP offerings at Atos

- **Kyle Bassett,** cloud native community member and open source advocate, collaborated with Google product and engineering to lead the original design partnership for Anthos
- **Melika Golkaram (Googler),** solutions architect in Google Cloud, with a focus on Kubernetes, Anthos, and Google Distributed Edge Cloud
- **Michael Madison,** cloud architect at World Wide Technology, with a background in software development and IaC
- **Onofrio Petragallo (Googler),** customer engineer at Google Cloud, focused on data analytics and artificial intelligence
- **Patricia Florissi (Googler),** technical director, Office of the CTO, Google Cloud, worked the past 10 years on federated computations, a superset of federated analytics and federated learning
- **Phil Taylor,** CTO at CDW Digital Velocity, started coding at age 13, relentless entrepreneur with a track record of taking products to market using the public Cloud and Kubernetes
- **Scott Surovich,** global container engineering lead at HSBC Bank, Google Fellow, Kubernetes advocate, and coauthor of *Kubernetes: An Enterprise Guide*

about this book

Anthos (https://cloud.google.com/anthos) is a multicloud containerized product working on-prem, on multiple public cloud platforms, on private clouds, and at the edge. It is also a managed application platform that extends Google Cloud services and engineering practices to many environments so you can modernize apps faster and establish operational consistency across them.

Who should read this book?

Readers should have a general understanding of distributed application architecture and a baseline understanding of cloud technologies. They should also have a basic understanding of Kubernetes, including commonly used resources, how to create a manifest, and how to use the kubectl CLI.

This book is designed for anyone interested in furthering their knowledge of Anthos and Kubernetes. After reading this book, the reader will have an increased knowledge of Anthos in GCP and multicloud platforms.

How this book is organized: A road map

- *Chapter 1*—An introduction to how Anthos and modern applications benefit businesses in driving transformation in multiple industries and how cloud native microservices architecture provides the scalability and modularity that provide the foundation and competitive edge that businesses need in today's world.
- *Chapter 2*—Most organizations can manage a small number of clusters easily but often run into support issues as they scale out environments, making management

a difficult task. In this chapter, you will learn how Anthos provides a single-pane-of-glass view to Kubernetes clusters running different cloud providers and on-prem clusters.

- *Chapter 3*—Kubernetes is becoming "the data center API" and is the main component behind Anthos, providing the compute environment we need to power portable, cloud native applications and, in the right use cases, monolithic applications. This chapter teaches the components of Kubernetes and the differences between declarative and imperative deployment models and advanced scheduling concepts to keep your workloads available if certain portions of the infrastructure experience failures.

- *Chapter 4*—Anthos provides a fully supported version of Istio, an open source service mesh that provides several features for workloads both running in an Anthos cluster and on external servers, like virtual machines. Learn about the components of ASM and how each provides features in the mesh and how to secure traffic using mutual TLS, provide advanced release cycles like A/B or canary testing, and offer visibility into mesh traffic using the GCP console.

- *Chapter 5*—Dive deeper into managing clusters and workloads using the GCP console. Learn about the different logging and monitoring considerations, how to manage clusters and workloads using the CLI, and how to scale and design operations management in a hybrid environment.

- *Chapter 6*—Using your knowledge from the previous chapters, learn about the Anthos components that provide tools for developers to create applications, including the Cloud Code plugin for IntelliJ, Visual Studio Code, and Google's Cloud Shell, and to deploy applications using versioning and Cloud Build.

- *Chapter 7*—Anthos allows an organization to standardize on Kubernetes, providing a unified pattern to develop, deploy, scale, and secure portability and high availability. Workloads can be secured using workload identity, which provides enhanced security across multiple clusters in hybrid and multicloud environments. Learn how to route traffic to clusters with load balancers and use Google's Traffic Director to route traffic across multiple clusters, and see how VPC service controls are used to secure your clusters.

- *Chapter 8*—Learn more about Anthos on the edge from telco examples and how they implement 5G to enhance quality checks, self-driving cars, and inventory tracking.

- *Chapter 9*—Serverless removes the complexity of Kubernetes for developers. In this chapter, you will learn about Cloud Run, which is based on Knative, and how its components are used to address different use cases, including eventing, versioning, and traffic management.

- *Chapter 10*—Anthos networking features multiple layers and options. In this chapter, you will learn about cloud networking and hybrid connectivity, including dedicated interconnects, Cloud VPC, and using standard public internet connections. Dive into the Anthos networking options and see how you can connect clusters running Anthos, or any compliant Kubernetes version, from other cloud service providers and on-prem.

- *Chapter 11*—As an organization grows, the complexities of managing and scaling multiple clusters increase along with it. Anthos Config Management (ACM) provides security using gatekeeper policies, configuration management with standard tools like Git, and additional namespace controls using the hierarchical namespace controller.

- *Chapter 12*—Continuous integration and continuous delivery are two of the main components to becoming an agile organization. To achieve your CI/CD goals, you will learn how to use Skaffold, Cloud Code, Cloud Source Repositories, Artifact Registry, and more to make your organization truly agile.

- *Chapter 13*—Build on the foundation of Anthos Config Management to secure your clusters from malicious or accidental incidents. To understand how to secure a system, you need to understand how it can be compromised, and in this chapter, you will learn how a person can deploy an escalated Pod to take over a host or an entire cluster. Then, using ACM, learn how to secure various components from attacks or mistakes like vulnerable libraries in your image(s).

- *Chapter 14*—You can run millions of images and products on Anthos, and your organization may maintain its own releases of products. Google makes it easier for you to use a collection of workloads that are curated by Google or other industry leaders like NetApp, IBM, Red Hat, and Microsoft. In this chapter, you will learn about the Google Marketplace and how you can use it to easily create solutions for your users.

- *Chapter 15*—Convincing developers or businesses to move from heritage applications running on virtual services can be difficult and time consuming. They may not have the staff or subject matter experts to assist with the work and prefer the status quo. Anthos includes a utility to help with the process, from identifying workload candidates for migration up to the actual migration of these workloads from virtual machines to containers.

- *Chapter 16*—To move a workload from any heritage technology to containers, you need to learn the best methods and the benefits of moving to microservices. This chapter will teach you how to use Anthos to modernize your applications through real-world examples and the antipatterns to avoid.

- *Chapter 17*—It is becoming increasingly common for more advanced workloads to move to Kubernetes, including workloads that may require GPUs, PCI cards, or external hardware components. Although you can accomplish this in a virtual environment, doing so has limitations and several complexities. In this chapter, you will learn how to deploy Anthos on bare metal, to provide a platform to address the requirements for which you may encounter limitations on VMware.

The following bonus appendixes are available in the ePub and Kindle versions of this book, and you can read them online in liveBook:

- *appendix A   Cloud is the new computing stack*
    Phil Taylor

- *appendix B   Lessons from the field*
    Kyle Basset

- *appendix C   Compute environment running on VMware*
    Jarosław Gajewski

- *appendix D   Data and analytics*
    Patricia Florissi

- *appendix E   An end-to-end example of ML application*
    Amita Kapoor

- *appendix F   Compute environment running on Windows*
    Kaslin Fields

liveBook discussion forum

Purchase of *Google Anthos in Action* includes free access to liveBook, Manning's online reading platform. Using liveBook's exclusive discussion features, you can attach comments to the book globally or to specific sections or paragraphs. It's a snap to make notes for yourself, ask and answer technical questions, and receive help from the authors and other users. To access the forum, go to https://livebook.manning.com/book/google-anthos-in-action/discussion. You can also learn more about Manning's forums and the rules of conduct at https://livebook.manning.com/discussion.

Manning's commitment to our readers is to provide a venue where a meaningful dialogue between individual readers and between readers and authors can take place. It is not a commitment to any specific amount of participation on the part of the authors, whose contribution to the forum remains voluntary (and unpaid). We suggest you try asking them some challenging questions lest their interest stray! The forum and the archives of previous discussions will be accessible from the publisher's website as long as the book is in print.

about the lead authors

ANTONIO GULLI has a passion for establishing and managing global technological talent for innovation and execution. His core expertise is in cloud computing, deep learning, and search engines. Currently, he serves as engineering director for the Office of the CTO, Google Cloud. Previously, he served as Google Warsaw Site leader, doubling the size of the engineering site.

So far, Antonio has enjoyed obtaining professional experience in four countries in Europe and has managed teams in six countries in Europe, the Middle East, Asia, and in the United States; in Amsterdam, as vice president at Elsevier, a leading scientific publisher; in London, as engineering site lead for Microsoft working on Bing; in Italy and the UK as CTO; in Europe and the UK for Ask.com; and in several cofounded startups, including one of the first web search companies in Europe.

Antonio has co-invented several technologies for search, smart energy, and AI, with 20-plus patents issued/applied for, and he has published several books about coding and machine learning, also translated into Japanese, Russian, Korean, and Chinese. Antonio speaks Spanish, English, and Italian, and he is currently learning Polish and French. Antonio is a proud father of two boys, Lorenzo, 22, and Leonardo, 17, and a little queen, Aurora, 13. They all share a passion for inventions.

SCOTT SUROVICH has been an engineer in one of the world's largest banks, HSBC, for the last 20 years. There he has had various engineering roles, including working with Citrix, Windows, Linux, and virtualization. For the last three years, he has been part of the hybrid integration platform team as the lead engineer and product owner for Kubernetes/Anthos.

Scott has always been passionate about training and writing about technology for anyone willing to learn. He was a certified trainer for years, teaching certified classes for multiple vendors, including Microsoft, Citrix, and CompTIA. In 2019, his first coauthored book, *Kubernetes and Docker: An Enterprise Guide*, was released. It was well received, and after the success of the first edition, an updated second edition was released on December 19, 2021, and became a number-one best seller in the first week of release.

He is also a huge 3D printing enthusiast (bordering on addiction), microcontroller tinkerer, and avid hockey player. When Scott has any downtime, he prefers to spend it with his wife, Kim, and his dog, Belle.

Scott also wants to thank Google for the opportunity to join the initial Google Fellow pilot group and entrusting him with participation in the creation of this book.

MICHAEL MADISON enjoys exploring new cloud technology and finding ways to use advancements in computing to streamline company operations and open new avenues for delivering value to customers. His current position as a Cloud Platform architect at World Wide Technology allows him to assist companies and organizations in beginning or continuing their cloud journeys.

Although he has been an IT professional for more than 15 years, Michael began in the entertainment sector, working for theme parks and cruise lines. Eventually, his hobby of programming became his primary career, and he expanded his domain to include infrastructure and cloud. When the opportunity arose, he focused on cloud initiatives fully, bringing his decade of software development experience to bear on the challenges surrounding cloud and hybrid deployments.

Originally from Texas, Michael lived and went to school in Georgia, Alaska, and Texas. He eventually wound up working in Missouri, where he currently lives outside Saint Louis. Michael and his wife own an RV and plan to tour the country in a few years, accompanied by their dog, Shenzi.

about the cover illustration

The figure on the cover of *Google Anthos in Action* is captioned "Habitante de Frascati," or "Resident of Frascati," taken from a collection by Jacques Grasset de Saint-Sauveur, published in 1797. Each illustration is finely drawn and colored by hand.

In those days, it was easy to identify where people lived and what their trade or station in life was just by their dress. Manning celebrates the inventiveness and initiative of the computer business with book covers based on the rich diversity of regional culture centuries ago, brought back to life by pictures from collections such as this one.

Overview of Anthos

Aparna Sinha

This chapter covers

- Anatomy of a modern application
- Accelerating software development with Anthos
- Standardizing operations at scale with Anthos
- Origins at Google
- How to read this book

Software has been running the world for a while. As consumers, we are used to applications that make it faster, smarter, and more efficient for us to do things like calling a cab or depositing a paycheck. Increasingly, our health, education, entertainment, social life, and employment are all enhanced by modern software applications. At the other end of those applications is a chain of enterprises, large and small, that deliver these improved experiences, services, and products. Modern applications are deployed not just in the hands of consumers but also at points along this enterprise supply chain. Major transactional systems in many traditional industries such as retail, media, financial services, education, and logistics are gradually being replaced by modern microservices that autoupdate frequently, scale efficiently, and incorporate more real-time intelligence. New digital-first startups are using this opportunity to disrupt traditional business models, whereas enterprise incumbents are rushing to modernize their systems so they can compete and avoid disruption.

This book will take you through the anatomy of Anthos—the platform, the development environment, the elements of automation and scaling, and the connection to patterns adapted from Google to attain excellence in modern software development in any industry. Each chapter includes practical examples of how to use the platform, and several include hands-on exercises to implement the techniques.

1.1   Anatomy of a modern application

What is a modern application? When you think of software that has improved your life, perhaps you think of applications that are interactive, fast (low latency), connected, intelligent, context aware, reliable, secure, and easy to use on any device. As technology advances, the capabilities of modern applications, such as the level of security, reliability, awareness, and intelligence, advance as well. For example, new development frameworks such as React and Angular have greatly enhanced the level of interactivity of applications, and new runtimes like Node.js have increased functionality. Modern applications have the property of constantly getting better through frequent updates. On the backend, these applications often comprise many services that are all continuously improving. This modularity is attained by breaking the older "monolith" pattern for writing applications, where all the various functions were tightly coupled to each other.

Applications written as a set of modules or microservices offer several benefits: constituent services can be evolved independently or replaced with other, more scalable or otherwise superior, services over time. Also, the modern microservices pattern is better at separating concerns and setting contracts between services, making it easier to inspect and fix problems. This approach to writing, updating, and deploying applications as microservices that can be used together but also updated, scaled, and debugged independently is at the heart of modern software development. In this book, we refer to this pattern as "modern" or "cloud native" application development. The term *cloud native* applies here because the microservices pattern is well suited to run on distributed infrastructure or the cloud. Microservices can be rolled out incrementally, scaled, revised, replaced, scheduled, rescheduled, and bin packed tightly on distributed servers, creating a highly efficient, scalable, reliable system that is responsive and frequently updated.

Modern applications can be written *greenfield* (from scratch) or refactored from existing *brownfield* applications by following a set of architectural and operational principles. The end goal of application modernization is typically revenue acceleration, and often this involves teams outside IT, in line-of-business (LOB) units. IT departments in most traditional enterprises have historically focused on reducing costs and optimizing operations. Although cost reduction and optimized operations can be by-products of application modernization, they are not the most important benefits. Of course, the modernization process itself requires up-front investment. Anthos is Google

Cloud's platform for application modernization in hybrid and multicloud environments. It provides the approach and technical foundation needed to attain high ROI application modernization. An IT strategy that emphasizes modularity through APIs, microservices, and cloud portability combined with a developer platform that automates reuse, experiments, and cost-efficient scaling along with secure, reliable operations are the basic critical prerequisites for successful application modernization.

One aspect of Anthos is a modern developer experience that accelerates line-of-business application development. It is optimized for refactoring brownfield apps and writing microservices and API-based applications. It offers unified local, on-prem, and cloud development with event-driven automation from source to production. Developers can write code rapidly using modern languages and frameworks with local emulation and testing and integrated CI/CD, and Anthos supports rapid iteration, experimentation, and advanced rollout strategies. The Anthos developer experience emphasizes cloud APIs, containers, and functions, but enterprise platform teams can also customize it. A key goal of the Anthos developer experience is for teams to release code multiple times a day, thereby enhancing both velocity and reliability. Anthos features built-in velocity and ROI metrics to help development teams measure and optimize their performance. Data-driven benchmarks are augmented with prepackaged best practice blueprints that teams can deploy to achieve the next level of performance.

Another aspect of Anthos is an operator experience for central IT. Anthos shines as the uniquely scalable, streamlined way to run operations across multiple clouds. This function is enabled by the remarkable foundation of technology invented and honed at Google over the past 20 years for running services with extremely high reliability on relatively low-cost infrastructure. This is achieved through the standardization of the infrastructure using a layer of abstraction comprising Kubernetes, Istio, Knative, and several other building blocks, along with Anthos-specific extensions and integrations for automated configuration, security, and operations. The operator experience on Anthos offers advanced security and policy controls, automated declarative configuration, highly scalable service visualization and operations, and automated resource and cost management. It features extensive automation, measurement and fault avoidance capabilities for high availability, secure service management across the cloud, and on-prem, edge, virtualized, and bare metal infrastructure.

Enterprise and small companies alike find that multicloud and edge is their new reality, either organically or through acquisitions. Regulations in many countries require proven ability to migrate applications between clouds and a demonstration of failure tolerance with support for sovereignty. Unregulated companies find multicloud necessary for providing developers' choice and access to innovative services. Opportunities for running services and providing greater intelligence at the edge add further surfaces to the infrastructure footprint. Some IT organizations roll their own cross-cloud platform integrations, but this job gets harder every day. It is extremely difficult to build a cross-cloud platform in a scalable, maintainable way, and, more importantly, that approach detracts from precious developer time for product innovation.

Anthos provides a solution rooted in years of time-tested experience and technical innovation at Google in software development and site reliability engineering (SRE) operations, augmented with Google Cloud's experience managing infrastructure for modern applications across millions of enterprise customers. Anthos is unique in serving the needs of LOB developers and central IT together, with advanced capabilities in both domains. Consistency of developer and operator experience across environments enables enterprises to obtain maximum ROI from application modernization with Anthos.

1.1.1 *Accelerating software development*

Software product innovation and new customer experiences are the engine of new revenue generation in the digital economy. But in the innovation process, only a few ideas lead to successful new products; most fail and disappear. As every industry transitions to being software driven, new product innovation depends on having a highly agile and productive software development process. Developers are the new kingmakers. Without an agile, efficient development process and platform, companies can fail to innovate, or innovate at very high costs and even negative ROI. An extensive DevOps Research Assessment[1] study (DORA) surveyed over 30,000 IT professionals over several years across a variety of IT functions. It shows that excellence in software development is a hallmark of business success. This is not surprising given the importance of modern applications in fueling the economy.

DORA quantifies these benefits, showing that "elite," or the highest-performing, software teams are two times more effective in attaining revenue and business goals than low-performing teams. The distinguishing characteristic of elite teams is the practice of releasing software frequently. DORA finds the following four key metrics provide an accurate measurement of software development excellence:

- Deployment frequency
- Lead time for changes
- Change fail rate
- Time to restore service

High-performance teams release software frequently, for example, several times a day. In comparison, low performers release less than once a month. The study also found that teams that release frequently have a lower software defect ratio and recover from errors more rapidly than others. As a result, in addition to being more innovative and modern, their software is more reliable and secure. Year over year, DORA results also show that an increasing number of enterprises are investing in the tools and practices that enable elite performance.

Why do teams with higher development velocity have better business results? In general, higher velocity means that developers can experiment more and test more, so they come up with a better answer in the same amount of time. But another reason exists. Teams with higher velocity have usually made writing and deploying code an

---

[1] https://www.devops-research.com/research.html.

automated, low-effort process, which has the side effect of enabling more people to become developers, especially those who are more entrenched in the business versus the tooling. As a result, high-velocity developer teams have more LOB thinking and a greater understanding of end user needs. The combination of rapid experimentation and focus on users yields better business results. Anthos is the common substrate layer that runs across clouds to provide a common developer experience for accelerating application delivery.

1.1.2   Standardizing operations at scale

Developers may be the new kingmakers, but operations is the team that runs the kingdom day in and day out. Operations includes teams that provision, upgrade, manage, troubleshoot, and scale all aspects of services, infrastructure, and the cloud. Typically, networking, compute, storage, security, identity, asset management, billing, and reliability engineering are part of the operations team of an enterprise. Traditional IT teams have anywhere from 15%–30% of their staff in IT operations. This team is not always visibly engaged in new product introductions with the line of business, but it often lays the groundwork, selecting clouds, publishing service catalogs, and qualifying services for use by the business. Failing to invest in operations automation often means that this team become the bottleneck and a source of fixed cost.

On the flip side, modernizing operations has a tremendous positive effect on velocity. Modern application development teams are typically supported by a very lean operations team, where 80%-plus of staff are employed in software development versus operations. Such a developer-centric ratio is achieved only through modern infrastructure with scaled, automated operations. This means operations are extremely streamlined and use extensive automation to bring new services online quickly. Perhaps the greatest value of Anthos is in automating operations at scale consistently across environments, which is enabled by a unique open cloud approach that has its origins in Google's own infrastructure underpinning.

1.2   Origins in Google

Google's software development process has been optimized and fine tuned over many years to maximize developer productivity and innovation, which attracts the best software developers in the world and leads to a virtuous cycle of innovation in software and software development and delivery practices. The Anthos development stack has evolved from these foundations and is built on core, open source technology that Google introduced to the industry.

At the heart of Anthos is Kubernetes, the extensive orchestration and automation model for managing infrastructure through the container abstraction layer. The layer above Kubernetes is grounded in Google's SRE or operations practices, which standardize the control, security, and management of services at scale. This layer of service management is rooted in Google's Istio-based Cloud Service Mesh. Enterprise policy and configuration automation is built in this layer using Anthos Config Management to provide automation and security at scale. This platform can run on multiple clouds and abstracts the disparate networking, storage, and compute layers underneath (see figure 1.1).

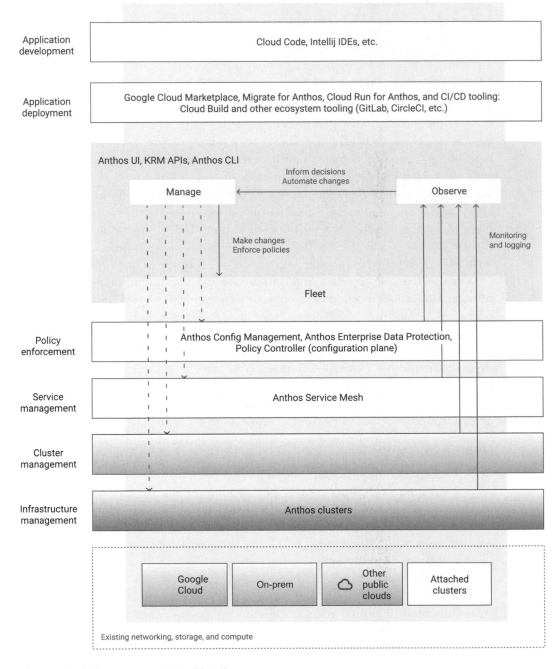

Figure 1.1   Anthos components and functions

Above this Anthos stack is developer experience and DevOps tooling, including a deployment environment that uses Knative and integrated CICD with Tekton.

Summary

- Modern software applications provide a host of business benefits and are driving transformation in many industries.
- The backend for these applications is typically based on the cloud native microservices architectural pattern, which allows for great scalability, modularity, and a host of operational and DevOps benefits that are well suited for running on distributed infrastructure.
- Anthos, which originated in Google Cloud, is a platform for hosting cloud native applications, providing both development and operational benefits.

One single pane of glass

Melika Golkaram

This chapter covers

- The advantages of having a single pane of glass and its components
- How different personas can use and benefit from these components
- Getting some hands-on experience configuring the UI and attaching a cluster to the Anthos UI

We live in a world where application performance is critical for success. To better serve their end users, many organizations have pushed to distribute their workloads from centralized data centers. Whether to be closer to their users, to enhance disaster recovery, or to take advantage of the benefits of cloud computing, this distribution has placed additional pressure on the tooling used to manage and support this strategy. The tools that have flourished under this new paradigm are those that have matured and become more sophisticated and scalable.

There is no one-size-fits-all tool. Likewise, no one person can manage the infrastructure of even a small organization. All applications require tools to manage

CI/CD, monitoring, logging, orchestration, deployments, storage, authentication/ authorization, and more. In addition to the scalability and sophistication mentioned earlier, most of the tools in this space offer an informative and user-friendly graphical user interface (GUI). Having an easily understood GUI can help people use the tool more effectively because it lowers the bar for learning the software and increases the amount of pertinent output the user receives.

Anthos itself has the capacity to support hundreds of applications and thousands of services, so a high-quality GUI and a consolidated user experience are required to use the ecosystem to its full potential and reduce the operational overhead. To this end, Google Cloud Platform offers a rich set of dashboards and integrated tools within the Google Cloud console to help you monitor, troubleshoot, and interact with your deployed Anthos clusters, regardless of their location or infrastructure provider. This single pane of glass allows administrators, operations professionals, developers, and business owners to view the status of their clusters and application workloads, all while benefiting from the capabilities of Google Cloud's Identity and Access Management (IAM) framework and any additional security provided on each cluster.

The Anthos GUI, its "single pane of glass," is not the first product to attempt to centralize the visibility and operations of a fleet of clusters, but it is the one that offers support to provide real-time visibility to a large variety of environments. To fully understand the benefits of the Anthos GUI, in this chapter, we are going to look at some of the options available to aggregate and standardize interactions with multiple Kubernetes clusters.

2.1 Single pane of glass

A single pane of glass offers the following three characteristics that are shared across all operators, industries, and operations scales:

- *Centralization*—As the name suggests, a single pane of glass should provide a central UI for resources, no matter where they run and to whom they are provided. The former aspect relates to the infrastructure and cloud provider on which the clusters are operating and the latter relates to inherently multitenant services, where one operator centrally manages multiple clients' clusters and workloads. With the benefits of a central dashboard, admins will be able to get a high-level view of resources and drill down to areas of interest without switching the view.

  However, a central environment might cause some concern in areas of privacy and security. Not every administrator is required to connect to all clusters, and not all admins should be able to have access to the UI. A central environment should come with its own safeguards to avoid any operational compromise with industry standards.

- *Consistency*—Let's go back to the scenario of an operator running clusters and customers in multicloud or hybrid architectures. Most infrastructure providers, whether they offer proprietary services or run on open source, attempt to offer a solid interface for their users. However, they use different terminology and have inconsistent views on priorities. Finally, depending on their UI philosophy and approach, they design the view and navigation differently. Remember, for a cloud provider, cluster and container management are only parts of the bigger suite of services and components of a predesigned dashboard. Although this might be a positive element in single operating environments (you can learn to navigate outside of the Kubernetes dashboard into the rest of the Cloud Services dashboard with minimum switching), it becomes a headache in multienvironment services and for those who focus only on Kubernetes.

- *Ease of use*—Part of the appeal of a single pane of glass in operation is how data coming from different sources is aggregated, normalized, and visualized. This brings a lot of simplicity in drilling down into performance management and triage, especially if it combines a graphical interface with it.

A graphical UI has always been an important part of any online application. First, at some point in an app management cycle, a team doesn't have either the skills or the interest for working with remote calls. They expect a robust, easy-to-navigate, and a highly device-agnostic UI for their day-to-day responsibilities.

Second, regardless of the team's skill sets, an aggregated dashboard has so much more to offer in one concentrated view than calling service providers and perhaps clusters individually given that the UI provides lots of data fields with the right installation and readability.

2.2 *Non-Anthos visibility and interaction*

Anthos is not the first solution to expose information about a Kubernetes cluster through a more easily digested form than the built-in APIs. Although many developers and operators have used the command-line interface (CLI), kubectl, to interact with a cluster, the information presented can be very technical and does not usually display potential problems in a friendly way. Extensions to Kubernetes, such as Istio or Anthos Config Management, typically come with their own CLIs as well (istioctl and nomos, for example). Cross-referencing information between all the disparate tools can be a substantial exercise, even for the most experienced developer or operator.

2.2.1 *Kubernetes Dashboard*

One of the first tools developed to solve this problem was the Kubernetes Dashboard (https://github.com/kubernetes/dashboard). Although this utility is not deployed by default on new Kubernetes clusters, it is easy to deploy to the cluster and begin using the information it provides. In addition to providing a holistic view of most of the components of a Kubernetes cluster, the dashboard also provides users with a GUI interface to deploy new workloads into the cluster. This makes the dashboard a convenient and quick way to view the status and interact with a new cluster.

However, it works on only one cluster. You can certainly deploy the Kubernetes Dashboard to each of your clusters, but they will remain independent of each other and have no cross-connection. In addition, because the dashboard is located on the cluster itself, accessing it remotely requires a level of effort similar to using the CLI tool, requiring services, load balancing, and ingress rules to properly route and validate incoming traffic. Although the dashboard can be powerful for proof of concept or small developer clusters, multiuser clusters need a more powerful tool.

2.2.2   Provider-specific UIs

Kubernetes was released from the beginning as an open source project. Though based on internal Google tools, the structure of Kubernetes allowed vendors and other cloud providers to easily create their own customized versions of Kubernetes, either to simplify deployment or management on their platforms or to add additional features. Many of these adaptations have customized UIs for either deployment or management operations.

For cloud providers, many of the user interfaces for their other products already existed and followed a particular style. Each provider developed a different UI for their version of Kubernetes. Although a portion of these UIs dealt with provisioning and maintaining the infrastructure of a cluster, some of each UI was dedicated to cluster operations and manipulation. However, each UI was implemented differently and couldn't manage clusters other than the native Kubernetes flavor for that cloud provider.

2.2.3   Bespoke software

Some companies have decided to push the boundaries and develop their own custom software and UIs to visualize and manage their Kubernetes installations and operations. Though always an option due to the open standards of the Kubernetes APIs, any bespoke development brings all the associated challenges that come with maintaining any custom operations software: maintaining the software for new versions, bug fixing, handling OS and package upgrades, and so on. For the highest degree of customization, nothing beats bespoke software, but the cost-versus-benefit calculation does not work out for most companies.

2.3   The Anthos UI

Each of the previous solutions has a fundamental flaw that prevents most companies from fully benefiting from it. The Kubernetes Dashboard has no multicluster capability and does not handle remote access easily. The provider-specific UIs work well for their flavor but cannot handle clusters that are not on their network or running their version of Kubernetes. And bespoke software comes with a high cost of development and maintenance. This is where the Anthos multicluster single pane of glass comes into play. This single pane of glass is an extension of, and embedded in, Google Cloud Platform's already extensive Cloud console that allows users to view, monitor, and manage their entire cloud infrastructure and workloads.

The solution Google has developed for multicluster visibility in Anthos depends on a new concept called *fleets* (formerly referred to as *environs*), the Connect framework, and the Anthos dashboard. The Anthos dashboard is an enhancement of the existing GKE dashboard that Google has provided for several years for its in-cloud GKE clusters. The Connect framework is new with Anthos and simplifies the communication process between Google Cloud and clusters located anywhere in the world. Fleets are methods of aggregating clusters to simplify common work between them. Let's take a moment to discuss a bit more about fleets.

2.3.1   *Fleets*

Fleets are a Google Cloud concept for logically organizing clusters and other resources, letting you use and manage multicluster capabilities and apply consistent policies across your systems. Think of them as a grouping mechanism that applies several security and operation boundaries to resources within a single project.[1] They help administrators build a one-to-many relationship between a fleet and its member clusters and resources to reduce the configuration burden of individual security and access rules. The clusters in a fleet also exist in a higher trust relationship with each other by belonging to the same fleet. This makes it easier to manage traffic into and between the clusters and join their service meshes together.

An Anthos cluster will belong to one and only one fleet and cannot join another without leaving the first. Unfortunately, this limitation can present a small problem in complex service communications. For example, assume we have an API service and a Data Processing service that need to run in distinct fleets for security reasons, but both need to talk to a bespoke Permissioning service. The Permissioning service can be placed in one of the two fleets, but whichever service does not belong to Permissioning's fleet will need to talk to the service using outside-the-cluster networking. However, this rule for fleets prevents users from accidentally merging clusters that must remain separate, because allowing the common service to exist in both fleets simultaneously would open additional attack vectors (see figure 2.1).

When multiple clusters are in the same fleet, many types of resources must have unique names, or they will be treated as the same resource. This obviously includes the clusters themselves but also covers namespaces, services, and identities. Anthos refers to this as *sameness*. Sameness forces consistent ownership across all clusters within a fleet, and namespaces that are defined on one cluster, but not on another, will be reserved implicitly.

When designing the architecture of your services, this sameness concept must be kept in mind. Anthos Service Mesh, for example, typically treats a service that exists in the same namespace with the same name as an identical service across the entire fleet and load balances traffic between clusters automatically. If the namespace and/or service in question has a unique name, this should not cause any confusion. However, accessing the Webserver service in the Demo namespace might yield unexpected results.

Finally, Anthos allows all services to use a common identity when accessing external resources such as Google Cloud services, object stores, and so on. This common

---

[1] A Google Cloud Platform project is a set of configuration settings that define how your app interacts with Google services and what resources it uses.

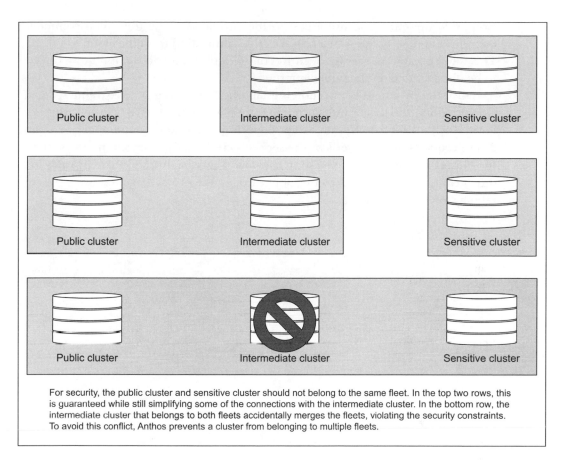

For security, the public cluster and sensitive cluster should not belong to the same fleet. In the top two rows, this is guaranteed while still simplifying some of the connections with the intermediate cluster. In the bottom row, the intermediate cluster that belongs to both fleets accidentally merges the fleets, violating the security constraints. To avoid this conflict, Anthos prevents a cluster from belonging to multiple fleets.

Figure 2.1   Example of fleet merging causing security problems

identity makes it possible to give the services within a fleet access to an external resource once, rather than cluster by cluster. Although this can be overridden and multiple identities defined, if resources are not architected carefully and configured properly, negative outcomes can occur.

2.3.2   Connect: How does it work?

Now that we have discussed fleets, we need to examine how the individual clusters communicate with Google Cloud. Any cluster that is part of Anthos, whether attached[2] or Anthos managed, has Connect deployed to the cluster as part of the installation or registration process. This deployment establishes a persistent connection from the cluster outbound to Google Cloud that accepts traffic from the cloud and provides

---

[2] Attaching clusters lets you view your existing Kubernetes clusters in the Google Cloud console along with your Anthos clusters and enable a subset of Anthos features on them, including configuration with Anthos Config Management. More details can be found at http://mng.bz/pdRE.

cloud-side operations secure access to the cluster. Because the initial connection is outbound, it does not rely on a fully routable connection from the cloud to the cluster. This setup greatly reduces the security considerations and does not require the cluster to be discoverable on the public internet.

Once the persistent connection is established, Anthos can proxy requests made by Google Cloud services or users using the Google Cloud UI to the cluster, whether it is located within Google Cloud, in another cloud provider, at the edge, or on-prem. These requests use the user's or the service's credentials, maintaining the security on the cluster and allowing the existing role-based access controls (RBAC)[3] rules to span direct connectivity as well as connections through the proxy. A request using the Anthos UI may look like figure 2.2.

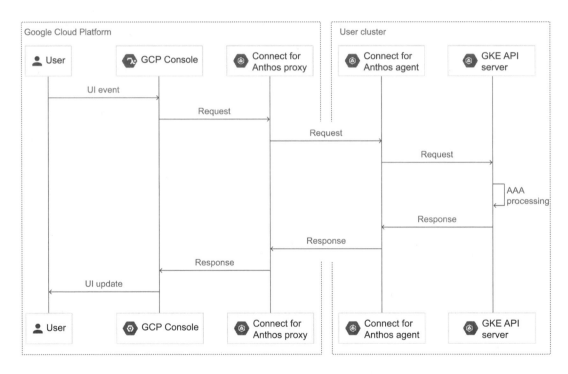

Figure 2.2   Flow of request and response from Google Cloud to cluster and back

While the tunnel from the Connect Agent to Google Cloud is persistent, each stage of each request is authenticated using various mechanisms to validate the identity of the requestor and confirm that layer is allowed to make the request. Skipping layers is not

---

[3] Role-based access control (RBAC) is a set of permissions and an authorization component that allows or denies admin or compute objects access to a set of requesting resources.

permitted and will be rejected by the next layer receiving the invalid request. An over-view of the request-response authentication is seen in figure 2.3.

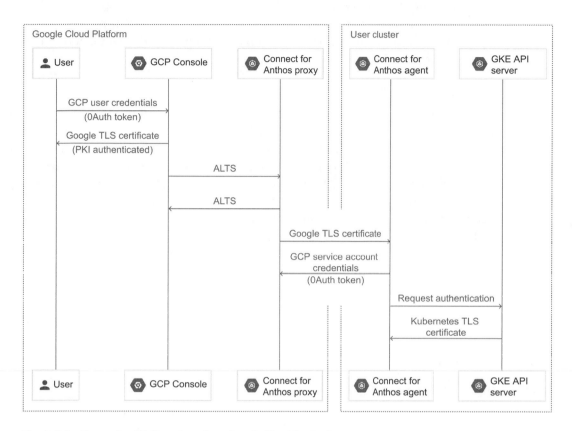

Figure 2.3   Request validation steps from Google Cloud to cluster

Regardless of any authorization measures at the cluster level, a user must still be allowed to view the Google Cloud project to which the cluster is attached to use the Connect functionality. This method uses the standard IAM processes for a given project, but having the separate permission allows the security team to grant a user access to a cluster through a direct connection (or some other tunnel) but not allow them remote access via Google Cloud.

Connect is compliant with Google's Access Transparency,[4] which provides transparency to the customer in the following two areas:

---

[4] Access Transparency–enabled services let customers control access to their organization's data by Google personnel. It also provides logs that capture the actions Google personnel take when accessing the customer's content.

- *Access approval*—Customers can authorize Google support staff to work on certain parts of their services. Customers can view the reasons a Google employee might need that access.
- *Activity visibility*—Customers can import access logs into their project cloud logging to have visibility into Google employees' actions and location and can query the logs in real time, if necessary.

2.3.3   *Installation and registration*

To use the Connect functionality, we obviously need to install the Connect Agent on our cluster. We also need to inform Google about our cluster and determine which project, and, therefore, which fleets, the cluster belongs to. Fortunately, Google has provided a streamlined utility for performing this task via the gcloud command-line tool (see http://mng.bz/Op72). This process uses either Workload Identity or a Google Cloud service account to enroll the cluster with the project's Connect pool and install and start the Connect Agent on the cluster.

Though these steps enroll the cluster with Google and enable most Anthos features, you still need to authenticate with the cluster from the Google Console to view and interact with the cluster from Google Cloud. Connect allows authentication via Cloud identity (when using the Connect gateway),[5] bearer token, or OIDC, if enabled on the cluster. The easiest, and recommended, method is to use Cloud Identity, but this requires the activation and configuration of the Connect Gateway for the cluster. For more information on Connect Gateway, please see chapter 5 on operations management with Anthos.

2.4   *The Anthos Cloud UI*

Now that we've done the plumbing, we can walk through and show off the UI. Google provides the Anthos UI via the Cloud console at the project level. Because the Anthos UI is visible only at the project level, only clusters registered to that project's fleets are visible. The Anthos UI menu contains multiple subpages, each focusing on a distinct aspect of cluster management. At the time of writing, these sections are the Dashboard, Service Mesh, Config Management, Clusters, Features, Migrate to Containers, Security, Cloud Run for Anthos, and Virtual Machines. Let's look at each of these pages.

2.4.1   *The Anthos dashboard*

The default page for the Anthos menu, and the central hub for the UI, is the dashboard. The dashboard is intended to give admins a wide-angle view of the clusters in the current fleet, while making it easy to drill down into details for the specific compo-

---

[5] Google Cloud Identity and Access Management (IAM) lets you grant more granular access to specific Google Cloud resources and prevents unwanted access to other resources.

nents. To start, go to the hamburger menu on the top-left corner of the console (figure 2.4). Select Anthos from the menu to enter the Anthos Features page.

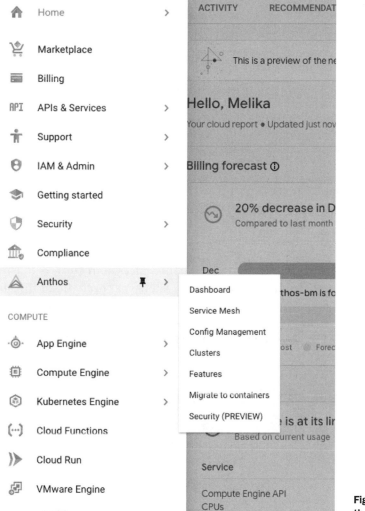

Figure 2.4   Navigation to the Anthos dashboard

Figure 2.5 shows an example of the Anthos dashboard view.

Although this example shows the current Anthos project cost, the dashboard still uses Google's IAM, and that information will appear only if the viewing user has the appropriate billing-related permissions. The remaining sections highlight critical errors or other user-involved problems for that aspect of Anthos. Following those links takes you to the appropriate subpage.

Figure 2.5   **Example of an Anthos dashboard**

2.4.2   *Service Mesh*

The Service Mesh page shows all services registered in any of the clusters in the current fleet. The initial list shows the names, namespaces, and clusters of each service, as well as basic metrics, such as error rate and latency, at predefined thresholds. You can also filter this list by namespace, cluster name, requests per second, error rate, latency, request size, and resource usage to allow admins to easily drill down for specific tasks. Figure 2.6 shows the Service Mesh screen filtered for services in the default namespace.

Services ❓

Is system object : False ✕   Namespace ; default ✕   Select a filter option

Status ❓	Name ↑	Namespace	Type	Clusters	Requests/sec (avg)	Error rate	50% latency	99% latency
ⓘ	adservice	default	K8s	cluster-gcp	1.5	0.0%	2ms	4ms
ⓘ	cartservice	default	K8s	cluster-gcp	2.5	0.0%	3ms	682ms
ⓘ	checkoutservice	default	K8s	cluster-gcp	0.1	0.0%	84ms	750ms
ⓘ	currencyservice	default	K8s	cluster-gcp	8.0	0.0%	1ms	4ms
ⓘ	emailservice	default	K8s	cluster-gcp	0.1	0.0%	2ms	4ms
ⓘ	frontend	default	K8s	❓ cluster-gcp	.	.	.	.
ⓘ	frontend-external	default	K8s	cluster-gcp	2.6	0.2%	49ms	826ms
ⓘ	paymentservice	default	K8s	cluster-gcp	0.1	0.0%	3ms	15ms
ⓘ	productcatalogservice	default	K8s	cluster-gcp	14.4	0.0%	1ms	22ms
ⓘ	recommendationservice	default	K8s	cluster-gcp	1.9	0.0%	6ms	77ms
ⓘ	redis-cart	default	K8s	❓ cluster-gcp	.	.	.	.

Figure 2.6   **Service Mesh UI with filters**

2.4.3   *Config Management*

Anthos Config Management, explored in depth in chapter 11, is Anthos's method of automatically adding and maintaining resources on a Kubernetes cluster. These resources can include most common Kubernetes core objects (such as Pods, Services, and Service Accounts) as well as custom entities such as policies and cloud-configuration objects. This tab displays the list of all clusters in the current fleet, their sync status, and which revision is currently enforced on the cluster (figure 2.7). The table also shows whether Policy Controller[6] has been enabled for the cluster.

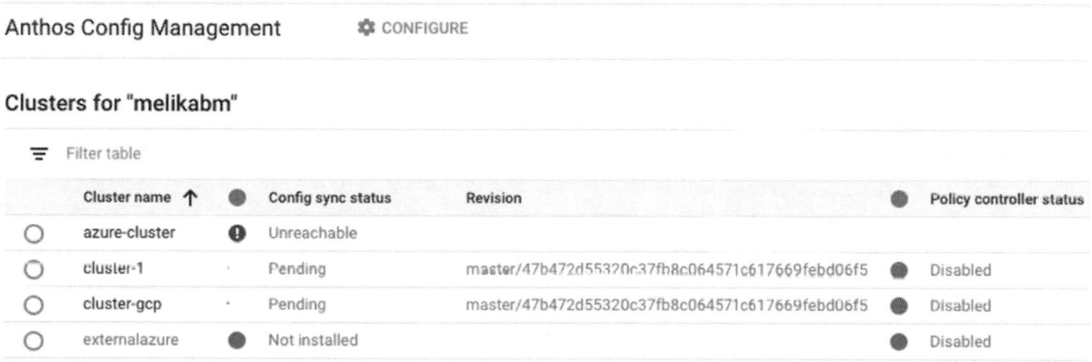

Anthos Config Management   ⚙ CONFIGURE

Clusters for "melikabm"

⇛ Filter table

	Cluster name ↑	●	Config sync status	Revision	●	Policy controller status
○	azure-cluster	❗	Unreachable			
○	cluster-1	·	Pending	master/47b472d55320c37fb8c064571c617669febd06f5	●	Disabled
○	cluster-gcp	·	Pending	master/47b472d55320c37fb8c064571c617669febd06f5	●	Disabled
○	externalazure	●	Not installed		●	Disabled

Figure 2.7   Clusters in Config Management view

Selecting a specific cluster opens the Config Management cluster detail, as shown in figure 2.8. This detailed view gives further information about the configuration settings, including the location of the repo used, the cycle for syncing, and the version of ACM running on the cluster.

---

[6] Policy Controller is part of Anthos Config Management, allowing administrators to define customized rules to place guardrails for security, resource management, or operational reasons.

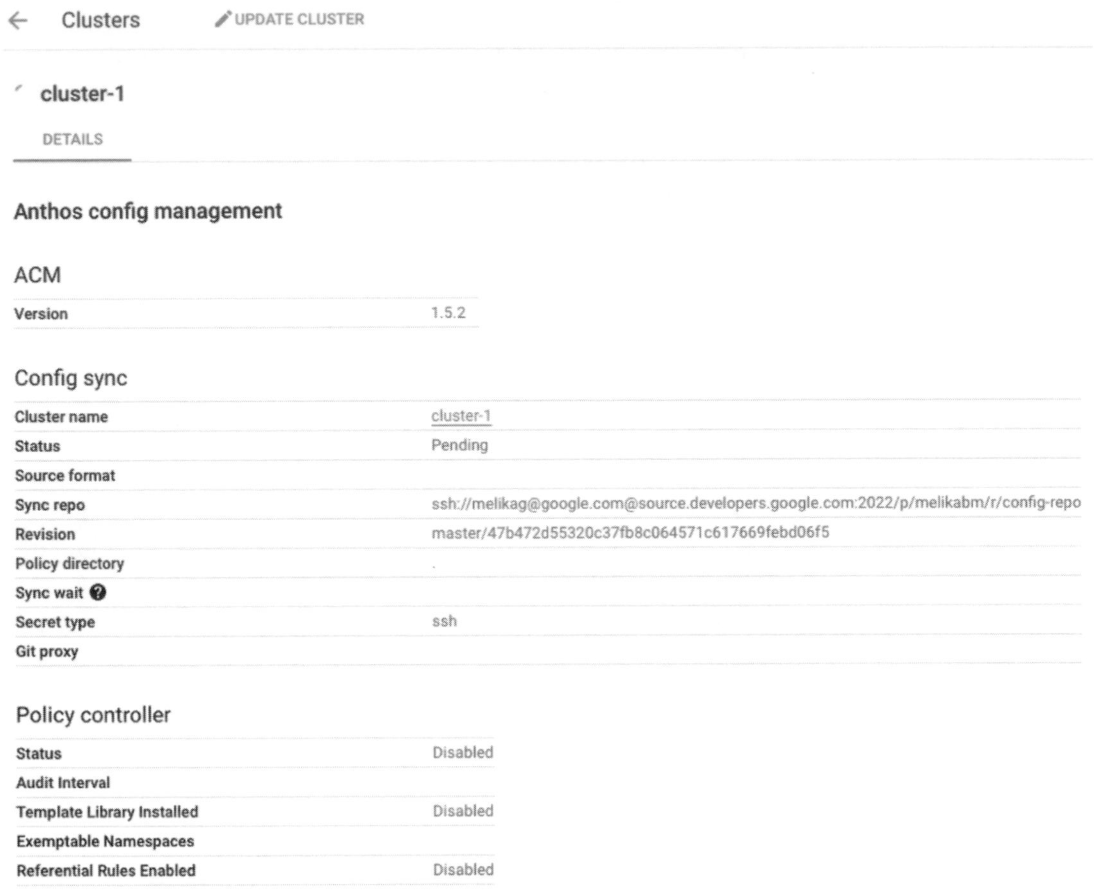

←   Clusters   ✎ UPDATE CLUSTER

cluster-1

DETAILS

Anthos config management

ACM

Version	1.5.2

Config sync

Cluster name	cluster-1
Status	Pending
Source format	
Sync repo	ssh://melikag@google.com@source.developers.google.com:2022/p/melikabm/r/config-repo
Revision	master/47b472d55320c37fb8c064571c617669febd06f5
Policy directory	.
Sync wait ❓	
Secret type	ssh
Git proxy	

Policy controller

Status	Disabled
Audit Interval	
Template Library Installed	Disabled
Exemptable Namespaces	
Referential Rules Enabled	Disabled

Figure 2.8   Cluster detail in Config Management view

2.4.4   *Clusters*

The Clusters menu lists all clusters in the current fleet, along with the location, type, labels, and any warnings associated with each cluster, as shown in figure 2.9. By selecting a cluster in the list, a more detailed view of the cluster, with the current Kubernetes version, the CPU and memory available, and the features enabled, will be displayed in the right sidebar, as shown in figure 2.10. Below the sidebar information, a Manage Features button will take you to the Features tab for that cluster. In figure 2.9, the following clusters are created on the project:

- GKE (cluster-gcp)
- Baremetal (cluster-1)
- Azure AKS (azure-cluster and externalazure)

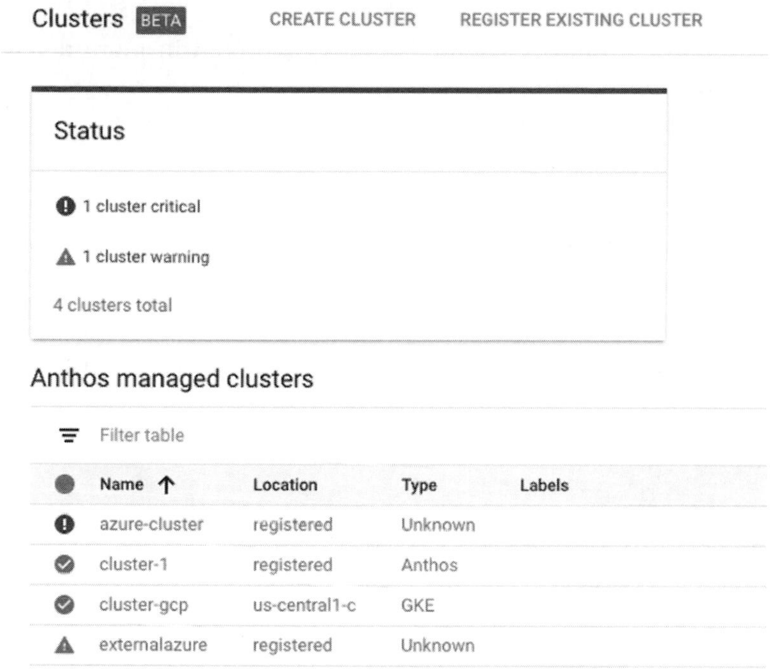

Clusters BETA   CREATE CLUSTER   REGISTER EXISTING CLUSTER

Status

! 1 cluster critical

⚠ 1 cluster warning

4 clusters total

Anthos managed clusters

≡ Filter table

●	Name ↑	Location	Type	Labels
!	azure-cluster	registered	Unknown	
✓	cluster-1	registered	Anthos	
✓	cluster-gcp	us-central1-c	GKE	
⚠	externalazure	registered	Unknown	

**Figure 2.9
List view in the
Clusters menu**

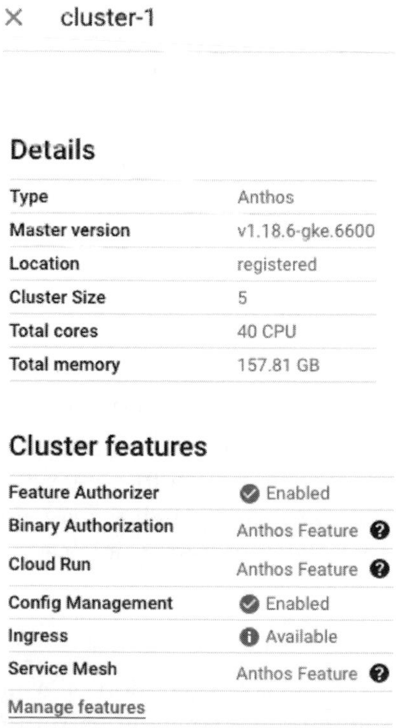

✕   cluster-1

Details

Type	Anthos
Master version	v1.18.6-gke.6600
Location	registered
Cluster Size	5
Total cores	40 CPU
Total memory	157.81 GB

Cluster features

Feature Authorizer	✓ Enabled
Binary Authorization	Anthos Feature ❓
Cloud Run	Anthos Feature ❓
Config Management	✓ Enabled
Ingress	ⓘ Available
Service Mesh	Anthos Feature ❓

Manage features

**Figure 2.10   Cluster detail
sidebar in the Clusters menu**

2.4.5   *Features*

The Anthos service encompasses several features (covered in more detail in other chapters), including:

- Configuration Management
- Ingress
- Binary Authorization
- Cloud Run for Anthos
- Service Mesh

The Features menu provides an easy way to enable and disable specific services for the entire fleet. Figure 2.11 shows the list of existing features for every cluster.

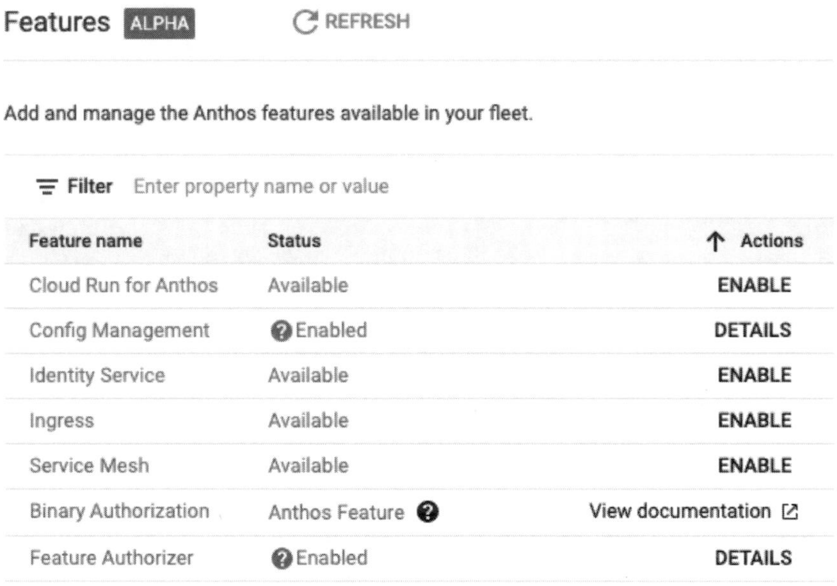

Features ALPHA   ↻ REFRESH

Add and manage the Anthos features available in your fleet.

⇉ Filter   Enter property name or value

Feature name	Status	↑ Actions
Cloud Run for Anthos	Available	ENABLE
Config Management	❷ Enabled	DETAILS
Identity Service	Available	ENABLE
Ingress	Available	ENABLE
Service Mesh	Available	ENABLE
Binary Authorization	Anthos Feature ❷	View documentation ↗
Feature Authorizer	❷ Enabled	DETAILS

Figure 2.11   Features menu

An admin also can disable or enable most of these features from the interface (some features are integral components of Anthos and cannot be disabled). The same possibility also exists through gcloud or the fleet management API for better automation. It's worth noting that if enablement is not fully possible through the visual interface, the console generates the right commands for the admin to seamlessly enter them into their CLI.

2.4.6   *Migrating to containers*

One of the major benefits of Anthos is the automatable migration of Windows and Linux VMs to containers and their deployment onto a compatible Anthos cluster.

Previously, this was primarily done via CLI and initiated from the source cluster, but this menu now provides a convenient, centralized process for shifting VMs to containers and into a different deployment scheme. The menu contains tabs for viewing and managing your migrations, sources, and processing clusters. For more information on the process of migrating your existing VMs to containers, see chapter 15, "Migrate."

2.4.7   Security

The Security menu is where you find multiple tools related to viewing, enabling, and auditing the security posture of the clusters in the current fleet. Figure 2.12 shows the basic view when you first select the Security menu.

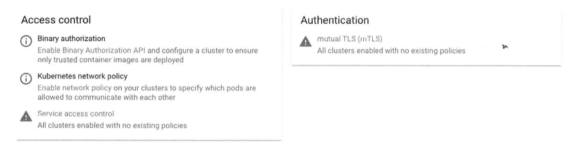

Figure 2.12   Security menu

As you can see, we do not currently have Binary Authorization[7] enabled, but Anthos provides us a shortcut to quickly turn it on. Once we do, we are presented with the configuration page for Binary Authorization (figure 2.13), enabling us to view and edit the policy, if needed.

2.5   Monitoring and logging

The Anthos menu in the GCP console is only part of the solution, however. Google also provides the operations suite, including Cloud Monitoring and Cloud Logging, to help with managing the operations of applications and infrastructure. Anthos simplifies the logging of application data and metrics to the operations suite as part of the default deployment. This can make it easy to add SLOs and SLAs based on these metrics.[8] In addition, several pages within the Anthos menu include shortcuts and buttons that trigger wizards to create SLOs in a guided fashion.

---

[7] Binary Authorization is explored in further detail in chapter 12, "Integrations with CI/CD."
[8] See chapter 4 for details on SLIs, SLOs, and SLAs with Anthos.

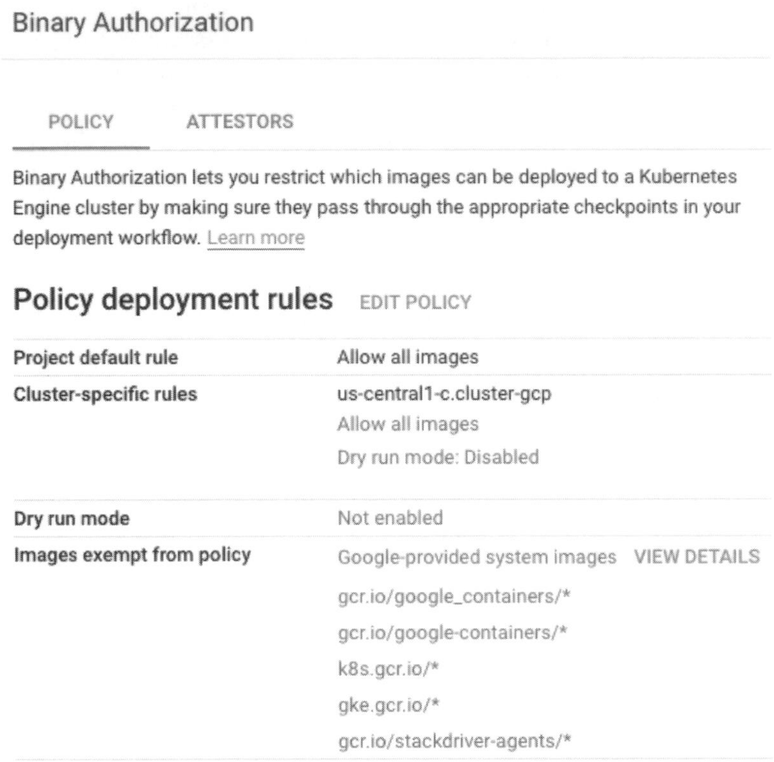

Binary Authorization

POLICY   ATTESTORS

Binary Authorization lets you restrict which images can be deployed to a Kubernetes Engine cluster by making sure they pass through the appropriate checkpoints in your deployment workflow. Learn more

Policy deployment rules   EDIT POLICY

Project default rule	Allow all images
Cluster-specific rules	us-central1-c.cluster-gcp
	Allow all images
	Dry run mode: Disabled
Dry run mode	Not enabled
Images exempt from policy	Google-provided system images VIEW DETAILS
	gcr.io/google_containers/*
	gcr.io/google-containers/*
	k8s.gcr.io/*
	gke.gcr.io/*
	gcr.io/stackdriver-agents/*

Figure 2.13   Binary Authorization policy details

2.6   *GKE dashboard*

Google has provided the GKE dashboard for several years to assist with viewing and managing your clusters for GKE in GCP. With the release of Anthos, the GKE dashboard has been expanded to display the details for Kubernetes clusters attached via GKE Connect. Although the Anthos menu is focused on the clusters at a high level and on the Anthos-specific features, such as the Service Mesh and Config Management, the GKE dashboard allows an admin to drill down to specific workloads and services. The next section presents a tutorial to register an Azure AKS cluster into an Anthos dashboard.

2.7   *Connecting to a remote cluster*

In this example, a cluster is already created in the Azure Kubernetes Service (AKS) engine. Google allows several cluster types to be registered remotely, referred to as *attached clusters* (see http://mng.bz/Y6ne). To attach these clusters, you will need to take the following steps:

1 Open a terminal window on a computer that has access to the cluster to be registered. Note the full path to the kubeconfig file used to connect to the cluster.
2 In the Google console, under the IAM section, create a Google Service account with the role GKE Connect Agent. Generate an account key and save it.
3 Decide on the official designation for the cluster in your Anthos project; this is the Membership Name.
4 Use the next command to register your cluster, replacing the `<FULLCAPS>` fields with the appropriate information:[9]

```
gcloud container fleet memberships register <MEMBERSHIP_NAME> \
  --context=<KUBECONFIG_CONTEXT> \
  --kubeconfig=<KUBECONFIG_PATH> \
  --service-account-key-file=<SERVICE_ACCOUNT_KEY_PATH>
```

In a few minutes, your cluster appears on the GCP console, as displayed in figure 2.14.

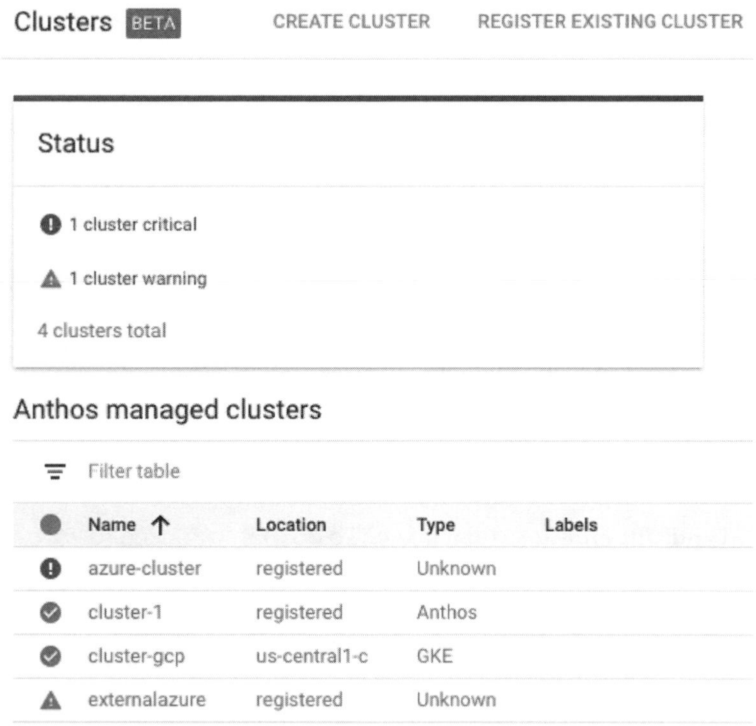

Clusters BETA   CREATE CLUSTER   REGISTER EXISTING CLUSTER

Status

⊘ 1 cluster critical

⚠ 1 cluster warning

4 clusters total

Anthos managed clusters

≡ Filter table

●	Name ↑	Location	Type	Labels
⊘	azure-cluster	registered	Unknown	
✓	cluster-1	registered	Anthos	
✓	cluster-gcp	us-central1-c	GKE	
⚠	externalazure	registered	Unknown	

Figure 2.14 Registered cluster view

---

[9] The `--kubeconfig` line is the local filepath where your kubeconfig containing an entry for the cluster being registered is stored. This defaults to $KUBECONFIG if that environment variable is set; otherwise, this defaults to $HOME/.kube/config.

5   Authenticate to the registered cluster. As you can see, a warning sign appears next to the recently created cluster (externalazure). That is normal and a reminder to sign in to the cluster to perform more operations on it. Figure 2.15 shows the view of the registration status of the cluster.

Kubernetes clusters   CREATE   DEPLOY   REFRESH   DEL

Filter table

		Name ↑	Location	Type	Number of nodes
☐	●				
☐	!	azure-cluster	registered	Unknown	unknown
☐	✓	cluster-1	registered	Anthos	5
☐	✓	cluster-gcp	us-central1-c	GKE	4
☐	⚠	externalazure	registered	Unknown	unknown

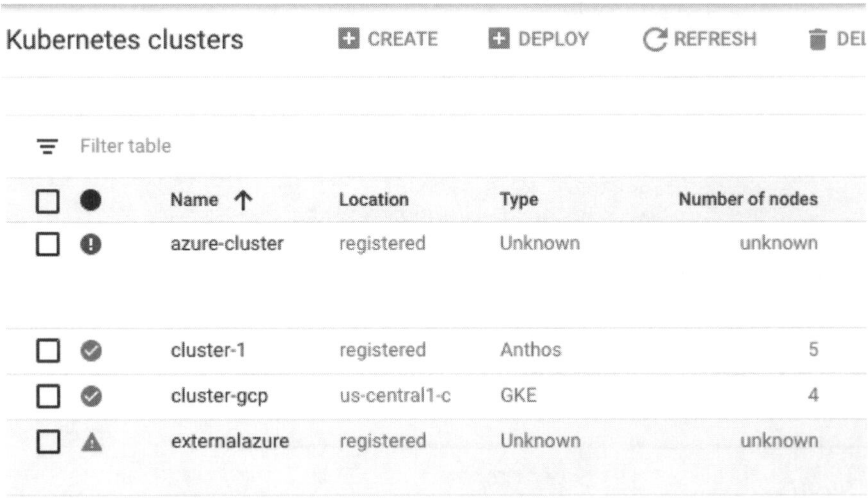

Figure 2.15   View of the registration status of the cluster

By clicking the three dots for a cluster, you can see the available actions. Click Login, and you can see the following login options are available:

- Use your Google identity to log in
- Token
- Basic authentication
- Authenticate with Identity Provider configured for the cluster

Let's go ahead and authenticate with a token. To do that, you need to have a Kubernetes Service Account (KSA) with the right permissions. If you do not already have one, create a KSA by typing the following in your terminal:

```
KSA_NAME=[KSA_NAME]
kubectl create serviceaccount ${KSA_NAME}
kubectl create clusterrolebinding [VIEW_BINDING_NAME] \
--clusterrole view --serviceaccount default:${KSA_NAME}
kubectl create clusterrolebinding [CLOUD_CONSOLE_READER_BINDING_NAME] \
--clusterrole cloud-console-reader --serviceaccount default:${KSA_NAME}
```

KSA permissions

All accounts logging in to a cluster need to hold at least the following Kubernetes RBAC roles in the cluster:

- `view`—Kubernetes primitive role that allows read-only access to see most objects in a namespace. It does not allow viewing roles or role bindings.
- `cloud-console-reader`—Users who want to view your cluster's resources in the console need to have the relevant permissions to do so. You define this set of permissions by creating a ClusterRole RBAC resource, `cloud-console-reader`, in the cluster. `cloud-console-reader` grants its users the get, list, and watch permissions on the cluster's nodes, persistent volumes, and storage classes, which allow them to see details about these resources.

Having created the KSA, acquire the KSA's bearer token:

```
SECRET_NAME=$(kubectl get serviceaccount [KSA_NAME] -o
    jsonpath='{$.secrets[0].name}')
kubectl get secret ${SECRET_NAME} -o jsonpath='{$.data.token}' | base64 --decode
```

After you have pasted the token in the login prompt in the Google console, you immediately get the same view in your AKS cluster (externalazure) that you would see in other cluster types. Figure 2.16 provides that view.

		Name ↑	Location	Type	Number of nodes
☐	●				
☐	❗	azure-cluster	registered	Unknown	unknown
☐	✔	cluster-1	registered	Anthos	5
☐	✔	cluster-gcp	us-central1-c	GKE	4
☐	✔	externalazure	registered	External	3

Figure 2.16   Anthos attached cluster authenticated

Figure 2.17 shows the nodes and their health status through the dashboard.

Several other types of Kubernetes clusters that are not managed by GCP can be attached to Anthos this way. Doing so gives operations simplicity and consistency, and permits access security to administrators from a single platform.

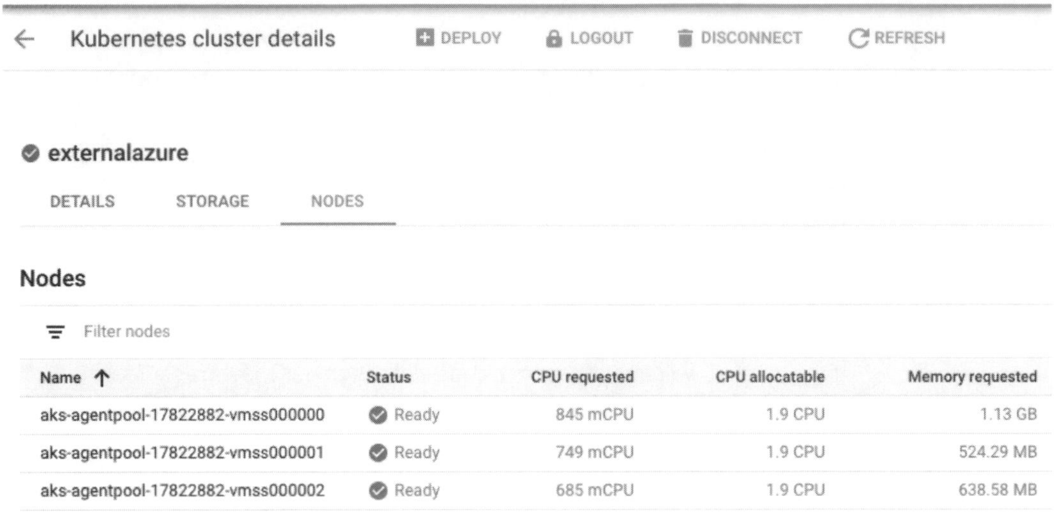

←   Kubernetes cluster details   ⊞ DEPLOY   🔒 LOGOUT   🗑 DISCONNECT   ↻ REFRESH

✓ **externalazure**

DETAILS   STORAGE   NODES

Nodes

⇶ Filter nodes

Name ↑	Status	CPU requested	CPU allocatable	Memory requested
aks-agentpool-17822882-vmss000000	✓ Ready	845 mCPU	1.9 CPU	1.13 GB
aks-agentpool-17822882-vmss000001	✓ Ready	749 mCPU	1.9 CPU	524.29 MB
aks-agentpool-17822882-vmss000002	✓ Ready	685 mCPU	1.9 CPU	638.58 MB

Figure 2.17   Node view on attached cluster

Summary

- Providing a single pane of glass to hybrid and multicloud Kubernetes for any organization who uses microservices is a stepping stone to a successful and global operation.
- One of the biggest benefits to a single pane of glass is that admins can use the same interface to configure service-level objectives and alerts to reassure service guarantees.
- The Anthos UI provides some major advantages including these:
  - Central operation of services and resources
  - Consistent operation experience across multiple service providers
  - Effortless navigation and easy staff training
  - A window to any organizational persona
- The Anthos UI provides multiple usages, including cluster management, service operation, and observability, using a unified interface.

Computing environment built on Kubernetes

Scott Surovich

This chapter covers

- Understanding Kubernetes management, architecture, components, and resources
- Declarative application management
- Understanding Kubernetes resources
- Controlling Pod scheduling
- Examples and case study

Like many new technologies, Kubernetes can be difficult to learn and implement. Creating a cluster manually requires an extensive skill set that includes public key infrastructure, Kubernetes, Linux, and networking. Many vendors recognized this problem and have automated cluster creation, allowing you to create Kubernetes clusters with little to no Kubernetes background. Although automation allows anyone to create a cluster, it also eliminates a lot of Kubernetes knowledge that can help you troubleshoot problems that you may encounter as a cluster administrator, or a developer, consuming the platform.

29

The question that comes up frequently is, "Do you really need to know Kubernetes?" The answer differs, depending on the role you will play in the cluster, but no matter what role you will have, you will need to have some understanding of how Kubernetes functions. For example, if you are a cluster admin, you should understand how all the cluster components interact. This understanding will help you troubleshoot cluster and workload deployment problems. As a developer, you should understand basic Kubernetes operations and the various Kubernetes resources, also referred to as Kubernetes *objects*, which can be used to deploy your workloads. It's also important to understand how to force your deployment to a node or a set of nodes by using options like selectors, tolerations, and affinity/anti-affinity rules.

In this chapter, you will learn how each component in a Kubernetes cluster interacts with the others. Once you understand the basic interaction, you will learn about the most used Kubernetes resources. Finally, to end the chapter, you will learn the details of how Kubernetes schedules workloads and how to constrain the scheduler to place workloads based on labels, selectors, and affinity/anti-affinity rules.

3.1   *Why do you need to understand Kubernetes?*

At the heart of Anthos is Kubernetes, which provides the compute engine for applications running in a cluster. Kubernetes is an open source project created by Google that has been around for years. At the time of this writing, the Cloud Native Computing Foundation has certified 90 Kubernetes offerings. Among the certified offerings are distributions from IBM, Canonical, SUSE, Mirantis, VMware, Rancher, Amazon, Microsoft, and, of course, Google.

Hearing the common complaint that deploying Kubernetes was "too difficult," most vendor solutions made it easier. Although making the installation easier is a necessary step for most enterprises and frees up time to focus on more important activities, it does lead to a problem: not understanding the basic components and resources included in a cluster.

Using a different service example, assume you have an application that requires a new database. You may not have any idea how to create a new database schema or SQL queries, but you know that Google offers MySQL, and you create a new instance for the application. The MySQL instance will be created automatically, and once it has been deployed, you can create a database using the GCP console.

Because you may not have a strong SQL background, you may stumble through and create a single table in the database with multiple fields that will work with the application. The database may perform well for a few days or weeks, but as it gets larger, the performance will start to slow down. A single-table database, though easy to implement, is not an optimized solution. If you had a SQL background, you would have created a database with multiple tables and relationships, making the database more efficient and scalable.

This scenario is like understanding how Kubernetes works and the features provided by the system. To use Kubernetes to its full potential, you should understand the underlying architecture and the role of each component. Knowing how components integrate with one another and what resources can be used will help you make good architectural decisions when deploying a cluster or deploying an application.

The details to cover each cluster component and the more than 60 resource types included with Kubernetes could fill a series of books. Because many of the topics in this chapter reference resources including Pods and DaemonSets, it will begin with a Kubernetes resource pocket guide, providing a brief definition of the most used API resources.

In this chapter, we will provide a background of Kubernetes components, resources, and commonly used add-on components, which provide the compute power that powers Anthos. If you are newer to Kubernetes, many books on the market today explain how to build a cluster and how to use kubectl and devote entire chapters to each Kubernetes resource. This chapter should be viewed as an introduction to resources, with an in-depth focus on how to control the placement of deployments in a cluster.

3.1.1 Technical requirements

The hands-on portion of this chapter will require you to have access to a Kubernetes cluster running in GCP with the following deployment pattern:

- The cluster must be deployed across at least two different zones in the same region. The examples shown in this chapter will be based on us-east4 zones, across us-east4-a, us-east4-b, and us-east4-c, but you can use different zones for your cluster.
- Each zone must contain at least one Kubernetes node.

This chapter is not specific to Kubernetes on GCP; the resources and constructs used in the exercises are applicable to any Kubernetes cluster.

3.1.2 History and overview

Because the audience for this book includes readers who may be newer to Kubernetes and readers who are seasoned Kubernetes administrators, we have added information covering some history and progression from physical servers to containers in the online appendix A.

3.1.3 Managing Kubernetes clusters

When a company decides to run a Kubernetes cluster in the cloud, they will often use the cloud provider's native offering, such as the following:

- Google Kubernetes Engine (GKE): https://cloud.google.com/kubernetes-engine/
- Amazon Elastic Kubernetes Service (EKS): https://aws.amazon.com/eks/
- Azure Kubernetes Service (AKS): http://mng.bz/GR7V

Using the native offering offers the quickest and easiest way to get a new cluster up and running, because the providers have automated the installation. To get from ground zero to a running cluster, you need to provide only a few pieces of information, like the number and size of the nodes, zones, and regions. With this information and a click or API call, you can have a cluster in a few minutes, ready to deploy your applications.

Google was the first cloud service provider to offer their Kubernetes solution across both the cloud and on-prem, without requiring any specialized hardware solution. Before Google did this, other offerings required organizations to deploy a different solution for each cloud provider and their on-prem clusters. Using a different solution for multiple installations often leads to a variety of different problems, including these:

- Increased staff to support each deployment
- Differences in the deployment of an application for on-prem and off-prem
- Different identity management solutions
- Different Kubernetes versions
- Different security models
- Difficulty in standardizing cluster operations
- No single view for all clusters

Each of these differences makes the job of running Kubernetes more difficult and, ultimately, more costly for an organization.

Google recognized these problems and created Anthos, which addresses the on-prem and off-prem challenges by providing a Kubernetes installation and management solution that not only works on GCP and on-prem clusters but also in other cloud providers like AWS and Azure running Anthos.

Using Anthos provides a common environment no matter where you deploy it. Imagine having a single support path and a common set of tools for all your clusters in GCP, AWS, Azure, and on-prem. Anthos provides an organization with many advantages, including the following:

- A consolidated view of clusters inside the Anthos console
- A common service mesh offering
- Configuration management using ACM
- All options supported by Google: a single point of contact for all cluster components

Best of all, Anthos is based on the upstream Kubernetes, so you get all the standard features but with the added tools and components that Anthos provides, making multiple cloud cluster management easier.

Next, we will jump into the architecture that makes up a Kubernetes cluster and how the components communicate with each other.

3.2   *Kubernetes architecture*

Like any infrastructure, Kubernetes consists of multiple components that communicate to create a cluster. The components are grouped into two layers: the control plane and the worker nodes. The control plane keeps the cluster state, accepting incoming requests, scheduling workloads, and running controllers, whereas the worker nodes communicate with the control plane to report available resources, run container workloads, and maintain node network rules.

   If you are running Anthos on GCP, you may not be familiar with the components of the control plane or the worker nodes, because you do not interact with them like you would with an on-prem installation. As this section will explain, Kubernetes clusters have a layer called the control plane that contains the components required to run Kubernetes. When a cluster is running in GCP, the control plane is created in a Google-managed project, which limits you from interacting with the admin nodes and the Kubernetes components.

   All GKE clusters can be viewed in your GCP console, located under the Kubernetes Engine section. For each cluster, you can view the details of the nodes by clicking on the cluster in the details pane, then selecting Nodes. The node details will be displayed, as shown in figure 3.1.

Kubernetes Engine	← Clusters	✏ EDIT	🗑 DELETE	⊞ ADD NODE POOL	⊞ DEPLOY	⊠ CONNECT	⧉ DUPLICATE

anthos-1

Details   Storage   Nodes

Nodes

Name ∧	Status	CPU requested	CPU allocatable	Memory requested	Memory allocatable	Storage requested	Storage allocatable
gke-anthos-1-default-pool-bb1016e5-f166	✅ Ready	203 mCPU	940 mCPU	262.14 MB	2.77 GB	0 B	0 B
gke-anthos-1-default-pool-bb1016e5-h2dj	✅ Ready	463 mCPU	940 mCPU	377.49 MB	2.77 GB	0 B	0 B
gke-anthos-1-default-pool-bb1016e5-hkdp	✅ Ready	639 mCPU	940 mCPU	730.86 MB	2.77 GB	0 B	0 B

Figure 3.1   GKE node details

Unlike GKE on GCP, an on-prem installation of GKE provides access to the control plane nodes and Kubernetes resources for the clusters. Of course, Google still supports the on-prem control plane, but you may be asked to look at components to troubleshoot any problems or configuration changes to a cluster. If you have only deployed GKE on GCP, you may not know all the components of the control plane and how they interact. Understanding this interaction is vital to troubleshooting and finding root causes to any problems.

   NOTE   When you deploy a GKE on-prem cluster, three Kubernetes config files are created. One will be named using the user cluster's name with a suffix of -kubeconfig, one is called kubeconfig, and the last one is called internal-cluster-kubeconfig-debug. The kubeconfig file is configured to target the load-balanced address of the admin cluster, whereas internal-cluster-kubeconfig-debug is configured to target the admin cluster's API server directly.

To view the multiple configuration files, see figure 3.2.

   With the importance of understanding the system, let's move on to each layer in a cluster, starting with the control plane.

GKE On-Prem Admin Cluster (Control Plane)

When a user cluster is added to an Admin cluster, a new namespace is created using the name that was given to the user cluster. In this example, the admin cluster is managing two user clusters, `cluster-001` and `cluster-002`. Each namespace contains the Control Plane components for the user cluster.

Cluster Namespace

NAME	STATUS	AGE
default	Active	65d
gke-system	Active	65d
cluster-001	Active	65d
cluster-002	Active	65d
kube-node-lease	Active	65d
kube-public	Active	65d

`Cluster-001` **Namespace**

NAME	READY
calico-controller-xxx	1/1
cluster-api-controller	2/2
kube-apiserver-0	3/3
kube-controller-manager-xxx	2/2
kube-etcd-0	2/2
kube-etcd-events-0	2/2
kube-scheduler-xxx	2/2
metrics-server-operator-xxx	1/1
monitoring-operator-xxx	1/1

`Cluster-002` **Namespace**

NAME	READY
calico-controller-xxx	1/1
cluster-api-controller	2/2
kube-apiserver-0	3/3
kube-controller-manager-xxx	2/2
kube-etcd-0	2/2
kube-etcd-events-0	2/2
kube-scheduler-xxx	2/2
metrics-server-operator-xxx	1/1
monitoring-operator-xxx	1/1

GKE Kubeconfig Files

Config File	API Server Used
kubeconfig	Admin Cluster
internal-cluster-kubeconfig-debug	Admin Cluster
cluster-001-kubeconfig	Cluster-001
cluster-002-kubeconfig	Cluster-002

Figure 3.2   Admin cluster and user cluster configuration files

3.2.1   *Understanding the cluster layers*

The first layer, the control plane, contains five or six components (in reality, the two controllers actually contain multiple components). The control plane includes the components that provide cluster management, cluster state, and scheduling features. We will detail each component in the next section, but for now, we just want to introduce the control plane components, shown here:

- ETCD
- The Kubernetes API server
- The Kubernetes scheduler
- The Kubernetes controller manager, which contains multiple controllers
  - Node controller
  - Endpoint controller
  - Replication controller
  - Service account/token controller
- The cloud controller manager, which contains multiple controllers
  - Route controller
  - Service controller
  - Node controller

To view a graphical representation of the control plane, see figure 3.3. At the end of this section, we will provide a complete component diagram, including how each component communicates.

Figure 3.3 Control plane components

The second layer in the cluster is the collection of worker nodes, which are responsible for running the cluster workloads. Each worker node has three components that work together to run applications, as shown in figure 3.4.

Figure 3.4 Worker node components

Up to this point, we haven't explained how each component interacts with the others. Before we show a full diagram of cluster interactions, we need to understand each component in the cluster. In the next section, we will explain each cluster component, and, to close out the section, we will combine the two diagrams to show the connectivity between all components.

3.2.2 The control plane components

As mentioned earlier, the control plane includes up to six components. Each of the components works together to provide cluster services. Understanding each component is key to delivering a robust, stable cluster.

ETCD

Every resource in the cluster and its state are maintained in the etcd key-value database. The entire cluster state is stored inside this database, making etcd the most important component in a cluster. Without a functioning etcd database, you do not have a functioning cluster.

Because etcd is so important, you should always have at least three replicas running in a cluster. Depending on the size of the cluster, you may want to have more than three, but no matter how many you decide to run, always run an odd number of replicas. Running an odd number of etcd nodes allows the cluster to elect a majority leader, minimizing the chance of the etcd cluster going into a split-brain state. If a cluster goes into a split-brain state, more than one node claims to be the majority leader, which leads to data inconsistencies and corruption. If you find yourself in a split-brain state, you will need to recreate the etcd cluster from an etcd backup.

Although running multiple copies will make etcd highly available, you also need to create a regular backup of your database and store it outside of the cluster in a safe location. If you lose your entire cluster or your etcd database gets corrupted, you will be able to restore your backup to restore a node or the entire cluster. We will explain the process to back up etcd later in this chapter.

The last consideration for etcd after making it highly available and creating regular backups is security. The etcd database contains every Kubernetes resource, so it will contain sensitive data like secrets, which may contain data like passwords. If someone gets a copy of your etcd database, they can easily pull any of the resources out because, by default, they are stored as clear text.

Covering etcd could require an entire chapter. For more information on etcd, head over to the main etcd site at https://etcd.io/docs/. Google also provides the steps and a script to back up GKE on-prem clusters. You can find the documentation and the script at http://mng.bz/zm1r.

THE KUBERNETES API SERVER

The API server is the front door to a cluster. All requests that come into the cluster enter through the API server, which will interact with the other component to fulfill requests. These requests come from users and services from the kubectl CLI, Kubernetes Dashboard, or direct JSON API calls.

It's really an event-driven hub-and-spoke model. The API server encapsulates etcd. All other components communicate with the API server. The API server doesn't communicate with controllers directly in response to requests. Instead, the controllers watch for relevant change events.

THE KUBERNETES SCHEDULER

If the API server receives a request to create a Pod, it will communicate with the Kubernetes scheduler, which decides which worker node will run the workload.

When a workload attempts to request a resource that cannot be met, or has constraints that cannot be matched, it will fail to schedule and the Pod will not start. If this happens, you will need to find out why the scheduling failed and either change your deployment code or add resources to your nodes to fulfill the request.

THE KUBERNETES CONTROLLER MANAGER

The controller manager is often referred to as a *control loop*. To allow Kubernetes to keep all resources in a requested, desired state, the state of each resource must be compared to its requested state. The process that makes this happen is known as a *control loop*.

The Kubernetes controller manager consists of a single binary that runs separate threads for each "logical" controller. The bundled controllers and their roles are shown in table 3.1.

Table 3.1 Bundled controllers and their roles

Controller	Description
Node	Maintains the status of all nodes
Replication	Maintains the number of pods for replication controllers
Endpoint	Maintains the mapping of pods to services, creating endpoints for services
Service accounts/token	Creates the initial default account and API tokens for namespaces

The main concept to take away from the table is that by using a control loop, the manager constantly checks the resource(s) that it controls to keep them in the declared state.

The Kubernetes controller manager deals with internal Kubernetes resource states. If you are using a cloud provider, your cluster will need a controller to maintain certain resources, which is the role of the cloud controller manager.

THE CLOUD CONTROLLER MANAGER

NOTE You may not see this controller on every cluster you interact with. A cluster will run a cloud controller only if it has been configured to interface with a cloud provider.

To allow cloud providers flexibility, the cloud controller manager is separate from the standard Kubernetes controller manager. By decoupling the two controllers, each cloud provider can add features to their offering that may differ from other providers or base Kubernetes components.

Like the Kubernetes controller manager, the cloud controller manager uses a control loop to maintain the desired state of resources. It is also a single binary that runs multiple controllers and their processes, as shown in table 3.2.

Table 3.2 Controllers run by the cloud controller manager

Controller	Description
Node	Creates node resources and maintains the status of the nodes located in the cloud provider
Route	Maintains network routes to provide node communication
Service	Maintains cloud provider components like load balancers, network filtering, and IP addresses

Finally, when we say *cloud provider*, we do not mean you are limited to only public cloud service providers. At the time of this writing, Kubernetes includes support for the following cloud providers:

- Amazon AWS
- Microsoft Azure
- Google Cloud Platform (GCP)
- OpenStack
- Huawei
- vSphere

Now that the control plane has been explained, let's move on to the worker node components.

3.2.3   *Worker node components*

From a high level, you should have a basic understanding of the components in the control plane. It's the layer responsible for cluster interaction and workload deployments. Alone, the control plane can't do very much—it needs to have a target that can run the actual workload once it's scheduled, and that's where the worker node comes in.

THE KUBELET

The kubelet is the component responsible for running a Pod and for reporting the node's status to the Kubernetes scheduler. When the scheduler decides which node will run a workload, the kubelet retrieves it from the API server, and the Pod is created based on the specs that were pulled.

KUBE-PROXY

We will mention this in more detail when we discuss services in the next section, but for now you only need to understand a basic overview of kube-proxy. kube-proxy is responsible for creating and deleting network rules, which allow network connectivity to a Pod. If the host operating system offers a packet filter, kube-proxy will use it, but if no packet filter is offered, the traffic will be managed by kube-proxy itself.

Depending on the network provider you decide to use for a cluster, you may have the option to run your cluster in a kube-proxyless mode. A Container Network Interface (CNI) like Cilium uses eBPF to provide the same functionality that kube-proxy provides but without requiring additional components outside of the base CNI deployment.

CONTAINER RUNTIME

The container runtime is the component responsible for running the actual container on the host. It has become common for people to refer to the container runtime as simply Docker. This is understandable because Docker did bring containers to the masses, but over the years, other alternatives have been developed. Two of the most popular alternatives are CRI-O and containerd.

At one time, the container runtime was integrated into the kubelet, which made adding a new runtime difficult. As Kubernetes matured, the team developed the Container Runtime Interface (CRI), which provides the ability to simply "plug in" a container runtime. No matter which runtime is in use, its responsibility is the same: to run the actual container on the node.

Now that we have reviewed each layer and their components, let's show the connectivity between the two layers and how the components interact, as illustrated in figure 3.5.

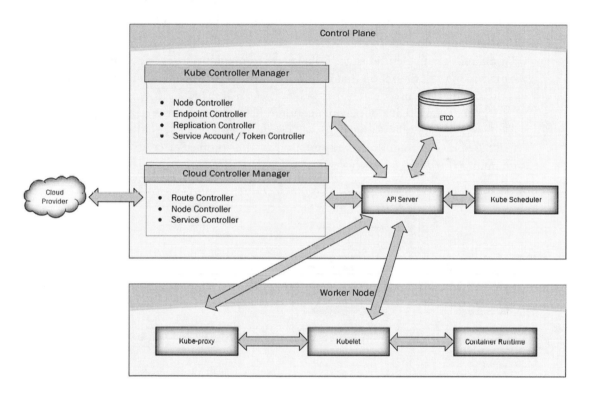

Figure 3.5   Cluster component communications

This concludes the section on Kubernetes cluster components. Knowing how the components interact will help you to diagnose problems and understand how the cluster interacts as a system.

Depending on your role, understanding the cluster components and how they interact may be less important than understanding cluster resources. Kubernetes resources are used by every user that interacts with a cluster, and users should understand, at the very least, the most used resources. For reference, you can read about Kubernetes resources on the Kubernetes website at http://mng.bz/0yRm.

To effectively deploy an application on Kubernetes, you need to understand the features of the infrastructure, starting with Kubernetes objects. Next, we will move on to DevOps paradigms and Kubernetes cluster components.

3.2.4 *Understanding declarative and imperative*

In DevOps, an automation framework can use two different implementation methods, referred to as *DevOps paradigms.* They include the declarative model and the imperative model.

Each of the paradigms will be explained in this chapter, but before diving into the differences between them, you should understand the concept of a control loop.

UNDERSTANDING CONTROL LOOPS

To maintain your desired state, Kubernetes implements a set of control loops. A control loop is an endless loop that is always checking that the declared state of a resource is the same as its current state.

If you declare that a deployment should have three replicas of a Pod, and one Pod is deleted accidentally, Kubernetes will create a new Pod to keep the states in sync. Figure 3.6 shows a graphical representation of the ReplicaSet control loop and how it maintains the desired replica count.

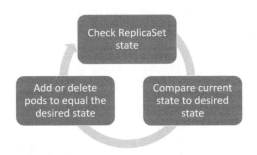

Figure 3.6   Control loop example

As you can see, a control loop doesn't need to be complex to maintain a desired state. The replication controller simply keeps looping through all the ReplicaSet resources in the cluster, comparing the currently available number of Pods to the desired number of Pods that is declared. Kubernetes will either add or delete a Pod to make the current replica count equal to the count that has been set on the deployment.

Understanding the features of Anthos and how Kubernetes maintains the declared state of a deployment is important for any user of Kubernetes, but it's only the beginning. Because deploying a cluster has been made so simple by many vendors, developers and administrators often overlook the advantages of understanding the entire system. As mentioned earlier, to design an effective cluster or application, you should understand the basic functionality of the cluster components. In the next section, the Kubernetes architecture will be covered, including the components of the control plane and worker nodes and how they interact with each other.

One of the first concepts to understand is the difference between the declarative and imperative models. Table 3.3 provides a brief description of each model.

Table 3.3   Declarative and imperative models

Model	Description
Declarative	Developers declare what they would like the system to do; there is no need to tell the system *how* to do it.
	The declarative model uses Kubernetes manifests to declare the application's desired state.
Imperative	Developers are responsible for creating each step required for the desired end state. The steps to create the deployment are completely defined by the developer.
	The imperative model uses kubectl commands like `create`, `run`, and `delete` to tell the API server what resources to manage.

In a declarative model, you can manage several resources in a single file. For example, if we wanted to deploy an NGINX web server that included a new namespace, the deployment, and a service, we would create a single YAML file with all the resources. The manifest would then be deployed using the kubectl `apply` command, which will create each resource and add an annotation that includes the last applied configuration. Because Kubernetes tracks the resources and you have all the resources in a single file, it is easier to manage and track changes to the deployment and resources.

In an imperative model, you must run multiple commands to create your final deployment. Using the previous example where you want to deploy an NGINX server, a service, and an Ingress rule, you would need to execute the following three kubectl commands:

```
kubectl create ns web-example
kubectl run ngnix-web --image=nginx:v1 -n web-example
kubectl create service clusterip nginx-web -tcp-80:80
```

Although this would accomplish the same deployment as our declarative example, it has some limitations that are not immediately noticeable using our simple example. One limitation is that the kubectl command does not allow you to configure every option available for each resource. In the example, we deploy a Pod with a single container running NGINX. If we needed to add a second container to perform a specialized task, like logging, we wouldn't be able to add it imperatively because the kubectl command does not have the option to launch two containers in a Pod.

It is a good practice to avoid using imperative deployments unless you are attempting to resolve a problem quickly. If you find yourself using imperative commands for any reason, you should keep track of your changes so that you can alter your declarative manifests to keep them in sync with any changes.

To understand how Kubernetes uses the declarative model, you need to understand how the system maintains the declared state with the currently running state for a deployment by using control loops.

3.2.5   *Understanding Kubernetes resources*

Throughout this book, you will see references to multiple Kubernetes resources. As mentioned earlier in the chapter, there are more than 60 resource types included with a new cluster, not including any custom resources that may be added through CRDs (custom resource definitions). Multiple Kubernetes books are available, so this chapter will provide only an introduction to each resource to provide a base knowledge that will be used in most of the chapters.

It's challenging to remember all the base resources, and you may not always have a pocket guide available to you. Luckily, you can use a few commands to look up resources and the options that are available for each. The first command, shown next, lists all the API resources available on a cluster:

```
kubectl api-resources
NAME                     SHORTNAMES    APIVERSION    NAMESPACED    KIND
bindings                               v1            true          Binding
componentstatuses        cs            v1            false         ComponentStatus
configmaps               cm            v1            true          ConfigMap
endpoints                ep            v1            true          Endpoints
events                   ev            v1            true          Event
limitranges              limits        v1            true          LimitRange
namespaces               ns            v1            false         Namespace
nodes                    no            v1            false         Node
persistentvolumeclaims   pvc           v1            true          PersistentVolumeClaim
persistentvolumes        pv            v1            false         PersistentVolume
pods                     po            v1            true          Pod
podtemplates                           v1            true          PodTemplate
replicationcontrollers   rc            v1            true          ReplicationController
resourcequotas           quota         v1            true          ResourceQuota
secrets                                v1            true          Secret
serviceaccounts          sa            v1            true          ServiceAccount
services                 svc           v1            true          Service
```

The output provides the name of the resource—any short name, if it can be used at a namespace level—and the kind of resource. This is helpful if you know what each one does, but you forgot the name or whether it can be set at a namespace level. If you need additional information for any resource, Kubernetes provides the next command, which provides the details for each one:

```
kubectl explain <resource name>
```

The explain command provides a short description of the resource and all the fields that can be used in a manifest. For example, next you see a brief description of what a Pod is and some of the fields that can be used when creating the resource:

```
KIND:   Pod
VERSION: v1

DESCRIPTION:
    Pod is a collection of containers that can run on a host. This resource is
       created by clients and scheduled onto hosts.
```

```
FIELDS:
 apiVersion  <string>
  APIVersion defines the versioned schema of this representation of an
  object. Servers should convert recognized schemas to the latest internal
  value, and may reject unrecognized values. More info:
  https://git.k8s.io/community/contributors/devel/sig-architecture/api-
    conventions.md#resources

 kind <string>
  Kind is a string value representing the REST resource this object
  represents. Servers may infer this from the endpoint the client submits
  requests to. Cannot be updated. In CamelCase. More info:
  https://git.k8s.io/community/contributors/devel/sig-architecture/api-
    conventions.md#types-kinds

 metadata   <Object>
  Standard object's metadata. More info:
  https://git.k8s.io/community/contributors/devel/sig-architecture/api-
    conventions.md#metadata
```

As you can see from the output, each field has a detailed explanation and a link to provide additional detailed information, when applicable.

You may not have access to a system with kubectl installed all the time, so table 3.4 provides a short description of most of the common resources you will use in a cluster.

Table 3.4 Resources used in a cluster

Kubernetes resource	Description
ConfigMaps	Hold configuration data for Pods.
EndpointSlice	A collection of Pods that are used as targets by services.
Namespace	Used to divide clusters between multiple developers or applications.
Node	Provides the compute power to a Kubernetes cluster.
PersistentVolumeClaim	Allows an application to claim a persistent volume.
PersistentVolume	A storage resource provisioned at the cluster layer. Claims to Persistent-Volume are provided by a PersistentVolumeClaim.
Pod	A container or a collection of containers.
ResourceQuota	Sets quota restrictions, enforced per namespace.
Secret	Holds secret data of a certain type. The total bytes of the values in the data field must be less than the MaxSecretSize bytes configuration value.
ServiceAccount	Provides an identity that can be authenticated and authorized to resources in a cluster.
Service	Provides a named abstraction of software service consisting of a local port that the proxy listens on and the selector that determines which Pods will answer requests sent through the proxy.
CustomResourceDefinition	Represents a resource that should be exposed on the API server.

Table 3.4   Resources used in a cluster *(continued)*

Kubernetes resource	Description
DaemonSet	Used to deploy a container to all nodes, or a subset of nodes, in the cluster. This includes any new nodes that may be added after the initial deployment.
Deployment	Enables declarative updates for Pods and ReplicaSets.
ReplicaSet	Ensures that a specified number of Pod replicas are running at any given time.
StatefulSet	StatefulSet represents a set of Pods with consistent identities and controlled Pod starting and stopping.
Ingress	A collection of rules that direct inbound connections to reach the Pod endpoints.
NetworkPolicy	Defines what network traffic is allowed for a set of Pods.
PodSecurityPolicy	Controls the ability to make requests that affect the security context that will be applied to a Pod and container.
ClusterRole	A cluster-level, logical grouping of PolicyRules that can be referenced as a unit by a RoleBinding or ClusterRoleBinding.
ClusterRoleBinding	Assigns the permissions defined in a ClusterRole to a user, group, or service account. The scope of a ClusterRoleBinding is cluster wide.
Role	A namespaced, logical grouping of PolicyRules that can be referenced as a unit by a RoleBinding.
RoleBinding	Assigns the permissions defined in a Role to a user, group, or service account. It can reference a Role in the same namespace or a ClusterRole in the global namespace. The scope of a RoleBinding is only to the namespace it is defined in.
StorageClass	Describes the parameters for a class of storage for which PersistentVolumes can be dynamically provisioned.

Understanding the resources available is one of the keys to creating the best application deployments and to helping troubleshoot cluster or deployment problems. Without an understanding of these resources, you may not know what to look at if an Ingress rule isn't working as expected. Using the resources in the table, you can find three resources that are required for an Ingress rule. The first is the Ingress itself, the second is the Service, and the last is the Endpoints/EndpointSlices.

Looking at the flow between resources for Ingress, an incoming request is evaluated by the Ingress controller, and a matching Ingress resource is found. Ingress rules route traffic based on the Service name defined in the Ingress rule, and, finally, the request is sent to a Pod from the Endpoints created by the Service.

3.2.6 *Kubernetes resources in depth*

A brief overview of resources and what they are used for is a great refresher, if you already have experience with resources. We realize that not every reader will have years of experience interacting with Kubernetes resources, so in this section, you will find additional details on some of the most commonly used cluster resources.

One thing that all GKE Kubernetes clusters have in common, on-prem or off-prem, is that they are built on the upstream Kubernetes code, and they all contain the base set of Kubernetes resources. Interacting with these base types is something you are likely to do daily, and having a strong understanding of each component, its function, and use case examples is important.

NAMESPACES

Namespaces provide a scope for names. Names of resources need to be unique within a namespace, but not across namespaces.

Namespaces create a logical separation between tenants in the cluster, providing a cluster with multitenancy. As defined by Gartner, "Multitenancy is a reference to the mode of operation of software where multiple independent instances of one or multiple applications operate in a shared environment. The instances (tenants) are logically isolated, but physically integrated" (http://mng.bz/Kl74).

Kubernetes resources that are created at a namespace level are referred to as being *namespaced*. If you read that a resource is namespaced, it means the resource is managed at a namespace level, rather than at a cluster level.

In a namespace, you can create resources that will provide security and resource limits. To provide a safe multitenant cluster, you can use the following categories of Kubernetes resources:

- RBAC
- Resource quotas
- Network policies
- Namespace security resources (previously Pod security policies)

We will discuss each of the resources in more detail in this section, but for now, you need to understand only that a namespace is a logical partition of a cluster.

Namespaces are also used when you create a service, which we will cover in the services section. The service is assigned a DNS name that includes the service name and the namespace. For example, if you created two services called myweb1 and myweb2 in a namespace called sales, in a cluster named `cluster.local`, the assigned DNS names would be as follows:

- `myweb1.sales.svc.cluster.local`
- `myweb2.sales.svc.cluster.local`

PODS

A Pod is the smallest deployable unit that Kubernetes can manage and may contain one or more containers. If a Pod has multiple containers running, they all share a common networking stack, allowing each container to communicate with the other containers in the Pod using localhost or 127.0.0.1. They also share any volumes that are mounted to the Pod, allowing each container access to a shared file location.

When a pod is created, it is assigned an IP address, and the assigned address should be considered ephemeral. You should never target the IP address of a Pod because it will likely change at some point when the Pod is replaced. To target an application that is running in a Pod, you should target a service name, which will use endpoints to direct traffic to the correct Pod where the application is running. We will discuss endpoints and services in their respective topics in this section.

Although no standard exists for how many containers should be in a single Pod, the best practice is to add containers that should be scheduled and managed together. Actions such as scaling and Pod restarts should be considered when deciding to add multiple containers to a Pod. Events like these are handled at a Pod level, not at a container level, so these actions will affect all containers in the Pod.

> **Example**
>
> You create a Pod with a web server and a database. You decide that you need to scale the web server to handle the current traffic load. When you scale the Pod, it will scale *both* the web server and the database server.
>
> To scale only the web server, you should deploy a Pod with the web server and a second Pod with the database server, which will allow you to scale each application independently.

Many design patterns use multiple containers in a Pod. A common use case for multiple containers in a Pod is referred to as a *sidecar*. A sidecar is a container that runs with the main container in your Pod, usually to add some functionality to the main container without requiring any changes to it. Some common examples that use sidecars to handle tasks follow:

- Logging
- Monitoring
- Istio sidecar
- Backup sidecar (i.e., Veritas NetBackup)

You can look at other examples on the Kubernetes site at http://mng.bz/91Ja.

Understanding Pods is a key point to understanding Kubernetes deployments. They will be the most common resource that you will interact with.

LABELS AND SELECTORS

Kubernetes uses labels to identify, organize, and link resources, allowing you to identify attributes. When you create a resource in Kubernetes, you can supply one or more key-value pair labels like `app:frontend-webserver` or `lob=sales`.

Selectors are used to reference a set of resources, allowing you to select the resource(s) you want to link, or select, using the assigned labels. You can think of selectors as a dynamic grouping mechanism—any label that matches the selector will be added as a target. This will be shown in the next section covering the services resource, which uses selectors to link the service to the Pods running the application.

SERVICES

We can use many of the previous resources to provide a full picture of how they connect to create an application. The last piece of the puzzle is the Service resource, which exposes an application to allow it to accept requests using a defined DNS name.

Remember that when you create a Pod with your application, it is assigned an IP address. This IP address will change when the Pod is replaced, which is why you never want to configure a connection to the Pods using an IP address.

Unlike Pods, which are ephemeral by nature, a Service is stable once created and is rarely deleted and recreated, providing a stable IP address and DNS name. Even if a Service is deleted and recreated, the DNS name will remain the same, providing a stable name that you can target to access the application. You can create a few Service types in Kubernetes, as shown in table 3.5.

Table 3.5   Services in Kubernetes

Service name	Description	Network scope
ClusterIP	Exposes the service internally to the cluster.	Internal External by using an Ingress rule
NodePort	Exposes the service internally to the cluster. Exposes the service to external clients using the assigned NodePort. Using the NodePort with any worker node DNS/IP address will provide a connection to the Pod(s).	Internal and external
LoadBalancer	Exposes the service internally to the cluster. Exposes the service externally to the cluster using an external load-balancer service.	Internal and external

Now let's use an example to explain how Kubernetes uses services to expose an application in a namespace called `sales` in a cluster using the name `cluster.local`:

1 A deployment is created for an NGINX server.
   - The deployment name is `nginx-frontend`.
   - The deployment has been labeled with `app: frontend-web`.
   - Three replicas have been created.

   The three running Pods have been assigned the IP addresses 192.10.1.105, 192.10.3.107, and 192.10.4.108.

2 To provide access to the server, a new service is deployed called `frontend-web`. In the manifest to create the service, a *label selector* is used to select any Pods that match `app: frontend-web`.

3   Kubernetes will use the service request and the selector to create matching
    endpoints.

    Because the selector matches the label that was used in the deployment for
    the NGINX server, Kubernetes will create an endpoint that links to the three
    Pod IPs: 192.10.1.105, 192.10.3.107, and 192.10.4.108.

4   The service will receive an IP address from the cluster's Service IP pool, and a
    DNS name that is created using the `<service name>.<namespace>.svc.<cluster`
    `domain>`.

    Because the application name is `nginx-frontend`, the DNS name will be
    `nginx-frontend.sales.svc.cluster.local`.

If any of the Pod IPs change due to a restart, the endpoints will be updated by the
kube-controller-manager, providing you a stable endpoint to the Pods, even when a
Pod IP address changes.

ENDPOINTSLICES
EndpointSlices map Kubernetes services to Pod(s) that are running the application,
linked by matching labels between the service selector and the Pod(s) with a matching
label. A graphical representation is shown in figure 3.7.

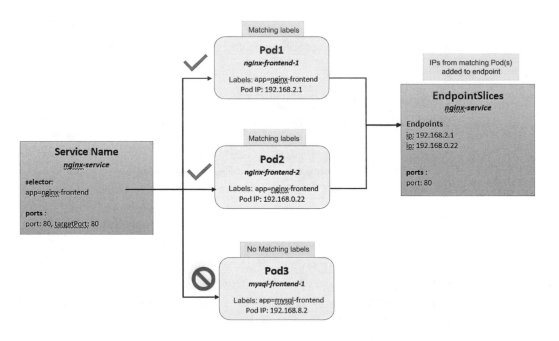

Figure 3.7   Kubernetes endpoints

In this figure, a service named `nginx-service` has been created in a namespace. The
service is using a selector for the key app, equal to the value `nginx-frontend`. Using

the selector, Kubernetes will look for any matching labels in the namespace equal to `app=nginx-frontend`. The namespace has three running Pods, and two of the Pods have been labeled with `app=nginx-frontend`. Because the selector matches, all matching Pod IP addresses are added to the EndpointSlices.

ANNOTATIONS

Annotations may look similar to selectors at a first glance. They are key-value pairs, just like labels are, but unlike labels, they are not used by selectors to create a collection of services.

You can use annotations to create records in a resource, like Git branch information, image hashes, support contacts, and more.

CONFIGMAPS

ConfigMaps are used to store application information that is not confidential, separate from the container image. Although you could store a configuration directly in your container image, it would make your deployment too rigid—any configuration change would require you to create your new image. This would lead to maintaining multiple images, one for each configuration.

A better method would be to store the configuration in a ConfigMap that is read in by your Pod when it is started. ConfigMaps can be mounted as a file in the container or as environment variables, depending on the application requirements. Deploying the image with a different configuration requires only a different ConfigMap, rather than an entire image build.

For example, imagine you have a web server image that requires a different configuration based on deployment location. You want to use the same image across your entire organization, regardless of the location where the container will run. To accomplish this, you create a web container image that is configured to use a ConfigMap for the web server configuration. By using an external configuration, you are making your image portable by allowing a configuration outside of the container itself.

SECRETS

Secrets are like ConfigMaps because they contain external information that will be used by Pods. Unlike ConfigMaps, secrets are not stored in cleartext; they are stored using Base64 encoding.

If you have worked with Base64 encoding before, you are probably thinking that it's not very different from, or more secure than, cleartext—and you would be right. Secrets in Kubernetes do not use Base64 encoding to hide the secret; they are Base64 encoded to allow secrets to store binary information. If a person has access to view the secret, it is trivial to decode the information. Because of this, it is suggested you encrypt your secrets using an external secret manager like Vault or Google Secret Manager.

> **Note**
>
> You can also encrypt secrets when they are stored in etcd, but this encrypts the value only in the database, not in Kubernetes. If you enable this feature, you are protecting the secrets in the etcd database only. To secure your secrets, you should use both encryption methods because this will protect your secrets both in the cluster and in etcd.
>
> etcd was discussed in section 3.2.2, "The control plane components."

RESOURCEQUOTAS

Remember that namespaces are used to provide a logical separation for applications or teams. Because a cluster may be shared with multiple applications, we need to have a way to control any effect a single namespace may have on the other cluster resources. Luckily, Kubernetes includes ResourceQuotas to provide resource controls.

A quota can be set on any standard Kubernetes resource that is namespaced; therefore, ResourceQuotas are set at a namespace level and control the resources that the namespace can consume, including the following:

- CPU
- Memory
- Storage
- Pods
- Services

Quotas allow you to control the resources that a namespace can consume, allowing you to share a cluster with multiple namespaces while providing a "guarantee" to cluster resources.

RBAC

Role-based access control (RBAC), is used to control what users can do within a cluster. Roles are created and assigned permissions, which are then assigned to users or groups, providing permissions to the cluster.

To provide RBAC, Kubernetes uses roles and binding resources. Roles are used to create a set of permissions to a resource or resources, whereas bindings are used to assign the permission set to a user or service.

ROLES AND CLUSTERROLES

A Role creates a set of permissions for a resource or resources. Two different types of Roles in Kubernetes are used to define the scope of the permissions, as shown in table 3.6.

Table 3.6   Roles used in Kubernetes

Role type	Scope	Description
Role	Namespace	Permissions in a Role can be used only in the namespace in which it was created.
ClusterRole	Cluster	Permissions in a ClusterRole can be used cluster wide.

The scope of Roles can be confusing for people who are new to Kubernetes. The Role resource is more straightforward than the ClusterRole resource. When you create a Role, it must contain a namespace value, which creates the role in the assigned namespace. Because a Role exists only in the namespace, it can be used to assign permissions only in the namespace itself—it cannot be used anywhere else in the cluster.

A ClusterRole is created at the cluster level and can be used anywhere in the cluster to assign permissions. When assigned to the cluster level, the permissions that are granted in the ClusterRole will be assigned to all defined resources in the cluster. However, if you use a ClusterRole at a namespace level, the permissions will be available only in the assigned namespace.

Two of the most common ClusterRoles are the built-in admin and view. By themselves, Roles and ClusterRoles do not assign a set of permissions to any user. To assign a Role to a user, you need to bind the Role using a RoleBinding or a ClusterRoleBinding.

ROLEBINDING AND CLUSTERROLEBINDING

Roles simply define the set of permissions that will be allowed for resources; they do not assign the granted permissions to any user or service. To grant the permissions defined in a role, you need to create a binding.

Similar to Roles and ClusterRoles, bindings have two scopes, as described in table 3.7.

Table 3.7   Binding types and their scopes

Binding type	Scope	Description
RoleBinding	Namespace	Can be used to assign permissions only in the namespace in which it was created
ClusterRoleBinding	Cluster	Can be used to assign permissions cluster wide

Now that we have discussed Kubernetes resources, let's move on to how you can control where a Pod will be scheduled to run.

3.2.7   *Controlling Pod scheduling*

In this section, we will explain how you can control where a workload is placed using features like node labels, affinity/anti-affinity rules, selectors, taints, and tolerations.

As Kubernetes has gained popularity, the use cases have grown and become more complex. You may run into deployments that requires special scheduling, such as the following:

- A Pod that requires a GPU or other specialized hardware
- Forcing Pods to run on the same node
- Forcing Pods to run on different nodes

- Specific local storage requirements
- Using locally installed NVMe drives

If you simply deploy a manifest to your cluster, the scheduler does not take any "special" considerations into account when selecting a node. If you deployed a Pod that required CUDA and the Pod was scheduled to run on a node that did not have a GPU, the application would fail to start because the required hardware would not be available to the application.

Kubernetes provides the ability to force a Pod to run on a particular node, or set of nodes, using advanced scheduling options that are set at the node level and in your deployment. At the node level, we use node labels and node taints to group nodes, and at the deployment level, we use node selectors, affinity/anti-affinity rules, and taints/tolerations to decide on Pod placement.

USING NODE LABELS AND TAINTS

At the node level, you can use two methods to control the Pods that will be scheduled on the node or nodes. The first method is by labeling the node, and the second is by tainting the node. Although both methods allow you to control whether a Pod will be scheduled on the node, they have different use cases—either attracting the Pods or repelling them.

ATTRACTING VERSUS REPELLING

You can use labels to group a set of nodes to target in your deployment, forcing the Pod(s) to run on that particular set of nodes. When you label a node, you are not rejecting any workloads. A label is an optional value that can be used by a deployment, if a value is set in the deployment to use a label. In this way, you are setting an attraction for Pods that may have a requirement that a label will provide, for example, gpu=true.

To label a node using kubectl, you use the following label option:

```
kubectl label nodes node1 gpu=true
```

If a deployment requires a GPU, it uses a selector that tells the scheduler that it needs to be scheduled on a node with a label gpu=true. The scheduler will look for nodes with a matching label and then schedule the Pod to run on one of the nodes with a matching label. If a matching label cannot be found, the Pod will fail to be scheduled and will not start.

Using a label is completely optional. Using the previous example label, if you create a deployment that does not select the gpu=true label, your Pod will not be excluded from nodes that contain the label.

Taints work differently: rather than creating a key value that invites the Pods to be run on it, you use a taint to repel any scheduling request that cannot tolerate the value set by the taint. To create a taint, you need to supply a key value and an effect, which controls whether a Pod is scheduled. For example, if you wanted to control the nodes that have a GPU, you could set a taint on a node using kubectl like this:

```
kubectl taint nodes node1 gpu=true:NoSchedule
```

This would taint `node1` with the key-value of `gpu=true` and the effect of `NoSchedule`, which tells the scheduler to repel all scheduling requests that do not contain a toleration of `gpu=true`. Unlike a label, which would allow Pods that do not specify a label to be scheduled, a taint setting with the effect `NoSchedule` will deny any Pod that does not "tolerate" `gpu=true` to be scheduled.

Taints have three effects that can be set: `NoSchedule`, `PreferNoSchedule`, and `NoExecute`. Each one sets a control on how the taint will be applied:

- `NoSchedule`—This is a "hard" setting that will deny any scheduling request that does not tolerate the taint.
- `PreferNoSchedule`—This is a "soft" setting that will attempt to avoid scheduling a Pod that does not tolerate the taint.
- `NoExecute`—This affects already running Pods on a node; it is not used for scheduling a Pod.

Now that we have explained how to create labels and taints on nodes, we need to understand how a deployment is configured to control Pod placement.

USING NODE NODESELECTORS

When a Pod is created, you can add a `nodeSelector` to your manifest to control the node on which the Pod will be scheduled. By using any label that is assigned to a node, you can force the scheduler to schedule the Pod on a node or a set of nodes.

You may not know all the labels available on a cluster. If you have access, you can use kubectl to get a list of the nodes and all labels by using the `get nodes` command with the `--show-labels` option as follows:

```
kubectl get nodes --show-labels
```

This will list each node and the labels that have been assigned, as shown here:

```
NAME                                    STATUS   ROLES    AGE    VERSION       LABELS
gke-cluster-1-default-pool-77fd9484-7fd6   Ready    <none>   3m28s  v1.16.11-gke.5    beta.kubernetes.io/arch=amd64,beta.kubernetes.io/instance-type=e2-medium
,beta.kubernetes.io/os=linux,cloud.google.com/gke-nodepool=default-pool,cloud.google.com/gke-os-distribution=cos,cloud.google.com/gke-preemptible=true,failure
-domain.beta.kubernetes.io/region=us-central1,failure-domain.beta.kubernetes.io/zone=us-central1-a,kubernetes.io/arch=amd64,kubernetes.io/hostname=gke-cluster
-1-default-pool-77fd9484-7fd6,kubernetes.io/os=linux
gke-cluster-1-default-pool-ca0442ad-hqk5   Ready    <none>   3m18s  v1.16.11-gke.5    beta.kubernetes.io/arch=amd64,beta.kubernetes.io/instance-type=e2-medium
,beta.kubernetes.io/os=linux,cloud.google.com/gke-nodepool=default-pool,cloud.google.com/gke-os-distribution=cos,cloud.google.com/gke-preemptible=true,failure
-domain.beta.kubernetes.io/region=us-central1,failure-domain.beta.kubernetes.io/zone=us-central1-b,kubernetes.io/arch=amd64,kubernetes.io/hostname=gke-cluster
-1-default-pool-ca0442ad-hqk5,kubernetes.io/os=linux
gke-cluster-1-default-pool-ead436da-8j7k   Ready    <none>   3m19s  v1.16.11-gke.5    beta.kubernetes.io/arch=amd64,beta.kubernetes.io/instance-type=e2-medium
,beta.kubernetes.io/os=linux,cloud.google.com/gke-nodepool=default-pool,cloud.google.com/gke-os-distribution=cos,cloud.google.com/gke-preemptible=true,failure
-domain.beta.kubernetes.io/region=us-central1,failure-domain.beta.kubernetes.io/zone=us-central1-c,kubernetes.io/arch=amd64,kubernetes.io/hostname=gke-cluster
-1-default-pool-ead436da-8j7k,kubernetes.io/os=linux
```

You can also see the node labels in the GCP console, as shown in figure 3.8, by clicking Details for a node.

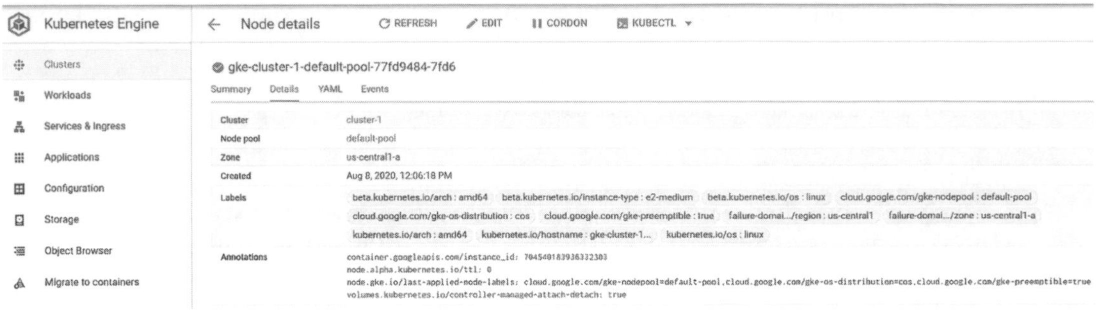

Figure 3.8 GCP node console view

Using a label from the cluster in the images, we can create a manifest that will deploy NGINX on the third node by using a `nodeSelector`, as shown next:

```
apiVersion: apps/v1
kind: Deployment
metadata:
 Labels:
   run: nginx-test
 name: nginx-test
spec:
 replicas: 1
 selector:
   matchLabels:
   run: nginx-test
 template:
   metadata:
   creationTimestamp: null
   labels:
     run: nginx-test
   spec:
    containers:
    - image: bitnami/nginx
     name: nginx-test
   nodeSelector:
     kubernetes.io/hostname: gke-cluster-1-default-pool-ead436da-8j7k
```

Using the value `kubernetes.io/hostname:gke-cluster-1-default-pool-ead436da-8j7k` in a `nodeSelector`, we forced the Pod to run the third node in the cluster. To verify the Pod did schedule on the correct node, we can use kubectl to get the Pods using the `-o wide` option, like this and as shown in figure 3.9:

```
kubectl get pods -o wide
```

```
NAME                         READY   STATUS    RESTARTS   AGE   IP          NODE
nginx-test-765fb5b456-nd66w  1/1     Running   0          9s    10.4.0.3    gke-cluster-1-default-pool-ead436da-8j7k
```

Figure 3.9 Getting Pods with wide output

The `nodeSelector` option allows you to use any label to control what nodes will be used to schedule your Pods. If the `nodeSelector` value does not match any nodes, the Pod will fail to schedule and will remain in a pending state until it is deleted or a label is updated on a node that matches the selector. In the next example, shown in figure 3.10, we tried to force a deployment to a `nodeSelector` that had a value of a host that does not exist in the cluster. First, we can look at all the Pods to check the status using kubectl `get pods`.

```
NAME                             READY   STATUS    RESTARTS   AGE
nginx-test-765fb5b456-nd66w      1/1     Running   0          3h25m
nginx-test2-6dccc98749-xng5h     0/1     Pending   0          2m55s
```

Figure 3.10   `get pods` output

Notice that the `nginx-test2` Pod is in a pending state. The next step in checking why the Pod fails to start is to describe the Pod:

```
kubectl describe pod nginx-test2-6dccc98749-xng5h
```

A description of the pod will be displayed, as illustrated in figure 3.11, including the current status at the bottom of the output.

```
Events:
  Type     Reason            Age                From                Message
  ----     ------            ---                ----                -------
  Warning  FailedScheduling  18s (x5 over 4m23s) default-scheduler  0/3 nodes are available: 3 node(s) didn't match node selector.
```

Figure 3.11   `kubectl describe` output

In the message area, the status shows `0/3 nodes are available: 3 node(s) didn't match node selector`. Because our `nodeSelector` did not match any existing label, the Pod failed to start. To resolve this, you should verify that the `nodeSelector` is correct and, if it is, verify that a node has the same label set.

USING AFFINITY RULES

Node affinity is another way to control which node your Pods will run on. Unlike a `nodeSelector`, an affinity rule can do the following:

- Contain additional syntax beyond a simple matching label.
- Schedule based on an affinity rule match, but if a match is not found, the Pod will schedule on any node.

Unlike a `nodeSelector`, which has a single value, a node affinity rule can contain operators, allowing for more complex selections. Table 3.8 contains a list of operators and a description of how they are evaluated.

Table 3.8   Operators and their descriptions

Operator	Description
In	Checks the label against a list. If any value is in the list, it is considered a match.
NotIn	Checks the label against a list, and if the value is not in the list, it is considered a match.
Exists	Checks whether the label exists; if it does, it is considered a match. Note: The value of the label does not matter and is not evaluated in the match.
DoesNotExist	Checks whether the label exists; if the label does not match any in the list, it is considered a match. Note: The value of the label does not matter and is not evaluated in the match.
Gt	Used to compare numeric values in a label; if a value is greater than (Gt) the label, it is considered a match. Note: This operator works only with a single number.
Lt	Used to compare numeric values in a label; if a value is less than (Lt) the label, it is considered a match. Note: This operator works only with a single number.

Using a node affinity rule, you can choose a soft or hard affinity based on your requirements. You can create affinity rules using two preferences: RequiredDuring-SchedulingIgnoredDuringExecution, also known as a hard affinity, and preferred-DuringSchedulingIgnoredDuringExecution, also known as a soft affinity. If you use a hard affinity, the affinity must match or the Pod will fail to schedule. However, if you use a soft affinity, the affinity rule will be used if it matches. If a match is not found, the Pod will schedule on any node in the cluster.

Creating node affinity rules

Node affinity is set in a manifest in the PodSpec, under the Affinity field, as node-Affinity. To better explain how to use a node affinity rule, let's use an example cluster to create a manifest that uses an affinity rule.

The cluster has three nodes, described in table 3.9. The labels we will use in the rule are in bold.

Table 3.9   Nodes in a cluster

Node	Node labels
Node 1	beta.kubernetes.io/arch=amd64,beta.kubernetes.io/instance-type=e2-medium,beta.kubernetes.io/os=linux,cloud.google.com/gke-nodepool=default-pool,cloud.google.com/gke-os-distribution=cos,cloud.google.com/gke-preemptible=true,failure-domain.beta.kubernetes.io/region=us-central1,**failure-domain.beta.kubernetes.io/zone=us-central1-a**,kubernetes.io/arch=amd64,kubernetes.io/hostname=gke-cluster-1-default-pool-77fd9484-7fd6,kubernetes.io/os=linux

Table 3.9 Nodes in a cluster *(continued)*

Node	Node labels

Node 2	`beta.kubernetes.io/arch=amd64,beta.kubernetes.io/instance-type=e2-`
	`medium,beta.kubernetes.io/os=linux,cloud.google.com/gke-`
	`nodepool=default-pool,cloud.google.com/gke-os-`
	`distribution=cos,cloud.google.com/gke-preemptible=true,failure-`
	`domain.beta.kubernetes.io/region=us-central1,`**`failure-`**
	`domain.beta.kubernetes.io/zone=us-central1-`
	`b``,kubernetes.io/arch=amd64,kubernetes.io/hostname=gke-cluster-1-`
	`default-pool-ca0442ad-hqk5,kubernetes.io/os=linux`

Node 3	`beta.kubernetes.io/arch=amd64,beta.kubernetes.io/instance-type=e2-`
	`medium,beta.kubernetes.io/os=linux,cloud.google.com/gke-`
	`nodepool=default-pool,cloud.google.com/gke-os-`
	`distribution=cos,cloud.google.com/gke-preemptible=true,failure-`
	`domain.beta.kubernetes.io/region=us-central1,`**`failure-`**
	`domain.beta.kubernetes.io/zone=us-central1-`
	`c``,kubernetes.io/arch=amd64,kubernetes.io/hostname=gke-cluster-1-`
	`default-pool-ead436da-8j7k,kubernetes.io/os=linux`

We want to create a deployment that will create an NGINX server in either the us-central1-a or us-central1-c zones. Using the following manifest, we can create a Pod in either of the zones using an affinity rule based on the `failure-domain.beta` `.kubernetes.io/zone` key:

```
apiVersion: v1
kind: Pod
metadata:
 name: nginx-affinity
spec:
 affinity:
  nodeAffinity:
   requiredDuringSchedulingIgnoredDuringExecution:
    nodeSelectorTerms:
    - matchExpressions:
     - key: failure-domain.beta.kubernetes.io/zone
      operator: In
      values:
      - us-central1-a
      - us-central1-c
 containers:
 - name: nginx-affinity
   image: bitnami/nginx
```

By using the key `failure-domain.beta.kubernetes.io/zone` in the `matchExpressions`, we set the affinity to evaluate to true if the node label matches either us-central1-a or us-central1-c. Because the second node in the cluster has a label value of us-central2-b, it will evaluate as false and will not be selected to run the Pod.

USING POD AFFINITY AND ANTI-AFFINITY RULES

A Pod affinity rule will ensure that deployed Pods are running on the same set of nodes as a matching label, and an anti-affinity rule is used to ensure that Pods will *not* run on the same nodes as a matching label. Pod affinity rules are used for different use cases than node affinity rules. Whereas node affinity allows you to select a node based on the cluster node labels, Pod affinity and anti-affinity rules use the labels of Pods that are already running in the cluster.

Creating Pod affinity rules

When you create an affinity rule, you are telling the scheduler to place your Pod on a node that has an existing Pod that matches the selected value in the affinity rule. Pod affinity rules, like node affinity rules, can be created as soft or hard affinity rules. They also use operators like node affinity rules, including In, NotIn, Exists, and DoesNot-Exist, but they *do not* support the Gt or Lt operators.

Pod affinity rules are specified in the PodSpec, under the affinity and podAffinity fields. They require an additional parameter that node affinity rules do not use—the topologyKey. The topologyKey is used by Kubernetes to create a list of nodes that will be checked against the affinity rule. Using a topologyKey, you can decide to look for matches based on different filters like zones or nodes.

For example, imagine you have a software package that is licensed per node, and each time a Pod that runs a portion of the software runs on another node, you need to purchase an additional license. To lower costs, you decide to create an affinity rule that will force the Pods to run where an existing licensed Pod is running. The existing Pod runs using a label called license with a value of widgets. An example manifest follows that creates a Pod on a node with an existing Pod with a label license=widgets. Because we need to be on the same node to maintain licensing, we will use a topology-Key that will filter by kubernetes.io/hostname:

```
apiVersion: v1
kind: Pod
metadata:
 name: widgets-license-example
spec:
 affinity:
  podAffinity:
   requiredDuringSchedulingIgnoredDuringExecution:
   - labelSelector:
     matchExpressions:
     - key: license
      operator: In
      values:
      - widgets
    topologyKey: kubernetes.io/hostname
 containers:
 - name: nginx-widgets
   image: nginx-widgets
```

The manifest tells Kubernetes to create the Pod `nginx-widgets`, running an image called `nginx-widgets` on a host that already has a Pod running using the label license with the value of `widgets`.

Creating Pod anti-affinity rules

Anti-affinity rules do the opposite of affinity rules. Whereas affinity rules group Pods based on a set of rules, anti-affinity rules are used to run Pods on different nodes. When you use an anti-affinity rule, you are telling Kubernetes that you *do not* want the Pod to run on another node that has an existing Pod with the values declared in the rule. Some common use cases for using anti-affinity rules include forcing Pods to avoid other running Pods or spreading Pods across availability zones.

Pod anti-affinity rules are specified in the `PodSpec`, under the `affinity` and `podAntiAffinity` fields. They also require the `topologyKey` parameter to filter the list of nodes that will be used to compare the affinity rules.

In our affinity example, we used a `topologyKey` that used the hostname of the node. If we used the same key for the deployment, zones wouldn't be considered; it would only avoid placing the Pod on the same node as another running Pod. Although the Pods would spread across nodes, the selected nodes could all be in the same zone, which would fail to spread the Pods across zones.

To spread the Pods across zones, we will use the label `failure-domain.beta.kubernetes.io/zone`, and we will use the operator `In` to compare the label app for the value of `nginx-frontend`, as shown in the next code snippet. We will also use a soft anti-affinity rule, rather than a hard rule, allowing Kubernetes to use the same zone, if there is no other choice:

```
apiVersion: v1
kind: Pod
metadata:
 name: nginx-frontend-antiaffinity-example
spec:
 podAntiAffinity:
  preferredDuringSchedulingIgnoredDuringExecution:
   podAffinityTerm:
    labelSelector:
     matchExpressions:
     - key: app
      operator: In
      values:
      - nginx-frontend
    topologyKey: failure-domain.beta.kubernetes.io/zone
 containers:
 - name: nginx-frontned
   image: bitnami/nginx
```

By using `failure-domain.beta.kubernetes.io/zone` as the `topologyKey`, we are telling Kubernetes that we want to avoid placing any Pod that has a label of `app=nginx-frontend` in the same zone.

USING TAINTS AND TOLERATIONS

Although you are more likely to require scheduling a Pod to a specific node, some use cases exist where you will want to reserve specific nodes to only certain workloads, essentially disabling default scheduling. Unlike `nodeSelector` and affinity rules, taints are used to automatically repel, rather than attract, a Pod to a node. This is useful when you want a node to reject any scheduling attempts by default, unless a deployment specifically states the correct "tolerations" to be scheduled on the node. For example, imagine you have a cluster that has a few hundred nodes and a few nodes have GPUs available. Because GPUs are expensive, we want to restrict Pods on these nodes to only applications that require a GPU, rejecting any standard scheduling requests.

Using controls like `nodeSelector` or affinity rules will not tell the Kubernetes scheduler to avoid using a node. These provide a developer the ability to control how Pods will be deployed, and if they don't provide either of these, the scheduler will attempt to use any node in the cluster. Because GPUs are expensive, we want to reject any scheduling attempt to run a Pod on a node with a GPU that doesn't require using a GPU.

Creating a node taint

To stop the scheduler from scheduling Pods on a node, you need to "taint" the node with a value. To create a taint, use kubectl with the `taint` command and the node you want to taint, the key-value, and the effect. The key-value can be any value that you want to assign, and the effect can be one of three values: `NoSchedule`, `PreferNoSchedule`, or `NoExecute`, described in table 3.10.

Table 3.10   Taint effects

Effect	Description
`NoSchedule`	If a Pod does not specify a toleration that matches the node taint, it will not be scheduled to run on the node.
`PreferNoSchedule`	If a Pod does not specify a toleration that matches the node taint, the scheduler will attempt to avoid scheduling the Pod on the node.
`NoExecute`	If a Pod is already running on a node and a taint is added, if the Pod does not match the taint, it will be evicted from the node.

For example, if we had a GPU in a node named `node1`, we would taint the node using the following command:

```
kubectl taint nodes node1 gpu=:NoSchedule
```

The key in the taint command tells the scheduler what taint must be matched to allow a Pod to schedule on the node. If the taint is not matched by a Pod request using a toleration, the scheduler will not schedule a Pod on the node, based on the effect `NoSchedule`.

Creating Pods with tolerations

By default, once a node has a taint set, the scheduler will not attempt to run any Pod on the tainted node. By design, you set a taint to tell the scheduler to avoid using the node in any scheduling, unless the deployment specifically requests running on the node. To allow a Pod to run on a node that has been tainted, you need to supply a *toleration* in the deployment. A toleration is used to tell the scheduler that the Pod can "tolerate" the taint on the node, which will allow the scheduler to use a node that matches the toleration with an assigned taint.

> **NOTE** Taints will not attract a Pod request—they only reject any Pod that does not have a toleration set. As such, to direct a Pod to run on a node with a taint, you need to set a toleration and a node selection, or a node affinity. The selector will tell the scheduler to use a node with a matching label, and then the toleration tells the scheduler that the Pod can tolerate the taint set on the node. Because tolerations tell the scheduler to "prefer" a node with a matching taint, if one cannot be found, the scheduler will use any node in the cluster with a matching label.

> **KEY TAKEAWAY** Tolerations and node selectors/affinity rules work together to select the node that the Pod will run on.

Tolerations are created in the pod.spec section of your manifest by assigning one or more tolerations that include the key to match, an operator, an optional value, and the taint effect.

The key must be assigned to the key that matches the node on which you want to schedule the Pod. The operator value tells the scheduler to simply look for the key (Exists) or to match a key value (Equals). If you use the Equals operator, your toleration must contain a value field. Finally, the effect needs to be matched for the Pod to be scheduled on the node.

To schedule a Pod that can tolerate the GPU taint for node1, you would add the following to your PodSpec:

```
spec:
 tolerations:
 - key: "gpu"
   operator: "Exists"
   effect: "NoSchedule"
```

Adding the toleration tells the scheduler that the Pod should be assigned to a node that has a taint key of gpu with an effect of NoSchedule.

Controlling where Pods will be scheduled is a key point to ensure that your application deployments can meet your assigned SLA/SLO objectives.

3.3   *Advanced topics*

This section contains a few advanced topics that we wanted to include in this chapter. We think these are important topics, but they aren't required to understand the main topics in the chapter.

3.3.1   *Aggregate ClusterRoles*

When a new component is added to the cluster, a new ClusterRole is often created and can be assigned to users to manage the service. Sometimes a role may be created, and you may notice that a user assigned the ClusterRole of admin has permissions to the new components by default. Other times, you may notice that a newly added component, like Istio, does not allow the built-in admin role to use any Istio resources.

It may sound odd that a role like admin would not have permissions to every resource by default. Kubernetes includes two ClusterRoles that provide some form of admin access: the `admin` ClusterRole and the `cluster-admin` ClusterRole. They may sound similar, but how permissions are assigned to them is very different.

The `cluster-admin` role is straightforward—it is assigned wildcards for all permissions, providing access to every resource, including new resources. The `admin` role is not assigned wildcard permissions. Each permission assigned to the `admin` role is usually explicitly assigned. Because the role does not use wildcards, any new permissions need to be assigned for new resources.

To make this process easier, Kubernetes has a concept called aggregated ClusterRoles. When a new ClusterRole is created, it can be aggregated to any other ClusterRole by assigning an `aggregationRule`. An example to help explain how aggregation works follows. The default `admin` ClusterRole looks similar to the next example:

```
kind: ClusterRole
apiVersion: rbac.authorization.k8s.io/v1
metadata:
 name: admin


...


aggregationRule:
 clusterRoleSelectors:
  - matchLabels:
     rbac.authorization.k8s.io/aggregate-to-admin: "true"
```

In this code snippet, you can see that the `admin` ClusterRole has an `aggregationRule` that contains `rbac.authorization.k8s.io/aggregate-to-admin: 'true'`. When a new ClusterRole is created, it can be automatically aggregated with the built-in admin ClusterRole if it uses the same `aggregationRule`. For example, a new CRD has been deployed to the cluster that creates a new ClusterRole. Because the permissions for the new ClusterRole should be assigned to admins, it has been created with an `aggregationRule` that matches `rbac.authorization.k8s.io/aggregate-to-admin:` `"true"`, as shown next:

```
apiVersion: rbac.authorization.k8s.io/v1
kind: ClusterRole
metadata:
 name: aggregate-example-admin
 labels:
   rbac.authorization.k8s.io/aggregate-to-admin: "true"
rules:
- apiGroups: ["newapi"]
 resources: ["newresource"]
 verbs: ["get", "list", "watch", "create", "update", "patch", "delete"]
```

This will create a new ClusterRole named `aggregated-example-admin` that assigns the actions `get`, `list`, `watch`, `create`, `patch`, and `delete` to the resource `newresource` in the `newapi` apiGroup. This new ClusterRole can be bound to any user that you want to assign permissions to, but because the permission is required by admins, it also has a label assigned of `rbac.authorization.k8s.io/aggregate-to-admin: "true"`, which matches the `aggregationRule` that is assigned in the `admin` ClusterRole. The labels match, so a controller on the API server will notice the matching labels and "merge" the permissions from the new ClusterRole with the `admin` ClusterRole.

3.3.2 *Custom schedulers*

One of the most misunderstood concepts in Kubernetes is how the cluster schedules workloads. You will often hear that applications deployed on a Kubernetes cluster are highly available, and they are, when deployed correctly. To deploy a highly available application, it's beneficial to understand how the kube-scheduler makes decisions and the options available to your deployments to help influence the decisions that it will make.

The default Kubernetes scheduler, kube-scheduler, has the job of scheduling Pods to worker nodes based on a set of criteria that include node affinity, taints and tolerations, and node selectors. Although Kubernetes includes the base scheduler, you are not stuck using only a single scheduler for all deployments. If you need special scheduling considerations that the base scheduler does not include, you can create custom schedulers by specifying a scheduler in the manifest, and if one is not provided, the default scheduler will be used. Creating a custom scheduler is beyond the scope of this book, but you can read more about custom schedulers on the Kubernetes site at http://mng.bz/jm9y.

An example of a Pod that sets the scheduler to a custom scheduler named `custom-scheduler1` follows:

```
apiVersion: v1
kind: Pod
metadata:
  name: nginx-web
spec:
 containers:
 - name: nginx
    image: bitnami/nginx
 schedulerName: custom-scheduler1
```

The Kubernetes scheduler watches the API server for Pods that require scheduling. Once it determines that a Pod needs to be scheduled, it will determine the most appropriate node by going through a multistage decision process that will filter out nodes and then assign a score to nodes that have not been filtered out.

3.4 Examples and case studies

Using the knowledge from the chapter, address each of the requirements in the case study found next. Remember, if you deployed your GKE cluster across different regions, replace the example regions in the exercises with your regions. To save on any potential cost, the examples require only a single node in each region.

3.4.1 FooWidgets Industries

You have been asked to assist FooWidgets Industries with a new GKE cluster that they have deployed. They quickly discovered that they did not have the internal skills to complete their deployment, and, therefore, the current state of the cluster is a simple, new cluster across three GCP zones.

CLUSTER OVERVIEW AND REQUIREMENTS

FooWidgets Industries has a GKE cluster that has been deployed across three zones: us-east4-a, use-east4-b, and us-east4-c. The company has various requirements for Pod placement based on internal standards and specialized hardware use. They have included a breakdown of the desired placement of workloads and the labels that should be assigned to nodes, outlined in table 3.11.

Table 3.11   Placement of workloads

Zone	Desired workloads	Label/taint	Node name
us-east4-a	Any workload Fast disk access	`disk=fast`	`gke-cls1-pool1-1d704097-4361`
us-east4-b	Only workloads that require a GPU	`workload=gpu`	`gke-cls1-pool1-52bcec35-tf0q`
us-east4-c	Any workload		`gke-cls1-pool1-e327d1de-6ts3`

The statement of work requires you to provide the requirements in the table. The cluster has not been configured past the initial deployment stage and will require you to complete the following configuration:

- Create any node labels or taints that are required to achieve workload placement based on the supported workloads documented in the table.
- Create an example deployment using an NGINX image to demonstrate successful placement of workloads based on the requirements provided by FooWidgets Industries.

The next section contains the solution to address FooWidgets' requirements. You can follow along with the solution or, if you are comfortable, configure your cluster to address the requirements and use the solution to verify your results.

FOOWIDGETS INDUSTRIES SOLUTION: LABELS AND TAINTS

The first requirement is to create any labels or taints that may be required. Using the requirements table, we can tell that we need to label the nodes in us-east4-a with `disk=fast`. This label will allow a deployment to force scheduling on a node that has the required fast disks for the application. The second requirement is to limit any running workloads in the us-east4-b zone to only applications that require a GPU. For this requirement, we have decided to taint all nodes in the us-east4-b zone with `workload=gpu`.

Why is a label used for one solution and a taint for the other? You may recall that labels and taints are used to accomplish different scheduling requirements: we use labels to attract workloads, whereas we use taints to repel them. In the requirements, FooWidgets clearly states that us-east4-a and us-east4-c can run any type of workload, but us-east4-b must run only workloads that require a GPU. If a deployment is created that does not specify a label on a node, the scheduler will still consider that node as a potential node for scheduling. Labels are used to force a deployment to a particular node, but they do not reject workloads that do not contain a label request. This behavior is far different from a node that has been assigned a taint. When a node is tainted, it will repel any workloads that do not contain a toleration for the assigned node taint. If a deployment is created without any tolerations for the node taint, the scheduler will automatically exclude the tainted nodes from scheduling the workload.

Creating the labels and taints

We need to label the node in us-east4-a with `disk=fast`. To label the node, we use the kubectl `label` command, supplying the node and the label:

```
kubectl label node gkc cls1-pool1-1d704097-4361 disk=fast
```

Next, we need to add a taint to the nodes in the us-east4-b zone with `workload=gpu`. Remember that a taint will repel any request that does not tolerate the assigned node taint, but it doesn't attract a workload. This means that you also need to add a label to direct the GPU Pods to the correct node. To taint the node, we use the kubectl `taint` command, supplying the node name and the taint:

```
kubectl taint node gke-cls1-pool1-52bcec35-tf0q workload=gpu:NoSchedule
```

Then, label the node to attract the GPU Pods:

```
kubectl label node gke-cls1-pool1-52bcec35-tf0q workload=gpu
```

Notice that we did not add a label or a taint to the node in us-east4-c because that zone can run any workload.

Now that the nodes are labeled, you need to create example deployments to verify that workload placement matches the requirements from the table.

Creating a deployment that requires fast disk access

To force a deployment that requires fast disk access to the us-east4-a zone, you need to add a `nodeSelector` to the deployment. The following code snippet creates an NGINX server that contains a `nodeSelector` using the label `disk=fast`, forcing the workload to run on a node in the us-east4-a zone:

```
apiVersion: v1
kind: Pod
metadata:
 labels:
  run: nginx-fast
 name: nginx-fast
spec:
 containers:
 - image: nginx
  name: nginx-fast
 restartPolicy: Always
 nodeSelector:
  disk: fast
```

When you create and execute the manifest, the `nodeSelector` tells the scheduler to use a node with the label `disk:fast`. To verify the selector is working correctly, we can list the Pods with `-o wide` to list the node that the Pod is running on. In us-east4-a we have a single node, `gke-cls1-pool1-1d704097-436`. The abbreviated output from `kubectl get pods` confirms that the Pod was scheduled correctly:

```
NAME         READY    STATUS     AGE      IP         NODE
nginx-fast   1/1      Running    4m49s    10.8.0.4   gke-cls1-pool1-1d704097-4361
```

Now that you have confirmed that Pods requiring fast disk access can be scheduled correctly, you need to create a deployment to test workloads that require GPUs.

Creating a deployment that requires a GPU

Any workload that requires a GPU needs to be scheduled on a node in us-east4-b. We already tainted the node in that zone, and to confirm that a workload requiring a GPU will be scheduled correctly, we need to create a test deployment with a toleration using the code that follows:

```
apiVersion: v1
kind: Pod
metadata:
 labels:
  run: nginx-gpu
 name: nginx-gpu
spec:
 containers:
 - image: nginx
  name: nginx-gpu
```

```
restartPolicy: Always
nodeSelector:
 workload: gpu
tolerations:
- key: "workload"
 operator: "Equal"
 value: "gpu"
 effect: "NoSchedule"
```

When this code snippet is applied, you can verify that the Pod is running on the correct node in us-east4-b using `kubectl get pods -o wide`:

```
NAME       READY   STATUS    AGE   IP          NODE
nginx-gpu  1/1     Running   3s    10.8.2.6    gke-cls1-pool1-52bcec35-tf0q
```

Comparing the output with the table that lists the nodes in each zone verifies that the Pod has been scheduled on a node in the us-east4-b zone.

Congratulations! You have successfully addressed the workload requirements and have proven that you understand how to schedule workloads based on node labels and taints.

Summary

- The control plan receives and stores objects and schedules workloads, whereas worker nodes are where the actual containers will execute once scheduled by the Kubernetes scheduler.
- Two different deployment models are available: declarative and imperative.
- You gained an understanding of Kubernetes resources and their functions.
- You can use selectors, taints, tolerations, and anti-affinity and affinity rules to control what nodes will be used for specific workloads.

Anthos Service Mesh: Security and observability at scale

Onofrio Petragallo

This chapter covers

- Sidecar proxy and proxyless architectures
- Introducing the main features of Istio
- Security and observability with Istio
- Exploring Anthos Service Mesh
- A practical example with code

One of the key aspects of being cloud native is to break up your application into microservices. This means an application that may have run on a single server now has multiple services, backed by multiple Pods, as separate components. As applications scale out their services, it becomes difficult to troubleshoot problems that you may encounter with the application. With this added complexity, we needed a tool to help organize, secure, and add resilience to the expanding complexities that microservices introduced. Another important problem is that enterprises often have a huge number of microservices and aren't always able to control, manage, and observe them—something a service mesh could fix.

68

In this chapter, we will discuss Anthos Service Mesh (ASM) and the features that ASM inherits from Istio (https://istio.io/), a popular open source framework for creating, managing, and implementing a service mesh.

The implementation of a service mesh not only facilitates communication between microservices using a dedicated communication management control plane; it also includes tools to observe communication between services—increase observability, enhance security, control application traffic flow, and simulate faults in an application.

Anthos Service Mesh is a Google-managed service that allows enterprise management of all the service meshes present in a hybrid cloud or multicloud architecture from a single point, providing complete and in-depth visibility of all microservices. The visualization of the topography of the service mesh and the complete integration with Cloud Monitoring provides users the tools to identify failing workloads or other problems, making problem resolution faster.

The security features made available by Anthos Service Mesh allow you to manage the authentication, authorization, and encryption of communications through mutual authentication (mTLS; http://mng.bz/1Mly), to secure and ensure trust in both directions for the communication between microservices; mTLS ensures a high level of security, minimizing the related risks. The traffic management features of Istio provide users the tools to manipulate traffic using request routing, fault injection, request timeouts, circuit breaking, and mirroring.

As you can see, Istio includes several complex features that may be difficult to troubleshoot. Few offerings in the market today include support for Istio, leaving you to support your service mesh on your own. Google has addressed this lack by including ASM in Anthos, providing a single support point for your Kubernetes clusters and Istio.

Before talking about the Anthos Service Mesh features and Istio in detail, let's start by explaining what a service mesh actually is.

4.1 Technical requirements

The hands-on portion of this chapter will require you to have access to a Kubernetes cluster running on GCP with the following deployment pattern: a GKE cluster with at least three nodes with four CPUs and 16 GB of RAM.

4.2 What is a service mesh?

To understand how a service mesh works and why it's becoming a standard tool in the microservices toolbox, you need to understand what a service mesh provides. The main advantages of adopting a service mesh are the ability to do the following:

- Observe and monitor all communications between the individual microservices
- Secure connections between the available microservices
- Deliver resilient services (distributed services) through multicluster and multicloud architecture patterns
- Provide advanced traffic management: A/B testing, traffic splitting, and canary rollouts

A service mesh is an infrastructure layer in a microservices architecture that controls the communication between services. We can not only create a mesh of services within a microservice's architecture that runs in a Kubernetes cluster, but we can also create a single service mesh that spans multiple clusters, or even nonmicroservice services running on virtual machines.

A service mesh manages all the ingress, or inbound traffic, and egress, or outbound traffic, for each microservice. Traffic management is a complex topic and something that most users do not want to deal with. To remove this burden, Istio doesn't require the developer to make any changes in their application logic; instead, the service mesh handles all of this by using a sidecar proxy approach or a proxyless approach.

The sidecar proxy is one of the main components of a service mesh that manages the ingress and egress traffic for each microservice, abstracting itself from the application logic of the microservices. Because all the traffic flows through the sidecar proxy, it can monitor this traffic to send metrics and logs to the centralized control plane.

The following three approaches are available, with the sidecar proxy the most common approach to creating a service:

- *Sidecar proxy*—Used in a microservices architecture where a proxy is connected to each microservice, with the same life cycle as the microservice itself, but executes as a separate process, as shown in figure 4.1.

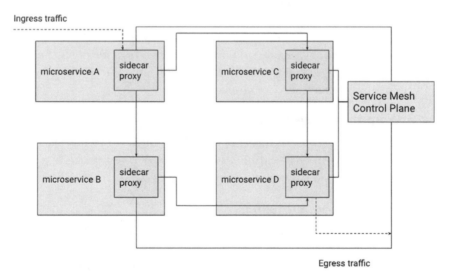

Figure 4.1   Sidecar proxy architecture

- *Proxyless*—Used in a microservices architecture where the microservice can send the telemetry directly to the control plane by using gRPC, a remote procedure call system developed by Google.

- *Proxy inside a VM*—An L7 proxy runs inside VMs as a process or an agent that can be added to the service mesh as if it were a sidecar proxy.

After seeing what a service mesh is and what the approaches are to create one, let's review how Anthos Service Mesh uses each of them. To monitor in real time the telemetry of all inbound and outbound communications between the microservices of the various service mesh networks, ASM uses the following two approaches:

- The sidecar proxy approach, using Envoy (https://www.envoyproxy.io/) proxies, an open source service proxy attached on each Pod to get the real-time telemetry, as shown in figure 4.2.

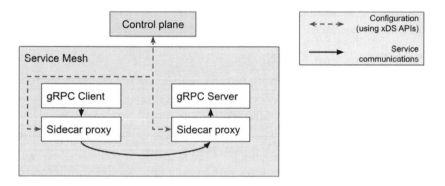

Figure 4.2   Sidecar proxy approach

- The proxyless approach using Google Cloud Traffic Director (https://cloud .google.com/traffic-director), which can use gRPC with xDS API (https://github .com/envoyproxy/data-plane-api), the same technology used by Envoy to communicate with the control plane, as shown in figure 4.3.

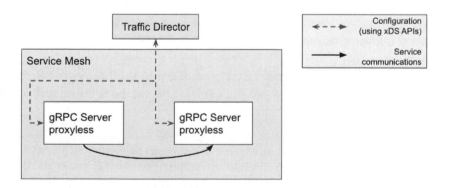

Figure 4.3   Proxyless approach

The proxyless approach removes the Istio sidecar from your deployments. By removing the sidecar, we are removing an extra hop in the network traffic to the service, leading to a reduction in network latency, enhancing the service overall response time.

A single service mesh can have services that use both the standard Istio sidecar and the proxyless approach. This flexibility allows you to use the correct approach for different applications, including gRPC using a proxyless approach, sidecars for services that do not use gRPC, and sidecars for services that use gRPC.

As discussed in previous chapters, Anthos is a complete platform from Google to build applications running on hybrid or multicloud platforms. Anthos Service Mesh is the main component that provides service management to developers and cluster administrators.

In the next section, we will examine the features of Istio, which is the basis for the Anthos Service Mesh.

4.3   *An introduction to Istio*

Istio is an open platform that offers a uniform way to integrate microservices, manage traffic flow across microservices, enforce policies, and aggregate telemetry data. Istio's control plane provides an abstraction layer over the underlying cluster management platform, such as Kubernetes. The main features of Istio (http://mng.bz/WA6x) follow:

- Automatic load balancing for HTTP, gRPC, WebSocket, and TCP traffic
- Fine-grained control of traffic behavior with robust routing rules, retries, failover, and fault injection
- A pluggable policy layer and configuration API supporting access controls, rate limits, and quotas
- Automatic metrics, logs, and traces for all traffic within a cluster, including cluster ingress and egress
- Secure service-to-service communication in a cluster with strong identity-based authentication and authorization

Given its open source nature, Istio is extensible and usable in various environments: for example, you can execute it on-prem, in the cloud, inside a VM, or with microservices, allowing you to customize the service mesh to your security and monitoring requirements.

To understand Istio, you need to understand the underlying architecture of the system. In the next section, we will explain the components of Istio and the features they provide.

4.3.1   *Istio architecture*

Istio's flexible architecture allows you to implement a service mesh from scratch. You do not have to have Istio installed before developers start using the cluster—a service mesh can be deployed before or after the developers have implemented and deployed their services. Remember, as shown in figure 4.4, Istio uses the sidecar proxy injection

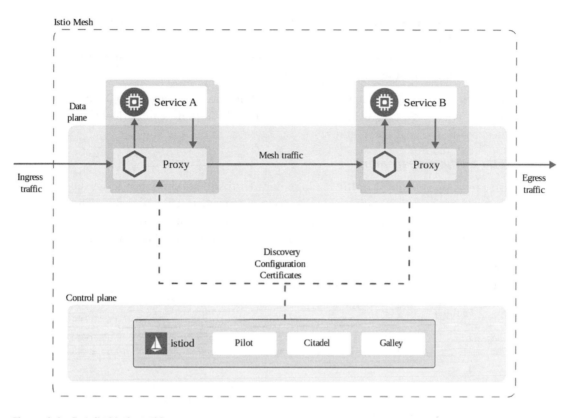

Figure 4.4   Detailed Istio architecture

to intercept the ingress and egress traffic from inside and outside the network of microservices, so there are no dependencies on the developers.

Starting with Istio version 1.5, the main components of Istio's architecture are the sidecar proxy and istiod, which contains three subcomponents: Pilot, Citadel, and Galley.

Istiod provides service discovery, configuration, and certificate management, as well as high-level routing rules that control traffic behavior into a specific configuration for the Envoy proxy, injecting them into the sidecars at runtime. It also acts as a certificate authority that generates certificates to allow secure mTLS communication in the data plane. Istiod contains the following three processes to provide its services:

- *Pilot*—Responsible for the life cycle of Envoy sidecar proxy instances deployed across the service mesh. Pilot abstracts platform-specific service discovery mechanisms and is conformant with any sidecar that can consume the Envoy API.
- *Galley*—Interprets the YAML files for Kubernetes and transforms them into a format that Istio understands. Galley makes it possible for Istio to work with environments other than Kubernetes—for example, virtual machine—because

it translates various configuration data into the common format that Istio understands.

- *Citadel*—Enables robust service-to-service and end user authentication with built-in identity and credential management.

So far, we have covered Istio at a high level, but now let's go through the features of Istio in detail. We can divide the features into three main categories: traffic management, security, and observability.

4.3.2 Istio traffic management

Istio provides powerful traffic management (https://istio.io/latest/docs/tasks/traffic-management/), which allows users to control ingress and egress traffic. This control is not limited to simply routing traffic to a specific service; it also offers the ability to split traffic between different versions and simulate failures and timeouts in applications. Table 4.1 shows Istio's traffic management features.

Table 4.1 Istio traffic management features

Feature	Description
Ingress	Controls the ingress traffic for the service mesh, to expose a service outside the service mesh over TLS or mTLS using the Istio gateway. In another chapter, we will deep-dive into ingress for Anthos.
Egress	Controls the egress traffic from the service mesh, routes traffic to an external system, performs TLS for outbound traffic, and configures the outbound gateway to use an HTTPS proxy.
Request routing and traffic splitting	Dynamically routes the traffic to multiple versions of the microservice or migrates traffic from one version to another version gradually and in a controlled way.
Fault injection	Provides configurable HTTP delays and fault injection with an HTTP status code, allowing developers to discover problems before they would occur in production.

Traffic management is a powerful feature of Istio, allowing developers to completely control traffic, down to the level where a single user could be directed to a new version of an application, while all other requests are directed to the current version. The fault injection feature enables developers to cause a delay between services, simulating an HTTP delay or faults, to verify how the application will react to unexpected problems. All these features can be used by users without any code changes to their application, providing a big advantage over the old "legacy" development days.

Security is everyone's job, but not everyone has a sufficient background in security to create the code to enhance application security. Just like the traffic management features, Istio provides extra security features, all without requiring developers to create any code.

In the next section, we will explain the security features included with Istio and ASM.

4.3.3 Istio security

Services in the mesh need to communicate with each other over a network connection, so you need to consider additional security to defend against various attacks, including man-in-the-middle and unknown service communication. Istio includes components to enhance your application security (https://istio.io/latest/docs/tasks/security/), ranging from an included certificate authority to peer authentication and authorization, helping you adopt a zero-trust posture.

The first component that Istio provides to increase your application security is the handling of certificate management, including an Istio certificate authority (CA) with an existing root certificate. In cryptography, a certificate authority or certification authority is an entity that issues digital certificates. A digital certificate certifies the ownership of a public key by the named subject of the certificate. This allows others to rely on signatures or assertions made about the private key that corresponds to the certified public key—proving the identity of the certificate owner. A CA acts as a trusted third party: trusted both by the owner of the certificate and by the party relying on the certificate.

In an organization, the root certificate signatory may want to remain responsible for signing all certificates issued for all entities in the organization. It is also possible that whoever has the responsibility of signing the root certificate wants to delegate the responsibility of signing the certificates to a subordinate entity. In this case, we refer to the subordinate entity as a *delegate CA*.

Istio's certificate authority can be configured in multiple ways. By default, the CA generates a self-signed root certificate and key, which is used to sign the certificates for microservices. Istio's CA can also sign certificates using an administrator-specified certificate and key and with an administrator-specified root certificate. The last configuration is most common in enterprise environments, where the CA is configured with an existing root certificate or delegated CA signing certificate and key.

The CA in Istio is used to securely provision strong identities to every workload in the mesh. Certificates are issued using X.509 certificates, which is a standard that defines the format of public key certificates. X.509 certificates are used in many protocols, including TLS/SSL, which is the basis for HTTPS, the secure protocol for browsing the web.

Istio agents, running alongside each Envoy proxy, work together with the Istio CA component of istiod to automate key and certificate rotation at scale. Because the rotation and distribution of certificates is automated, once configured, little overhead remains for operators or users of the cluster—a powerful feature of Istio to secure communications between services.

Certificates are the building block for additional security in our service mesh. In the next section, we will discuss authentication and mutual TLS encryption—a security layer that relies on the issued certificates to secure the mesh workloads.

ISTIO AUTHENTICATION

Istio uses peer authentication for service-to-service authentication and to verify the client initiating the connection. Istio also makes mTLS available as a full-stack solution for transport authentication, which can be enabled without requiring changes to any application code. Peer authentication provides the following benefits:

- Each service has a strong identity that represents its role to enable interoperability inside the clusters.
- Encryption of all communication between services.
- A key management system to automate the generation, distribution, and rotation of keys and certificates.

Istio allows request-level authentication with JSON Web Token (JWT) validation with many authentication providers (e.g., Google Auth [https://developers.google.com/identity]).

ISTIO AUTHORIZATION

Istio provides a mechanism for operators to define authorization policies to control access to the service mesh, namespace, and workloads within the service mesh, as shown in figure 4.5. Traffic can be restricted by type, such as TCP or HTTP, and the identity of the requestor. The advantages that authorization provides follow:

- *Authorization*—Between workloads and from user to workload.
- *Flexible semantics*—Operators can define custom conditions on Istio attributes and use the DENY and ALLOW actions to tune the policies to suit their needs.
- *High performance*—Istio authorization is applied natively on the Envoy proxy.

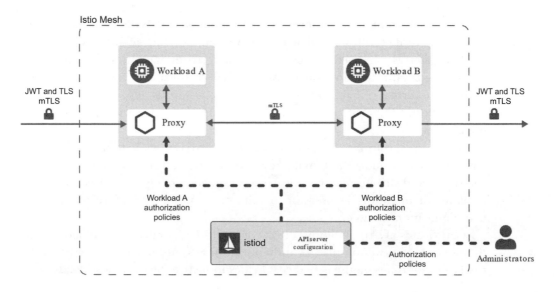

Figure 4.5   Istio authorization architecture

- *Flexibility*—Supports gRPC, HTTP, HTTPS, and HTTP2 natively as well as all regular TCP protocols.
- *Distributed*—Each Envoy proxy runs its own authorization engine that authorizes each request to be executed.

At the beginning of the chapter, we mentioned that one advantage of a service mesh was the ability to organize microservices. As your number of services grows, so does your architecture's complexity. The only way to maintain health and to troubleshoot problems in services is to have a powerful set of tools that allow you to look deep into the mesh activities. In the next section, we will go over the tools that you can use with Istio to view the activities in the mesh.

4.3.4 Istio observability

To offer a view into the service mesh, Istio features multiple add-on components (https://istio.io/latest/docs/tasks/observability/) that provide distributed tracing, metrics and logging, and a dashboard.

Istio contains a few options that provide a mesh with distributed tracing. Distributed tracing allows you to track the user through all the services and understand request latency, serialization, and parallelism. You can configure Istio to send distributed metrics to different systems, including Jaeger (https://www.jaegertracing.io/), Zipkin (https://zipkin.io/), and Lightstep (https://lightstep.com/).

Jaeger, a distributed tracing system released as open source by Uber Technologies, is used for monitoring and troubleshooting microservices-based distributed systems, including the following features: distributed context propagation, distributed transaction monitoring, root cause analysis, service dependency analysis, and performance optimization.

Zipkin and Lightstep are other distributed tracing systems. They help gather timing data needed to troubleshoot latency problems in service architectures. Features include both the collection and lookup of this data.

You can collect all the metrics and logs from Envoy proxies and TCP sessions and customize the metrics using Istio metrics, making available all the data via Kiali (https://kiali.io/), Prometheus (https://prometheus.io/), or Grafana (https://grafana.com/).

Kiali, shown in figure 4.6, is a management console for Istio-based service meshes that can build a service graph based on the telemetry data sourced from Envoy sidecar proxies. Kiali provides dashboards and observability and lets you operate your mesh with robust configuration and validation capabilities. It shows the structure of your service mesh by inferring traffic topology and displays the health of your mesh. Kiali provides detailed metrics, powerful validation, Grafana access, and strong integration for distributed tracing with Jaeger. This application allows you to use Kubernetes JWT tokens to provide native RBAC permission. The JWT presented by the user allows access to all namespaces they have access to in the cluster while denying all

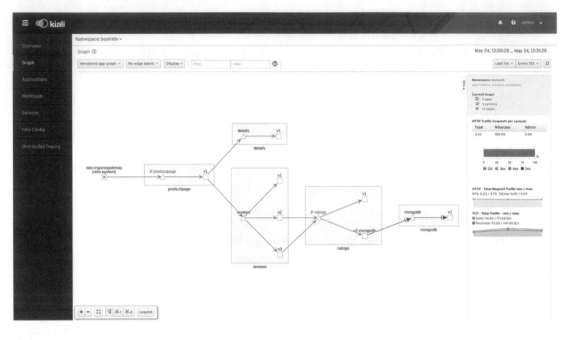

Figure 4.6   Kiali console UI

users that do not have permissions to the namespaces—all without any configuration required by cluster admins.

Prometheus is an open source system-monitoring and -alerting application that has the following features: a multidimensional data model with time-series data identified by metric name and key-value pairs, and a flexible query language to use this dimensionality named PromQL. The time-series collection happens via a pull model over HTTP, and pushing time series is supported via an intermediary gateway.

Grafana is open source visualization and analytics software application. It allows you to query, visualize, alert on, and explore your metrics, no matter where they are stored. It provides you with tools to turn your time-series database data into beautiful graphs and visualizations. Grafana can connect with Prometheus and Kiali.

Now that we have looked at Istio, let's see what features and advantages Istio offers when it is used by Anthos Service Mesh, managed by Google Cloud.

4.4   *What is Anthos Service Mesh?*

Anthos Service Mesh has a suite of features and tools that help you observe and manage secure, reliable services in a unified way. With Anthos Service Mesh, you get an Anthos-tested and -supported distribution of Istio, managed by Google, letting you create and deploy a service mesh on GKE on Google Cloud and other platforms, with full Google support.

The use of Istio features in Anthos Service Mesh varies according to the architecture you want to design and implement, including full cloud, multicloud, hybrid cloud, or edge. Each implementation has different available features; therefore, it is necessary to check the availability of the supported features for the various scenarios (see http://mng.bz/81R2).

Before installing Anthos Service Mesh, always check the documentation and choose the most suitable and updated configuration profile. The configuration profiles, YAML files that are used by the `IstioOperator` API, define and configure the features installed with Anthos Service Mesh. At time of writing, you can install ASM in the following scenarios:

- Anthos cluster (GKE) on Google Cloud in a single project
- Anthos cluster (GKE) on Google Cloud between different projects
- Anthos cluster (GKE) on VMware
- Anthos cluster (GKE) on bare metal
- Anthos cluster (GKE) on AWS
- Attached cluster Amazon Elastic Kubernetes Service (Amazon EKS)
- Attached cluster Microsoft Azure Kubernetes Service (Microsoft AKS)

4.5   *Installing ASM*

You install ASM differently on GKE clusters on GCP and on-prem. You can view the most current installation procedures on the ASM site at http://mng.bz/El7l. Explaining each option of the installation is beyond the scope of a single chapter, but the steps to deploy ASM on a GKE cluster with all components for testing requires only a few steps, as described next for ASM 1.12 in a cluster:

1 Download the ASM installation script as follows:

```
curl https://storage.googleapis.com/csm-artifacts/asm/asmcli_1.12 > asmcli
```

2 Make the script executable like this:

```
chmod +x asmcli
```

3 Install ASM using `asmcli`:

```
./asmcli install --project_id PROJECT_ID --cluster_name CLUSTER_NAME
--cluster_location CLUSTER_LOCATION --output_dir ./asm-downloads
--enable_all
```

After Istio is deployed into the Kubernetes cluster, you can start configuring and using it right away. One of the first things to do is define which approach you want to follow to make proxies communicate within the service mesh.

In the next section, we will define how Istio handles the sidecar proxy injection.

4.5.1   *Sidecar proxy injection*

Activating Anthos Service Mesh features is an easy, transparent process, thanks to the possibility of injecting a sidecar proxy next to each workload or microservice. You can inject a sidecar proxy manually by updating your Pods' Kubernetes manifest, or you can use automatic sidecar injection. By default, sidecar autoinjection is disabled for all namespaces. To enable autoinjection for a single namespace, execute

```
kubectl label namespace NAMESPACE istio.io/rev=asm-managed --overwrite
```

where NAMESPACE is the name of the namespace for your application's services and rev=asm-managed is the release channel (see http://mng.bz/Nm72).

All channels are based on a generally available (GA) release (although individual features may not always be GA, as marked). New Anthos Service Mesh versions are first released to the Rapid channel and over time are promoted to the Regular and Stable channels. This progression allows you to select a channel that meets your business, stability, and functionality needs.

Because sidecars are injected when Pods are created, after you execute the command, you must restart any running Pods for the change to take effect. When Kubernetes invokes the webhook, the admissionregistration.k8s.io/v1beta1#Mutating-WebhookConfiguration configuration is applied. The default configuration injects the sidecar into Pods in any namespace with the istio-injection=enabled label. The label should be consistent with the previous command. The istio-sidecar-injector configuration map specifies the configuration for the injected sidecar.

The way you restart Pods depends very much on the way they were created, as described here:

1 If you used a deployment, you should update or recreate the deployment first like this, which will restart all Pods, adding the sidecar proxies:

```
kubectl rollout restart deployment -n YOUR_NAMESPACE
```

2 If you didn't use a deployment, you should delete the Pods as follows. They will be automatically recreated with sidecars:

```
kubectl delete pod -n YOUR_NAMESPACE --all
```

3 Check that all the Pods in the namespace have sidecars injected:

```
kubectl get pod -n YOUR_NAMESPACE
```

4 In the following example, output from the previous command, you will notice that the READY column indicates two containers exist for each of your workloads: the primary container and the container for the sidecar proxy:

```
NAME            READY  STATUS   RESTARTS  AGE
YOUR_WORKLOAD    2/2   Running  0         20s
```

We have now seen how to install Anthos Service Mesh, using the approach with a side-car proxy, and how important it is to choose the right profile. Now let's see what the other features of Anthos Service Mesh are and the advantages of using them.

4.5.2   Uniform observability

One of the most important and useful features of the Anthos Service Mesh is observability. Implementing a service mesh through the proxy architecture and taking advantage of the Google Cloud Monitoring services ensures in-depth visibility of what is happening among the various microservices present in the mesh.

Through the proxy, each microservice can send telemetry automatically, without the developers having to add any code in their application. All traffic is intercepted by proxies, and the telemetry data is sent to Anthos Service Mesh. In addition, each proxy sends the data to Google Cloud Monitoring and Google Cloud Logging without any extra development, using the APIs that Google makes available.

The Anthos Service Mesh control plane discussed in chapter 1 provides two main dashboards: table view and topology view. In the table view, you have a complete view of all the services deployed in the cluster. You can see all the metrics, and you can add SLI and SLO to better monitor your services.

In the topology view, service meshes are represented as a graphical map. All the services such as workloads, Pod, systems services, and relative owners are connected as a network of nodes. This view provides a comprehensive look at the overall performance of the entire service mesh and an inside look into each node with detailed information.

4.5.3   Operational agility

If observability is one of the most "visible" features for managing a service mesh, then the management of traffic within a microservices architecture is another fundamental asset to manage operations easily. Because Anthos Service Mesh is based on Istio, it inherits most of the traffic and network management features that Istio provides (http://mng.bz/DZ79), so let's look at these features next.

REQUEST ROUTING AND TRAFFIC SPLITTING

Using Istio, you can redirect traffic to multiple versions of the same microservice deployed in the cluster and safely (under a possible quota) control part of the traffic from an old version of the microservice to a newly installed version. Both options allow you to be agile in the deployment of new features or to fix bugs that may affect the business.

For example, let's imagine we need to urgently fix a microservice. After the deployment of the new version, we can redirect a small part of the incoming traffic, verify that the fix works correctly, and then completely redirect the traffic to the new version without any downtime. If the fix is carried out only for a specific case, it is possible to keep both versions of the microservice active, redirecting traffic to both versions based on preestablished rules, without necessarily having to delete the old version, which is working well for most cases.

Through these traffic management features, Anthos Service Mesh can manage A/B testing, allowing you to direct a particular percentage of traffic to a new version of a service. This practice is helpful when you want to introduce a new version of a service by first testing it using a small percentage of user traffic and, if all goes well, then increasing the percentage while simultaneously phasing out the old version.

Thanks to these functionalities, it is possible to implement canary deployments or progressive rollout strategies, directly testing the new versions of the services released. If the new version of the service experiences no problems with a small percentage of the traffic directed toward it, you could move all traffic to the new version and discard the old one.

In figure 4.7, a canary deployment with traffic splitting is used to redirect 5% of the traffic to test the new release of Service A.

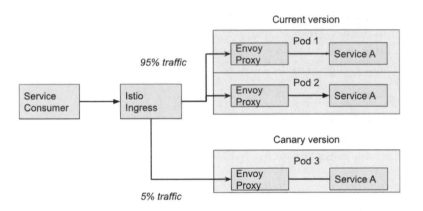

Figure 4.7   Istio canary deployment feature based on traffic

In figure 4.8, a canary deployment with traffic splitting is used to redirect the iPhone's traffic to test the new release of Service A.

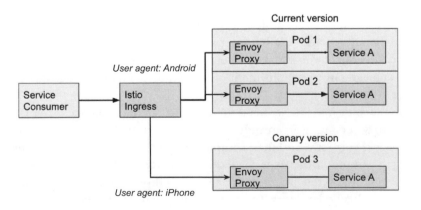

Figure 4.8   Istio canary deployment feature based on user-agent

The operations departments that manage the production environment take advantage of these features as they release plans for fixes and new versions of microservices. Each of these scenarios can be executed on the fly without disrupting the end users.

Circuit breaking

Microservices architectures were born to be scalable, agile, and resilient, but it is not always easy to design and implement these architectures to manage high workloads or manage integration with external services with consequent possible downtime or timeout. As mentioned earlier, the service mesh is independent of the application code and the programming language used, and, consequently, this facilitates the adoption of functions dedicated to the management of the office.

The functionality that allows you to manage timeouts, failures, and loads on the architecture is called *circuit breaking* (http://mng.bz/lJAM). When you design a microservices architecture, you must always put yourself in position to manage faults correctly. These faults may have been caused not only by bugs in the application code but also from external factors, for example, in the network or infrastructure. In the event of a fault or failure to reach the SLA (on availability and/or performance of a given service), circuit breaking automatically allows you to redirect traffic to another microservice or external service to limit downtime or to limit the loss of functionality by the end user.

Let's see an example. In figure 4.9, the service consumer is invoking Istio Ingress to call Service A, which is distributed in two Pods. Let's assume that Service A inside Pod 1 has a load problem and becomes unreachable. Thanks to the circuit breaking feature, Istio will close the connection of the proxy to Service A inside Pod 1 and redirect all traffic to the proxy inside Pod 2, until Service A in Pod 1 works properly again.

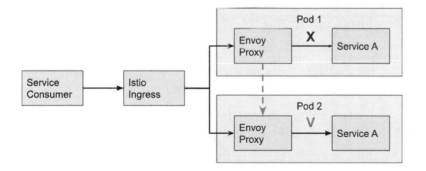

Figure 4.9   Istio circuit breaking feature example

Egress control

Usually, when it comes to service mesh, an important feature is the control of the Ingress gateway to ensure absolute security to the network. However, if we find ourselves in situations for which the regulations (e.g., PCI [http://mng.bz/Bl7g]) or the customer's requirements require us to also control the outgoing traffic from the service mesh, then, thanks to Istio and thanks to the egress gateway control, we can cover the security required.

With Anthos Service Mesh, you can configure the routing of the traffic from the service mesh to the external services (HTTP or HTTPS) using a dedicated Egress gateway or an external HTTPS proxy, if necessary, to perform TLS origination (SDS or file mount) from the service mesh for the connection on those external services. See figure 4.10 for an illustration.

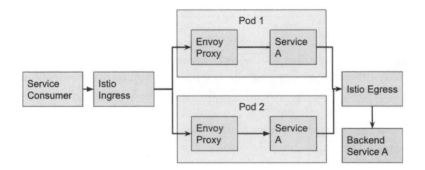

Figure 4.10   Istio egress control example

4.5.4   *Policy-driven security*

Since the adoption of containers, shared services, and distributed architectures, it has become more difficult to mitigate insider threats and minimize and limit data breaches, ensuring that communications between workloads remain encrypted, authenticated, and authorized. Anthos Service Mesh security features (http://mng.bz/dJOX) help mitigate these threats, configuring context-sensitive service levels or context-sensitive networks.

Before offerings like Istio, securing an application was the responsibility of the application developer, and many of the tasks were complex and time consuming, including the following:

- Encrypting the communications between the application and other services, which required certificate management and maintenance
- Creating modules that were language specific to authenticate access based on open identity standards like JSON web tokens (JWTs)
- Implementing a complex authorization system to limit the permissions allowed using the assertions on the presented JWT

Instead of a developer taking time to create and manage this security, they can take advantage of the features of Istio, which address each of these tasks without any additional code required.

With Anthos Service Mesh, it is possible to adopt an in-depth defense posture consistent with zero-trust security principles via declarative criteria and without modifying any application code. The principal security features in ASM are the managed private certificate authority, Identity-Aware access controls, request claims–aware access control policies, user authentication with Identity-Aware Proxy, and access logging and monitoring.

The first feature, the managed private certificate authority (Mesh CA), includes a Google-managed multiregional private certificate authority for issuing certificates for mTLS. The Mesh CA is a highly reliable and scalable service, optimized for dynamically scaled workloads on a cloud platform. Mesh CA lets you rely on a single root of trust across Anthos clusters. When using Mesh CA, you can rely on workload identity pools to provide coarse-grained isolation. By default, authentication fails if the client and the server are not in the same workload identity pool.

The next feature, Identity-Aware access control (firewall) policies, allows you to configure network security policies based on the mTLS identity versus the IP address of the peer. This lets you create policies that are independent of the network location of the workload. Only communications across clusters in the same Google Cloud project are currently supported.

The third feature, request claims–aware access control (firewall) policies, enables you to grant access to services based on request claims in the JWT header of HTTP or gRPC requests. Anthos Service Mesh lets you assert that a JWT is signed by a trusted entity, so you can configure policies that allow access from certain clients only if a request claim exists or matches a specified value.

The fourth feature, user authentication with Identity Aware Proxy, authenticates users accessing any service exposed on an Anthos Service Mesh Ingress gateway by using Identity-Aware Proxy (IAP). IAP can authenticate users that log in from a browser, integrate with custom identity providers, and issue a short-lived JWT token or an RCToken that can then be used to grant access at the Ingress gateway or a downstream service (by using a sidecar).

The final features, access logging and monitoring, ensure that access logs and metrics are available in Google Cloud's operations suite and provides an integrated dashboard to understand access patterns for a service or workload based on this data. You can also choose to configure a private destination. Anthos Service Mesh lets you reduce noise in access logs by logging only successful accesses in a configurable time window. Requests that are denied by a security policy or result in an error are always logged, letting you significantly reduce the costs associated with ingesting, storing, and processing logs, without the loss of key security signals.

4.6   Conclusion

In this chapter, we have seen what a service mesh is, what the advantages of implementing it are, and how Anthos Service Mesh exploits the potential of Istio to manage the entire service mesh. Thanks to Anthos Service Mesh, developers can be more agile in implementing microservices architectures and don't need to worry about implementing monitoring probes within the application code, by taking advantage of sidecar proxy and proxyless approaches.

The operations structures can monitor everything that happens within the service mesh in real time, guaranteeing the required service levels. The traffic splitting and rolling release features allow you to efficiently release new versions of the services, ensuring that everything works correctly. Thanks to the security features, the service mesh is protected from risks that can come from outside or inside the network, implementing effective authentication and authorization policies.

4.7   Examples and case studies

Using the knowledge from the chapter, address each of the requirements in the following case study.

4.7.1   Evermore Industries

Evermore Industries has asked you to enable ASM on a GKE cluster running in GCP. The cluster will be used for initial service mesh testing and should be installed with all features to allow the developers to test any feature. They have also asked you to deploy an online Boutique application to prove that the service mesh is up and running as expected.

Because they are new to Istio and the advantages of using a service mesh, they do not have any special requirements outside of deploying ASM and the Boutique demo application. The only additional requirement is to provide proof that the Boutique application is running in the mesh as expected, from the GCP console.

The next section contains the solution to address Evermore's requirements. You can follow along with the solution, or, if you are comfortable, you can configure your cluster to address the requirements and use the solution to verify your results.

EVERMORE INDUSTRIES SOLUTION: INSTALLING ASM

To install ASM, you can download the ASM installation script to deploy ASM with all components installed. Follow the next steps to install ASM with all components on your GKE cluster running in GCP:

1 Download the ASM installation script:

```
curl https://storage.googleapis.com/csm-artifacts/asm/asmcli_1.12 > asmcli
```

2 Make the installer executable:

```
chmod +x asmcli
```

3 You will need the following information from your project and GKE cluster to execute the installation script: Project ID, GKE cluster name, and the GKE cluster location.

4 Execute the installation script with the information from your cluster to install ASM:

```
./asmcli install --project_id gke-test1-123456 --cluster_name gke-dev-
001 --cluster_location us-central1-c --output_dir ./asm-downloads --
enable_all
```

5 The installation will take a few minutes. Once the installation is complete, you will see a message like the one shown here:

```
asmcli: Successfully installed ASM.
```

6 Verify that the `istio-system` namespace has healthy Pods that have been started successfully using the following code:

```
kubectl get pods -n istio-system
```

7 This should show you that there are four running Pods: two `istio-ingress-gateway` Pods and two `istiod` Pods. Example output follows:

```
NAME                          READY   STATUS
istio-ingressgateway-68fb877774-9tm8j  1/1    Running istio-ingressgateway-
68fb877774-qf5dp  1/1    Running
istiod-asm-1124-2-78fb6c7f98-n4xpp     1/1     Running
istiod-asm-1124-2-78fb6c7f98-sgttk     1/1     Running
```

Now that Istio has been deployed, you need to create a namespace and enable Istio for sidecar injection.

EVERMORE INDUSTRIES SOLUTION: ENABLING SIDECAR INJECTION

To enable the namespace for sidecar injection, follow the steps shown here:

1 Create a namespace that will be used to deploy the Boutique application. In our example, we will use a namespace called `demo`:

```
kubectl create namespace demo
```

2 Next, we need to label the namespace with the correct label to enable sidecar injection. Starting with Istio 1.7, the label used to enable sidecar injection changed from a generic `istio-injection` to using the value of the control plane version.

3 To find the control plane version we will use in the label, retrieve the labels in the `istio-system` namespace:

```
kubectl -n istio-system get pods -l app=istiod --show-labels
```

4 This will return the labels of the istiod Pods, which contains the value we need. The output will look similar to the following example. (Note: The label value we will need is in bold.)

```
NAME                       READY  STATUS  RESTARTS  AGE  LABELS
istiod-asm-1124-2-78fb6c7f98-n4xpp  1/1  Running  0     44m
app=istiod,install.operator.istio.io/owning-
resource=unknown,istio.io/rev=asm-1124-
2,istio=istiod,operator.istio.io/component=Pilot,pod-template-
hash=78fb6c7f98,sidecar.istio.io/inject=false
istiod-asm-1124-2-78fb6c7f98-sgttk  1/1  Running  0     44m
app=istiod,install.operator.istio.io/owning-
resource=unknown,istio.io/rev=asm-1124-2,istio=istiod,opera-
tor.istio.io/component=Pilot,pod-template-hash=78fb6c7f98,side-
car.istio.io/inject=false
```

5 Using the istio/io value, label the demo namespace to enable sidecar injection as follows:

```
kubectl label namespace demo istio.io/rev=asm-1124-2
```

EVERMORE INDUSTRIES SOLUTION: INSTALLING THE BOUTIQUE APPLICATION

Now that ASM has been installed and we have created a new namespace with the correct label to enable sidecar injection, we can deploy the Boutique application. Follow the next steps to deploy the Boutique demo:

1 Download the Boutique demo application from the Git repository. The following command will download the GIT repo into a directory called online-boutique:

```
kpt pkg get https://github.com/GoogleCloudPlatform/microservices-
demo.git/release online-boutique
```

2 Deploy the application using the files in the online-boutique directory:

```
kubectl apply -n demo -f online-boutique
```

This command will install several deployments and services into the demo namespace. It will take a few minutes for the Pods to start up. You can watch the namespace or list the Pods in the namespace to verify that each Pod enters a running state and that each Pod shows two containers. (Remember that each Pod will have a sidecar injected for the Istio proxy.)

3 Once all Pods are running, the demo namespace output should look similar to the following:

```
NAME                       READY  STATUS
adservice-6b74979749-2qd77       2/2   Running
cartservice-6fc79c6d86-tvncv     2/2   Running  checkoutservice-
7c95787547-8dmzw    2/2   Running  currencyservice-67674dbdf7-hkw78
2/2   Running  emailservice-799966ff9f-qcb6s    2/2   Running  frontend-
597d957cdf-dmdwr       2/2   Running  loadgenerator-88f7dbff5-cn78t
2/2   Running  paymentservice-5bdd645d9f-4w9f9    2/2   Running
productcatalogservice-7ffbf4fbf5-j98sq  2/2   Running
recommendationservice-599dfdc445-gpmww  2/2   Running  redis-cart-
57bd646894-tdxwb       2/2   Running  shippingservice-5f4d856dc-cwtcl
2/2   Running
```

4 As part of the deployment, a load balancer service was created that allows connectivity to the Boutique application from the internet. To find the IP address that has been assigned, get the service called `frontend-external` in the demo namespace:

```
kubectl get services frontend-external -n demo
```

This code will output the service details, which will contain the external address you can use to verify the application is working.

5 Use the address from the output in step 3 to connect to the application from a web browser. Once you connect, you should see the main Boutique page, shown in figure 4.11.

Figure 4.11 Online Boutique web application

EVERMORE INDUSTRIES SOLUTION: OBSERVING SERVICES USING THE GCP CONSOLE

The final requirement from Evermore is to prove that the Boutique application is running in the mesh, using the GCP console. To prove this, you can navigate to Anthos > Service Mesh from the GCP console, as shown in figure 4.12.

This interface will provide a list of all services in the service mesh. The default table view, shown in figure 4.13, will show each service and metrics including requests, latency, and failures.

You can change the view from the table view to a topology view by clicking the topology button in the upper-right corner of the console. This will provide a graphical topology layout of the mesh services, shown in figure 4.14.

Both views will show services in the service mesh. Because we see the expected services for the Boutique application, this proves that the deployment is successfully

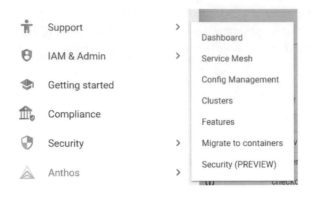

Figure 4.12   Google Cloud Console: Anthos menu

Services   ❓

Status ❓	Name ↑	Namespace	Types	Clusters	Requests/sec (avg)
ⓘ	adservice	demo	K8s	gke-dev-001	0.9
ⓘ	cartservice	demo	K8s	gke-dev-001	1.5

Figure 4.13   Anthos Service Mesh: list of services

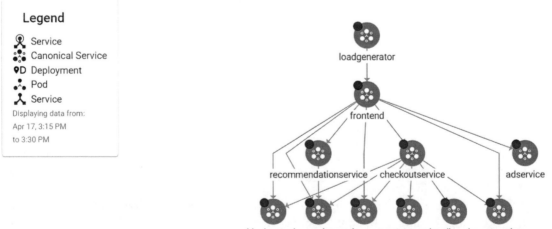

Figure 4.14   Anthos Service Mesh: topology view

working inside of the mesh. In this exercise, you deployed ASM in a GKE cluster, created a new namespace that was enabled for sidecar injection, and deployed a test application into the service mesh.

Summary

- A service mesh based on Anthos Service Mesh helps organizations run microservices at scale.
- We covered all the components of Istio and what each component does to provide the service mesh features.
- ASM increases security between workloads using mutual TLS (mTLS) to encrypt all communication between mesh resources and by using native Istio authentication and authorization policies.
- ASM provides traffic-routing abilities, allowing for a more flexible release process, including A/B testing and canary deployments.
- You can discover application failures before releasing any new code, which increases availability and resilience, using circuit breakers and fault injection to proactively find problems with how an application will handle common problems like network delays or HTTP errors.
- ASM provides visibility, monitoring, security, and control of the entire service mesh and between multiple environments.
- To use the features of ASM, developers do not need to modify their code, thanks to the Envoy proxy sidecar, which handles the traffic flow for the application.

Operations management 5

Jason Quek

This chapter covers

- Using the Unified Cloud interface to manage Kubernetes clusters
- Managing Anthos clusters
- Logging and monitoring
- Anthos deployment patterns

Operations is the act of ensuring your clusters are functioning, active, secure, and able to serve the application to the users. To that end, one prevailing school of thought has gained adoption and momentum in the cloud era: an operations practice known as DevOps.

The simplest definition of DevOps is "the combination of developers and IT operations." DevOps aims to address two major points. The first is to enable continuous delivery through automated testing, frequent releases, and management of the entire infrastructure as code. You can use frameworks such as Terraform or Pulumi to implement this, depending on the developer's skill set. The second, an often overlooked part of DevOps, is IT operations, which includes tasks like logging and monitoring and then using those indicators to scale and manage the system.

You can use open source projects such as Prometheus and Grafana to manage these tasks. Teams can further improve performance by implementing an additional security tool chain to build a modern DevSecOps practice.

Before the development of DevOps, Google developed an approach called *site reliability engineering (SRE)*. This approach automates and codifies all tasks in operating the infrastructure to enhance reliability in the systems, and if something goes wrong, it can be repaired automatically through code. An SRE team is responsible for not only keeping the environment stable but also for handling new operational features and improvements to the infrastructure.

Both DevOps and SRE have different responsibilities assigned to different teams; however, they have the same goal: to be able to implement changes rapidly and efficiently, automate where possible, and continuously monitor and enhance the system. This commonality underlies the "desire" from the engineering and operations teams to break silos (closed teams) and take common responsibility for the system.

Either approach will deliver many of the same advantages, but they solve problems in different ways. For example, in a DevOps approach, a dedicated operations team may take care of the operations management aspect of the infrastructure, handing off problems to another development team to resolve. This differs from the SRE approach, where operations are driven by the development team and approached from a software engineering point of view, allowing for a single SRE team to address problems within their own team.

Anthos provides a path to build a strong DevOps or SRE culture using the tools provided in the framework. This chapter will show product owners, developers, and infrastructure teams that, through using Anthos, they are able to build a DevOps/SRE culture that will help to reduce silos in their company, build reliable systems, and enhance development efficiency.

In the next section, we will explain the tools that Anthos includes, starting with the unified user interface through Google Cloud console, then centralized logging and monitoring, and, finally, environs, which are all key concepts that will provide the building blocks to enable an operations practice.

5.1 Unified user interface from Google Cloud console

With everything-as-code these days, a software engineer takes pride in doing everything from the command line or as code. However, when a production problem occurs affecting real-life services, an intuitive and assistive user interface can help an engineer identify the problem quickly. This is where Google's unified user interface comes in handy, as shown in figure 5.1.

These tools allow you to view multiple items, like Kubernetes clusters, in a single view. Having this view available to an administrator gives them oversight of all the resources available, without having to log in to three separate clusters, as shown in figure 5.1. This view also shows where resources are located, who their providers are, and any actions required to manage the clusters.

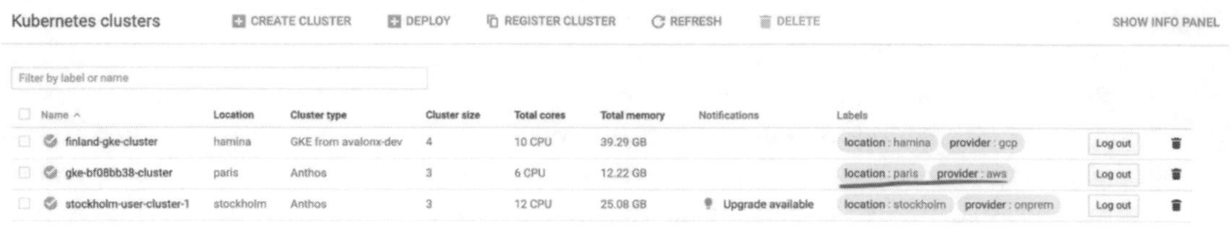

Figure 5.1   Multiple clusters registered to Google Cloud console

Accessing this view requires that the user is already logged in to Google Cloud console, which is secured by Google Cloud Identity, providing an additional layer of security to build defense against malicious actors. Having access to this type of view fulfills one of the DevOps principles: using tooling to provide observability into the system.

To have a single-pane-of-glass view, you need to register your clusters with your GCP project. In the next section, we will cover how to register a cluster that is running Anthos on any of the major cloud service providers or on-prem.

5.1.1   *Registering clusters to Google Cloud console*

The component responsible for connecting clusters to Google Cloud console is called Connect and is often deployed as one of the last steps after a cluster is created. If a cluster is deployed by Anthos on GKE, AWS, or Azure, the Connect Agent is automatically deployed at the time of cluster creation. However, if the cluster is not deployed by Anthos—such as EKS, AKS, OpenShift, and Rancher clusters—the agent will have to be deployed separately, because Anthos is not involved in the installation process. This process will be covered later in this chapter.

Because Anthos is built following best practices from Kubernetes, the Connect Agent is represented as a Kubernetes deployment, with the image provided by Google as part of the Anthos framework. The agent can also be seen in the Google Cloud console and can be managed like any other Kubernetes object, as shown in figure 5.2.

The Connect Agent acts as a conduit for Google Cloud console to issue commands to the clusters in which it has been deployed and to report vCPU usage for licensing. This brings up one important point: the clusters need to be able to reach Google Cloud APIs (egress); however, the clusters do not need to be reachable by Google Cloud APIs (ingress). The impact on latency is minimal due to the unidirectional tunnel initialized after the first connection.

So, how does Google Cloud console issue Kubernetes API commands, such as listing Pods to display on the Google Cloud console? The answer is through the Connect Agent, which establishes a persistent TLS 1.2 connection to GCP to wait for requests, eliminating the need for having an inbound firewall rule for the user cluster.

Transport Layer Security (TLS) is a cryptographic protocol designed to provide privacy and data integrity between the sender and receiver. It uses symmetric encryption based on a shared secret to ensure that the message is private. Messages are

⊘ gke-connect-agent-20200515-02-00

Overview Details Revision history Events YAML

Cluster	finland-gke-cluster
Namespace	gke-connect
Labels	app : gke-connect-agent hub.gke.io/project : anthos-sandbox-256114 version : 20200515-02-00
Replicas	1 updated, 1 ready, 1 available, 0 unavailable
Pod specification	Revision 1, containers: gke-connect-agent-20200515-02-00 , volumes: creds-gcp, http-proxy

Active revisions

Revision ⌄	Name	Status	Summary	Created on	Pods running/Pods total
1	gke-connect-agent-20200515-02-00-5865ddc9f5	⊘ OK	gke-connect-agent-20200515-02-00: gcr.io/gkeconnect/gkeconnect-gce:20200515-02-00	25 May 2020, 01:32:41	1/1

Managed pods

Revision	Name	Status	Restarts	Created on ⌃
1	gke-connect-agent-20200515-02-00-5865ddc9f5-jpgfr	⊘ Running	0	28 May 2020, 21:33:34

Figure 5.2 A Connect Agent deployed on a GKE cluster

signed with a public key to ensure authenticity and include a message-integrity check to make sure messages are complete. In short, the communication channel to the Connect Agent over the internet is as secure as internet bank transfers. The full communication flow can be seen in chapter 2, figure 2.2.

One important point to note is that the outbound TLS-encrypted connection over the internet is used for Anthos deployments to communicate with Google Cloud, as shown in figure 5.3. This setup simplifies things, because no inbound firewall rules have to be added to Anthos deployments—only outbound traffic to Google Cloud—without any virtual private networks (VPN) required.

One great thing about Kubernetes is its standardization, which means this agent will be able to issue Kubernetes API commands on clusters created by Google or *any* provider that provides a Kubernetes-compliant distribution as defined by the Cloud Native Computing Foundation.

In large enterprises, IT security usually wants to know what the Connect Agent is sending to Google Cloud APIs, and this is a tricky problem to overcome, due to the perceived worry that if Google shares the keys to decrypt the traffic, it is effectively overriding the security put into place. More details of what information is actually sent from the Connect Agent to Google Cloud can be found in this white paper by Google (http://mng.bz/rdAZ). Google has also stated unequivocally that no customer data is sent via the Connect Agent and that it is used only to provide functionality to communicate with the Kubernetes API and also provide licensing metrics for Anthos billing.

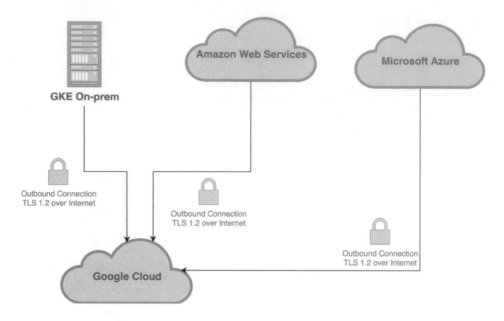

Figure 5.3   The outbound connection to Google Cloud from Anthos deployments

5.1.2   *Authentication*

Authentication to Google Kubernetes Engine should use Identity and Access Management (IAM) roles to govern access to the GKE clusters. The following section pertains to GKE on-prem, GKE on AWS, GKE on Azure, and Anthos attached clusters.

To access Anthos clusters, users with access to the project will always have to provide either a Kubernetes Service Account (KSA) token or basic authentication or authenticate against an identity provider configured for the cluster.

Using a KSA token would be the easiest to set up, but it requires token rotation and a secure way to distribute tokens regularly to the users who need access to the clusters. Using basic authentication would be the least secure due to having password management requirements, but it is still supported as an authentication method if an identity provider is not available. If you must use basic authentication, one tip would be to implement a password-rotation strategy in the event of password leaks.

The recommended practice would be to set up OpenID Connect (OIDC) with Google Cloud Identity so that users can benefit from their existing security setup to manage access to their clusters as well. As of September 2020, OIDC is supported on GKE on-prem clusters from the command line (not from the console). A solid KSA token rotation and distribution strategy is highly recommended. This can be as simple as utilizing Google Secret Manager, where permissions to retrieve the token can be controlled via IAM permissions, and the token can be updated every seven days using Cloud Scheduler.

Once OIDC with Google Cloud Identity has been set up, users can authenticate the user clusters using the gcloud CLI or from the Google Cloud console, as shown in figure 5.4.

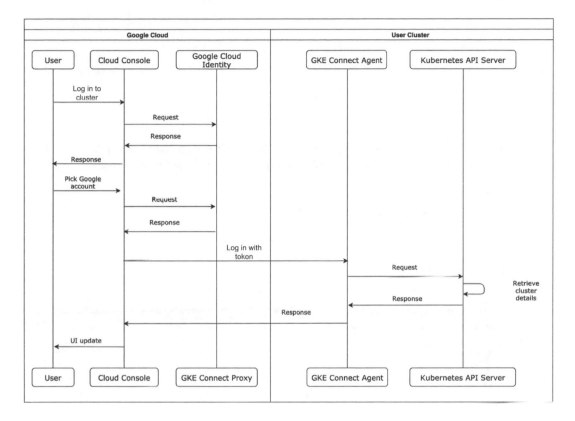

Figure 5.4   Authentication flow for OIDC with Google Cloud Identity

In figure 5.4, we show the identity flow using OIDC with Google Cloud Identity. With Anthos Identity Service, other providers that follow the OIDC and Lightweight Directory Access Protocol (LDAP) protocols can provide identity. This process allows a seamless user administration with technologies such as Microsoft Active Directory or an LDAP server and follows the principle of having one single source of truth of identity.

5.1.3   Cluster management

After registering the clusters and authenticating, users will be able to see Pods, Services, ConfigMaps, and persistent volumes, which are normally available from GKE native clusters. In this section, the cluster management options available via the Google Cloud console will be covered. However, to build a good SRE practice, cluster management should be automated and scripted. It is nice, however, to be able to modify these from a user-friendly interface.

Administrators who have experience in Google Kubernetes Engine on GCP know how easy it is to connect to the cluster from the Google Cloud console. They just navigate to the cluster list, as seen in figure 5.5, and click the Connect button.

Name ^	Location	Cluster size	Total cores	Total memory	Notifications	Labels	
⊘ anthos-primary-cluster	europe-north1-a	4	10 vCPUs	37.50 GB	🔔 Low resource requests	mesh_id : proj-710282601588	Connect

Figure 5.5   Cluster list in the GCP console

Once they click Connect, a pop-up window, as shown in figure 5.6, provides the command to run in a Google Cloud Shell to connect to the selected cluster.

Connect to the cluster

You can connect to your cluster via command-line or using a dashboard.

Command-line access

Configure kubectl command-line access by running the following command:

```
$ gcloud container clusters get-credentials primary-cluster --region europe-west1 --project msp-cc-prod
```

Run in Cloud Shell

Cloud Console dashboard

You can view the workloads running in your cluster in the Cloud Console Workloads dashboard.

Open Workloads dashboard

OK

Figure 5.6   One of the best features in GKE— generating kubectl credentials via gcloud

For on-prem and other cloud clusters, the Connect gateway functionality, discussed later in this chapter, allows operations administrators to manage their clusters remotely but through a different command.

Google Cloud console provides a user-friendly interface to edit and apply YAML deployments, as shown in figure 5.7. Through this interface, administrators can modify Kubernetes configurations without having to go through the kubectl command

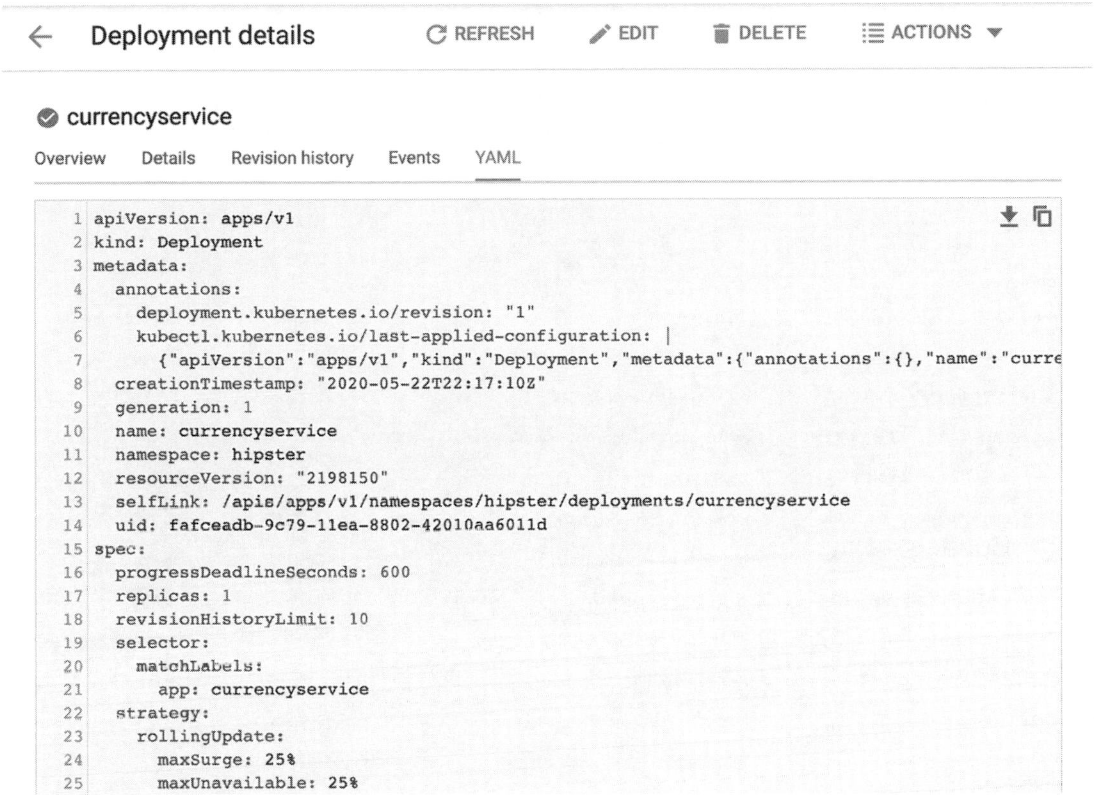

Figure 5.7   Editing a YAML definition from the Google Cloud console

line, which can save some time in emergency situations. These actions on Google Cloud console translate to Kubernetes API calls, or kubectl edit commands, and are issued via the Connect Agent to the Anthos clusters. Of course, this method should be used only in triage or development situations, not necessarily in production, but it shows the future possibilities of opening up access to the Connect Agent from the local command line.

Google Cloud console also provides useful information about the underlying Docker, kubelet, and memory pressure for the nodes, as seen in figure 5.8. Using this, administrators can run a quick root cause analysis if a fault occurs with one of the nodes, and they can cordon off and drain the node.

When listing the workloads in Google Cloud console, a user can see deployments across all clusters and filter them by cluster. This ability provides an overview of what services are running across all clusters and indicates if problems arise with any services and scaling limits. A common problem is that Pods cannot be provisioned due to lack of CPU or memory. This is clearly visible as a bright red error message in the console, as seen in figure 5.9.

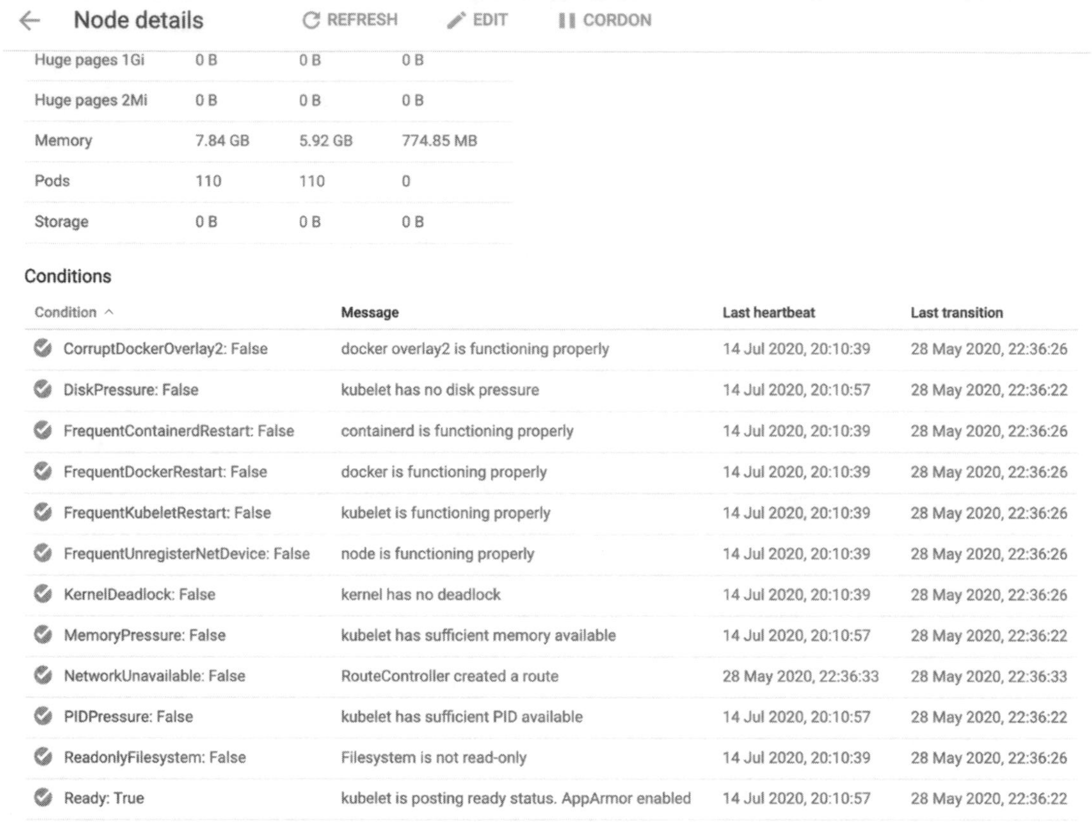

Node details   C REFRESH   ✎ EDIT   ‖ CORDON

Huge pages 1Gi	0 B	0 B	0 B
Huge pages 2Mi	0 B	0 B	0 B
Memory	7.84 GB	5.92 GB	774.85 MB
Pods	110	110	0
Storage	0 B	0 B	0 B

Conditions

Condition ^	Message	Last heartbeat	Last transition
✅ CorruptDockerOverlay2: False	docker overlay2 is functioning properly	14 Jul 2020, 20:10:39	28 May 2020, 22:36:26
✅ DiskPressure: False	kubelet has no disk pressure	14 Jul 2020, 20:10:57	28 May 2020, 22:36:22
✅ FrequentContainerdRestart: False	containerd is functioning properly	14 Jul 2020, 20:10:39	28 May 2020, 22:36:26
✅ FrequentDockerRestart: False	docker is functioning properly	14 Jul 2020, 20:10:39	28 May 2020, 22:36:26
✅ FrequentKubeletRestart: False	kubelet is functioning properly	14 Jul 2020, 20:10:39	28 May 2020, 22:36:26
✅ FrequentUnregisterNetDevice: False	node is functioning properly	14 Jul 2020, 20:10:39	28 May 2020, 22:36:26
✅ KernelDeadlock: False	kernel has no deadlock	14 Jul 2020, 20:10:39	28 May 2020, 22:36:26
✅ MemoryPressure: False	kubelet has sufficient memory available	14 Jul 2020, 20:10:57	28 May 2020, 22:36:22
✅ NetworkUnavailable: False	RouteController created a route	28 May 2020, 22:36:33	28 May 2020, 22:36:33
✅ PIDPressure: False	kubelet has sufficient PID available	14 Jul 2020, 20:10:57	28 May 2020, 22:36:22
✅ ReadonlyFilesystem: False	Filesystem is not read-only	14 Jul 2020, 20:10:39	28 May 2020, 22:36:26
✅ Ready: True	kubelet is posting ready status. AppArmor enabled	14 Jul 2020, 20:10:57	28 May 2020, 22:36:22

Figure 5.8   Node information from Google Cloud console

❗ Pod errors: Unschedulable	SHOW DETAILS

Figure 5.9   Unschedulable Pods error

Viewing a cluster interactively with tools is beneficial for real-time views of object states, node statuses, and more. Although this tool can be helpful in the right scenario (e.g., when diagnosing a previously unknown problem that impacts production and a user-friendly interface reduces the need to remember commands in a high-stress situation), you will find yourself looking at logs and creating monitoring events more often than real-time views. In the next section, we will detail the logging and monitoring features that Anthos includes.

5.1.4   Logging and monitoring

Kubernetes offers different kinds of logs, which are useful for administrators to investigate when managing a cluster. One type is system logs, to which Kubernetes system services such as kube-apiserver, etcd, kube-scheduler and kube-controller-manager log. Clusters also have application logs, which contain log details for all the workloads running on the Kubernetes cluster. These logs can be accessed through the Connect Agent, which communicates with the Kubernetes API and essentially issues a kubectl `logs` command.

Both of these log types, shown in figure 5.10, are not stored in the cloud but are retrieved on demand from the Kubernetes API, which translates to an increased retrieval latency but is at times necessary in case of IT security requests.

✅ **adservice-84449b8756-n54d5**

| DETAILS | EVENTS | LOGS | YAML |

☰ Filter logs   ❓

Container	Timestamp ↓	Message
istio-proxy	14 Jul 2020, 20:42:23	[2020-07-14T18:38:12.810Z] "- - -" 0 - "-" "-" 1428 3415 240859 - "-" "-" "-" "-" "173.194.222.95:443" outbound|443||*.googleapis.com 10.10.4.11:38954 173.194.222.95:443 10.10.4.11:38952 cloudtrace.googleapis.com -
istio-proxy	14 Jul 2020, 20:40:08	[Envoy (Epoch 1)] [2020-07-14 18:40:08.150][38][warning][filter] [src/istio/mixerclient/report_batch.cc:110] Mixer Report failed with: UNAVAILABLE:upstream connect error or disconnect/reset before headers. reset reason: connection failure
istio-proxy	14 Jul 2020, 20:29:37	[Envoy (Epoch 1)] [2020-07-14 18:29:37.449][31][warning][config] [bazel-out/k8-opt/bin/external/envoy/source/common/config/_virtual_includes/grpc_stream_lib/common/config/grpc_stream.h:91] gRPC config stream closed: 13,
istio-proxy	14 Jul 2020, 20:13:23	[2020-07-14T18:13:20.731Z] "GET /computeMetadata/v1/instance/service-accounts/default/token HTTP/1.1" 200 - "-" "-" 0 210 26 25 "-" "Google-HTTP-Java-Client/1.24.1 (gzip)" "f8ef3aea-0512-43e3-9c79-5148e0802f7c" "169.254.169.254" "169.254.169.254:80" PassthroughCluster - 169.254.169.254:80 10.10.4.11:55300 - -
istio-proxy	14 Jul 2020, 20:09:07	[Envoy (Epoch 1)] [2020-07-14 18:09:07.886][38][warning][filter] [src/istio/mixerclient/report_batch.cc:110] Mixer Report failed with: UNAVAILABLE:upstream connect error or disconnect/reset before headers. reset reason: connection failure
istio-proxy	14 Jul 2020, 20:06:03	[2020-07-14T17:34:10.309Z] "- - -" 0 - "-" "-" 948462 7830 1904930 - "-" "-" "-" "-" "173.194.73.95:443" outbound|443||*.googleapis.com 10.10.4.11:49044 173.194.73.95:443 10.10.4.11:49042 monitoring.googleapis.com -

Figure 5.10   Container logs

Logs are primarily about errors—warnings that are output to the standard output stream during the execution of any Kubernetes Pod. These logs are written to the node itself, and if the Google Cloud operations suite (formerly Stackdriver) agent is enabled on the GKE cluster, the logs are aggregated and forwarded to the Cloud Logging API and written to the cloud.

Metrics are observations about a service, such as memory consumption or requests per second. These observations are saved as a historical trend, which can be used to scale services or identify possible problems in implementation. Given that each service can potentially have tens of observations occurring every second or minute, depending on the business requirements, managing this data in a usable manner is nontrivial. We propose a couple of solutions in the next subsection involving Google's Cloud

Logging and Monitoring services. You can also use partner technology such as Elastic Stack, Prometheus, Grafana, or Splunk to make sense of the metrics. See http://mng.bz/VpmO or http://mng.bz/xdAY for more information.

LOGGING AND MONITORING GKE ON-PREM

Administrators can choose between a few different options for observability when installing GKE on on-prem clusters. The first option is to use Google's native Cloud Logging and Cloud Monitoring solutions. Cloud Logging and Cloud Monitoring handle infrastructure and cloud services, as well as Kubernetes logging and monitoring. All logged data can be displayed in hierarchical levels according to the Kubernetes object types. By default, GKE logging collects logs and metrics only from the `kube-system`, `gke-system`, `gke-connect`, `istio-system`, and `config-management` system namespaces, which are used to track cluster health and are sent to Cloud Logging and Cloud Monitoring in Google Cloud. This service is fully managed and includes dashboarding and alerting capabilities to build a useful monitoring control panel. Cloud Logging and Cloud Monitoring are often used to monitor Google Cloud resources and issue alerts on certain logged events and also serve as a single pane of glass for monitoring service health. This is the recommended option if an organization is open to using and learning a new logging and monitoring stack and wants a low-cost and fully managed option.

Certain organizations may want to disable Cloud Logging and Cloud Monitoring due to internal decisions. Although they can be disabled, the Google Support SLA will be voided and Google support will be able to help only as a best effort when resolving GKE on-prem operation problems.

The second option is to use Prometheus, Alertmanager, and Grafana, a popular open source collection of projects, to collect application and system-level logs, and provide alerting and dashboarding capabilities. Prometheus and Grafana are deployed as Kubernetes monitoring add-on workloads and, as such, benefit from the scalability and reliability of running on Kubernetes. When using this solution, support from Google is limited to basic operations and basic installation and configuration. For more information on Prometheus and Alertmanager, visit https://prometheus.io, and for Grafana, please visit https://grafana.com.

This option can be used across any Kubernetes setup, and many prebuilt Grafana packages can be used to monitor Kubernetes cluster health. One downside is that administrators would have to manage Prometheus, ensure its health, and manage its storage of historical metrics as it is running, as with any other application workload. Other tools such as Thanos can be used to query, aggregate, downsample, and manage multiple Prometheus sources, as well as store historical metrics in object storage such as Google Cloud Storage or any S3-compatible object stores. For more information on Thanos, please visit https://thanos.io/.

This option is easy for organizations that have built logging and monitoring services using open source technologies and have deployed this stack before. It also improves portability and reduces vendor lock-in due to the open source technologies used.

The third option is to use validated solutions, such as Elastic Stack, Splunk, or Datadog, to consume logs and metrics from Anthos clusters and make them available to the operations team. This option is attractive if these current logging methods are already in place and the organization relies on partners to manage the logging and monitoring systems' uptime. Organizations that choose this option often have already purchased this stack and use it for their overall operations with many heterogeneous systems.

A fourth option is also a tiered telemetry approach, which is recommended for organizations embarking on a hybrid journey with Anthos. Multiple reasons exist for this approach, the first being that platform and system data from Anthos clusters is always tightly coupled with Cloud Monitoring and Cloud Logging, so administrators would have to learn Cloud Monitoring and Cloud Logging to get the most up-to-date logs and metrics anyway. In addition, it does not have any extra costs and is part of the Anthos suite. The second reason is that building a hybrid environment often requires migrating applications to the hybrid environment, with developers who are used to working with these partner solutions and have built debugging and operating models around that stack. This makes it a supported option that reduces the operational friction of moving workloads to a hybrid environment. The third reason is to build the ability to balance points of failure among different providers and have a backup option.

5.1.5 Service Mesh logging

Anthos Service Mesh is an optional component but included in the Anthos platform, as explained in depth in chapter 4. It is an extended and supported version of open source Istio, included with Anthos and supported by Google. Part of what Google extended is the ability to upload telemetry data from sidecar proxies injected with your Pods directly to the Cloud Monitoring API and Cloud Logging API on Google Cloud. These metrics are then used to visualize preconfigured dashboards in the Google Cloud console. For more details, please refer to chapter 3.

Storing these metrics on Google Cloud also allows you to have historical information on latency, errors, and traffic between microservices, so that you can conduct a postmortem on any problems. You can further use these metrics to drive your service-level indicators and Pod-scaling strategy and identify services for optimization.

5.1.6 Using service-level indicators and agreements

Anthos Service Mesh service-level indicators (SLIs), service-level objectives (SLOs), and service-level agreements (SLAs) are features that you can use to build an SRE practice where Anthos is deployed. It is necessary to consider these concepts when designing operations management procedures in Anthos.

Two indicators measure service levels: latency and availability. Latency is how long the service takes to respond, whereas availability represents how often the service responds. When the system is designed from a DevOps view, administrators must consider Anthos upgrade and scaling needs and plan accordingly so they do not affect these indicators.

For service-level objectives, you should think from the angle of the worst-case scenario, and not the best-case scenario, making that decision as data driven as possible. For example, if the latency is unrealistic and does not affect the user experience, there will be no way to even release the service. Find the highest latency acceptable according to the user experience and then work on reducing that based on business needs. Educate your business stakeholders that a target approaching 99.99999% availability is very expensive to attain and that a practical trade-off often must be agreed on. An important concept mentioned in the SRE book by Google is to strive to make a service reliable enough but no more than it has to be. You can find more information on the SRE book by Google at http://mng.bz/Al77. Understanding the procedures and risks of Anthos upgrades, rollbacks, and security updates is essential input to determine whether a service-level objective is realistic.

You should also define a compliance period for the service-level objective to be measured against. The set SLO can be any period of measurement—a day, a week, or a month. This allows for the teams responsible for the service to decide when it is time to roll back, make a hotfix, or slow down development to prioritize fixing bugs. The SLI and SLO also empower product owners to propose service-level agreements with users that require them and offer a realistic latency and availability agreement.

5.2   *Anthos command-line management*

You can use various command-line tools to deal with cluster creation, scaling, and upgrading of Anthos versions, such as gkectl, gkeadmin and anthos-gke. This chapter is not meant to replace the documentation on Google Cloud, but it summarizes the actions and some of the gotchas to look out for.

Reminder: Admin clusters are deployed purely to monitor and administer user clusters. Think of them as the invisible control plane analogous to GKE, and do not deploy services that can affect it there.

> **TIP**   You can use a kubeconfig manager like ktx from https://github.com/heptiolabs/ktx, which allows administrators to switch between admin and user cluster contexts easily.

In the next section, we'll break up the segments into GKE on-prem and GKE on AWS because the tools and installation process differ.

5.2.1   *Using CLI tools for GKE on-prem*

GKE on-prem installation uses the APIs from VMware[1] to build an admin workstation, admin cluster nodes, and user cluster nodes programmatically. Persistent volumes are powered from individual VMware datastores or vSAN, and networking is provided by

---

[1] In addition to VMware, it is possible to use Anthos on bare metal. That is the topic discussed in chapter 17.

either distributed or standard vSphere switches. These act like the IaaS components provided by Google Cloud when building a GKE cluster: thus the name, GKE on-prem. The concept of having an admin cluster with user clusters and node pools mirrors GKE best practices.

The current installation process is to download a tool named gkeadm, which creates an admin workstation. It is from this admin workstation that the admin cluster and user clusters are installed, as described next. Although versions of gkeadm are available for Windows, Linux, and macOS, this section will explain only an abbreviated process for Linux:

1 The first step is to download the tool from the cloud storage bucket:

```
gsutil cp gs://gke-on-prem-release-public/gkeadm/<anthos
version>/linux/gkeadm ./chmod +x gkeadm
```

2 Next, create a prepopulated config file:

```
./gkeadm create config
```

3 Fill in the vCenter credentials, GCP whitelisted service account key path (after purchasing Anthos, customers are asked to provide a service account, which Google will whitelist to be able to download images and other proprietary tools), and vCenter Certificate Authority certification path.

The vCenter Certificate Authority certifications can be downloaded as follows:

```
curl -k "https://[SERVER_ADDRESS]/certs/download.zip" > download.zip
```

After unzipping the download.zip file, the relevant certifications can be found in the certs/lin folder. The file with the .0 suffix is the root certificate. Rename it to vcenter.crt, and use it in the reference from the installation config file.

The vCenter and F5 Big-IP credentials are saved in plain text in the config file when you create new user clusters or on installation. One way to secure the F5 credentials is through using a wrapper around Google Cloud Secret Manager and gcloud.

To create a password secured by Google Secret Manager, use the following code:

```
echo "vcenterp455w0rd" | gcloud secrets create vcenterpass --data-file=- --
    replication-policy=user-managed --locations=us-east1
```

To retrieve a password secured by Google Secret Manager, enter the following code:

```
gcloud secrets versions access latest --secret="vcenterpass"
```

This secret is now protected via Google IAM policies and a wrapper script can be written to retrieve the secret, replace the placeholder in the config file, apply it, and then delete the file.

The process to create Anthos cluster components is quickly evolving, and it's not uncommon for a newer version to have some changes to the config file. You can learn about the latest release procedures at http://mng.bz/Zova.

CLUSTER MANAGEMENT: CREATING A NEW USER CLUSTER

The gkectl command is used for this operation. As a rule of thumb, admins should constrain their setups so that they contain a ratio of one admin cluster to 10 user clusters. User clusters should have a minimum of three nodes, with a maximum of 100 nodes. As previously mentioned, newer releases may increase these numbers. When a new Anthos release is published, you can check the new limits in the Quotas and Limits section of the respective release.

The general advice is to leave some space for at least one cluster, which can be created in your on-prem environment. This gives the operations team space to recreate clusters and move Pods over when upgrading or during triage.

Keep good documentation, like which IP addresses have been already assigned for other user clusters, so that nonoverlapping IPs can be determined easily. Consider that user clusters can be resized to 100 nodes, so reserve up to 100 IP addresses per range to keep that possibility.

Source control your configuration files, but do not commit the vSphere username and passwords. Committing such sensitive information to repositories can open security risks because anyone with access to the repository will be able to get those login details. Tools like ytt can be used to template configuration YAML and perform code reviews, and you should use repository scanners to prevent such mistakes from taking place (e.g., http://mng.bz/Rl7O).

Node pools can also be created with different machine shapes, so size them correctly to accommodate your workloads. Doing so also gives you granular control over which machine types to scale and saves costs. For production workloads, use three replicas for the user cluster master nodes for high availability, but for development, one should be fine.

Validate the configuration file to make sure the file is valid. The checks are both syntactic and programmatic, such as checking for IP range clashes and IP availability using the gkectl check-config command:

```
gkectl check-config --kubeconfig [ADMIN_CLUSTER_KUBECONFIG] --config
    [CONFIG_FILE]
```

After the first few validations, most time-consuming validations can be skipped by passing the --fast flag.

Next, the seesaw load balancer should be created if the bundled load balancer is chosen. If you do not create the seesaw node(s) before attempting a cluster build that has been configured with the integrated load-balancer option, you will receive an error during the cluster precheck. To create the seesaw node(s), use the gkectl create loadbalancer command:

```
gkectl create loadbalancer --kubeconfig [ADMIN_CLUSTER_KUBECONFIG] --config
    [CONFIG_FILE]
```

After the creation of a new user cluster, remember that for the bundled load-balanced seesaw version, the user will then be able to create the user cluster as follows:

```
gkectl create cluster --kubeconfig [ADMIN_CLUSTER_KUBECONFIG] --config
    [CONFIG_FILE]
```

You can also add the `--skip-validation-all` flag if the config file has already been validated.

The whole user cluster process, which consists of starting up new VMware virtual machines with the master and worker node images and joining them into a cluster, can take 20–30 minutes, depending on the hardware. The administrator is also able to see the nodes being created from the VMware vCenter console.

High-availability setup
High availability is necessary for Anthos deployments in production environments because failures can occur at different parts of the stack, ranging from networking, to hardware, to the virtualization layer.

High availability (HA) for admin clusters makes use of the vSphere HA in a vSphere cluster setup to protect GKE on-prem clusters from going down in the event of a host failure. This ensures that admin cluster nodes are distributed among different physical nodes in a vSphere cluster, so in the event of a physical node failure, the admin cluster will still be available.

To enable HA user control planes, simply specify `usercluster.master.replicas: 3` in the GKE on-prem configuration file. This will create three user cluster masters for each user cluster, consuming three times the resources but providing an HA Kubernetes setup.

CLUSTER MANAGEMENT: SCALING
Administrators can use the gkectl CLI to scale up or down nodes. They change the config file to set the number of expected replicas and execute the following command to update the node pool:

```
gkectl update cluster --kubeconfig [USER_CLUSTER_KUBECONFIG] --config
    [CONFIG_FILE]
```

CLUSTER MANAGEMENT: UPGRADING ANTHOS
Like any upgrade process, failures can occur during the process. A lot of effort has been put into making the upgrade process robust, including the addition of prechecks before executing the upgrade to catch potential problems before they occur. Each product team at Google works closely together when an upgrade is being developed to avoid any potential incompatibilities between components like Kubernetes, ACM, and ASM. For ease of access, bookmark this link for quick access: http://mng.bz/nJV8.

New Anthos versions appear frequently due to industry demand for new features, and so upgrading Anthos is a common activity. That can also mean upgrading to a new version of Kubernetes, which impacts Anthos Service Mesh due to Istio dependency on Kubernetes. The upgrade chain is complex, which is why we recommend keeping some spare hardware resources that can be used to create new versions of Anthos clusters and then move workloads to the new cluster before tearing down the older-version cluster. This process reduces the risk associated with upgrades by providing an easy rollback path in case of a failed upgrade. In this type of upgrade path, you should have a load balancer in front of the microservices running in the old cluster to be upgraded, which can direct traffic from the old cluster to the new cluster, because they will exist at the same time. However, if this is not an option, administrators can upgrade Anthos clusters in place.

First, consult the upgrade paths. From GKE on-prem 1.3.2 onward, administrators can upgrade directly to any version in the same minor release; otherwise, sequential upgrades are required. From version 1.7 onward, administrators can keep their admin cluster on an older version, while only upgrading the admin workstation and the user cluster. As a best practice, administrators should still schedule the admin cluster upgrades to keep up to date.

Next, download the gkeadm tool, which must be the same as the target version of your upgrade, and run gkeadm to upgrade the admin workstation and gkectl to upgrade your user cluster and, finally, the admin cluster.

When upgrading in place, a new node is created with the image of the latest version, and workloads are drained from the older version and shifted over to the latest version, one node after the other. Administrators should plan for additional resources in their physical hosts to accommodate at least one user node for upgrade purposes. The full flow can be seen in figure 5.11.

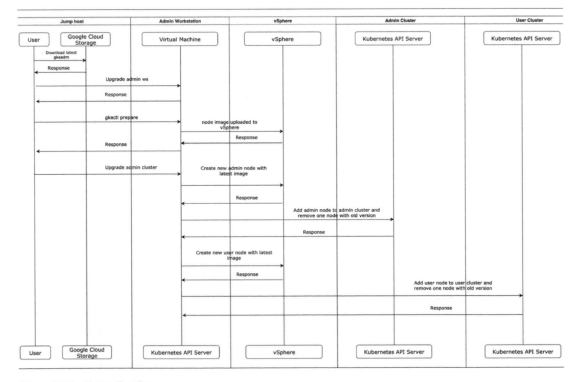

Figure 5.11   Upgrading flow

For a detailed list of commands, consult the upgrade documentation at http://mng .bz/Px7v for exact details.

CLUSTER MANAGEMENT: BACKING UP CLUSTERS

Anthos admin clusters can be backed up by following the steps found at http:// mng.bz/Jl7a. It is recommended you do this as part of a production Anthos environment setup to regularly schedule backups and to do on-demand backups when upgrading Anthos versions.

An Anthos user clusters' etcd can be backed up by running a backup script, which you can read more about at http://mng.bz/wPAa. Do note that this backs up only the etcd of the clusters, meaning the Kubernetes configuration. Google also states this should be a last resort. Backup for GKE promises to make this simpler, and was recently made available (http://mng.bz/X5MM).

Any application-specific data such as persistent volumes are not backed up by this process. Those should be backed up regularly to another storage device using one of the several available tools, like Velero.

You should treat your cluster backups the same as any data that is backed up from a server. The recommendation is to practice restoring an admin and user cluster from backup, along with application-specific data, to gain confidence in the backup and recovery process.

Google has several additions in development for Anthos. One important feature being added will be named Anthos Enterprise Data Protection and will provide the functionality to back up clusterwide config such as custom resource definitions, and namespace-wide configuration and application data from Google Cloud console into a Cloud storage bucket, as well the ability to restore using the backup.

5.2.2 GKE on AWS

GKE on AWS uses AWS EC2 instances and other components to build GKE clusters, which means these are not EKS clusters. If a user logs in to the AWS console, they will be able to see the admin cluster and user cluster nodes only as individual AWS EC2 instances. It is important to differentiate this from managing EKS clusters in Anthos because the responsibilities assigned to the various cloud providers according to each cluster type differ.

GKE on AWS installation is done via the gcloud CLI with the command `gcloud container aws clusters create`. For Terraform users, sample terraform code is available to install GKE on Anthos in the following repository: http://mng.bz/71R7. This sample code will further simplify the installation process and remove the need for a bastion host and management server mentioned in the steps that follow.

The installation process is to first get an AWS Key Management Service (KMS) key, then use anthos-gke, which in turn uses Terraform to generate Terraform code. Terraform, offered by HashiCorp, is an Infrastructure as Code open source tool to define a target state of a computing environment. Terraform code is declarative and uses Terraform providers, which are often contributed by cloud providers such as Google,

AWS, and Microsoft, to map their cloud provisioning APIs to Terraform code. The resulting Terraform code describes how the GKE on AWS infrastructure will look. It has components analogous to GKE on-prem, such as a load balancer and EC2 virtual machines, but it uses the Terraform AWS provider to instantiate the infrastructure on AWS. You can learn more about Terraform at https://www.terraform.io/.

The architecture of GKE on AWS can be seen in figure 5.12, which is from the Google Cloud documentation at http://mng.bz/mJAW.

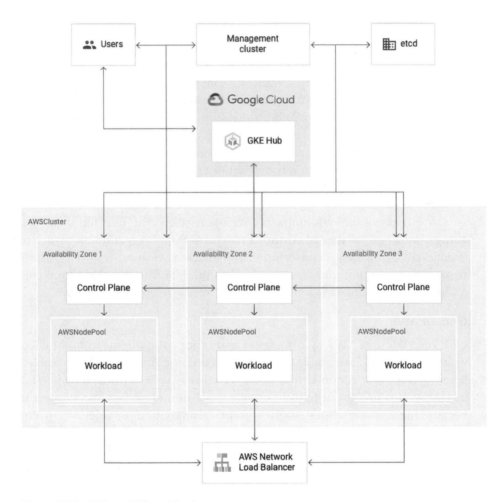

Figure 5.12   GKE on AWS architecture

The use of node pools is like GKE, with the ability to have different machine sizes within a cluster.

> **NOTE**   To do any GKE on AWS operations management, the administrator will have to log in to the bastion host, which is part of the management service.

CONNECTING TO THE MANAGEMENT SERVICE

When doing any management operations, the administrator needs to connect to the bastion host deployed during the initial installation of the management service. This script is named bastion-tunnel.sh and is generated by Terraform during the management service installation.

CLUSTER MANAGEMENT: CREATING A NEW USER CLUSTER

Use the bastion-tunnel script to connect to the management service. After connecting to the bastion host, the administrator uses Terraform to generate a manifest, configuring an example cluster in a YAML file:

```
terraform output cluster_example > cluster-0.yaml
```

In this YAML file, the administrator then changes the AWSCluster and AWSNodePool specifications. Be sure to save the cluster file to a code repository because it will be reused for scaling the user cluster.

Custom resources are extensions of Kubernetes to add additional functionality, such as for provisioning AWS EC2 instances. AWS clusters and objects are represented as YAML files, referencing the AWSCluster and AWSNodePool custom resources in the management service cluster, which interpret this YAML file and adjust the resources in AWS accordingly. To read more about custom resources, refer to http://mng .bz/51R8.

CLUSTER MANAGEMENT: SCALING

You may experience a situation where a cluster requires additional compute power, and you need to scale out the cluster. Luckily, an Anthos node pool can scale a cluster, including a minimum and maximum node count. If you created a cluster with the same count in both the minimum and maximum nodes, you can change that setting at a later date to grow your cluster. To scale a cluster for GKE on AWS, you just require the administrator to modify the YAML file by updating the minNode-Count while creating the user cluster and applying it to the management service:

```
apiVersion: multicloud.cluster.gke.io/v1
kind: AWSNodePool
metadata:
 name: cluster-0-pool-0
spec:
 clusterName: cluster-0
 version: 1.20.10-gke.600
 minNodeCount: 3
 maxNodeCount: 10
```

CLUSTER MANAGEMENT: UPGRADING

Upgrading GKE on AWS is done in two steps, with the management service handled first, and then the user clusters. To upgrade a GKE on the AWS management service, the administrator must upgrade a GKE on the AWS management service from the directory with the GKE on AWS configuration. Then, the user must first download the latest version of the anthos-gke binary. Next, the user will have to modify the anthos-gke.yaml file to the target version:

```
apiVersion: multicloud.cluster.gke.io/v1
kind: AWSManagementService
metadata:
 name: management
spec:
 version: <target_version>
```

Finally, to validate and apply the version changes, run the next code:

```
anthos-gke aws management init
anthos-gke aws management apply
```

The management service will be down, so no changes to user clusters can be applied, but user clusters continue to run their workloads.

To upgrade the user cluster, the administrator switches context in the management service from the GKE on the AWS directory using the following command:

```
anthos-gke aws management get-credentials
```

Then, upgrading the version of the user cluster is as easy as using the following:

```
kubectl edit awscluster <cluster_name>
```

Edit the YAML file to point to the right GKE version:

```
apiVersion: multicloud.cluster.gke.io/v1
kind: AWSCluster
metadata:
 name: cluster-0
spec:
 region: us-east-1
 controlPlane:
  version: <gke_version>
```

On submission of this change, the CRD starts to go through the nodes in the control plane one by one and upgrades them to the latest version of GKE on AWS. This upgrade process causes a downtime of the control plane, which means the cluster may be unable to report the status of the different node pools until it is completed.

Finally, the last step is to upgrade the actual node pool. The same procedure applies: the administrator just edits the YAML file to the version required and applies the YAML file to the management service as follows:

```
apiVersion: multicloud.cluster.gke.io/v1
kind: AWSNodePool
```

```
metadata:
 name: cluster-0-pool-0
spec:
 clusterName: cluster-0
 region: us-east-1
 version: <gke-version>
```

5.3 Anthos attached clusters

Anthos attached clusters let you view your Kubernetes clusters and are provisioned and managed by Elastic Kubernetes Service (EKS) by AWS, Azure Kubernetes Service (AKS), or any conformant Kubernetes cluster. In this case, the scaling and provisioning of the clusters are done from the respective clouds. However, these clusters can still be attached and managed by Anthos by registering them to Google Cloud through deploying the Connect Agent, as illustrated in figure 5.13.

Figure 5.13   Adding an external cluster (bring your own Kubernetes)

GKE is also handled in the same way and can be attached from another project into the Anthos project as follows:

1   The administrator must generate a kubeconfig to the EKS or AKS cluster and then provide that kubeconfig in a generated cluster registration command in gcloud. Consult the documentation from AWS and Azure on how to generate a kubeconfig file for the EKS or AKS clusters. The administrator can also generate one manually using the following template and providing the necessary certificate, server info, and service account token:

```
apiVersion: v1
kind: Config
users:
- name: svcs-acct-dply
 user:
   token: <replace this with token info>
clusters:
- cluster:
   certificate-authority-data: <replace this with certificate-authority-
data info>
   server: <replace this with server info>
 name: self-hosted-cluster
contexts:
- context:
   cluster: self-hosted-cluster
   user: svcs-acct-dply
 name: svcs-acct-context
current-context: svcs-acct-context
```

2 The administrator must create a Google service account and a service account key to provide for the registration, as shown in figure 5.14.

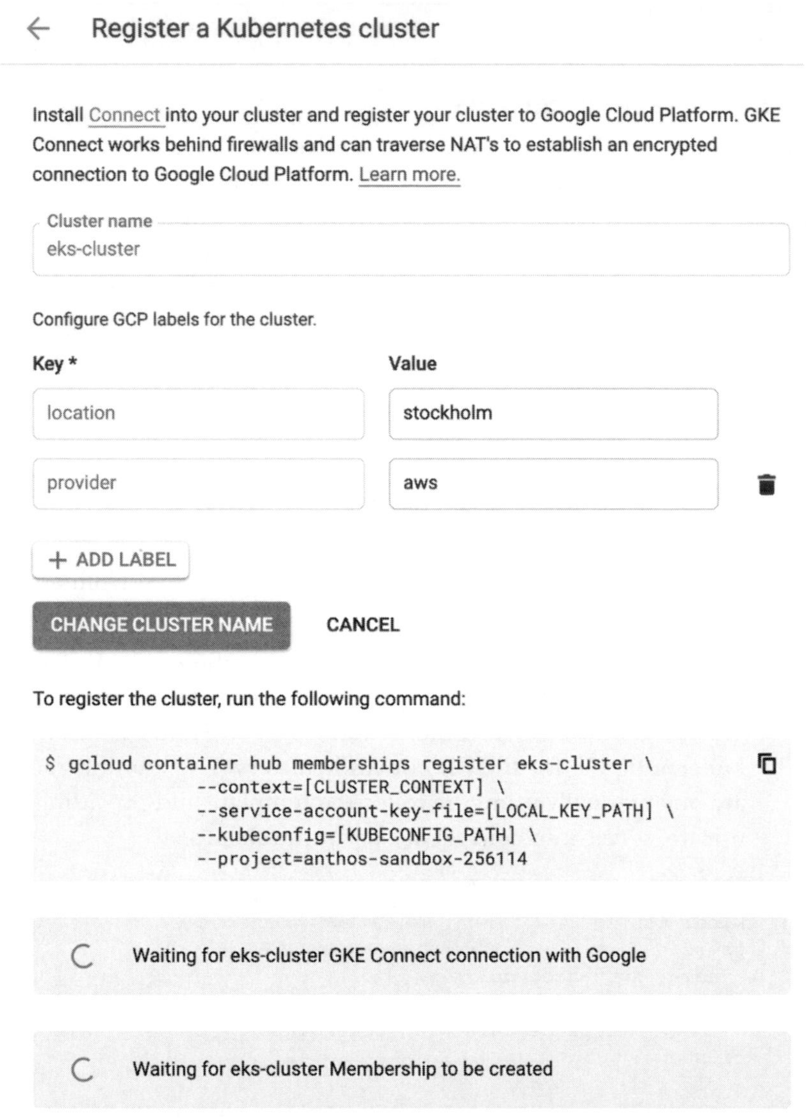

← **Register a Kubernetes cluster**

Install Connect into your cluster and register your cluster to Google Cloud Platform. GKE Connect works behind firewalls and can traverse NAT's to establish an encrypted connection to Google Cloud Platform. Learn more.

Cluster name
eks-cluster

Configure GCP labels for the cluster.

Key *	Value	
location	stockholm	
provider	aws	🗑

\+ ADD LABEL

CHANGE CLUSTER NAME   CANCEL

To register the cluster, run the following command:

```
$ gcloud container hub memberships register eks-cluster \
          --context=[CLUSTER_CONTEXT] \
          --service-account-key-file=[LOCAL_KEY_PATH] \
          --kubeconfig=[KUBECONFIG_PATH] \
          --project=anthos-sandbox-256114
```

C   Waiting for eks-cluster GKE Connect connection with Google

C   Waiting for eks-cluster Membership to be created

Figure 5.14   Generating a registration command for the external cluster

3 The administrator will provide these two items in the generated registration command, and after the Connect Agent has been deployed to the external cluster, it will be visible in the Google Cloud console.

5.4 Anthos on bare metal

Operating and managing Anthos on bare metal often requires additional skill sets in the OS configuration space because it is based on installing Anthos on RHEL, Ubuntu, or CentOS. For the detailed steps for installing and upgrading Anthos on bare metal, consult chapter 17.

Anthos on bare metal is similar to Anthos on VMware but with more flexibility in its deployment models and no dependency on VMware. The benefits of using Anthos on bare metal versus managing Kubernetes running on a set of virtualized machines include the performance gain, the support provided by Google during installation of all Anthos components, and the ability to deploy applications from the Google Cloud Marketplace directly into the Anthos cluster. However, the team will have to manage their own storage devices to provide durable and performant storage to Anthos on bare metal clusters, compared to having that natively supported with Anthos on VMware with custom-built storage drivers.

You must make a few key decisions when designing the operations management procedures for Anthos on bare metal. First is capacity planning and resource estimation. Unlike the rest of the setups, where new nodes need to be provisioned using either public cloud resources or a pool of VMware resources, new bare metal nodes must be provisioned. This requires additional capacity requirements if there is a zero-downtime requirement during upgrades of the nodes because there is always a risk of nodes failing during upgrade and causing a decrease in capacity.

Second is automating the prerequisite installation of the nodes as much as possible. Many companies also require a golden image of a base operating system, which must be vetted by a security team and continuously updated with security patches and latest versions. This should be built into the Anthos on bare metal provisioning process to verify compatibility with Anthos installation. One option is to set up PXE boot servers and have newly provisioned bare metal servers point to the PXE boot servers to install the operating system of bare metal nodes to the right configuration.

Third is determining the different deployments to run Anthos on bare metal, in standalone, multicluster, or hybrid cluster deployments. Flexibility also means complexity and having to build different operational models for the different deployments. Chapter 17 goes into more detail about the differences, but this chapter highlights the following operational considerations when choosing the different deployment models:

- *Standalone cluster deployment*—This deployment model, shown in figure 5.15, has the admin and user clusters in the same cluster. In such a configuration, workloads run in the same nodes, which have SSH credentials and in which Google service account keys are stored. This configuration is well suited for edge deployment, and as such, operational models should introduce SSH credential and service account key generation for each new standalone cluster provisioned and deployed, as well as a plan to decommission those credentials when a cluster is compromised or lost. There is a minimum requirement of five nodes for a high-availability setup.

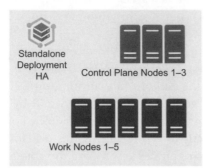

Figure 5.15   Standalone deployment

- *Multicluster deployment*—This deployment model, illustrated in figure 5.16, has an admin cluster and one or more user clusters, like Anthos on VMware. This model features many benefits, such as admin/user isolation for the clusters, multitenanted setups (i.e., each team can have their own cluster), and a centralized plan for upgrades. The downside is the increased footprint in node requirements and a minimum of eight nodes for a high-availability setup. Because of this, this model requires more effort when setting up for multiple edge locations and is more for a data center setup.

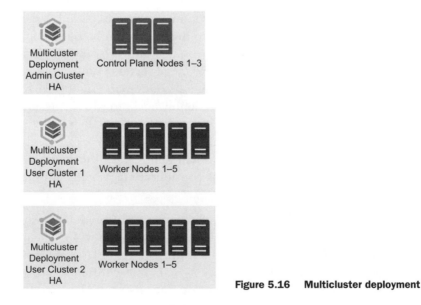

Figure 5.16   Multicluster deployment

- *Hybrid cluster deployment*—This deployment model, shown in figure 5.17, allows for running user workloads on the admin clusters and managing other user clusters. This model reduces the footprint required for multicluster deployment to five nodes for a high-availability setup, but it has the same security concern of running user workloads on nodes that may contain sensitive data from the standalone cluster deployment. Using a hybrid cluster deployments grants flexibility to tier workloads by security levels and introduces user clusters for workloads that require higher security.

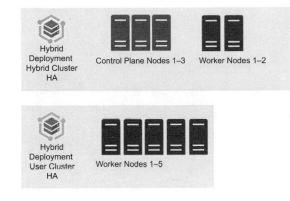

Figure 5.17   Hybrid deployment

5.5   Connect gateway

Registering Anthos clusters allows the user to interact with them through the UI, but administrators often have a toolbox of scripts, which they use to work with clusters through the kubectl command line. With GKE on-prem, on AWS, or on Azure, these clusters often can be accessed only via the admin workstation or a bastion host. GKE users, on the other hand, can use gcloud and generate kubeconfig details from kubectl to their clusters on their local machines. With Connect gateway, this problem is solved.

Administrators can connect to any Anthos-registered cluster and generate kubeconfig that enables the user to use kubectl for those clusters via the Connect Agent. With this feature, administrators will not be required to use jump hosts to deploy to the GKE on clusters, but instead can run a gcloud command to generate a kubeconfig to connect via kubectl.

The setup requires an impersonation policy, which allows the Connect Agent service account to impersonate a user account to issue commands on their behalf. An example of the YAML file, which creates the ClusterRole and ClusterRoleBinding for impersonation, can be seen here:

```
# [USER_ACCOUNT] is an email, either USER_EMAIL_ADDRESS or GCPSA_EMAIL_ADDRESS
$ USER_ACCOUNT=foo@example.com
$ cat <<EOF > /tmp/impersonate.yaml
apiVersion: rbac.authorization.k8s.io/v1
kind: ClusterRole
metadata:
 name: gateway-impersonate
```

```
rules:
- apiGroups:
  - ""
  resourceNames:
  - ${USER_ACCOUNT}
  resources:
  - users
  verbs:
  - impersonate
---
apiVersion: rbac.authorization.k8s.io/v1
kind: ClusterRoleBinding
metadata:
 name: gateway-impersonate
roleRef:
 kind: ClusterRole
 name: gateway-impersonate
 apiGroup: rbac.authorization.k8s.io
subjects:
- kind: ServiceAccount
 name: connect-agent-sa
 namespace: gke-connect
EOF
```

After the impersonation policy has been set up, the administrator must run the command shown in figure 5.18 to generate a kubeconfig, which appears in figure 5.19.

```
gcloud alpha container hub memberships get-credentials stockholm-gke-cluster
```

Figure 5.18   Command to get credentials to the GKE on-prem cluster

```
- cluster:
    server: https://connectgateway.googleapis.com/v1alpha1/projects/74668819743/memberships/stockholm-gke-cluster
  name: connectgateway_anthos-sandbox-256114_stockholm-gke-cluster
```

Figure 5.19   kubeconfig generated via gcloud

With this kubeconfig in place, administrators can manage GKE on-prem workloads, even from their local machine, while being secured by Google Cloud Identity. This method also opens the possibility for building pipelines to deploy to the different Anthos clusters.

5.6   *Anthos on Azure*

Anthos GKE clusters can be installed on Azure with an architecture consisting of a multicloud API hosted on GCP that provides life cycle management capabilities to GKE clusters in Azure, as shown in figure 5.20. You can also access Azure GKE clusters via the Connect gateway mentioned in this chapter. Anthos on Azure uses Azure-native technologies like the Azure Load Balancer, Azure Active Directory, and Azure Virtual Machines but relies on Anthos via the multicloud API to manage GKE cluster life cycle operations. This creates a uniform way to deploy applications across the three major public clouds and on-prem.

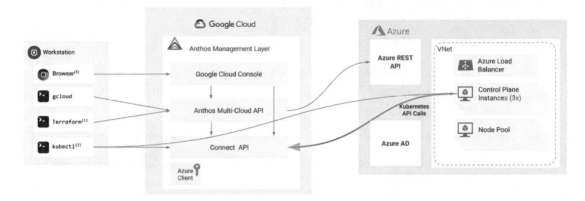

Figure 5.20   Anthos on Azure architecture

As a prerequisite, the administrator must install the gcloud CLI. In addition, the administrator has to have the following Azure built-in roles shown here:

- Application administrator
- User access administrator
- Contributor

The next steps would be to create an Azure Active Directory application, a virtual network, and a resource group for the clusters, and grant the necessary permissions to the Azure Active Directory application. Detailed prerequisite information can be found in the public documentation at http://mng.bz/61Rp.

5.6.1   Cluster management: Creation

To create a new user cluster, the administrator must first set up an Azure client with an SSH key pair:

```
export SUBSCRIPTION_ID=$(az account show --query "id" --output tsv)
export TENANT_ID=$(az account list \
 --query "[?id=='${SUBSCRIPTION_ID}'].{tenantId:tenantId}" --output tsv)
export APPLICATION_ID=$(az ad app list --all \
 --query "[?displayName=='APPLICATION_NAME'].appId" --output tsv)

gcloud alpha container azure clients create CLIENT_NAME \
 --location=GOOGLE_CLOUD_LOCATION \
 --tenant-id="${TENANT_ID}" \
 --application-id="${APPLICATION_ID}"

CERT=$(gcloud alpha container azure clients get-public-cert --
     location=GOOGLE_CLOUD_LOCATION \
   CLIENT_NAME)
```

```
az ad app credential reset --id "${APPLICATION_ID}" --cert "${CERT}" --append

ssh-keygen -m PEM -t rsa -b 4096 -f KEY_PATH

SSH_PUBLIC_KEY=$(cat KEY_PATH.pub)

ssh-keygen -m PEM -t rsa -b 4096 -f ~/.ssh/anthos-multicloud-key
SSH_PUBLIC_KEY=$(cat ~/.ssh/anthos-multicloud-key.pub)
```

Next, the administrator will need to assign Azure resource groups, VNet, and subnet IDs to environment variables; add IAM permissions; and run the gcloud command to create the Anthos on Azure cluster:

```
CLUSTER_RG_ID=$(az group show --resource-group=CLUSTER_RESOURCE_GROUP_NAME \
 --query "id" -otsv)
VNET_ID=$(az network vnet show --resource-group=VNET_RESOURCE_GROUP_NAME \
 --name=VNET_NAME --query "id" -otsv)
SUBNET_ID=$(az network vnet subnet show \
 --resource-group=VNET_RESOURCE_GROUP_NAME --vnet-name=VNET_NAME \
 --name default --query "id" -otsv)

PROJECT_ID="$(gcloud config get-value project)"
gcloud projects add-iam-policy-binding "$PROJECT_ID" \
 --member="serviceAccount:$PROJECT_ID.svc.id.goog[gke-system/gke-multicloud-
    agent]" \
 --role="roles/gkehub.connect"


gcloud alpha container azure clusters create CLUSTER_NAME \
  --location GOOGLE_CLOUD_LOCATION \
  --client CLIENT_NAME \
  --azure-region AZURE_REGION \
  --pod-address-cidr-blocks POD_CIDR \
  --service-address-cidr-blocks SERVICE_CIDR \
  --vm-size VM_SIZE \
  --cluster-version 1.19.10-gke.1000 \
  --ssh-public-key "$SSH_PUBLIC_KEY" \
  --resource-group-id "$CLUSTER_RG_ID" \
  --vnet-id "$VNET_ID" \
  --subnet-id "$SUBNET_ID"
```

This cluster should then be available on the administrator's GKE console. Finally, the admin adds a node pool to deploy workloads to the cluster:

```
SUBNET_ID=$(az network vnet subnet show \
 --resource-group=VNET_RESOURCE_GROUP_NAME --vnet-name=VNET_NAME \
 --name default --query "id" -otsv)
SSH_PUBLIC_KEY=$(cat KEY_PATH.pub)

gcloud alpha container azure node-pools create NODE_POOL_NAME \
  --cluster=CLUSTER_NAME \
  --location GOOGLE_CLOUD_LOCATION \
  --node-version=1.19.10-gke.1000 \
```

```
--vm-size=VM_SIZE \
--max-pods-per-node=110 \
--min-nodes=MIN_NODES \
--max-nodes=MAX_NODES \
--ssh-public-key="${SSH_PUBLIC_KEY}" \
--subnet-id="${SUBNET_ID}"
```

5.6.2 *Cluster management: Deletion*

To delete a cluster, administrators must first delete all the node pools that belong to a cluster:

```
gcloud alpha container azure node-pools delete NODE_POOL_NAME \
  --cluster CLUSTER_NAME \
  --location GOOGLE_CLOUD_LOCATION

gcloud alpha container azure clusters delete CLUSTER_NAME \
  --location GOOGLE_CLOUD_LOCATION
```

With an autoscaler ready to go with Anthos on Azure, it is easy for the administrator to control costs and manage minimum resource requirements for each cluster. It is recommended to have a security device like HashiCorp Vault to store the SSH keys for retrieval and rotation.

Summary

- The best way to learn is by trying, and the best advice is to try building clusters on the various providers to understand the optimizations available and the actions that an administrator would need to do in their day-to-day life managing operations in Anthos. This is key to building a continuous improvement process because new features in Anthos are released frequently to make Kubernetes cluster management easier and faster.
- We covered how to use the Google Cloud console to operate and manage workloads of the various Anthos cluster types.
- You read about the various logging and monitoring options available with Anthos deployments and the criteria to consider.
- You now understand how to operate and manage various types of Anthos deployments through the command line and how and what kind of communication happens between Google Cloud and the deployments.
- You learned how to upgrade, scale, and design operations management procedures in Anthos across a hybrid environment.

Bringing it all together

Onofrio Petragallo

This chapter covers

- How Anthos components provide a unique and powerful developer experience
- Deploying applications using different Anthos offerings
- Using policy enforcement for management and consistency
- Using Anthos Service Mesh to observe and secure applications

As we have seen in the previous chapters, Anthos is a modern application platform that provides a consistent development and operations experience for cloud and hybrid environments. In this chapter, you will get an overview of the main layers of the platform and the main functionalities. Figure 6.1 illustrates the Anthos components and features and how they provide Anthos's functionality across your environments, from infrastructure management to supporting application development.

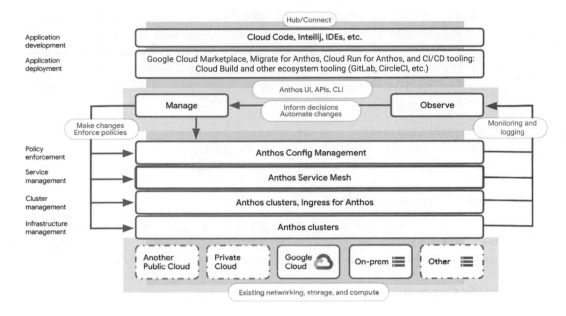

Figure 6.1   Anthos components and features

6.1   *Application development*

For the developer, Anthos provides a state-of-the-art container management platform based on Kubernetes. Developers can use this platform to quickly and easily build and deploy existing container-based applications and microservices-based architectures. The key benefits to developers include the following:

- Git-compliant management and CI/CD workflows for configuration as well as code, using Anthos Config Management
- A code-free abstraction layer, using Anthos Service Mesh and Cloud Monitoring and Cloud Logging to provide uniform observability
- Code-free protection of services, using mTLS and throttling

Developers can develop modern applications using the IDEs they prefer: for example, they can use IntelliJ (https://www.jetbrains.com/idea/) or Visual Studio Code for the implementation of cloud native applications that can run on Anthos.

Google Cloud provides Cloud Code (https://cloud.google.com/code), which is a plug-in for IntelliJ, Visual Studio Code, and Google Cloud Shell that allows you to obtain a Kubernetes development and debugging environment fully integrated with the IDE. Thanks to Cloud Code, you can create and manage clusters directly from the IDE, and you can deploy your code in an Anthos cluster or Cloud Run for Anthos in a few clicks. You can also do the following:

- Debug the code within your IDEs using Cloud Code, taking advantage of built-in IDE debugging features

- View underlying resources and metadata for your Kubernetes clusters and Cloud Run services. You're a click away from acting on these resources: you can fetch a description, view logs, manage secrets, or get a terminal directly into a Pod.
- While interacting with Google Cloud configuration files, get out-of-the-box support for IDE features including code completion, inline documentation, linting, and snippets.

Under the covers, Cloud Code for IDEs uses popular tools such as Skaffold (https:// skaffold.dev/), Jib (https://github.com/GoogleContainerTools/jib), and kubectl (http://mng.bz/Nm9X) to provide continuous feedback on your code in real time.

6.2   Application deployment

Once your application has been developed, you can reuse your favorite CI/CD tools for full application testing and deployment. Google Cloud provides several cloud native tools that allow you to speed up the build, test, and release applications.

6.2.1   Cloud Source Repositories

Cloud Source Repositories are Git repositories managed by Google (see https://cloud .google.com/source-repositories). Git (https://git-scm.com) is a free, open source, distributed version-control system designed to handle everything from small to very large projects with speed and efficiency. With Cloud Source Repositories, you get free access to unlimited private repositories to organize your code the way you want. Mirror code from GitHub or Bitbucket repositories to use powerful code search, code exploration, and diagnostics.

Figure 6.2 shows the first page of the Google Cloud console, where we can select to create a new repository or connect an existing one.

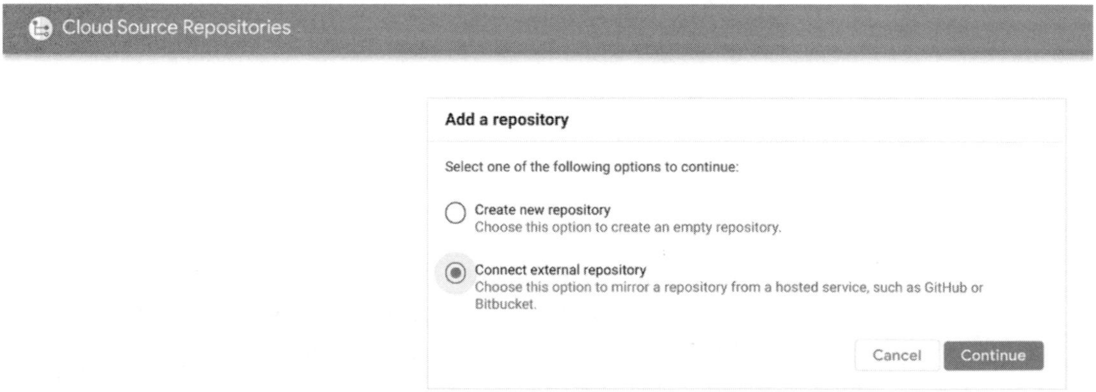

Figure 6.2   Connection of an existing Git repository from the Google Cloud console

Assuming we would like to create a new repository, figure 6.3 shows the list view of the Git repository inside the project "onofrio." "hello-world" is the new Git repository created inside the project.

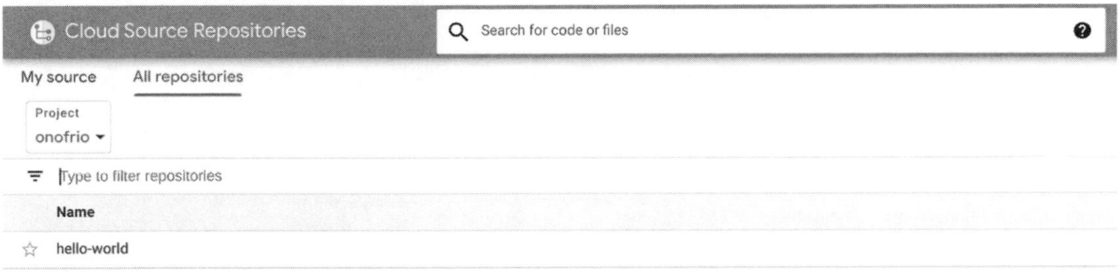

Figure 6.3   List of Git repositories

Figure 6.4 shows the content of the new repository, thc cxample.py file.

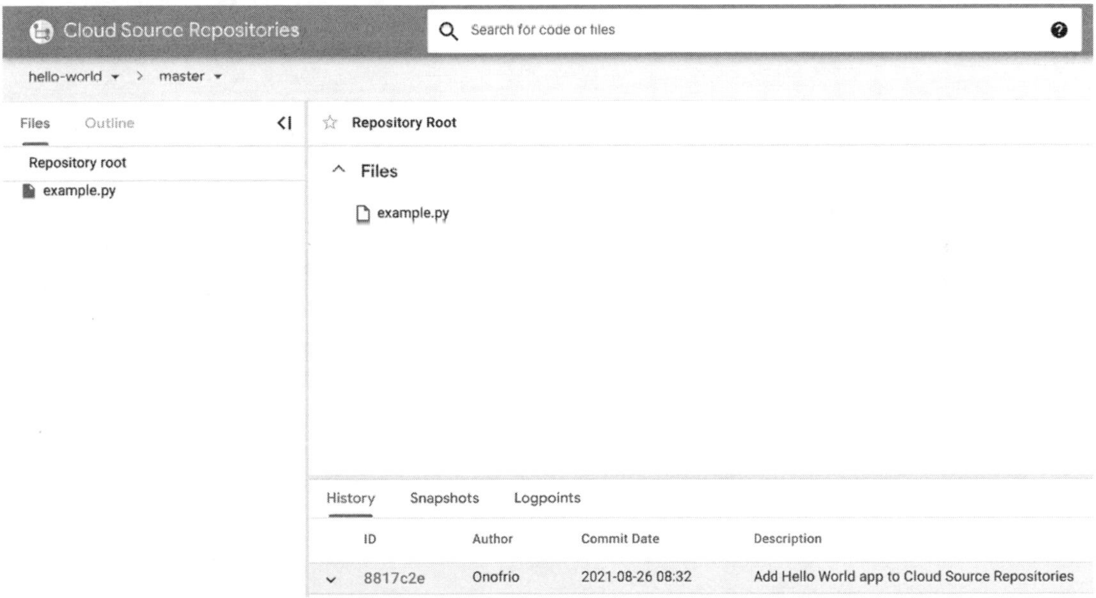

Figure 6.4   Repository root view

If we click the single file, we can see the content of the file, as shown in figure 6.5.

With Cloud Source Repositories, you get feedback on code changes quickly with built-in integrations for continuous integration. You can easily configure triggers to automatically build and test with Cloud Build when you push changes to Cloud Source Repositories.

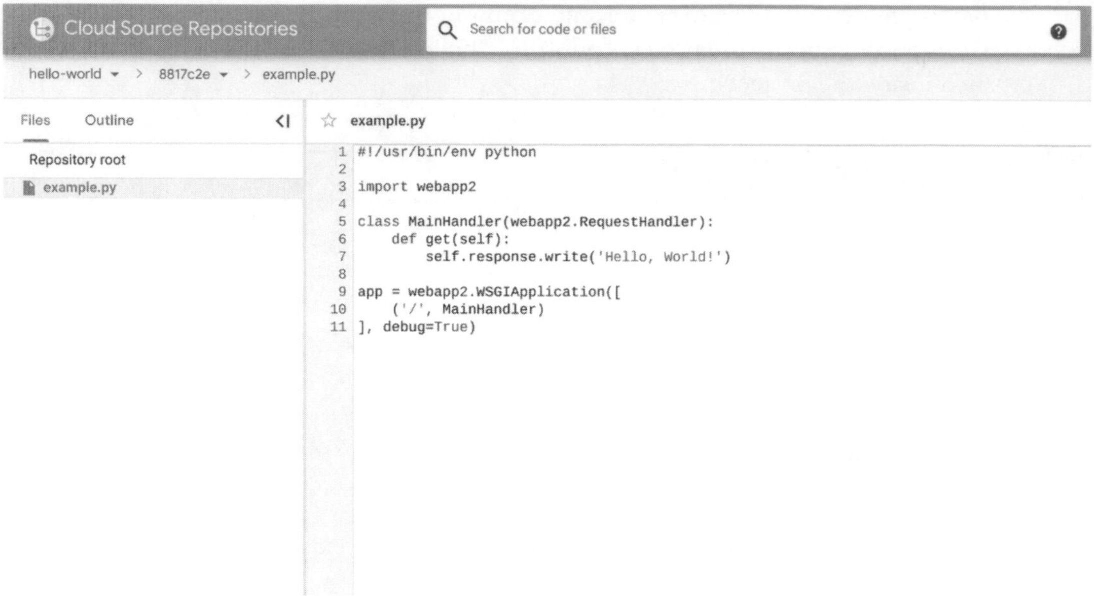

Figure 6.5   File content view

You can also use powerful regular expressions to search across multiple directories, as displayed in figure 6.6. Regular expressions (regex) allow you to refine your search or perform a single targeted search across projects, files, and code repositories.

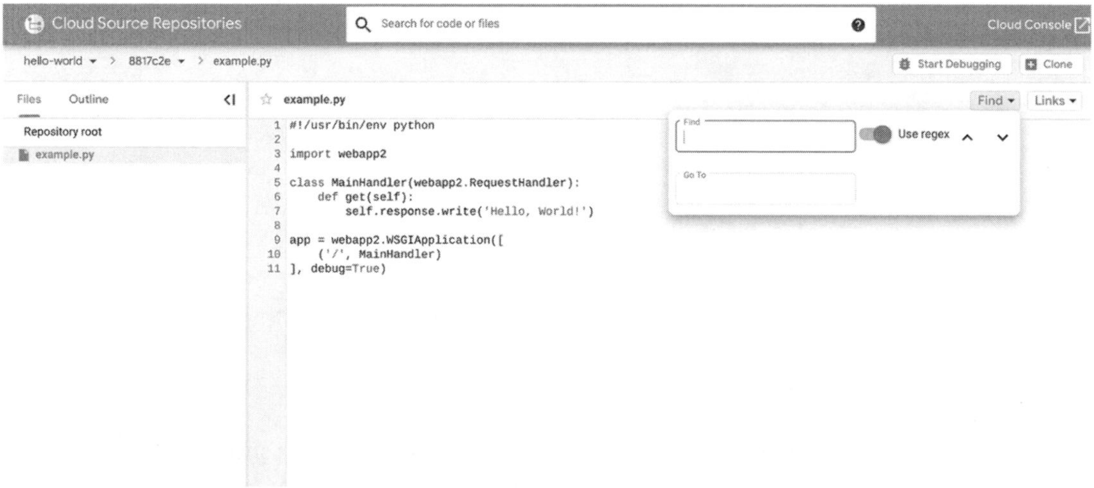

Figure 6.6   File search with regex

6.2.2   Cloud Build

Cloud Build (https://cloud.google.com/build) is a service that runs your builds on Google Cloud Platform infrastructure. Cloud Build can import source code from a variety of repositories or cloud storage spaces, build to your specifications, and produce artifacts such as Docker containers or Java Archives. With Cloud Build, you access connected machines via Google's global network to significantly reduce the build time of your applications. You can run builds on high CPU VMs or cache source code, images, or other dependencies to further increase build speed. Figure 6.7 shows the history of a build in Cloud Build.

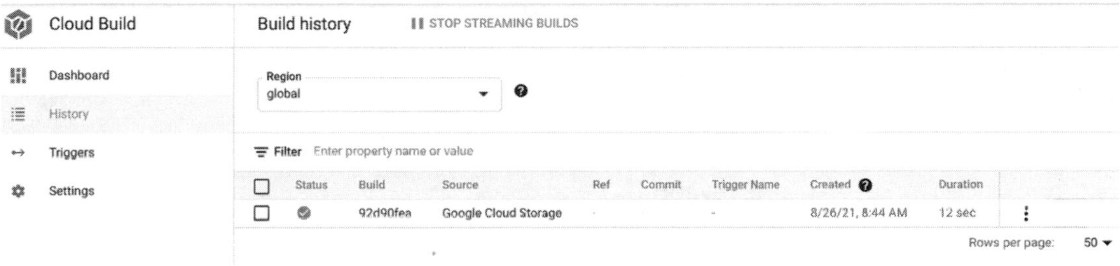

Figure 6.7   History of a build

The process of pulling requests from the Git repository for building, testing, and deployment is easy. You can set up a trigger on the Google Cloud console to automatically create, test, or deploy source code when you push changes to a Cloud Source repository, Bitbucket, or GitHub. Figure 6.8 shows how to integrate Cloud Build with an existing Cloud Source repository. Inside the dashboard, you can find all the Git repositories on Cloud Source Repositories. You can create a trigger by clicking Add Trigger, as shown in figure 6.8.

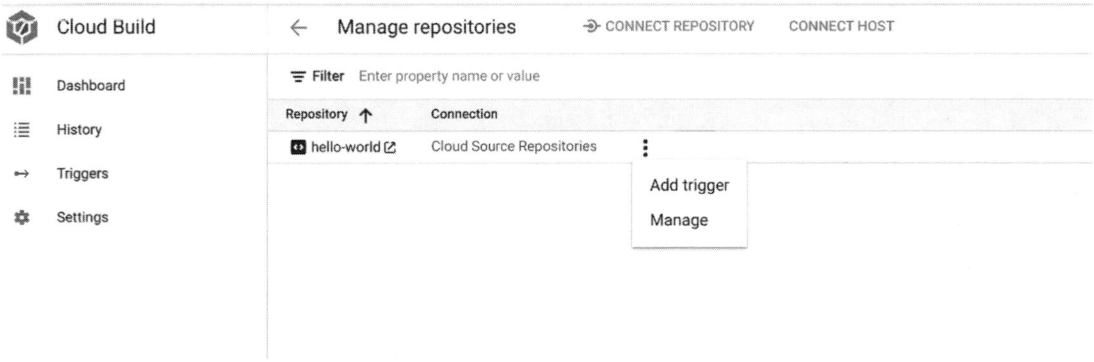

Figure 6.8   Adding a trigger from an existing repository

After selecting the repository, you can create a trigger that will build the software. As shown in figure 6.9, the trigger with the tag "prod" will build each time a push is done in the repository.

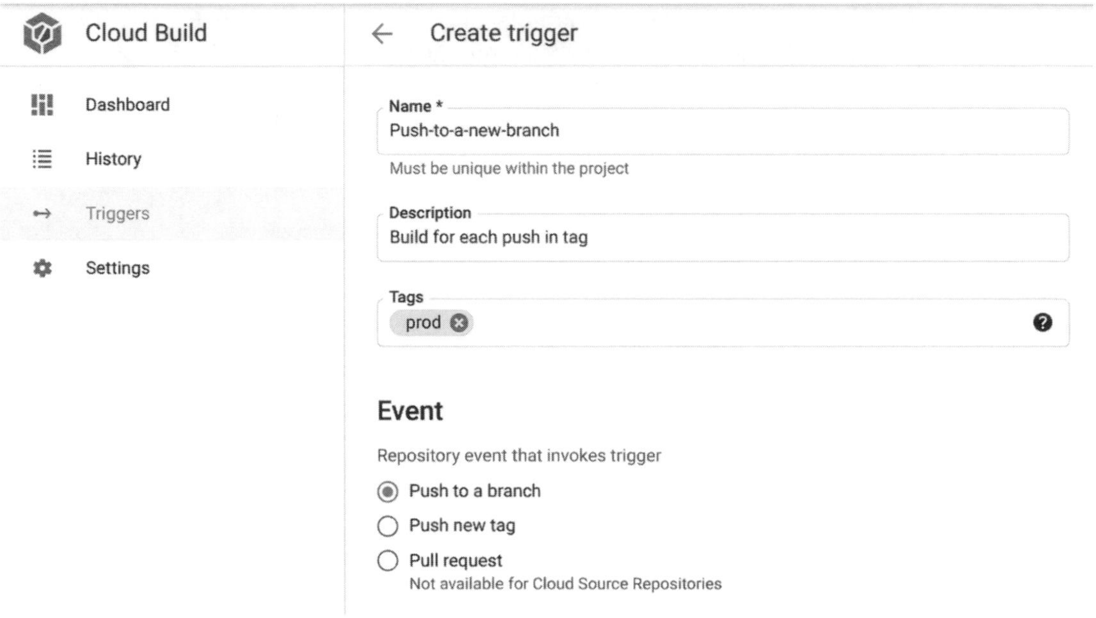

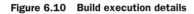

Figure 6.9   Trigger configuration

For each build, you can see the details of the execution with all the logs, as illustrated in figure 6.10.

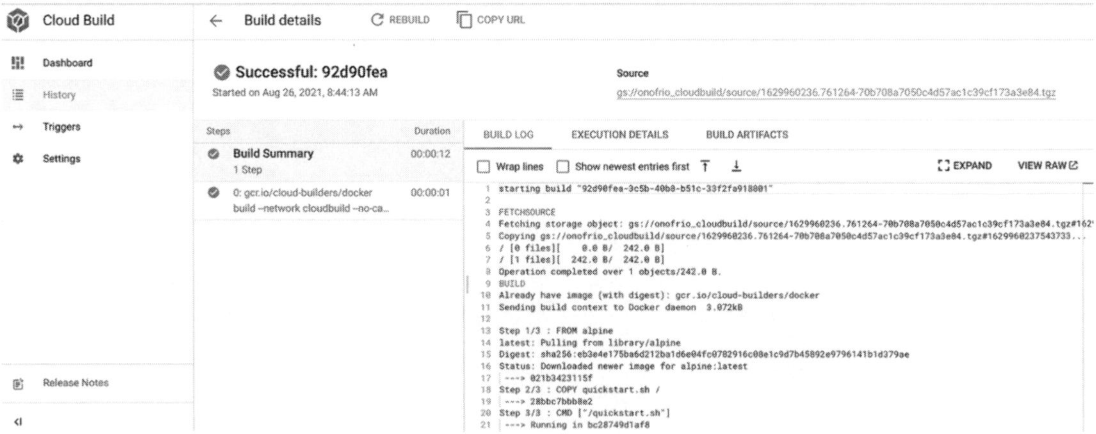

Figure 6.10   Build execution details

Cloud Build helps you secure your containers by allowing you to identify package vulnerabilities. You can automatically run package vulnerability scans for Ubuntu, Debian, and Alpine.

Once you've built your containerized application, you can deploy to multiple clouds via Anthos as part of your CI/CD pipeline. Cloud Build includes builder images with languages and tools already installed.

You can also run builds locally on your development machine before sending them to Cloud Build. You build and debug on the local machine with the local open source builder.

6.2.3   *Artifact Registry*

Once you've built your containerized application, Artifact Registry (https://cloud .google.com/artifact-registry) offers a single location from which your team can manage Docker images, perform vulnerability scans, and decide who has access to what with granular access control. You can automatically create and push images to the private registry when you commit code to Cloud Source Repositories, GitHub, or Bitbucket.

Artifact Registry allows you to scan Docker containers for package vulnerabilities in Linux distributions. You can also add and remove image tags with a single click in the Google Cloud console web interface, as well as perform the following tasks:

- Create triggers to automatically save your builds
- Create containers based on code or tag changes in a repository
- Search all previous builds from the Google Cloud console
- View information about a build, such as trigger, source, steps, and logs

6.2.4   *Google Cloud Marketplace*

In addition to applications developed by you, you can deploy ready-to-market applications that Google partners and vendors make available on Google Cloud Marketplace (https://cloud.google.com/marketplace). You can find integrated solutions reviewed by Google Cloud to meet all your IT needs. Thanks to the tight integration with Anthos, you can choose solutions and applications that can be deployed on-prem and multicloud. Using the Google Cloud Marketplace allows you to speed up the acquisition process for you and your teams. You can make purchases without needing an internal vendor review if Google is already one of your preferred partners. You can build a scalable and repeatable procurement process with deployments integrated with Google Cloud without having to contact the product vendor separately. All the details relating to the deployment modalities of containerized and ready-to-use applications and solutions for Anthos can be found in chapter 14.

6.2.5   *Migrate for Anthos*

If you already have an application running in VM on-prem or in another cloud and you want it to be deployed on Anthos, you can take advantage of the exclusive Migrate for Anthos technology (https://cloud.google.com/migrate/anthos). Migrate for Anthos simplifies and speeds up the modernization of traditional applications by allowing them to be moved from virtual machines to native containers. This unique automated approach allows you to extract critical application elements from the VM so you can easily place them in containers in Google Kubernetes Engine or an Anthos cluster. The details of Migrate for Anthos can be found in chapter 15.

6.3   *Policy enforcement*

Extending multiple hybrid, on-prem, and multicloud environments adds complexity in terms of resource management and consistency. Anthos provides a unified declarative model for computing, networking, and even managing cloud and data center services.

Configuration as data is a common approach to managing this complexity, allowing you to store the desired state of your hybrid environment under version control and apply it directly with repeatable results. Anthos makes this possible with Anthos Config Management, which integrates with Anthos clusters locally or in the cloud, allowing you to deploy and monitor configuration changes stored in a central Git repository, as shown figure 6.11.

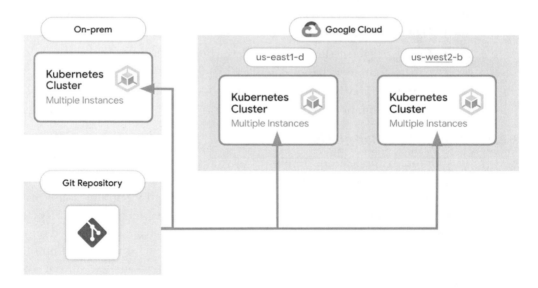

Figure 6.11   Apply and enforce common policy with Anthos Config Management.

This approach uses core Kubernetes concepts, such as namespaces, labels, and annotations, to determine how and where to apply configuration changes to all of your Kubernetes clusters, from where they reside. Anthos Config Management offers the following advantages for your Anthos environments:

- Single source of truth, control, and management
- One-step deployment across all clusters

- Rich inheritance model for applying changes
- Advanced policy enforcement and control with Policy Controller

You can find all the details about Anthos Config Management in chapters 11 and 13.

6.4 Service management

As we saw in chapter 4, Anthos Service Mesh manages your service mesh environment by offering you the following features and services:

- Service metrics and logs for all traffic within your mesh's GKE cluster are automatically imported into Google Cloud.
- It automatically generates in-depth telemetry in the Anthos Service Mesh dashboard.
- Service-to-service relationships at a glance—understand who connects to each service and which services they depend on.
- Protect your traffic between services through the Anthos Service Mesh Certificate Authority (Mesh CA), automatically generating and rotating certificates so you can easily enable TLS authentication (mTLS) with Istio policies.
- Quickly view the communication security status of not only your service but also its relationships with other services.
- Dig deeper into your service metrics, and combine them with other Google Cloud metrics using Cloud Monitoring.
- Get clear and simple insights into your service health with service-level objectives, which allows you to easily define and send alerts on your service health standards.

Summary

- The Anthos components provide all the tools a developer requires to develop and deploy their applications.
- Anthos application development features include Cloud Code, a plug-in for IntelliJ, Visual Studio Code, and Google Cloud Shell.
- Various components can be used for deploying an application, including versioning using Cloud Source Repository and Cloud Build to build the source code.
- Policy enforcement provides management and consistency across multiple cloud providers and hybrid cloud environments.
- Anthos Service Mesh provides service metrics and logs to communicate security status and health.

Hybrid applications

Jason Quek

This chapter covers

- Highly available applications
- Geographically distributed applications
- Hybrid multicloud applications
- Applications regulated by law
- Applications that must run on the edge

In the real world, applications are bound by rules such as data locality requirements, resource constraints, situations where a stable connection to the cloud cannot be guaranteed—such as at a baseball stadium, a construction site, or on a fighter jet—to do low-latency computation locally on the edge to avoid large amounts of data transfer. The application must be available and survive a regional disaster or cloud outage.

However, a need to run applications with the same consistency and stability that the Kubernetes platform provides still exists. Thus, solutions such as Anthos are designed to create this conformant distributed cloud platform for such applications.

In this chapter, we will go over these different situations and show various architectures involving the use of Anthos and its suite of products to support these types of applications.

7.1 *Highly available applications*

This class of applications must run 24 hours a day, 7 days a week. Financial institutions managing transactions, health care applications, and traffic management are just some of the examples of applications that affect the real world if they are unavailable for a short period of time.

In Google Kubernetes Engine, you can create clusters to span availability zones within a region. This practice provides insurance in the event one of the availability zones within a region goes down—the other availability zones are still running the application. The Kubernetes scheduler would then spin up additional replicas on the nodes still active on the other availability zones to meet replica requirements defined in the Kubernetes configuration.

However, what if an entire region, or an entire cloud provider, was down? An article found in Forbes (http://mng.bz/DZa0) mentioned a scenario where a banking client wanted to use a single cloud and the regulator was concerned about what would happen during an outage. The client estimated they would have a maximum of two hours of downtime during the cloud outage, but the plan was rejected by the regulator as an unviable option.

In this situation, companies would have to span multiple clouds and regions, but doing so would introduce complexity and overhead in managing multiple cloud providers and require double the skill set across their operations, development, and security management at the same time.

With Anthos, companies can standardize on Kubernetes with one unified pattern of deployment, scaling, security, and development, while still being able to take advantage of the availability of multiple cloud providers and move workloads across regions and availability zones.

7.1.1 *Architecture*

The setup shown in figure 7.1 is simple: installing Anthos GKE, GKE on AWS, and GKE on-prem, and including them all in a service mesh. Such a setup would give high availability not just on the regional level but also at the cloud provider level.

Note that this structure assumes that the application just has to be available but may not be required to be accessible from the internet. This distinction is important because this architecture will survive even in the extremely unlikely event that one of the cloud providers has a severe outage. Anthos clusters can still function, even if they cannot reach Google Cloud APIs for a limited amount of time.

7.1.2 *Benefits*

Installation of the managed Kubernetes service across all three clouds may seem simple, but each has different processes, options, and best practices. Versions of Kubernetes

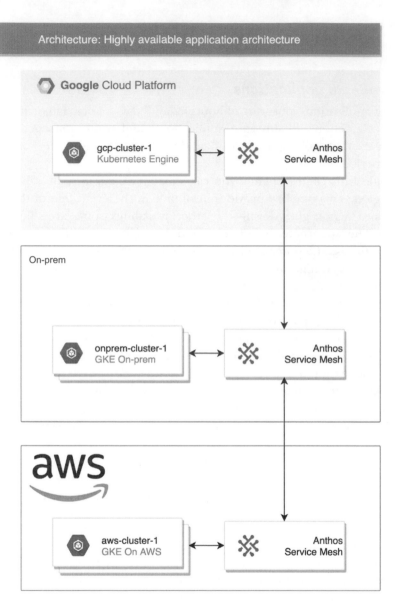

Figure 7.1   Multicloud availability with Service Mesh connectivity

available also differ across cloud providers. By using Anthos, such problems are handled by Google engineers who work behind the scenes to make sure that everything works on the different clouds. Solutions such as Workload Identity can be deployed across hybrid and multiclouds to provide a unified authentication framework. This situation provides a true sense of a multicloud managed service where the customer says to Google, "Take my budget and help me manage my clusters everywhere, even on your competitors' services."

7.1.3   Limitations

Such applications normally require somewhere to persist state, which then creates a dependency on a provider, unless the organizations choose to host their own data solution on the cloud. With the emergence of Kubernetes-native databases such as CockroachDB, which can be deployed across multiple clusters, or using MirrorMaker to replicate messages across Kafka deployments in multiple clusters, this problem is beginning to have robust solutions.

Anthos does not manage the underlying networks, storage, and compute used to build the clusters, and organizations still need to manage networking and ensure storage and compute availability across hybrid and multiple clouds. It is all about the Kubernetes API and making it available to developers on any surface throughout the organization—a shared responsibility that differs from competing products.

It is important to understand that such architecture might not be easy to build and maintain, but for organizations that have regulatory, financial, and reputational reasons to have their applications always available and disaster resistant, Anthos provides a path to that.

7.2   *Geographically distributed applications*

These applications must be located around the world to serve a worldwide audience. Having a managed service be able to route to the nearest cluster from one single IP from anywhere in the world makes application scaling across the world much simpler.

The most important point for this setup is to provide the user access to this application from the location nearest to them to minimize latency. The application is often an exact copy of microservices deployed to clusters in different regions but with no requirement that it span multiple clouds. This is coupled with multigeographical databases, which can be used either as a managed service from Google, (e.g., Spanner) or CockroachDB, which can be deployed across multiple Kubernetes clusters spanning the globe.

However, with Anthos, the same application can be deployed in multiple regions, which opens new opportunities in various markets. One important component that ties this together is Ingress for Anthos, a cloud-hosted gateway for distributed clusters.

With Ingress for Anthos, all users of the application can access it through an anycast IP and get routed to the cluster nearest to the user. One use case where this ability is important is the retail sector, where customer churn is proven to be directly related to the latency of the e-commerce site.

7.2.1   *Ingress for Anthos architecture*

Ingress for Anthos builds on top of the existing Google HTTP load-balancing architecture, using Google Cloud points of presence to route traffic efficiently to the nearest available cluster, as can be seen in figure 7.2. With such an architecture, you can deploy applications that need to serve a new audience in a different region on an

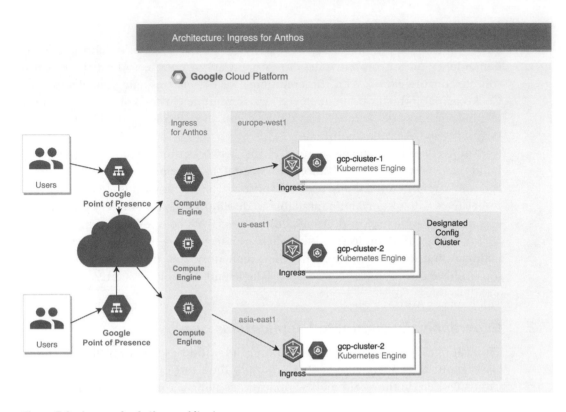

Figure 7.2   Ingress for Anthos architecture

Anthos cluster on that specific region and configure Ingress for Anthos to send traffic to that new region, while keeping the same IP address and domain name.

Any cluster can be designated as a config cluster, and two custom Kubernetes objects, `MultiClusterIngress` and `MultiClusterService`, are deployed on this one, which is just a centralized configuration storage for the Anthos Ingress controller to read from.

The Anthos Ingress controller is a set of Compute Engine instances that sit in multiple Google Cloud regions outside of the user's control and are managed by Google. These instances must be placed nearest to the Google points of presence where traffic enters to make routing decisions based on Anthos clusters that are members in the same Anthos fleet[1] and Pod availability.

The key concept of Ingress for Anthos is the use of network endpoint groups (NEGs). NEGs are groups of backend endpoints or services, which can be deployed on Anthos clusters. The Compute Engine instances in the Ingress for Anthos service seen in figure 7.2 route to the correct NEG, based on the availability of the service.

To understand more about Ingress for Anthos networking, please refer to chapter 10.

---

[1] See chapter 2 for the definition of a fleet.

7.2.2   Ingress for Anthos benefits

Creating load balancers to route traffic to clusters from points of presence that are also aware of the state of service availability of each cluster is a complex task. This process breaks down the problem into a single cluster problem, so developers can concentrate on building more features and know that they can be deployed in a standardized way across the globe and be accessible to their users with low latency.

7.2.3   Ingress for Anthos limitations

Ingress for Anthos is currently restricted to only Anthos Google Kubernetes Engine clusters and does not support GKE on-prem or GKE on AWS clusters. It is possible, however, to have a solution that also supports GKE on-prem clusters—using the Traffic Director would be a possible solution.

7.3   Hybrid multicloud applications with internet access

Some enterprises have invested in remote data centers or have a multicloud strategy, which makes Anthos a good fit as a product for them. However, when exposing their services to the public internet, they need to protect these applications so bad actors are unable to disrupt their availability and latency. One limitation of Ingress for Anthos is that these clusters must be on Google Cloud, but they also need to route to applications deployed across private and public clouds. Thus, they can use the Traffic Director, which can route traffic to clusters in a hybrid multicloud architecture.

7.3.1   Traffic Director architecture

Traffic Director architecture looks similar to the Ingress for Anthos setup, with a key difference being that all the services must be in a Service Mesh for Traffic Director to work. For more details on Service Mesh, please refer to chapter 4. See figure 7.3 for an overview of using the Traffic Director for routing hybrid applications.

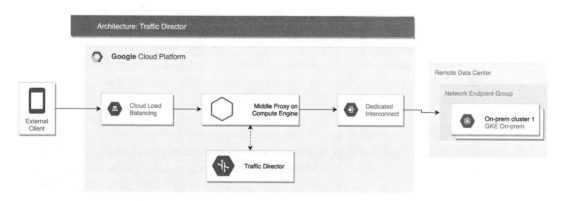

Figure 7.3   Traffic Director architecture for hybrid applications

In figure 7.3, the GKE on-prem cluster provides backend services to be used with the Traffic Director. The Traffic Director then directs the Google Cloud load balancer to direct traffic to the GKE on-prem cluster. This paradigm works for Anthos clusters on other clouds as well.

7.3.2 Traffic Director benefits

The Traffic Director allows the use of Google Cloud load balancers to front hybrid applications, and, in doing so, can use cloud native services such as Google Cloud Armor (https://cloud.google.com/armor), Cloud CDN (https://cloud.google.com/cdn), Identity-Aware Proxy (https://cloud.google.com/iap), and managed certificates (http://mng.bz/lJPz).

All traffic coming into the application, regardless of where the services are hosted, will enter via a Google point of presence to a Google Cloud load balancer, which is then proxied via Envoy proxies programmed by the Traffic Director to a service that is part of the service mesh. The service can be hosted on-prem or across multiple clouds but is known through the service mesh. By using these services, hybrid applications on-prem can be protected from denial of service (DDoS) attacks, which can be a problem for hybrid applications.

The Traffic Director can also direct traffic to Google Compute Engines if the application is not running on Google Kubernetes Engine. The Traffic Director can also be used to split traffic between cloud services and on-prem services, to aid migration of services from on-prem to the cloud with no downtime.

7.3.3 Traffic Director limitations

In figure 7.3, the middle proxy is deployed on a managed instance group, which scales according to traffic from the external load balancer before forwarding it to the GKE on-prem cluster. This additional compute cost is borne by the application owner.

7.4 Applications regulated by law

One set of applications belongs to highly regulated industries, which are bound to data locality restrictions. A list of these industries includes financial institutions, health care providers, pharmaceutical companies, and government agencies.

Such applications require constant monitoring and complicated audit and security policies, which are aided using GKE on-prem, Anthos Config Management, Anthos Service Mesh, and VPC Service Controls.

7.4.1 Architecture

VPC Service Controls enable administrators to restrict access to certain Google Cloud APIs to allowed IP addresses, identities, and client devices. Such APIs include gke-hub.googleapis.com, gkeconnect.googleapis.com, meshca.googleapis.com, and containerregistry.googleapis.com, which are the GKE Hub, GKE Connect, Anthos Service Mesh, and Container Registry services used throughout the Anthos offering. This process uses BeyondCorp (https://cloud.google.com/beyondcorp), a concept made popular by Google Cloud: that trust should be built on identity, not on networking, and a zero-trust policy is used within a network. This allows users to work more securely from any trusted locations without a VPN. See figure 7.4 for a visualization of the setup.

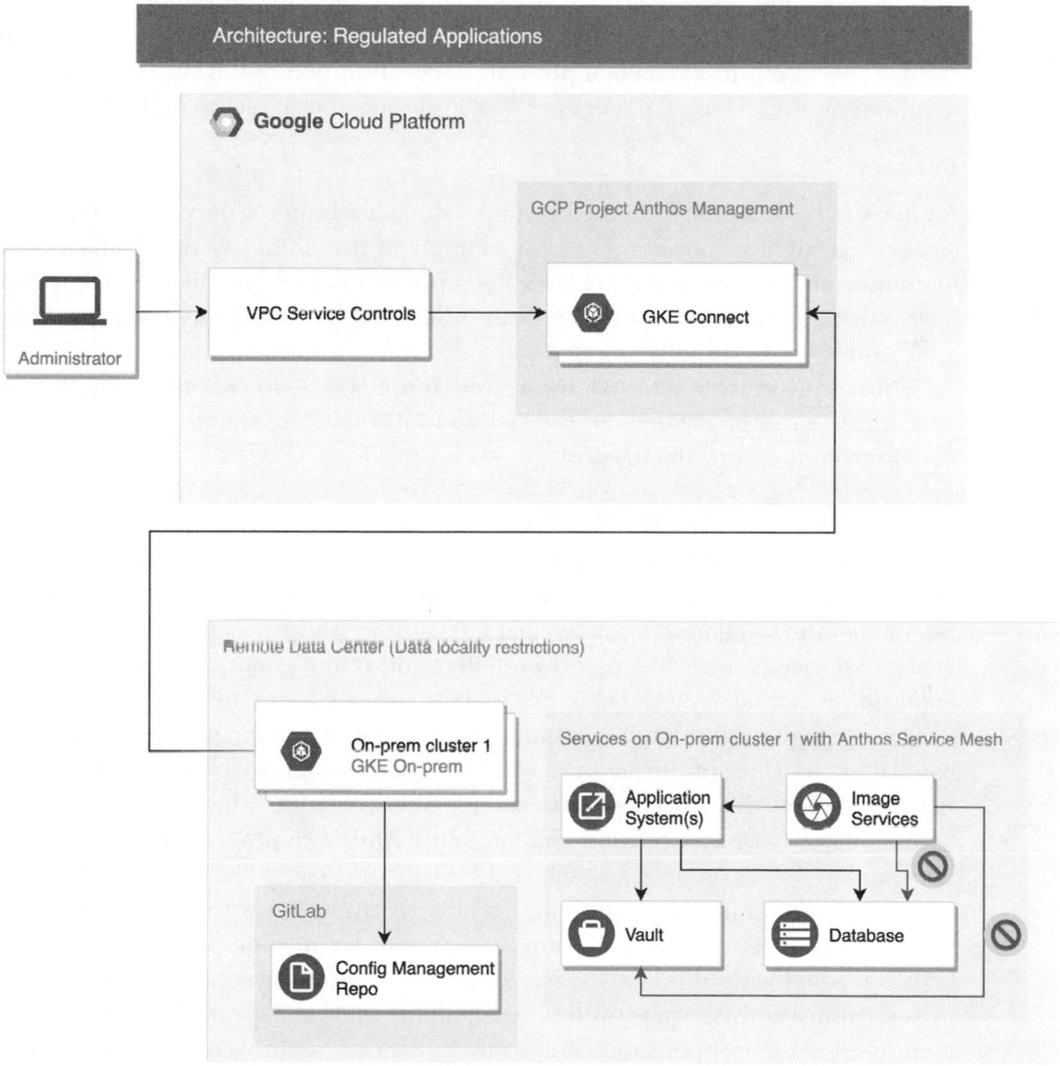

Figure 7.4 Regulated application with VPC Service Control, ACM, and ASM

Enterprises can configure Anthos clusters to read config management from a repository hosted on-prem, set up role-based access controls in one location, and have that setup propagated through a continuous sync. With the Policy Controller deployed with Anthos Config Management, administrators and security teams can define policies to restrict the use of unapproved container registries, prevent the creation of privileged Pods, and define read-only operating system filesystems. To understand how to do this in detail, please refer to chapter 13.

With Anthos Service Mesh, administrators can enforce mutual TLS communication between all Pods as well as define which Pods can communicate with each other—and only with each other, nothing more. This restriction prevents unauthorized access to sensitive data and prevents data exfiltration in the event a rogue Pod is deployed on the system. For a deeper dive into this subject, please refer to chapter 4.

7.4.2   Benefits

All the services mentioned in the previous section are built for purpose and have security as their highest consideration. For example, if the Anthos Config Management is disconnected from the repo, the last synced policies are still in effect. All components have also been tested to work with each other, and any problems are a quick ticket away from Google Support.

This architecture is also extensible and automatable, so that new on-prem regulated clusters can be created, be hooked up to the same ACM and ASM artifacts, and benefit from the work already done.

7.5   Applications that must run on the edge

Edge devices mean different things for different companies and business use cases. For example, a telecom edge use case would refer to computing requirements for 5G capabilities. See chapter 8 for a detailed look at how Anthos enables this case.

Edge devices can also be used by retailers and remote manufacturing sites, where applications can be deployed closer to users to provide a low-latency experience while delivering high-performance compute. One example is calculating statistics for a baseball game right in the stadium while the game is going on and delivering those statistics in real time to commentators and the audience. This was a driving force behind Major League Baseball's decision to use Anthos to process and analyze data in the cloud as well as on-prem at each of their ballparks (see http://mng.bz/Blyq).

These applications must run on edge appliances with low resource requirements and without depending on a continuous internet connection. The biggest problem relates to deploying the latest versions of your software over the air to these edge nodes. Anthos at the edge provides this capability while still giving developers the ability to deploy their applications uniformly in a cloud native way and trust that their applications will work in the same way as on the cloud due to the conformant deployment of Kubernetes.

7.5.1   Architecture

The architecture shown in figure 7.5 represents retail stores of the future, where shoppers can shop without any cashiers. The retailer can still monitor purchases securely

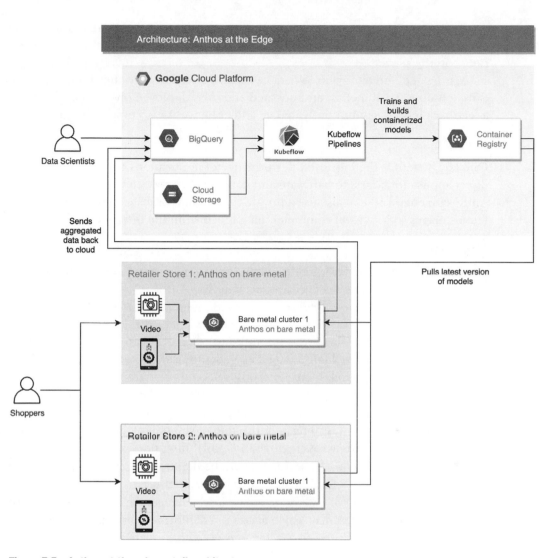

Figure 7.5   Anthos at the edge retail architecture

through video and transact via an application in the store, as well as identify hot spots of traffic, identify when to restock goods, and comply with privacy regulations while providing a real-time low-latency experience.

For such a use case, many machine learning models would be used for detection of theft, detection of low stocks, recommendations, and determining traffic hot spots. Models such as RetailNet can be used for people counting and hot spot detection in retail stores, referenced here: http://mng.bz/dJ9z. What is required for this setup is a way to continuously train and update the model and deploy it reliably on the edge with high performance compute for inference. As can be seen in figure 7.5, you can use Anthos on bare metal to deliver just that. Streaming video data back to the cloud for inference requires large bandwidth and causes a lag, degrading the real-time experience in the store.

Aggregated and anonymized data can then be sent back to the cloud, and models can be trained via Kubeflow and updated and then deployed on-prem again, creating a feedback loop to continuously update and enhance the accuracy of the models.

7.5.2 Benefits

One key benefit is the improved performance of applications on the edge due to the direct application access to hardware and skipping the cost of a virtual machine license. Anthos on edge 1.9+ can also use a private registry mirror instead of gcr.io to pull container images so it can run completely air-gapped from the internet.

7.5.3 Limitations

Without a virtualization layer, node scaling requires you to install new hardware nodes and connect them to the fleet of bare metal devices.

Summary

- The different Google Cloud and Anthos services play an important role in the different use cases of high availability, geographical spread, regulated industries, and edge computing. Many enterprises need these different use cases to enrich their digital offerings and can use the prescribed architectures to do this.
- With Anthos, companies can standardize on Kubernetes with one unified pattern of deployment, scaling, security, and development and maintain the ability to move workloads across regions and availability zones.
- Solutions such as Workload Identity can be deployed across multiple and hybrid clouds to provide a unified authentication framework.
- Ingress for Anthos allows you to create load balancers to route traffic to clusters from points of presence, which allows the deployment of features in a standardized way globally, with accessibility to users with low latency.
- The Traffic Director allows the use of Google Cloud load balancers to front hybrid applications and use cloud native services, which are part of the service mesh.
- VPC Service Controls enable administrators to restrict access to certain Google Cloud APIs to specific IP addresses, identities, and client services.
- Anthos on the edge improves performance of applications via direct application access to hardware, thus bypassing the cost of a virtual machine license.

Working at the edge and the telco world

Giovanni Galloro

This chapter covers

- Evolution of telco network functions toward cloud native network functions
- Edge application use cases
- Anthos specific capabilities for supporting telco and edge workloads
- Google Distributed Cloud Edge

This chapter is about using Anthos as an enabling platform for edge and telco workloads, which fall into the following two categories:

- *Cloud native network functions*—An evolution of telecom network functions, either already virtualized or still deployed as physical appliances, toward containerized workloads to reach greater efficiency, performance, and ease of management. This evolution will be driven also by new 5G-related network functions.
- *New edge applications*—Workloads to be deployed in edge locations, near the end customer, to reduce latency and enable new types of applications such as

autonomous driving, smart cities, smart video surveillance, augmented reality, virtual reality, and remote healthcare/surgery. Often this type of application will benefit and be powered by 5G networks and, in large part, will be deployed as containerized workloads.

8.1 *Evolution of telecom applications*

In this section, you will find a recap of the evolution of telecom network functions toward network functions virtualization and cloud native network functions.

8.1.1 *Introduction to network functions virtualization*

Traditionally, network operators used to implement network functions on dedicated, proprietary hardware appliances. From the mid 2010s, the concept of network functions virtualization (NFV) emerged as telcos looked at virtualizing their networking functionality, following the same pattern that led to the virtualization of IT servers, to consolidate the many network equipment types into industry-standard high-volume servers, switches, and storage to reduce costs and increase efficiency, agility, and resilience.

A trend started to transform network appliances in virtual network functions (VNFs): virtual machines deployed on industry standard x86 servers through a hypervisor. As depicted in figure 8.1, the three main working domains of an NFV architecture follow:

- *Virtualized network functions (VNFs)*—x86-compliant virtual machine versions of the network appliances
- *Network function virtualized infrastructure (NFVI)*—All hardware (servers, storage, network gear) and software components (virtualization software) that build up the environment hosting the virtual network functions
- *Management and orchestration (MANO)*—Life cycle management and orchestration of physical or software resources that support the infrastructure virtualization and the life cycle management of the virtual network functions

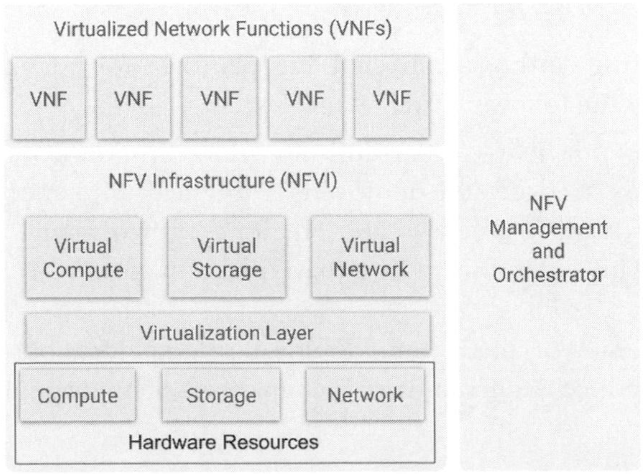

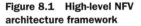

Figure 8.1   High-level NFV architecture framework

8.1.2   NFV use cases

Some virtualized network functions created as part of this initiative, with different success in the adoption, follow:

- *vCPE (virtualization of home and enterprise CPE [customer premises equipment])*— Routers into the operator network. With this approach, the advanced routing and network functions are moved from the access router, which service providers traditionally deployed in enterprise premises or in consumer homes, to VNFs running on industry-standard hardware in the provider's own NFVI. The customer's on-prem appliance is replaced with simpler hardware.
- *vPE (virtualization of PE [provider edge] routers*—In this approach, the routers deployed in the service provider edge, which typically connect with those deployed on customer premises, are also virtualized.
- *vEPC (evolved packet core) virtualization*—Virtualization of network functions that are part of the mobile core networks and IP multimedia subsystem: mobility management entity, serving gateway, and packet data network gateway.
- *vCDN*—Virtualization of CDNs. This use case aims to virtualize third-party CDN appliances that are usually deployed on-prem.
- *vRAN*—Virtualization of mobile base stations in radio access networks (RANs) was initially considered a use case for NFV, mainly because mobile base stations account for most of the total cost of ownership and energy consumption of mobile networks. This approach didn't effectively materialize in NFV, but the aim to get the benefits of containerized workloads described earlier and the need for new radio network functions related to 5G is pushing the transformation of these functions to CNFs.

8.1.3   Evolution to cloud native network functions

Telco operators and network functions vendors are looking at container-based cloud native network functions, as an evolution of VNFs, to fully realize the above-mentioned NFV benefits and add the improvements carried by cloud native applications in terms of portability, agility, manageability, and efficiency.

Various initiatives inside Cloud Native Computing Foundation (CNCF) aim to support telecom operators (and network vendors) in obtaining the benefits touted by cloud native technologies. These are mainly led by the Telecom User Group (https:// github.com/cncf/telecom-user-group), which produced various assets, including a white paper available in the repository and the following definition for cloud native network functions:

> *A cloud-native network function (CNF) is a cloud-native application that implements network functionality. A CNF consists of one or more microservices and has been developed using Cloud Native Principles including immutable infrastructure, declarative APIs, and a "repeatable deployment process."*

8.2   *New edge applications*

The following paragraphs contain a description of the characteristics of new edge applications, which take advantage of 5G networks' higher bandwidth and lower latency.

8.2.1   *5G as the enabler of new edge applications*

Characteristics of the 5G network, including its larger contiguous spectrum, more advanced radio antenna technologies (Massive MIMO), better modulation schemes, and changes to/optimization of signaling flows between the core and RAN, provide network capabilities with significantly higher bandwidth and lower latency. Telco service providers and applications/digital services developers are looking to use these characteristics in applications that will have more devices connected and will exchange information at a very high speed, enabling improved scenarios: autonomous driving, smart cities, smart factories, smart video surveillance, augmented reality, virtual reality, and remote health care/surgery.

To align with these requirements, workloads will be deployed, in many cases, in edge locations, near the end devices or user, to do near-real-time data processing and analysis of data, allowing smart devices to act and respond to inputs without sending that data to the cloud and back. This kind of application will largely be deployed as containerized workloads. Generally, 5G will be mainly software defined, continuing the transformation started with NFV; will have a further need for automation, due the speeds and volumes it will handle; and will be based on open source software.

8.2.2   *Edge computing*

Edge computing will allow applications to respond quickly, provide near-real-time insights, be less dependent on the network connection to the central datacenter or cloud, and reduce the amount of data that is transmitted centrally. Gartner predicts that by 2025, 75% of enterprise-generated data will be created and processed outside a traditional centralized data center or cloud (see http://mng.bz/rdDE).

As shown in figure 8.2, edge infrastructure will be deployed in locations with widespread distribution and, in many cases, smaller than a central datacenter, as follows:

- *Telco edge*—Telco operators' small data centers, points of presence, and network cabinets
- *Public cloud edge*—Cloud providers'/global broadcasters' points of presence and CDN edges
- *Enterprise edge*—Enterprise/end users' locations as branch offices, retail stores, warehouses, and factories

Compute node numbers will typically grow, and the need will arise to have a central management plane capable of managing a larger compute fleet in the order of tens of thousands.

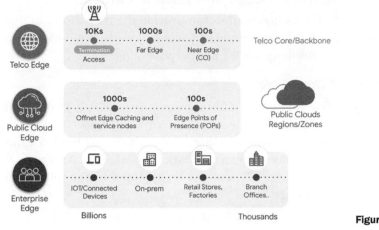

Figure 8.2   Edge deployment

8.2.3   Edge application examples

Some examples follow of applications and use cases that will take advantage of deployed-at-edge locations and perform analysis and predictions on images, video, audio, and other types of data through local execution of AI models:

- *Predictive maintenance*—Analyzing manufacturing plants and machine data on-site to predict faults before they happen and optimize uptime and maintenance team work
- *Manufacturing quality check*—Analyzing pictures and videos of products on the assembly line to check conformance to quality standards
- *Worker safety*—Analyzing correct security measure implementation and safety equipment usage through pictures and videos
- *Diagnostic services and patient monitoring*—Using a computer vision solution deployed to the edge to process imaging, which could improve diagnostic accuracy and exam efficiency
- *Queue and shelf management in retail stores*—Analyzing video feeds to check how many people are in line or the availability of goods on shelves and open cash registers or fill goods accordingly
- *Self-driving cars and industrial vehicles*—Low-latency processing for data ingested and gathered by autonomous vehicles
- *Manufacturing workers' guidance and training through AR/VR*—AI models deployed on the edge with object detection and recognition, live capture, and the like
- *Logistics tracking*—AI models that recognize packages, items, pallets, and vehicles in transit from images and videos and update tracking systems
- *Inventory management and production planning*—Near-real-time analysis of asset status through images to provide inputs to production and supply chain fulfillment

8.3   Anthos as a platform for edge and telco workloads

In this section, we'll discuss how Anthos can provide the foundation to support edge Anthos deployments and the execution of telco workloads. We'll also delve into specific solutions Google has designed for this purpose.

8.3.1   Google Distributed Cloud Edge

Google Distributed Cloud Edge (GDCE), shown in figure 8.3, is a fully managed solution from Google, designed to support telco virtualized and cloud native network functions and edge applications, including software, OS, and hardware (servers and TOR network switches) in Google-managed racks. It's based on Anthos on bare metal (described in detail in chapter 17) and can be deployed in the following site types, described in the previous sections:

- *Public cloud edge*—Google edge locations
- *Telco edge*—Owned by telco providers
- *Enterprise edge*—Owned by the final customer (such as in retail stores, factory floors, branch offices, and stadiums)

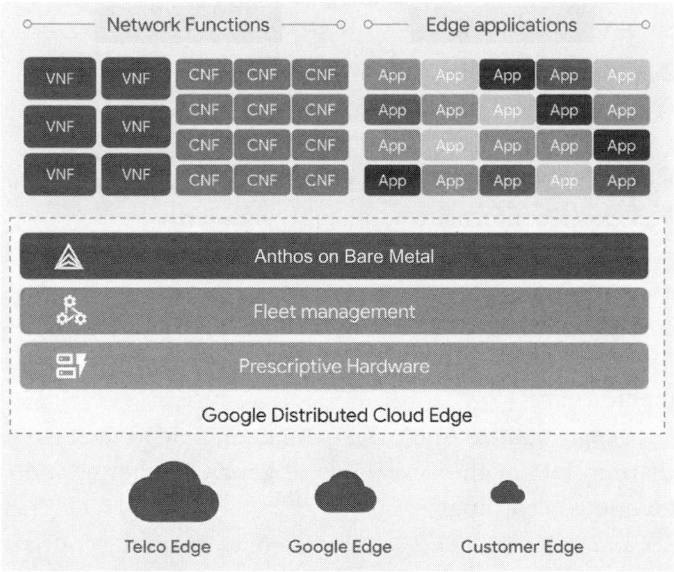

Figure 8.3   Google Distributed Cloud Edge high-level architecture

GDCE provides fleet management capabilities to manage all the hardware and software assets and supports both containerized workloads and virtual machines through Anthos on bare metal capabilities.

GDCE also provides users a VPN connection to GCP, allowing users to interact with other applications running in a customer's VPC and other GCP services. To service high-performance and low-latency workloads, GDCE also provides several high network performance features such as SR-IOV and DPDK. Google Cloud operates and manages the underlying infrastructure, extending the cloud experience to the customer premises.

Google provides the compute, network, and storage hardware. Those are shipped to the target location and managed by Google. The Google operations team manages and monitors the Google gear remotely.

The customer needs to have a designated contact person (part of the customer personnel, not a Google person) at the target location with access to the gear and permissions to perform basic administrative tasks. Those include, for example, cold restart, replacing of parts, ability to run local diagnostics on the gear, and common system administration tasks. After the hardware is connected and operational, users can consume the service using standard Google API tools and use the service.

A GDCE Kubernetes cluster consists of a control plane and worker nodes. Worker nodes are organized into node pools. The control plane is hosted on GCP in a single compute region. Worker nodes are servers on GDCE racks, with each worker node using a full physical server. A rack or a group of racks with shared space, power, cooling, and contiguous network fabric is defined as a GDCE zone.

GOOGLE DISTRIBUTED CLOUD EDGE CONTAINER RESOURCE MODEL

GDCE has a different resource model compared to Anthos and other Anthos deployment options. Here you will find a list of the container resources used to describe, implement, and manage the compute architecture of a GDCE implementation, described schematically in the figure 8.4:

- *Zone*—A zone represents a set of machines sharing a network fabric or a single fault domain. A zone can represent one rack or a number of racks placed in the same location. The GDCE zone resource is different from GCE compute zones.

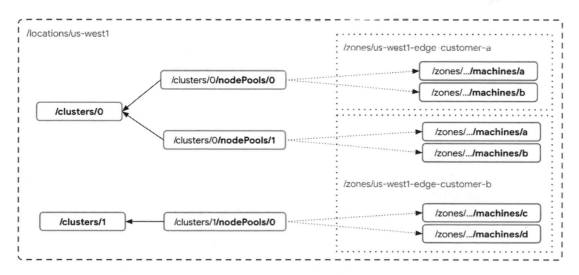

Figure 8.4   Google Distributed Cloud Edge container resource model

Listing the GCE compute zones will not return the GDCE zones. A zone represents a single failure domain. To deploy fault-tolerant applications with high availability and help protect against failures, users need to deploy applications across multiple zones linked to the same region.

- *Machine*—A machine represents a physical server. The machine resource metadata includes which rack it is on and other properties and tags. Machines are read-only resources for users. At deployment, a machine is assigned to a specific region based on the physical location of the GDCE system. Each physical machine is a node within the Distributed Cloud Edge cluster. A machine can be part of a Kubernetes cluster deployed only in its designated region.
- *Cluster*—A cluster consists of a control plane and zero or more node pools. It is housed in a specific region and can connect node pools only from that region. If a user tries to connect a node pool with machines homed in a different region, the operation will fail.
- *Node pool*—A node pool is a logical grouping of machines in a GDCE zone and is used to add worker nodes to clusters.
- *VPN connection*—GDCE supports setting up a VPN connection to a GCP project allowing workloads running on a GDCE Kubernetes cluster to connect directly to GCP resources. At least one node pool should be created in the cluster before establishing a VPN connection.

GOOGLE DISTRIBUTED CLOUD EDGE NETWORK RESOURCE MODEL

In addition to Kubernetes cluster resources, APIs, and the default Kubernetes Pod network, GDCE also allows customers to provision additional networks in a GDCE zone and connect them with customer networks for different purposes. For example, in a network functions use case, a customer might create an operations, administration, and management network and a signal network, each with different multiple subnets that connect to the secondary interfaces of the network function Pods.

Figure 8.5 describes the resources and their relationships for the network model in GDCE. From the high level, the following five types of resources are related to the edge network configuration:

- *Network*—A virtual network in a GDCE zone with private address space, which may contain one or more subnetworks. A network is isolated from other networks in the same GDCE zone.
- *Subnetwork*—A layer-2 (VLAN) subnet in a GDCE network. A subnetwork has its own broadcast domain and customer-assigned classless interdomain routing. Subnetworks within a network can reach each other. Subnetworks of different networks in a GDCE zone cannot reach each other.
- *Interconnect*—Represents a bundled logical link of one or more physical links between GDCE and a customer network. An interconnect can be created only at GDCE site initiation time. Multiple interconnects are typically configured to provide high availability.

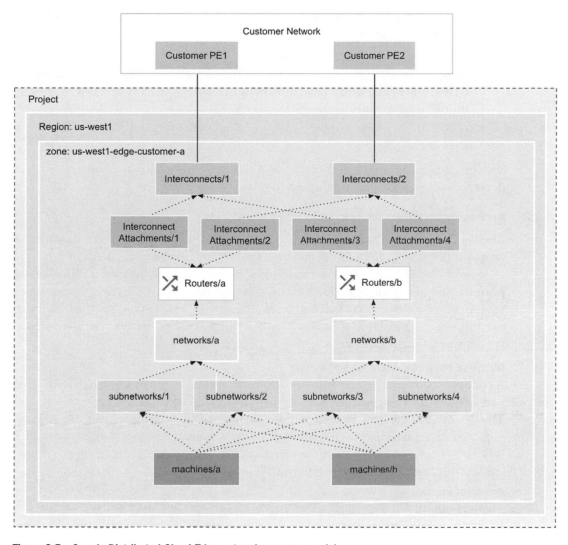

Figure 8.5   Google Distributed Cloud Edge network resource model

- *Interconnect attachment*—A virtual link provisioned on top of an interconnect based on customer requests, to provide an isolated connection between a GDCE network and a customer network (e.g., a VRF). Packets flowing through an interconnect attachment will be untagged or tagged with a customer-specified VLAN ID.
- *Router*—A virtual routing instance to configure routing functionalities for a network in a GDCE zone. For example, customers can use it to configure a BGP peering session over an interconnect attachment between a GDCE network and a customer network, or over a Pod subnet, so that certain Pods can advertise prefixes to GDCE. By default, the routes received from subnetworks will be readvertised.

These resources are similar to the Google Cloud network abstractions, with a few differences, described here:

- All network resources created for GDCE are local to the GDCE zone. A GDCE network doesn't have direct connectivity to a GCP VPC. Networks in different GDCE zones also don't have direct connectivity to each other, unless they are intentionally connected by the customer.
- GDCE subnetworks support VLAN and are thus isolated from each other in layer 2.

System administrators should create and maintain all network resources. An app developer/owner has only view access to network resources.

8.3.2   *Anthos capabilities for telco and edge workloads*

Besides the specific characteristics of GDCE, Anthos capabilities are available in the standard product to help the deployment, execution, and management of edge and telco workloads. Some of these capabilities have been designed specifically for this purpose and are mainly provided with Anthos on bare metal, which is the most suitable version for these workloads and is also the core of GDCE. Other capabilities, such as Anthos Config Management, are provided for general purpose but can be adapted for edge and telco applications.

MULTIPLE NETWORK INTERFACES FOR PODS

A common containerized network functions (CNFs) requirement is to have additional network interfaces provisioned to Pods on top of the default Kubernetes interface. This is often needed to keep separation between the data plane and the management/control plane, for performance or security reasons, or to isolate network flows for other reasons. Anthos provides this capability on Anthos on bare metal, using a specific implementation of the Multus CNI plug-in.

Architecture

This capability allows a single Pod to connect to multiple networks. The default Kubernetes interface will be seen in the Pod as eth0, whereas additional interfaces, created through the Multus CNI, will be seen by default as net1, net2, and so on, and can be configured. The CNI used for the additional interfaces can be as follows:

- IPvlan
- MacVLAN
- Bridge
- SR-IOV

Setup

To enable this feature, the user must perform the following three actions:

1 *Enable multi-NIC.* Enable multi-NIC for pods by adding the `multipleNetwork-Interfaces` field to the `clusterNetwork` section of the Anthos bare metal cluster custom resource and setting it to `true`, as shown here:

```
...
clusterNetwork:
 multipleNetworkInterfaces: true
 pods:
  cidrBlocks:
  - 192.168.0.0/16
 services:
  cidrBlocks:
  - 10.96.0.0/12
...
```

2 *Specify network interfaces.* Use the `NetworkAttachmentDefinition` custom resources to specify additional network interfaces. The `NetworkAttachmentDefinition` custom resources correspond to the networks that are available for the Pods. It's possible to specify these custom resources within the cluster configuration manifest at cluster creation time or add them directly to an existing target cluster:

```
apiVersion: "k8s.cni.cncf.io/v1"
kind: NetworkAttachmentDefinition
metadata:
 name: gke-network-1
spec:
 config: '{
 "type": "ipvlan",
 "master": "ens224",
 "mode": "l2",
 "ipam": {
  "type": "whereabouts",
  "range": "172.120.0.0/24"
 }
}'
```

3 *Assign network interfaces to Pods.* You can enable multiple NICs in the Pod or deployment manifest through the `k8s.v1.cni.cncf.io/networks:` annotation, using the value corresponding to the specific `NetworkAttachmentDefinition` custom resource and its namespace, as in the following example where the network interfaces are specified by names of two `NetworkAttachmentDefinition` custom resources, `gke-network-1` and `gke-network-2`, in the default namespace of the target cluster:

```
---
apiVersion: apps/v1
kind: Deployment
metadata:
 name: sample-deployment
spec:
 ...
 template:
```

```
      metadata:
       annotations:
        k8s.v1.cni.cncf.io/networks: default/gke-network-1, default/gke-network-2
        labels:
         app: sample-deployment
      ...
```

Restricting network interfaces to a node pool

Use the k8s.v1.cni.cncf.io/nodeSelector annotation to specify the pool of nodes for which a NetworkAttachmentDefinition custom resource is valid. Anthos clusters on bare metal force any Pods that reference this custom resource to be deployed on those specific nodes. In the following example, Anthos clusters on bare metal force deployment of all Pods that are assigned the gke-network-1 network interface to the multinicNP node pool. Anthos clusters on bare metal labels a node pool with the baremetal.cluster.gke.io/node-pool label accordingly:

```
apiVersion: "k8s.cni.cncf.io/v1"
kind: NetworkAttachmentDefinition
metadata:
 annotations:
  k8s.v1.cni.cncf.io/nodeSelector: baremetal.cluster.gke.io/node-
     pool=multinicNP
 name: gke-network-1
spec:
 ...
```

A note on the SR-IOV plug-in

SR-IOV is a specification that essentially enables the virtualization of physical PCIe devices. It allows you to segment a compliant network device, recognized on the host node as a physical function (PF, which usually represents a single NIC port), into multiple virtual functions (VFs) that can be directly accessed by a virtualized workload. SR-IOV direct access to network hardware provides enhanced performance, so it is widely used in VM-based VNFs.

The SR-IOV CNI plug-in (https://github.com/intel/sriov-cni) enables a Kubernetes Pod to attach directly to an SR-IOV VF and also bind the VF to a DPDK driver, which provides enhanced network performance for cloud native network functions as previously done for VNFs.

In figure 8.6, you can see an example diagram showing multiple CNFs chained together to provide different services (firewall, deep packet inspection, SD-WAN) using multi-NIC Pods to connect multiple network segments.

RUNNING VM-BASED WORKLOADS ON ANTHOS ON BARE METAL

Not all the network functions will be deployed as CNFs, and some will stay as VNFs, so a coexistence between the two deployment models will be required for some time. To cater to this situation and other requirements of running part of a workload as a VM

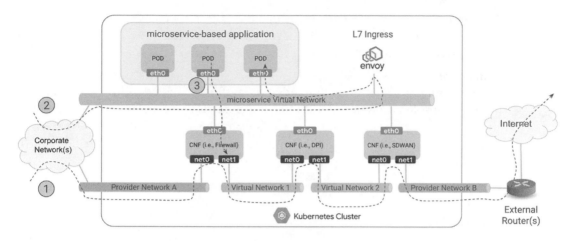

Figure 8.6 CNF using multiple NICs to connect different network segments

rather than as a container, Anthos on bare metal provides the possibility of running VM-based workloads through Anthos VM Runtime, based on KubeVirt.

A synthetic description of the task you need to perform to run VMs on Anthos on bare metal is shown in the next sections.

Enabling Anthos VM Runtime

To enable Anthos VM Runtime you need to do the following:

1 Update the `VMRuntime` custom resource to set `enabled` to `true` as shown in the next example:

```
apiVersion: vm.cluster.gke.io/v1
kind: VMRuntime
metadata:
 name: vmruntime
Spec:
 enabled: true
 # useEmulation default to false if not set.
 useEmulation: true
 # vmImageFormat default to "qcow2" if not set.
 vmImageFormat: qcow2
```

2 If your node doesn't support hardware virtualization, or you aren't sure, set `useEmulation` to `true`. If available, hardware virtualization provides better performance than software emulation. The `useEmulation` field defaults to `false`, if it isn't specified.

3 You can change the image format used for the VMs you create by setting the `vmImageFormat` field that supports two disk image format values: `raw` and `qcow2`. If you don't set `vmImageFormat`, the Anthos VM Runtime uses the raw disk image format to create VMs. The raw format may provide improved performance over `qcow2`, a copy-on-write format, but may use more disk.

4 Save the configuration and verify that the VMRuntime custom resource is enabled: you can execute kubectl describe vmruntime vmruntime and check that the description shows VMRuntime.Status.Ready set to true.

Creating a VM

Before creating a VM, it's recommended to configure a cloud-init file to ensure that you have console access to the VM once it's created. You can create a custom cloud-init file in two ways. The easiest way is to specify the --os=<OPERATING_SYSTEM> flag when creating the VM. This method automatically configures a simple cloud-init file and works for the following operating systems:

- Ubuntu
- CentOS
- Debian
- Fedora

Once your VM is created, you can access it for the first time with the following credentials and then change the password:

```
user: root
password: changeme
```

If your image contains a different Linux-based OS or you need a more advanced configuration, you can manually create a custom cloud-init file and specify the path to that file by specifying the --cloud-init-file=<path/to/file> flag. In its most basic form, the cloud-init file is a YAML file that contains the following:

```
#cloud-config
user: root
password: changeme
lock_passwd: false
chpasswd: {expire: false}
disable_root: false
ssh_authorized_keys:
- <ssh-key>
```

To create a VM using kubectl, you need to use the following steps:

1 Install the virtctl plug-in with the following command: sudo -E ./bmctl install virtctl.

2 Execute the command kubectl virt create vm. The next example contains parameters:

```
kubectl virt create vm VM_NAME \
   --boot-disk-access-mode=MODE \
   --boot-disk-size=DISK_SIZE \
   --boot-disk-storage-class="DISK_CLASS" \
   --cloud-init-file=FILE_PATH \
   --cpu=CPU_NUMBER \
   --image=IMAGE_NAME \
   --memory=MEMORY_SIZE
```

The parameters are explained here:

- *VM_NAME*—The name of the VM that you want to create.
- *MODE*—The access mode of the boot disk. Possible values are `ReadWriteOnce` (default) or `ReadWriteMany`.
- *DISK_SIZE*—The size you want for the boot disk. The default value is `20Gi`.
- *DISK_CLASS*—The storage class of the boot disk. The default value is `local-shared`.
- *FILE_PATH*—The full path of the customized cloud-init file. Depending on the image, this may be required to gain console access to the VM after it is created.
- *CPU_NUMBER*—The number of CPUs you want to configure for the VM. The default value is `1`.
- *IMAGE_NAME*—The VM image, which can be `ubuntu20.04` (default), `centos8`, or a URL of the image.
- *MEMORY_SIZE*—The memory size of the VM. The default value is `4Gi`.

If parameters are not specified, the default values are used.

Alternatively, it's possible to apply a manifest defining a `VirtualMachine` custom resource, which also enables popular GitOps deployment methods (declarative and asynchronous management).

ORCHESTRATION AND AUTOMATION FOR LARGE COMPUTE FLEETS

One of the impacts of edge and radio access network CNFs deployments is the need to have a central control plane capable of managing a wider and more granularly distributed compute fleet, and, moreover, deploying several application instances that could be orders of magnitude bigger than what is typically deployed in traditional data centers or public clouds. In some cases, you will need to deploy instances of the same application on tens, hundreds, or thousands of compute clusters, distributed in edge locations. Often, you'll need to define the locations where the instances must be deployed, dynamically based on specific criteria, with very short notice to adapt to changing needs from network, monitored objects, or application users. Central configuration and policy management capabilities provided by Anthos Config Management will be key to satisfying this requirement.

Anthos Config Management

Anthos Config Management capabilities are described extensively in chapter 11. Here we discuss a couple of them that are especially useful for managing applications and network functions deployments on a large fleet of clusters:

- Multiple repository mode
- Cluster selectors

Multiple repository mode

Enabling multirepository mode on Anthos Config Management allows you to sync configuration from multiple repositories to the same set of clusters, as shown in figure 8.7. A single *root repository*, typically managed by a central platform team, hosts cluster and centrally defined namespace-scoped configurations, whereas optional *namespace repositories* are used to configure objects in specific namespaces. This capability extends ACM usage, beyond platform configuration and policies management, to the deployment of applications: it is possible to delegate the setup and control of a namespace repository to an application release team. Centrally defined namespaces resources are inherited, whereas the application team is free to configure application-related ones (deployments, config maps, etc.). If conflicts arise between the root and the namespace repository, only the declaration in the root repository is applied to the cluster.

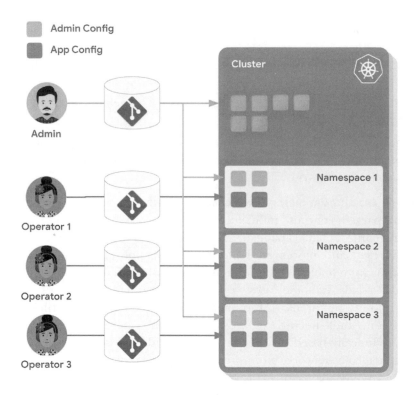

Figure 8.7   Anthos Config Management with multiple repositories

Namespace repositories are defined by a `RepoSync` resource, deployed in the specific namespace by the central platform team or directly by the application team, if delegated by the central team.

The diagram in figure 8.8 represents the structures of a root repository and two namespace repositories where numbers identify the following:

1   The root configuration defined by the central admin/platform team.
2   The configuration defined by the central team, common to multiple namespaces because it's placed in their parent folder and is inherited by the namespaces.

3   Resources defined by the central team in each specific namespace folder, including the `RepoSync` resource. (This can be delegated to the applications team, too.)

4, 5   Application configuration manifests managed by the application team.

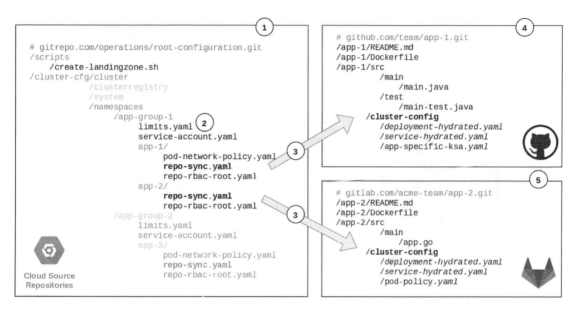

Figure 8.8   ACM example config with multiple repositories

Cluster selectors

ACM provides two specific resource objects that allow you to selectively choose clusters where a specific configuration or deployment is applied, using the Kubernetes label and selector approach.

Cluster objects identify specific clusters managed by ACM and assign them arbitrary labels to identify all cluster-relevant attributes (location, hardware capabilities, purpose, etc.):

```
kind: Cluster
apiVersion: clusterregistry.k8s.io/v1alpha1
metadata:
 name: edge-cluster-112a
 labels:
  location: london-12
  environment: production
  kind: edge
  gpu: yes
```

ClusterSelector objects are used to select only clusters with a given label or combination of labels. The following ClusterSelector selects only clusters with the environment: production and kind: edge labels—useful, for example, to target all production clusters deployed in edge locations:

```
kind: ClusterSelector
apiVersion: configmanagement.gke.io/v1
metadata:
 name: production-edge
spec:
 selector:
  matchLabels:
    environment: production
    kind: edge
```

ClusterSelector objects can be referenced, using the configmanagement.gke.io/cluster-selector: annotation, from any ACM-managed Kubernetes resource to select on which cluster that resource will be deployed.

The following ClusterRole will be created only on production clusters deployed in edge locations:

```
kind: ClusterRole
apiVersion: rbac.authorization.k8s.io/v1
metadata:
 name: node-reader
 annotations:
   configmanagement.gke.io/cluster-selector: production-edge
rules:
- apiGroups: [""]
 resources: ["nodes"]
 verbs: ["get", "list", "watch"]
```

ClusterSelector objects can also be referenced by application-specific resources to selectively define the clusters that will host the application instance, and, if multiple repositories are used, in RepoSync resources to sync the specific namespace repository only to specific clusters.

In figure 8.9, you can see an example of a distributed unit CNF, defined by an operator-managed custom resource (kind: DU), deployed on hundreds of Anthos clusters labeled with cnfs: du-slice-1 but not on the ones dedicated to central units (cnfs: cu-cp-slice1, cu-up-slice-1).

All these configurations are driven by continuously synchronizing with a Git repository (root and, if present, namespace) that acts as the source of truth. All the fleet will regularly converge to the desired state, so, for example, the following things occur:

- Any cluster assigned the cnfs: du-slice-1 label will immediately have the CNF deployed.
- Any cluster that changes destination or purpose by changing any of the labels will have the CNF deleted and the new desired configuration immediately applied.
- Any update to the CNF configuration will be immediately deployed on all the desired clusters.

Figure 8.9   ACM example config using cluster selectors to deploy different CNFs to different clusters

8.3.3   Solution architecture example: Smart retail

In addition to the deployment examples provided in this chapter, here we will describe an edge application architecture built on Anthos for a retailer.

One of the goals of the retailer is to have the smallest possible infrastructure deployed in stores, leaving only video cameras as endpoints. The application deployed is a real-time queue management, as shown in figure 8.10. It starts with a video camera

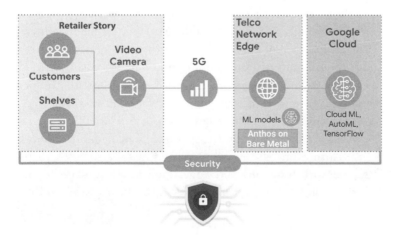

Figure 8.10   High-level architecture for an edge smart retail solution

monitoring the checkout line at the cash register and streaming the video feed in real time through a 5G modem in the store over a 5G connection to a telecom operator edge location. The telecom operator network edge receives all 5G traffic, and the software there intelligently sends the retail store traffic to an Anthos bare metal cluster deployed in this edge. There, a container-based ML app runs machine learning inference on the incoming video feed and detects how many people are in line at the retail store. If that number crosses a certain threshold, a notification to open another cash register is sent back to the store over the same low-latency 5G path on which the video feed came in.

In addition, the AI/ML app also sends metadata about this and other events to Google Cloud. Later, Google Cloud securely processes this information to provide insight to the retailer and to train future iterations of the models. With Google Cloud's sophisticated AI/ML product suite, we can easily train and deploy highly accurate models for any applications anywhere.

This architecture can be extended to other smart retail applications, such as per-customer personalization and digital signage, real-time recommendations, contactless checkout, and automatic restocking of shelves. All the latency-sensitive processing, such as video or image ML inference, happens at the telecom edge, whereas all the non-real-time components, like model training and data analytics, run in the cloud.

Summary

- Market trends and continuously evolving platform capabilities drive telco network functions and edge applications toward Kubernetes and Anthos as the ideal deployment platform.
- NFV had the goal of transitioning telco network functions from dedicated, proprietary hardware appliances to virtual machines deployed on industry-standard x86 servers. This transformation has started but has not completely materialized as expected.
- 5G is driving the rise of new applications, deployed on edge locations as containerized workloads and using 5G networks' higher bandwidth and lower latency, providing near-real-time data processing and allowing smart devices to act and respond to inputs without sending that data to the cloud and back.
- Anthos provides specific capabilities that are key enablers for the deployment, execution, and management of edge and telco workloads: VM runtime, hardware accelerators, multiple network interfaces per Pod, and large fleet management.
- Google Distributed Cloud Edge (GDCE) is a fully managed solution from Google, based on Anthos on bare metal, designed to support telco virtualized and cloud native network functions and edge applications and including software, OS, and hardware in Google-managed racks. It can be deployed in Google, telco, or enterprise edge.

Serverless compute
engine (Knative)

Konrad Cłapa

This chapter covers

- Introduction to serverless
- Knative Serving and Eventing components
- Knative on Anthos

Before we get into the details, let's set the scene. In this chapter, we're going to talk about Google Cloud Platform's managed service based on an open source project called Knative. The project was started to allow for quicker development of Kubernetes applications without the need to understand the complex Kubernetes concepts they use. With this service, Google installs and manages Knative serving inside your Anthos GKE cluster. One of the benefits of using Knative with Anthos instead of open source Knative is that Google's automation and site reliability engineers handle all installation and maintenance. Anthos integrates with numerous GCP services like Cloud Load Balancing (https://cloud.google.com/load-balancing), Cloud Armor (https://cloud.google.com/armor), Cloud CDN (https://cloud.google.com /cdn/docs/overview), and many others, making an enterprise-ready Knative a reality.

We have already discussed Kubernetes in chapter 3, so we understand how complex the installation and maintenance of it can be. This problem is solved for us with Google Kubernetes Engine. In addition to Kubernetes, we still need to know how to run and operate cloud native applications. What Knative does is abstract those implementation details and allow you to serve your serverless container-based workloads on any Kubernetes cluster.

In this chapter, we will look at what serverless is, introduce you to Knative, and discuss how Anthos delivers an enterprise-grade container-based serverless platform.

9.1   Introduction to serverless

A lot of discussion occurs about what serverless is. Comparisons between serverless and function as a service (FaaS) are common—it is almost an ideological dispute. To keep this simple, let's look at the Cloud Native Computing Foundation's definition:

> *Serverless computing refers to a new model of cloud-native computing, enabled by architectures that do not require server management to build and run applications.*

Google's fully managed cloud-run service perfectly fits into this definition because it abstracts the compute layer from the developer and operator. It allows you to deploy the containers that will be serving HTTP(S) requests. The scaling of the application is handled by the platform itself.

Although Google Cloud Functions deliver similar capabilities, they are more opinionated about the runtime languages you can use. With Cloud Run, you can use any language that can run a service that answers HTTPS calls. Cloud Run does not require you to use Anthos.

When we think about Cloud Run, we can think about the following set of serverless features:

- *No server*—Developers don't need to worry about underlying compute infrastructure.
- *Multilanguage*—The application can be written in any language.
- *Event-driven*—The container/function is triggered by an external event.
- *Autoscaling*—The container can automatically scale based on requests.
- *Portability*—Your container/application should be able to run on any Kubernetes platform.

9.2   Knative

Because you already know Kubernetes is a platform for building platforms, why not use it for building serverless platforms based on containers? Knative runs on top of Kubernetes like any other Kubernetes application. You can even see some statements from Knative contributors that it should not be called "serverless," so let's look at Knative as a platform to deliver serverless anywhere where you run Kubernetes. Sound fair?

9.2.1 *Introduction*

Say you would like to build your own Kubernetes-based serverless platform. You might come up with the diagram shown in figure 9.1 showing all the required components. Clearly some duplication of effort exists related to building the primitives like autoscalablity, observability, rollouts, and many others. What Knative is doing is providing all these primitives for you so you have a common experience of running a serverless workload on Kubernetes.

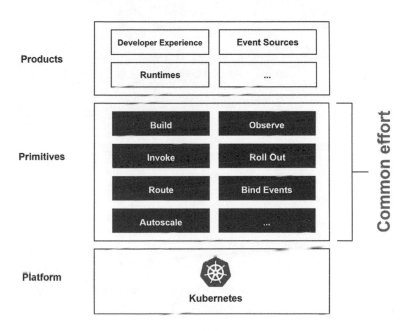

Figure 9.1 Kubernetes serverless stack architecture

Now think of it from the developer's perspective. All they have to do is define the dependencies, write their code, and put it in a container. Then they deploy the application to Knative. The details of how it is served is not their concern. This does not mean, however, that they lose the capability to fine tune the service. They can set multiple parameters like concurrency (how many requests can be served per container), minimum/maximum instances (minimum/maximum container instances that can be provisioned for the Knative service), and many others. Knative hides all the complexities of Kubernetes involved with scaling and traffic management and provides a means to observe the workloads. That is what you call an easy start with development of Kubernetes applications, right?

KNATIVE VS. CAAS, FAAS, AND PAAS

In the second section of this chapter, we learn what problems Knative is trying to solve: enable serverless workloads to run anywhere with the flexibility of Kubernetes but hiding the complexity. Table 9.1 presents a comparison of Knative against platform as a service (PaaS; http://mng.bz/WAKX), container as a service (CaaS; http://mng.bz/81gg), and function as a service (FaaS; https://www.ibm.com/topics/faas), with various features being supported. Do-it-yourself (DIY) means you need to do some development to be able to use that feature.

Table 9.1   Knative vs. PaaS, CaaS, and FaaS

Feature	Knative	PaaS	CaaS	FaaS
Simple UX/DX	Yes	Yes		Yes
Event driven	Yes	Yes		Yes
Container based	Yes	Yes	Yes	Yes
Autoscaling	Yes	Yes	DIY	Yes
Scale resources to 0	Yes	Yes		Yes
Load balancing	Yes	Yes	DIY	Yes
Unrestricted execution time	Yes*	Yes	Yes	
Unrestricted compute/memory limits	Yes**	Yes**	Yes**	
Variety of programming languages support	Yes	Yes	Yes	Limited

* Might be restricted for managed services like Cloud Run.
** Depends on the platform.

As we can see, Knative provides all the advantages of FaaS but also gives you the ability to run your application in almost any language. The limits on the execution time are much higher compared to FaaS. In many cases, where there is a need for longer request-processing time, Knative is a solution. You finally have access to advanced features like volumes and networking so you can tweak your workload if needed. Like with all compute services with greater flexibility, the responsibility demarcation line shifts more toward you. You need to build your own container and make sure you can make use of all the advanced features. But let's be honest: who does not like to be in more control of your application until you get all the benefits of FaaS?

9.2.2 *Knative history*

Google started Knative but now has multiple companies contributing to it, like IBM, RedHat, and SAP. The full documentation and source code can be found here: https://github.com/knative. Knative started as a set of components that allows you to build and run stateless workloads together with subscriptions to events. The following two active projects, shown in figure 9.2, are in progress on GitHub:

- *Knative Serving*—Allows you to serve serverless containerized workloads
- *Knative Eventing*—Allows subscriptions to external events

Build   Serving   Eventing

Figure 9.2
Knative components

The third project, *Knative Build*, which helped build containers, was deprecated and turned into the Tekton Pipelines (https://github.com/tektoncd/pipeline) project. As you will learn in chapter 9, it was used by Google to build Cloud Build for Anthos.

At the time of writing, both Knative Serving and Eventing are already in version 1.x, with Eventing being slightly behind Serving. Knative was developed with the vision to deliver the simplicity of App Engine (https://cloud.google.com/appengine) but allowing for the flexibility that Kubernetes brings. As an example, with Knative you can modify the routing to different versions of the application by setting the traffic configuration on a Knative Serving[1] object rather than changing the low-level network object's configuration (e.g., Istio). This setup resembles App Engine, where you simply run one command to perform a task, and it can be used for canary deployments and A/B testing. Knative gives you the ability to run your serverless containers anywhere, whether in the cloud or in an on-prem data center.

As you will shortly learn, multiple Knative-based, fully managed services already exist that make it even easier to avoid getting into the complexity of Kubernetes. The most interesting one for this book is, of course, Knative for Anthos, which is one of the most advanced offerings existing on the market.

9.3   Knative architecture

Let's look at Knative architecture, presented in figure 9.3. As you can see, multiple layers exist, with some of the components being plug and play or optional.

Knative can run on any compute platform that can run Kubernetes. It can be based on either virtual machines or bare metal servers. For traffic routing, Service Mesh Gateway is used. Obviously, the most popular is Istio, but alternative solutions are also supported, including Gloo, Ambassador, Contour, and Kourier, with more to come. To learn more about Istio, refer to chapter 4. On top of that, we have Knative components installed as a Kubernetes application. Note that each of those components can be installed and operated separately. If you are not interested in managing the Knative installation yourself, you can use one of the many already existing managed services—Google Cloud Run and Google Cloud Run for Anthos, OpenShift

---

[1] Knative Serving is explained in the next section of this chapter.

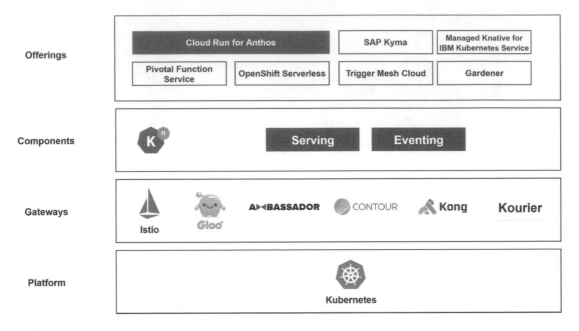

Figure 9.3   Knative architecture

Serverless, managed Knative for IBM Cloud Kubernetes Service—where both Knative and underlying Kubernetes are managed by the provider. A list of those services can be found here: http://mng.bz/El6r.

9.3.1   Knative Kubernetes resource types

Knative comes with a set of controllers and custom resource definitions (CRDs) that extend the native Kubernetes API. Therefore, integration with Knative is very much like interaction with the Kubernetes API itself. We will look at the Knative resources in the next section.

If you think of a simple Kubernetes application, you should have objects like Pods, Deployments, and Services. If you include Service Mesh, you will have additional resources to handle the traffic management like virtual services and destination rules. With Knative, you control your deployment with a single resource—Knative Service— which allows you to both deploy the workload and handle the traffic. All the required Kubernetes and Service Mesh resources are created for you.

9.3.2   Knative Serving

Knative Serving allows you to easily deploy container-based serverless workloads and serve them to users via HTTP(s) requests (with gRPC recently announced). As an example, you can serve an entire e-commerce website frontend using Knative Serving. It automatically scales your workload as per demand (from 0 to N) and routes or splits traffic to the version (revision) you choose. To achieve this with native Kubernetes, you would need to use additional Kubernetes resources like HorizontalPodAutoscaler (HPA; http://mng.bz/NmaX). Knative Serving extends the Kubernetes API with new CRDs like Knative Serving Service, Configuration, Route, and Revision. Figure 9.4 shows how the Knative resources depend on each other.

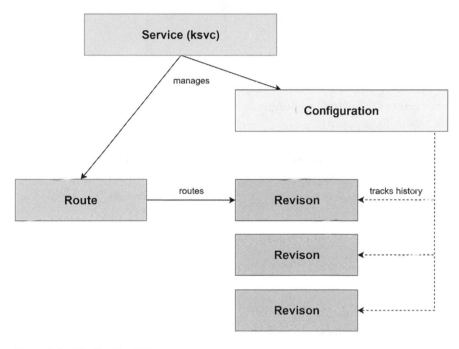

Figure 9.4   Knative Serving resources

Each of the CRDs is described next:

- *Service (API path service.serving.knative.dev)*—The most important resource in Knative Serving. It automatically creates other Knative resources needed for the entire life cycle of your workload. With the update of the services, a new Revision is created. Within the Knative Service, you define both the container version and the traffic rules.

NOTE   This is different from the native Kubernetes Service *object*, which might be confusing to new users at first.

For example, a Service definition that deploys a simple Hello World workload to Knative Serving will automatically create other resources: Revision, Configurations, and Route:

```
apiVersion: serving.knative.dev/v1
kind: Service
```

```
metadata:
  name: helloworld
  namespace: default
spec:
  template:
    spec:
      containers:
        - image: docker.io/{username}/helloworld
          env:
            - name: TARGET
              value: "Python Sample v1"
```

- *Revision (API path revision.serving.knative.dev)*—An immutable snapshot of the container version and its configuration. It defines what is actually served to the user.
- *Configuration (API path configuration.serving.knative.dev)*—The configuration part of your application that enforces the desired state of your workload. It allows you to separate your code (container) from the configuration piece. Modification of the configuration results in new Revision creation.
- *Route (API path route.serving.knative.dev)*—Maps the endpoints to one or more revisions.

When you use Knative, you no longer need to worry about the native Kubernetes and Service Mesh resources like Deployments, Services, and VirtualServices. You define your application as a Knative Service and all the "backend" resources are created for you.

TRAFFIC MANAGEMENT

When you want to update your Knative Service with a new image, a new revision is created, and by default, the traffic is directed to the new revision, as shown in figure 9.5. You can perform A/B (http://mng.bz/DZ50) testing on a canary (https://martinfowler .com/bliki/CanaryRelease.html) release, controlling how much traffic should be directed to a particular revision by defining the `metadata.spec.traffic` attribute. You can also just tag a particular revision to be accessible by a dedicated URL.

To achieve the routing shown in figure 9.5, you would set up the `metadata.spec .traffic` attribute in the Knative Service:

```
traffic:
  - tag: current
    revisionName: helloworld-v1
    percent: 95%
  - tag: candidate
    revisionName: helloworld-v2
    percent: 5%
  - tag: latest
    latestRevision: true
    percent: 0
```

As you can see, with a single Kubernetes object, a developer can control how the entire workload is served. There is no need to dive deep into the Kubernetes backend.

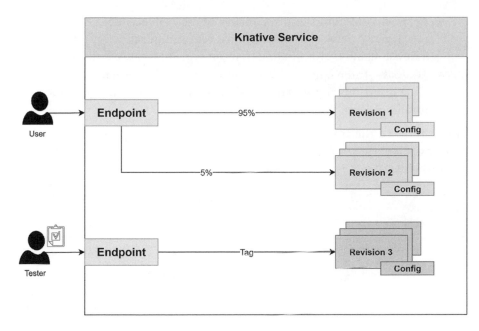

Figure 9.5   Knative Service traffic flows

KNATIVE SERVING CONTROL PLANE

Now let's look at the Knative Serving control plane, which allows for all this magic to happen. As we've already said, Kubernetes uses Istio, or any other supported service mesh, for traffic management. It also comes with several services that take care of running and scaling the workload.

To retrieve the list of the services in the `knative-serving` namespace you installed with Knative, use `kubectl get services n knative-serving`. It will show the following services:

```
NAME                TYPE        CLUSTER-IP        EXTERNAL-IP    PORT(S)                  AGE
activator-service   ClusterIP   10.96.61.11       <none>         80/TCP,81/TCP,9090/TCP   1h
autoscaler          ClusterIP   10.104.217.223    <none>         8080/TCP,9090/TCP        1h
controller          ClusterIP   10.101.39.220     <none>         9090/TCP                 1h
webhook             ClusterIP   10.107.144.50     <none>         443/TCP                  1h
```

As you can see, for such a complex service, it doesn't have many supporting services. Let's look at them one by one:

- *Activator*—Receives and buffers requests for inactive revisions and reporting metrics to the Autoscaler. It also retries requests to a Revision after the Autoscaler scales the revision based on the reported metrics.
- *Autoscaler*—Sets the number of Pods required to handle the load based on the defined parameters.

- *Controller*—Monitors and reconciles Knative objects defined in CRDs. When a new Knative Service is created, it creates Configuration and Route. It will create a Revision and corresponding Deployment and Knative Pod Autoscaler.
- *Webhook*—Intercepts, validates, and mutates Kubernetes API calls, including CRD insertions and updates. Sets the default value and rejects inconsistent and invalid objects.

If you retrieve the list of the deployments in the namespace you installed Knative to using `kubectl get deployments -n knative-serving`, you will see the following deployments:

```
NAME                     DESIRED   CURRENT   UP-TO-DATE   AVAILABLE   AGE
activator                1         1         1            1           1h
autoscaler               1         1         1            1           1h
controller               1         1         1            1           1h
networking-certmanager   1         1         1            1           1h
networking-istio         1         1         1            1           1h
webhook                  1         1         1            1           1h
```

We have already discussed four of these services, but we have not yet seen the following two deployments:

- *Networking-certmanager*—Reconciles cluster ingresses into cert manager objects.
- *Networking-istio*—Reconciles a cluster's ingress into an Istio virtual service.

9.3.3   *Knative Eventing*

Eventing is the Knative component that orchestrates events originating from various sources inside or outside of the Kubernetes cluster. This important element of event-driven architecture allows you to trigger your service using existing event sources and build new ones for scenarios where you need a custom source not already available. This process is different from FaaS, where the functions are triggered using only HTTP requests or other predefined triggers, like Google Cloud Storage events.

All the Knative Eventing objects are defined as CRDs. This ensures that the events are handled as defined in the Knative objects using controllers. Scalability is taken care of automatically as events trigger calls to your container. It gives you scalability similar to Knative Serving, so you can start with a small load of a few events and scale to handle a stream of events.

You can use around 20 predefined sources, and the list is growing. You can also develop your own source. Knative Eventing is also pluggable, so you can choose how you want to store your event—whether in memory or persistent storage—while it's being processed. Knative uses an open CNCF standard, CloudEvents, to parse the original events. The target for the events can be both Knative and Kubernetes Services. The Eventing pipelines are simple—like a simple event being sent to a single Service—but they can also get very complex. For the sake of understanding Cloud Run, let's concentrate on the basics first.

KNATIVE EVENTING RESOURCES

The most essential component of Knative events are Brokers and Triggers. If we look at figure 9.6, we see that the events are generated from external sources and are captured by the Broker. There, one or more Triggers receives the events, filters them, and passes them to the Service.

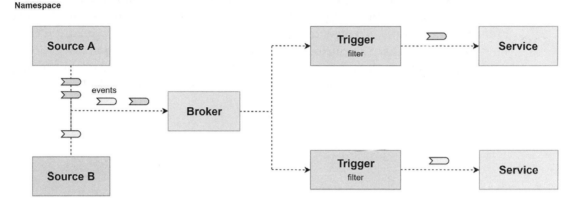

Namespace

Figure 9.6   Knative Eventing resources

The architecture of Knative clearly separates concerns. Knative Eventing Broker is an event mesh that pulls or receives events, whereas Knative Trigger filters and routes events to targets. Event sources are the control plane of Knative Eventing that makes sure events are sent to the Broker. Now let's look more closely at the resources.

The Broker API path `broker.eventing.knative.dev` is essentially an addressable event delivery system that you install by setting a label on your namespace, similar to what you do with Istio when you want to do sidecar injections into the Pods. Events are received by the Broker and then sent to subscribers. The messages are stored in a channel managed by the Broker.

The channel can be a simple in-memory channel or it can use persistent storage for reliability purposes. Examples of these are Pub/Sub and Kafka. The configuration of the channels is stored in ConfigMaps. If you want to have different types of messages, you can install Broker into multiple namespaces. You can also filter which events are accepted by the Broker. An example definition of a Knative Broker follows:

```
apiVersion: eventing.knative.dev/v1
kind: Broker
metadata:
  annotations:
    eventing.knative.dev/broker.class: MTChannelBasedBroker
  name: default
  namespace: default
```

```
spec:
  config:
    apiVersion: v1
    kind: ConfigMap
    name: config-br-default-channel
    namespace: knative-eventing
```

The Triggers API path `trigger.eventing.knative.dev` matches the event with a Service, so it is defined for the type of event (e.g., a Cloud Storage object sending the event to that Service). Triggers can filter events based on one or more attributes. If multiple attributes exist, all attribute values need to match. This method can also produce new event types from the received event. This can be a nice use case for filtering events with sensitive data. An example definition of a Knative Trigger is shown next:

```
apiVersion: eventing.knative.dev/v1alpha1
kind: Trigger
metadata:
  name: helloworld-python
  namespace: knative-samples
spec:
  broker: default
  filter:
    attributes:
      type: dev.knative.samples.helloworld
      source: dev.knative.samples/helloworldsource
  subscriber:
    ref:
      apiVersion: v1
      kind: Service
      name: helloworld-python
```

The Source API path `<source_name>.eventing.knative.dev` is defined as a CRD. The list is still growing and includes AWS SQS, Google Cloud Pub/Sub, Google Cloud Scheduler, Google Cloud Storage, GitHub, and GitLab. A full list of events appears at https://knative.dev/docs/eventing/sources/. You can either use an existing Source or create your own. The following example shows how to configure a `CloudPubSubSource` event source. The event will be generated whenever a message is published to a Pub/Sub topic named `testing`:

```
apiVersion: events.cloud.google.com/v1
kind: CloudPubSubSource
metadata:
  name: cloudpubsubsource-test
spec:
  topic: testing
  sink:
    ref:
      apiVersion: v1
      kind: Service
      name: event-display
```

In figure 9.7, you can see how an event source works.

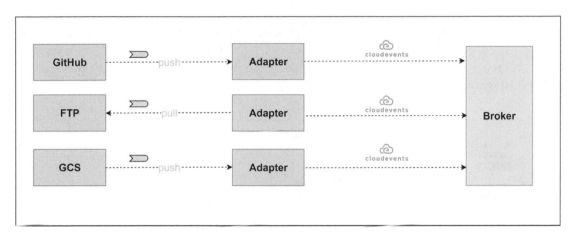

Figure 9.7   How an event source works

The events are pulled or pushed to the adapters, depending on whether the source is capable of pushing events. If it is not, the events need to be pulled. The adapters are developed to understand the events and translate them into a common Cloud-Events format. Once translated, they are available for the Broker to pick them up in the new format.

HOW EVENT SOURCES WORK

Event sources consist of control and data planes. The control plane is responsible for configuration of the event delivery with the authoritative source, the setup of the data plane, and the cleanup—put simply, it creates the webhooks and subscriptions. The data plane performs the push/pull operations, then validates and converts the data into CloudEvents.

On top of existing sources, you can create your own event sources using Kubernetes operators, container sources, or existing services. To see how you can develop your own source, refer to the Knative Eventing documentation (http://mng.bz/lJBz).

KNATIVE USE CASES

With Knative, you can cover several use cases, from a simple single service to very complex multimicroservice applications. Using Knative Serving, you can create both HTTP and gRPC (https://grpc.io/docs/what-is-grpc/introduction/) services, webhooks, and APIs. You can also manage rollouts and rollbacks and control the traffic to your application. With Knative Eventing, you can create simple or very complex eventing pipelines. By combining those two services, you can deliver a fully cloud native, event-driven application.

Let's look at a simple example of binding running services to a Cloud IoT Core (https://cloud.google.com/iot-core), as shown in figure 9.8. The messages from the IoT devices are sent to the Google Cloud IoT Core and synced to Pub/Sub. The Knative Eventing service uses the Pub/Sub source to get the messages from the topic. The messages are sent to a Broker and converted to CloudEvents. A Trigger ensures the events are sent to the proper service that can further process, log, or display them to the user.

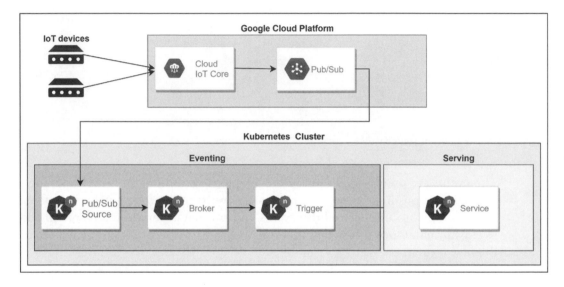

Figure 9.8   Binding running services to IoT Core

If you would like to try the Pub/Sub example yourself, we encourage you to follow the step-by-step tutorial at http://mng.bz/Bljq.

9.3.4   *Observability*

Knative comes with logging and tracing capabilities, as shown in figure 9.9. The following open source software is supported:

- Prometheus and Grafana for metrics
- ELK (Elasticsearch, Logstash, and Kibana) stack for logs
- Jaeger or Zipkin for distributed tracing

To learn more about metrics and tracing, see chapter 4.

You can also integrate with Google Cloud Logging (formerly Stackdriver Logging) for logs using the *Fluent Bit* agent. The installation procedure for each of the components is well described in the article found at http://mng.bz/dJlz.

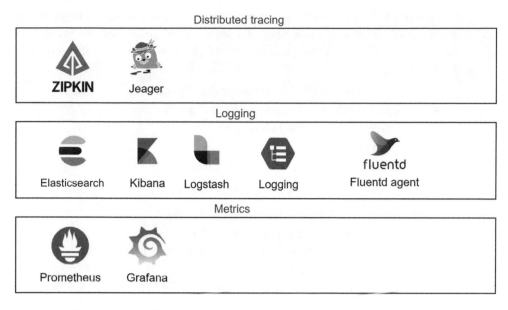

Figure 9.9   Knative observability ecosystem

Because these components are deployed like any other Kubernetes application, you can access them by exposing the Kubernetes service. An example of Pods running on a cluster after deployment follows:

```
NAME                                   READY   STATUS    RESTARTS   AGE
grafana-798cf569ff-v4q74               1/1     Running   0          2d
kibana-logging-7d474fbb45-6qb8x        1/1     Running   0          2d
kube-state-metrics-75bd4f5b8b-8t2h2    4/4     Running   0          2d
node-exporter-cr6bh                    2/2     Running   0          2d
node-exporter-mf6k7                    2/2     Running   0          2d
node-exporter-rhzr7                    2/2     Running   0          2d
prometheus-system-0                    1/1     Running   0          2d
prometheus-system-1                    1/1     Running   0          2d
```

9.3.5   *Installing Knative*

You can install Knative on multiple cloud platforms or on-prem, if you run a Kubernetes cluster that includes but is not limited to the following:

- Amazon EKS
- Google GKE
- IBM IKS
- Red Hat OpenShift Cloud Platform
- Minikube

In the end, Knative is nothing but a Kubernetes application. You can install it either using YAML files or an operator. To learn more about operators, see http://mng .bz/rdRE. The installation process for the Knative Serving component consists of the following:

- Installation of the custom resource definitions
- Installation of the core components of Serving
- Installation of the networking layer
- Configuration of DNS
- Installation of optional Serving extensions

Installation of the Knative Eventing component consists of the following:

- Installation of the custom resource definitions
- Installation of the core components of Eventing
- Installation of the default channel (messaging) layer
- Installation of a Broker (Eventing) layer
- Optional Eventing extensions (sources)

Once you are done with the installation of Serving and Eventing, you can install the observability components described in the previous section. The step-by-step procedure for end-to-end installation is available at http://mng.bz/Vp0r.

9.3.6   *Deploying to Knative*

You can follow a simple guide to deploy your first application to Knative, which is as simple as applying a single Knative Service object, as follows. This is assuming you already have a containerized Python application that responds with the response "Hello Python Sample v1!" stored in Docker Hub (see http://mng.bz/xdRq to check the source code for that application):

1   Run the following command to create a Knative Service:

```
kubectl apply -f service.yaml
```

where Service is defined in the service.yaml file as follows:

```
apiVersion: serving.knative.dev/v1
kind: Service
metadata:
  name: test
  namespace: default
spec:
  template:
    spec:
      containers:
        - image: docker.io/<user>/<image_name>
          env:
            - name: TARGET
              value: "v1"
```

2 Once deployed, multiple objects are created for you, including Pods, Knative Service, Configuration, Revision, and Route. You can verify them by running the next code:

```
kubectl get pod,ksvc,configuration,revision,route
```

3 You can access the service and get the IP address of the Istio ingress gateway as follows:

```
kubectl get ksvc helloworld-python  --output=custom-
columns=NAME:.metadata.name,URL:.status.url
```

This will return the following URL:

```
NAME                URL
helloworld-python   http://helloworld-python.default.1.2.3.4.xip.io
```

4 Now test the application by running a curl query:

```
curl http://helloworld-python.default.1.2.3.4.xip.io
```

Note that the xip.io domain is called a magic DNS. You can configure it when installing Knative (see http://mng.bz/Al9E).

5 You should see the following output:

```
Hello Python Sample v1!
```

You have successfully deployed your first Knative application!

To get some hands-on experience with Knative, we suggest you check out the examples shown in table 9.2. They cover end-to-end Knative app development and deployment scenarios with multiple language support. We especially recommend the Mete Atamel tutorial on Knative, which takes you by hand from a very simple deployment to very complex ones, including usage of Google Cloud services like Pub/Sub, AI APIs, and BigQuery. We are sure you will have a lot of fun!

Table 9.2 References for deploying to Knative

Title	URL
Knative Serving code samples	https://knative.dev/docs/serving/samples/
Knative Eventing code samples	https://knative.dev/docs/eventing/samples/
Mete Atamel Knative tutorial with multiple examples	https://github.com/meteatamel/knative-tutorial

KNATIVE SUMMARY

With Knative service, you no longer must choose between the flexibility of Kubernetes and the simplicity of function as a service—you get the best of both worlds. You can run your serverless workload anywhere. With Knative Eventing, you can subscribe and receive events from several predefined sources as well as define your own source using cloud native architecture.

CLOUD RUN VS. KNATIVE ON ANTHOS

Cloud Run is a fully managed serverless offering, whereas Knative on Anthos runs on top of your Anthos clusters, as shown in figure 9.10. You can interact with Cloud Run, whichever version you go for. Cloud Run, however, runs on Google infrastructure, so you don't need to worry about the underlying platform.

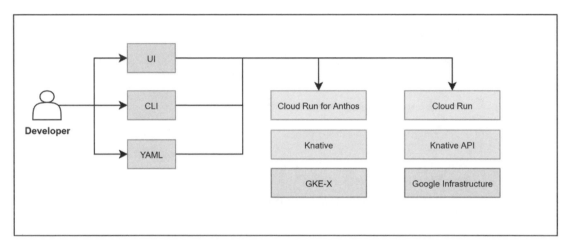

Figure 9.10   Cloud Run and Knative on Anthos architecture

> **NOTE**   For the purposes of this book, we will refer to Cloud Run (fully managed) as Cloud Run.

Although we know what the main differences are, you still might be wondering which service better fulfills your workload needs. Table 9.3 shows a little bit more detail on the differences.

Table 9.3   Cloud Run vs. Knative on Anthos

Feature	Cloud Run	Knative on Anthos
Price	Pay per use	GKE Anthos cost
Compute	CPU and memory limits	As per GKE cluster nodes capabilities (includes GPU)
Isolation	Based on gVisor or other sandbox	Default GKE isolation
Scaling	1,000 containers with extensible quota	As per GKE cluster
URL/SSL	URL and SSL autogenerated	Can configure custom domain

Table 9.3   Cloud Run vs. Knative on Anthos *(continued)*

Feature	Cloud Run	Knative on Anthos
Domains	Custom domain can be created	
Network	Access to VPC via serverless VPC access	Direct access to VPC
Service mesh	Integrated with service mesh	Services connected to Istio Service Mesh
Execution environment	Google infrastructure	GKE cluster

So, when to choose each of the offerings? This very much depends on how much control you want to have over your application execution and whether you need custom hardware for GKE nodes. As an example, you might want to use GPUs to boost the performance of your ML pipelines. In such a case, Knative on Anthos is the way to go.

Summary

- Knative abstracts away the complexity of Kubernetes.
- Workloads are portable to any Kubernetes cluster.
- Knative has multiple components that can address multiple use cases.
- Eventing is the component that orchestrates events originating from various sources.
- Serving is the component that allows you to deploy container-based serverless workloads and serve them to users.
- Serverless Kubernetes workloads can be deployed and served using Knative on Anthos.
- Versions of the application can be controlled using revisions.
- Traffic to the application can be managed using revision parameters.
- You can get insights into your application using a rich, open source ecosystem of tools for monitoring, logging, and tracing.

Networking environment 10

Ameer Abbas

This chapter covers

- Anthos cloud networking and hybrid connectivity between multiple cloud environments
- Anthos Kubernetes and GKE networking, including Dataplane v2
- Anthos multicluster networking, including service discovery and routing
- Service-to-service and client-to-service connectivity

Anthos networking can be divided into four sections. Each section provides a layer of connectivity between entities such as environments (e.g., public cloud and on-prem), Anthos GKE clusters, and service-to-service communications. The four layers, shown in figure 10.1, follow:

- *Cloud networking and hybrid connectivity*—Addresses the lowest layer of networking and covers how different infrastructure environments can be interconnected.

182

- *Anthos GKE networking*—Anthos GKE clusters come in a variety of implementations, depending on the infrastructure in which they are deployed. This section covers Anthos GKE cluster networking, including how ingress works in various environments.

- *Multicluster networking*—Addresses how various Anthos GKE clusters connect to each other. Anthos GKE clusters may be deployed in a single infrastructure environment (e.g., in GCP), or they can be deployed across multiple infrastructure environments (e.g., GCP and in an on-prem data center).

- *Service and client connectivity*—Addresses how applications running on Anthos connect to each other. This section also addresses how clients and services running outside of Anthos can connect to services running inside the Anthos platform.

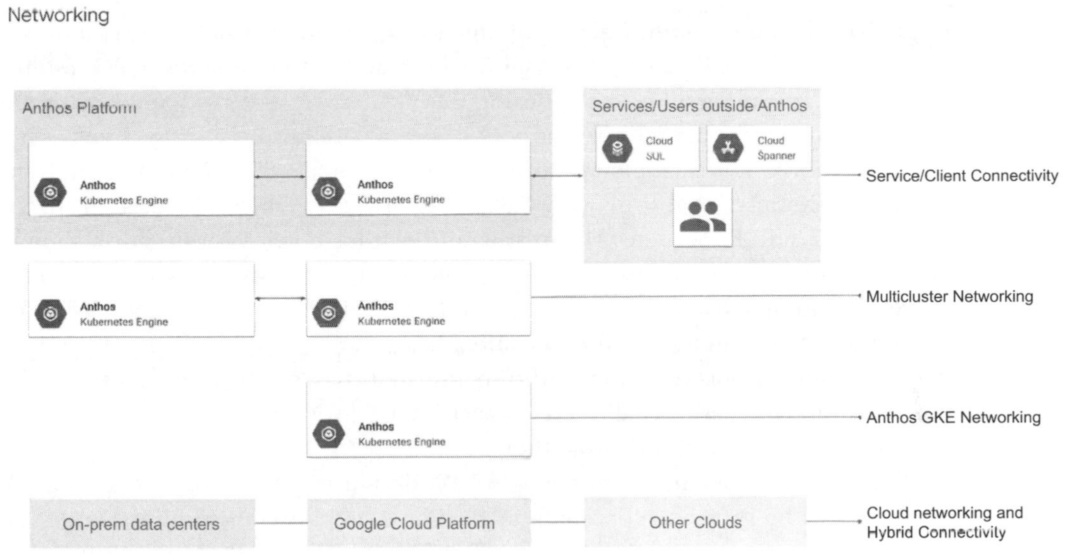

Figure 10.1   Four layers of Anthos networking

10.1   *Cloud networking and hybrid connectivity*

This section addresses various aspects of network connectivity at the infrastructure environment level. Anthos is a multicloud platform and can run in one or more public and private cloud environments. At the infrastructure layer, you can deploy Anthos in the following ways:

- *In a single cloud environment*—For example, GCP or on-prem data center or even in another public cloud
- *In a multi-/hybrid cloud environment*—For example, a platform deployed in GCP and in one or more on-prem data centers

10.1.1 *Single-cloud deployment*

The Anthos platform can be deployed in a single-cloud environment. The single-cloud environment can be on GCP, another public or private cloud, or on-prem data centers.

ANTHOS ON GCP

Anthos on GCP uses resources that are placed within a virtual private cloud (VPC; https://cloud.google.com/vpc). You can configure VPCs in GCP in multiple ways. Depending on the needs of the company, a single VPC (in a single GCP project) might suffice. In a more complex design, shared VPC, peered VPC, or even multiple disparate VPCs are required. The Anthos platform can work with a variety of VPC designs. Choosing the right VPC architecture up front is important because it may pose scalability and operational consequences later. We discuss various VPC design and decision criteria next.

Single VPC

Single VPC is the simplest design. For small environments, where everything is contained in a single GCP project, you may choose a single VPC. A single VPC results in a flat network, meaning all resources using the VPC are on the same network. You can control connectivity between resources via security features at various layers in the Anthos platform. For example, you can use a VPC firewall (https://cloud.google.com/vpc/docs/firewalls) at the network layer, Kubernetes NetworkPolicies (http://mng.bz/ZoWj) inside Kubernetes Dataplane, and Anthos Service Mesh (http://mng.bz/RlOn) authentication and authorization policies at the service mesh layer. With this approach, multiple teams use resources in the same GCP project and same VPC. Single VPC design, shown in figure 10.2, also simplifies network administration. All resources, whether inside or outside of the Anthos platform, reside on the same flat network and can communicate easily as allowed via security rules. No additional configuration is required to connect resources together.

The primary challenge with a single VPC design is scale. Although a single VPC design might be sufficient for small- to medium-sized implementations, large implementations may not be possible because you will start to hit VPC limits (https://cloud.google.com/vpc/docs/quota). As the organization grows, separate projects may need to be created for separate products, teams, or environments. A single VPC design does not support multiproject environments. Depending on the industry, regulations might exist that prohibit hosting all resources in a single VPC and require some level of network or project separation.

When designing your network structure for Anthos, you must understand and account for the longevity of the platform up front. For example, in two to four years, how much will the platform scale, and will any other restrictions arise that need to be considered, quota- or regulation-wise?

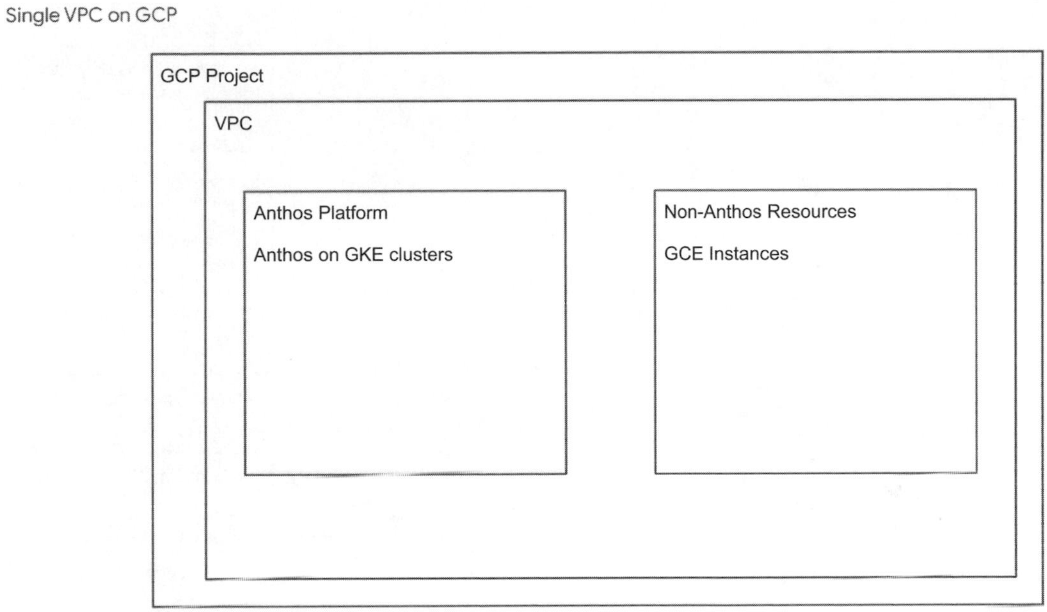

Single VPC on GCP

GCP Project

VPC

Anthos Platform

Anthos on GKE clusters

Non-Anthos Resources

GCE Instances

Figure 10.2   Single VPC architecture in GCP

Shared VPC

Using a shared VPC (https://cloud.google.com/vpc/docs/shared-vpc) is the recommended way to provision a network on GCP for the Anthos platform. You can use a shared VPC design, shown in figure 10.3, for both simple and complex (large-scale and multitenant) Anthos environments. A shared VPC allows a single VPC to be shared across multiple projects, which results in a single flat network space shared by multiple tenants, each within their own project. Separating GCP projects by products/tenants allows for granular IAM permissioning at the project level. At the same time, resources in multiple projects can still connect to each other (if allowed) as if they were on a single network.

A network host project contains a centralized "shared" VPC. All network resources are located in this network host project, including subnets, firewall rules, and network permissions. A centralized networking team owns and controls the network host project. This arrangement ensures that the organization's network best practices are enforced by a single qualified team of networking experts. Multiple service projects can then use network resources from the host project. Subnets are shared from the network host project to multiple service projects and are used by resources inside each service project.

For Anthos on GCP, it is recommended to create a service project and name it similar to platform_admins. The Anthos platform (all GKE clusters) resides inside the platform_admins project. The platform_admins project (as the name suggests) is

Shared VPC on GCP

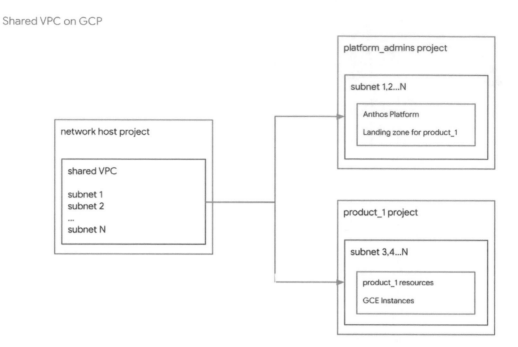

Figure 10.3   Shared VPC architecture in GCP

owned by the platform administrator team who manages and maintains the life cycle of the Anthos platform. Platform administrators are one of many tenants of the network host project. Similarly, products and environments get their own service projects. Anthos is a shared multitenant platform where each tenant gets a "landing zone" in which to run their services on Anthos. A landing zone is a set of resources required to run a service on the Anthos platform and is typically one (or more) namespaces in one (or more) Anthos GKE clusters and a set of policies required to run that service. All non-Anthos resources (belonging to a service) are provisioned and managed in the individual service's GCP project. This way, multiple tenants can have their own projects for non-Anthos resources, and they can all share a single Anthos GKE on GCP clusters. Using a shared VPC allows Anthos and non-Anthos resources to connect to each other.

Multiple VPC
The two previous VPC implementations result in a flat network where all resources are provisioned in a single logical VPC. In some cases, security or regulatory restrictions may require the separation of resources into multiple VPCs. The company or organization may also want each team or product to manage their own network.

The Anthos GKE on GCP platform can be installed in one VPC. Multitenancy allows you to share the Anthos GKE on GCP with multiple tenants, as shown in figure 10.4. You might have to connect services running on the Anthos platform to services

Multiple VPC on GCP

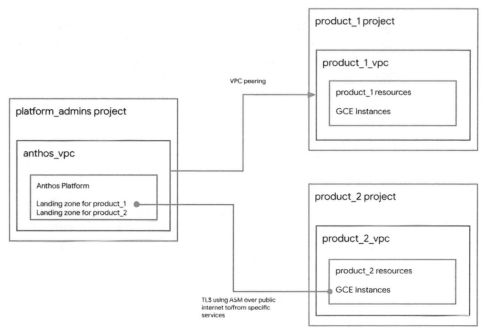

Figure 10.4   Multiple VPC architecture in GCP

outside of the platform. In this design, these services run in different VPCs. For example, services running on Anthos GKE in GCP may be running on a VPC called anthos_vpc and non-Anthos resources may be running on a VPC called product_1_ vpc. You can connect these services in the following ways:

- *IPsec VPN* (http://mng.bz/2a4N)—You can create an IPsec VPN tunnel between two VPCs. IPsec VPN traffic flows over the public internet in a secure manner. Traffic traveling between the two networks is encrypted by one VPN gateway and then decrypted by the other VPN gateway to protect your data as it travels over the internet. Flowing through the public internet may result in performance degradation, however. IPsec VPN can be helpful for large-scale environments.
- *VPC Network Peering* (http://mng.bz/1MvZ)—You can peer multiple VPCs to allow VPC interconnectivity without having to connect VPCs via IPsec VPN. VPC peering offers the same data plane and performance characteristics as a single VPC but with boundaries for administration (security and configurations), resulting in better security and performance for VPC-to-VPC traffic. VPC Network Peering requires coordination between the network admins of the two VPCs. It does not allow for overlapping IP addresses. Also, both VPC owners maintain separate firewalls with desired rules allowing traffic between subnets belonging to the two VPCs.

- *Public internet and secure ingress*—If VPC peering or VPN is not an option, services can communicate over the public internet. In this case, higher-level functionality like Anthos Service Mesh can be used to encrypt traffic between networks using TLS or mTLS (mutual TLS). This method works well if only a small number of services require connectivity across VPCs because this method requires per-service (destination service) configuration as opposed to the previous two methods, which connect two networks at the TCP/IP layer.

ANTHOS ON A SINGLE NON-GCP ENVIRONMENT

You can deploy Anthos in a variety of non-GCP environments, including on-prem data centers, public clouds, and private clouds. At the infrastructure layer, you should consider two primary network designs: single and multiple.

Single flat network

As the name suggests, flat networks are composed of a single logical network space where both Anthos and non-Anthos resources (e.g., VMs running outside of the Anthos platform) reside on the same network. A flat network is a set of subnets connected by routers and switches where each IP endpoint can switch or route to another endpoint given the correct routing (and firewall) rules. A single GCP VPC is an example of a flat network where you may have multiple subnets and routing/firewall rules to allow routing between any two endpoints.

Flat networks are easier to manage compared to multiple disparate networks, but they require more rigor when it comes to security because all entities are on the same logical network space. Firewall rules, network policies, and other functionality can ensure only the allowed entities have network access. Flat networks may also run into scalability problems. Typically, these networks use RFC1918 address space (https://datatracker.ietf.org/doc/html/rfc1918), which provides a finite number of IP addresses (just under 18 million addresses). Typically, a flat logical network requires all resources use the same RFC1918 space. Exceptions to this general rule arise where large organizations may use their own public IP address space for internal addressing. Regardless of the IP address usage, it is important to note that, in a flat network, no two endpoints may have the same IP address.

Multiple networks

Anthos can also be deployed in a multinetwork environment. Anthos GKE clusters can be deployed on single or multiple networks as required. Typically, it is easier to manage network connectivity for applications running on an Anthos platform if Anthos is deployed in the same network. You can deploy the Anthos platform across multiple disconnected networks, though, in some cases, it may be required to connect these multiple networks. You have the following ways to connect applications running on an Anthos platform across multiple networks:

- *VPN/ISP*—You can connect multiple networks together via a VPN, or the chosen ISP may provide this connectivity. These are the typical choices for connecting multiple on-prem data centers.

- *VPC peering*—You can use VPC peering if Anthos is deployed on a public cloud that offers VPC peering functionality.
- *Gateways or mTLS*—Services may be connected securely over the public internet using TLS, mTLS, or a secured API gateway. This functionality exists through service meshes like Anthos Service Mesh (ASM; https://cloud.google.com/service-mesh/docs/overview) or API gateways like Apigee (https://cloud.google.com/apigee). This is done on a per-service level, whereas the first two options are configured at the network layer.

10.1.2 Multi/hybrid cloud deployment

Anthos is a multicloud platform and can be deployed to multiple environments, for example, public/private clouds and on-prem data centers. Managing networking across multiple environments is challenging because each environment is unique, and managing resources differs depending on the provider. For instance, the way a GCP VPC is provisioned is different from an AWS VPC or a data center network. Anthos provides a common interface across multiple environments. You can deploy the Anthos platform to multiple environments in the following three ways:

- *Multicloud deployment*—You can deploy the Anthos platform to multiple public cloud environments, for example, GCP and one or more public clouds like AWS and Azure.
- *Hybrid cloud deployment*—You can deploy the Anthos platform to GCP and one or more on-prem data centers.
- *Multi and hybrid cloud deployment*—This deployment is a combination of the two deployments previously mentioned. For example, you can deploy the Anthos platform to GCP, to one or more on-prem data centers, and to one or more non-GCP public clouds.

MULTI/HYBRID NETWORKING

When you deploy Anthos across multiple infrastructure environments, these environments must have network connectivity to GCP. Three network connectivity options are available to connect multiple infrastructure environments: Cloud Interconnect, Cloud VPN, and public internet.

Cloud Interconnect

Cloud Interconnect (http://mng.bz/Pxe2) extends an on-prem network to Google's network through a highly available, low-latency connection. You can use Dedicated Interconnect to connect directly to Google or use Partner Interconnect to connect to Google through a supported service provider. Dedicated Interconnect provides direct physical connections between your on-prem network and Google's network. Dedicated Interconnect enables you to transfer large amounts of data between networks, which can be more cost effective than purchasing additional bandwidth over the public internet.

For Dedicated Interconnect, you provision a Dedicated Interconnect connection between the Google network and your own router in a common location (see http://mng.bz/JlQp). Figure 10.5 shows a single Dedicated Interconnect connection between a VPC network and your on-prem network.

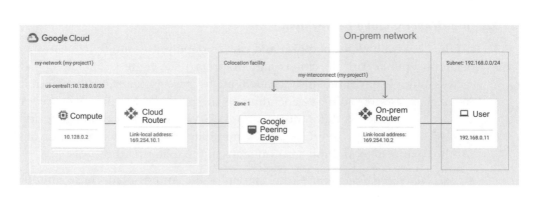

Figure 10.5   Dedicated Interconnect between GCP and an on-prem data center

For this basic setup, a Dedicated Interconnect connection is provisioned between the Google network and the on-prem router in a common colocation facility.

When you create a VLAN attachment (http://mng.bz/wPR7), you associate it with a Cloud Router (http://mng.bz/qdlK). This Cloud Router creates a BPG session for the VLAN attachment and its corresponding on-prem peer router. The Cloud Router receives the routes that your on-prem router advertises. These routes are added as custom dynamic routes in your VPC network. The Cloud Router also advertises routes for Google Cloud resources to the on-prem peer router.

Depending on your availability needs, you can configure Dedicated Interconnect to support mission-critical services or applications that can tolerate some downtime. To achieve a specific level of reliability, Google offers the following two prescriptive configurations:

- Achieve 99.99% (52.60 minutes per year) availability for Dedicated Interconnect (http://mng.bz/71ax) (recommended)
- Achieve 99.9% availability for Dedicated Interconnect (http://mng.bz/516q)

Cloud Interconnect is the most robust and secure option to connect GCP and non-GCP environments and is the recommended option to connect GCP and one or more on-prem data centers.

Cloud VPN

Cloud VPN (http://mng.bz/mJPn) securely connects your peer network to your VPC network through an IPSsec VPN connection. Traffic traveling between the two networks is encrypted by one VPN gateway, and then decrypted by the other VPN gateway, which protects your data as it travels over the internet. Google Cloud offers high-availability VPN, which provides higher uptime and throughput with an additional/redundant VPN connection at a higher cost.

Each Cloud VPN tunnel can support up to 3 gigabits per second total for ingress and egress. You can use multiple Cloud VPN tunnels to increase your ingress and egress bandwidth.

You can use Cloud VPN between GCP and on-prem data centers as well as between GCP and other public cloud vendors. This is the easiest option to set up, and you can be running without any delays. Cloud VPN can also be used in conjunction with Cloud Interconnect as a secondary connectivity option.

Public internet

Applications running on the Anthos platform on multiple environments can be connected over the public internet without using Cloud Interconnect or VPN. Applications running on the platform connect over the public internet using TLS/mTLS.

Anthos Service Mesh (ASM) is part of the Anthos platform. ASM uses client-side proxies injected into each Pod to connect services. One of the security features of these proxies is to secure connectivity using mTLS. Using a common root certificate authority on multiple environments, the sidecar proxies can connect using a secure mTLS connection via gateways (e.g., ingress or east-west gateways) across the public internet. For details on Anthos Service Mesh, please refer to chapter 4.

If many services require connectivity between environments, then this option might not be operationally scalable. In such a case, it is recommended you use one of the network connectivity options mentioned earlier.

Disconnected environments

In some situations, you may be required to have environments that are completely disconnected from each other. Anthos platform supports disconnected environments. The disconnected environments must have network connectivity to GCP so that the platform (i.e., Anthos clusters) can be registered to a GCP project. This is required for control plane traffic only. For certain Anthos functionalities, registering a cluster is required. For example, to use multicluster ingress on Anthos clusters, all participating clusters must be registered to GCP. The services across disconnected environments will not be able to communicate to each other.

10.2 *Anthos GKE networking*

Anthos GKE clusters can be deployed to a variety of environments, for example, on GCP, on VMware in an on-prem data center, on bare metal servers, and on AWS. In addition to the supported Anthos clusters, you can also register any conformant Kubernetes cluster to the Anthos platform. For example, you can register EKS clusters running in AWS and AKS clusters running in Azure to the Anthos platform. Currently, the following six types of Anthos clusters are available:

- Anthos clusters on GCP (GKE)
- Anthos clusters on VMware (GKE on-prem)
- Anthos clusters on bare metal
- Anthos clusters on AWS (GKE on AWS)
- Anthos clusters on Azure (GKE on Azure)
- Anthos attached clusters (conformant Kubernetes clusters)

10.2.1 *Anthos cluster networking*

CLUSTER IP ADDRESSING

All Anthos GKE clusters require the following three IP subnets:

- Node and API server IP addresses
- Pod IP addresses
- Services or ClusterIP addresses

Node and API server IP addresses are LAN (for on-prem data centers) or VPC (for public clouds) IP addresses. Each node and API server gets a single IP address. Depending on the number of nodes/API servers required, ensure you have the required number of IP addresses.

Pod IP addresses are assigned to every Pod in an Anthos GKE cluster. Each node in an Anthos cluster is assigned a unique IP address range, which is used to assign Pod IP addresses (running inside that node). If the Pod moves from one node to another, its IP address changes based on the IP address range of the new node. The API server takes a large IP range, often called the Pod CIDR IP range, for example a /14 or a /16 (you can learn about IP subnets at http://mng.bz/610G). The server then equally divides this range into smaller IP ranges and assigns a unique range to each node. You define the desired number of Pods per node, which is used by the API server to slice the large subnet into smaller subnets per node. For example, if you want 30 Pods per node, each node requires a minimum of a /27. Your Pod IP range must be large enough to account for N subnets with 32 addresses each, where N is the maximum number of nodes in the cluster.

Pod IP addresses are routable within the cluster. They may or may not be routable from outside of the cluster, depending on the type and implementation of the cluster. This is discussed in detail in the next section.

Service or ClusterIP addresses are assigned to every Kubernetes Service. Unlike Pod IP addresses, which may change as Pods move between nodes, ClusterIP addresses remain static and act as a load-balancing virtual IP address (VIP) to multiple Pods representing a single Kubernetes Service. As the name suggests, service IPs or ClusterIPs are locally significant to the cluster and cannot be accessed from outside of the cluster. Services inside the cluster can access services using ClusterIPs.

CLUSTER NETWORKING DATA PLANE

Anthos GKE clusters provide two options for networking data planes.

GKE Dataplane v1: kube-proxy and Calico

Kubernetes manages connectivity among Pods and Services using the kube-proxy component. This is deployed as a static Pod on each node by default. Any GKE cluster running version 1.16 or later has a kube-proxy deployed as a DaemonSet.

kube-proxy is not an in-line proxy but an egress-based load-balancing controller. It watches the Kubernetes API server and continually maps the ClusterIP to healthy Pods by adding and removing destination NAT rules to the node's iptables subsystem. When a container running in a Pod sends traffic to a Service's ClusterIP, the node selects a Pod at random and routes the traffic to that Pod.

When you configure a Service, you can optionally remap its listening port by defining values for `port` and `targetPort`. The `port` is where clients reach the application. The `targetPort` is the port where the application is listening for traffic within the Pod. kube-proxy manages this port remapping by adding and removing iptables rules on the node.

In GKE Dataplane v1, Kubernetes NetworkPolicies are implemented using the Calico component. Calico is an open source networking and network security solution for containers, virtual machines, and native host–based workloads. This implementation uses components that rely heavily on iptables functionality in the Linux kernel. Dataplane v2 addresses and resolves some of these problems.

GKE Dataplane v2: eBPF and Cilium

GKE Dataplane v2, shown in figure 10.6, is an opinionated data plane that harnesses the power of extended Berkeley Packet Filter (eBPF) and Cilium, an open source project that makes the Linux kernel Kubernetes aware using eBPF.

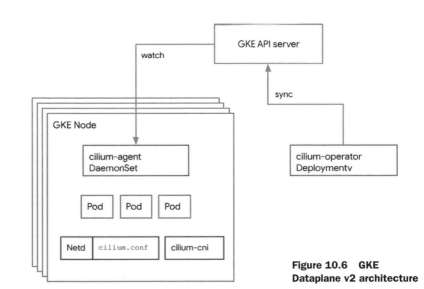

Figure 10.6   GKE Dataplane v2 architecture

Dataplane V2 addresses the observability, scalability, and functional requirements by providing a programmable data path. eBPF, a new Linux networking paradigm, exposes programmable hooks to the network stack inside the Linux kernel. The ability to enrich the kernel with user-space information—without jumping back and forth between user and kernel spaces—enables context-aware operations on network packets at high speeds.

The new data plane adds two new cluster components: the `cilium-agent` DaemonSet that programs the eBPF data path and the `cilium-operator` Deployment that manages the Cilium-internal CRDs and helps the `cilium-agent` avoid watching every Pod.

The data plane also eliminates both Calico cluster components—the `calico-node` DaemonSet and the `calico-typha` Deployment. These components provide NetworkPolicy enforcement, which is provided by the `cilium-agent` DaemonSet.

The data plane also removes the kube-proxy static Pod from the nodes. kube-proxy provides service resolution functionality to the cluster, which is also provided by the `cilium-agent`.

Dataplane V2 offers networking programmability and scalability to Anthos clusters, as shown in figure 10.7. Enterprises use Kubernetes NetworkPolicies to declare how Pods can communicate with one another. However, there previously was no scalable way to troubleshoot and audit the behavior of these policies. With eBPF in GKE, you can now enforce real-time policies as well as correlate policy actions (allow/deny) to Pod, namespace, and policy names at a line rate with minimal impact on the node's CPU and memory resources. As packets come into the VM, specialized eBPF programs can be installed in the kernel to decide how to route the packet. Unlike iptables, eBPF programs have access to Kubernetes-specific metadata, including network policy information. This way, they can not only allow or deny the packet, they can also report annotated actions back to the user space. These events make it possible for you to generate network policy logs.

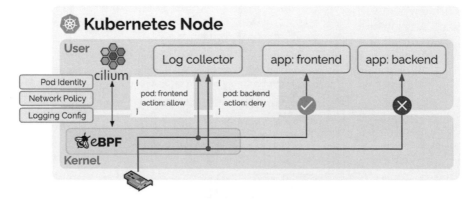

Figure 10.7   GKE Dataplane v2: Network policy flow logging

Table 10.1 shows a comparison of networking features between GKE Dataplane v1 and v2.

Table 10.1

Network feature	Existing	New Dataplane
ClusterIP service resolution	kube-proxy using iptables	`cilium-agent` using eBPF on sockets
NodePort service resolution	kube-proxy using iptables	`cilium-agent` using eBPF on eth0 TC hooks
Load balancer service resolution	kube-proxy using iptables redirecting to service chain	`cilium-agent` using eBPF on eth0 TC hooks (same hook as previously)
Network policy enforcement	Calico using iptables	`cilium-agent` using eBPF on socket as well as eth0 TC hooks

Depending on the type and implementation of the Anthos cluster, networking design and requirements vary. In the next section, we look at each type of Anthos cluster in terms of networking requirements and best practices.

ANTHOS GKE ON GCP

An Anthos GKE cluster runs on GCP and uses GCP VPC functionality for Kubernetes networking. Two types of implementations of Anthos GKE on GCP are available: VPC-native clusters and routes-based clusters.

VPC-native clusters

This is the default and recommended implementation for Anthos GKE on GCP clusters. A cluster that uses alias IP address ranges is called a VPC-native cluster. VPC-native clusters use real VPC IP addresses for Pod IP ranges. This option allows Pod-to-Pod communication within a single cluster as well as across multiple (VPC-native) clusters in the same VPC. It also allows direct Pod connectivity to any routable VPC entity, for example, GCE instances. VPC-native clusters use secondary IP address ranges for Pod IP and Service IP ranges. VPC-native clusters offer the following benefits:

- Pod IP addresses are natively routable within the cluster's VPC network and other VPC networks connected to it by VPC Network Peering.
- Pod IP addresses are reserved in the VPC network before the Pods are created in your cluster. This prevents conflict with other resources in the VPC network and allows you to better plan IP address allocations.
- Pod IP address ranges do not depend on custom static routes. They do not consume the system-generated and custom static routes quota. Instead, automatically generated subnet routes handle routing for VPC-native clusters.
- You can create firewall rules that apply to just Pod IP address ranges instead of any IP address on the cluster's nodes.
- Pod IP address ranges, and subnet secondary IP address ranges in general, are accessible from on-prem networks connected with Cloud VPN or Cloud Interconnect using Cloud Routers.

Routes-based clusters

A cluster that uses Google Cloud Routes is called a routes-based cluster. Google Cloud routes define the paths that network traffic takes from a VM instance to other destinations. The Pod IP address ranges in a routes-based cluster are not VPC IP addresses and, therefore, are not natively routable inside the VPC. Cloud Routes are created for each Pod IP address range so that Pods within a cluster can communicate with other Pods running on different nodes. Routes-based clusters do not provide Pod-to-Pod intercluster connectivity for multiple Anthos GKE clusters. To create a routes-based cluster, you must explicitly turn off the VPC-native option.

In a routes-based cluster, each node is allocated a /24 range of IP addresses for Pods. With a /24 range, you have 256 addresses, but the maximum number of Pods per node is 110. By having approximately twice as many available IP addresses as possible Pods, Kubernetes can mitigate IP address reuse as Pods are added to and removed from a node.

A routes-based cluster has a range of IP addresses that are used for Pods and Services. Even though the range is used for both Pods and Services, it is called the *Pod address range*. The last /20 of the Pod address range is used for Services. A /20 range has 4,096 addresses that are used for Services as well as Pods.

In command output, the Pod address range is called clusterIpv4Cidr, and the range of addresses used for Services is called servicesIpv4Cidr. For example, the output of `gcloud container clusters describe` includes output like this:

```
clusterIpv4Cidr: 10.96.0.0/16
...
servicesIpv4Cidr: 10.96.240.0/20
```

For GKE version 1.7 and later, the Pod address range can be from any RFC1918 block: 10.0.0.0/8, 172.16.0.0/12, or 192.168.0.0/16. For earlier versions, the Pod address range must be from 10.0.0.0/8.

The maximum number of nodes, Pods, and Services for a given GKE cluster is determined by the size of the cluster subnet and the size of the Pod address range. You cannot change the Pod address range size after you create a cluster. When you create a cluster, ensure that you choose a Pod address range large enough to accommodate the cluster's anticipated growth.

Anthos GKE cluster IP allocation

Kubernetes uses the following IP ranges to assign IP addresses to nodes, Pods, and Services:

- *Node IP*—In Anthos GKE clusters, a node is a GCE instance. Each node has an IP address assigned from the cluster's VPC network. This node IP provides connectivity from control components like kube-proxy and the kubelet to the Kubernetes API server. This IP is the node's connection to the rest of the cluster.
- *Pod IP CIDR*—Each node has a pool of IP addresses that GKE assigns to Pods running on that node (a /24 CIDR block by default). You can optionally specify

the range of IPs when you create the cluster. The Flexible Pod CIDR range feature allows you to reduce the size of the range for Pod IPs for nodes in a given node pool. Each Pod has a single IP address assigned from the Pod CIDR range of its node. This IP address is shared by all containers running within the Pod and connects them to other Pods running in the cluster. The maximum number of Pods you can run on a node is equal to half of the Pod IP CIDR range. For example, you can run a maximum of 110 Pods on a node with a /24 range—not 256 as you might expect. This number of Pods provides a buffer so that Pods don't become unschedulable due to a transient lack of IP addresses in the Pod IP range for a given node. For ranges smaller than /24, half as many Pods can be scheduled as IP addresses in the range.

- *Service IP*—Each Service has an IP address, called the ClusterIP, assigned from the cluster's VPC network. You can optionally customize the VPC network when you create the cluster. In Kubernetes, you can assign arbitrary key-value pairs called *labels* to any Kubernetes resource. Kubernetes uses labels to group multiple related Pods into a logical unit called a Service. A Service has a stable IP address and ports and provides load balancing among the set of Pods whose labels match all the labels you define in the label selector when you create the Service.

Egress traffic and controls

For VPC-native clusters, traffic egressing a Pod is routed using normal VPC routing functionality. Pod IP addresses are preserved in the TCP header as the source IP address. You must create the appropriate firewall rules to allow traffic between Pods and other VPC resources. You can also use NetworkPolicy to further control the flow of traffic between Pods within a cluster, as well as traffic egressing Pods. These policies are enforced by the GKE Dataplane implementation explained in the previous section. At the Service layer, you can use egress policy through ASM to control what traffic exits the clusters. In this case, an Envoy proxy called the istio-egressgateway exists at the perimeter of the service mesh through which all egress traffic flows. For routes-based clusters, all Pod egress traffic goes through NAT via the node IP address.

Load balancers and ingress

GKE provides the following three types of load balancers to control access and to spread incoming traffic across your cluster as evenly as possible. You can configure one Service to use multiple types of load balancers simultaneously:

- External load balancers manage traffic coming from outside the cluster and outside your Google Cloud VPC network. They use forwarding rules associated with the Google Cloud network to route traffic to a Kubernetes node.
- Internal load balancers manage traffic coming from within the same VPC network. Like external load balancers, they use forwarding rules associated with the Google Cloud network to route traffic to a Kubernetes node.

- HTTP(S) load balancers are specialized external load balancers used for HTTP(S) traffic. They use an Ingress resource rather than a forwarding rule to route traffic to a Kubernetes node.

The external and internal load balancers described here are TCP/L4 load balancers. If your Service needs to be reachable from outside the cluster and outside your VPC network, you can configure your Service as a load balancer by setting the Service's type field to Loadbalancer. GKE then provisions a network load balancer in front of the Service. The network load balancer is aware of all nodes in your cluster and configures your VPC network's firewall rules to allow connections to the Service from outside the VPC network, using the Service's external IP address. You can assign a static external IP address to the Service.

For traffic that needs to reach your cluster from within the same VPC network, you can configure your Service to provision an internal load balancer. The internal load balancer chooses an IP address from your cluster's VPC subnet instead of an external IP address. Applications or services within the VPC network can use this IP address to communicate with Services inside the cluster. An example of a Service manifest that creates an internal load balancer follows. You can configure an external load balancer in the same way by removing the annotation (which creates an internal load balancer):

```
apiVersion: v1
kind: Service
metadata:
  name: ilb-service
  annotations:
    cloud.google.com/load-balancer-type: "Internal"      ⬅  The annotation
  labels:                                                     creates an internal
    app: hello                                                Google load balancer.
spec:
  type: LoadBalancer      ⬅  Creates a
  selector:                  Google load
    app: hello              balancer
  ports:
  - port: 80
    targetPort: 8080
    protocol: TCP
```

Many applications, such as RESTful web service APIs, communicate using HTTP(S). You can allow clients external to your VPC network to access this type of application using a Kubernetes Ingress resource. An Ingress resource allows you to map hostnames and URL paths to Services within the cluster. An Ingress resource is associated with one or more Service objects, each of which is associated with a set of Pods. When you create an Ingress resource, the GKE Ingress controller creates a Google Cloud HTTP(S) load balancer and configures it according to the information in the Ingress and its associated Services. To use Ingress, you must have the HTTP load balancing add-on enabled. GKE clusters have HTTP load balancing enabled by default. GKE Ingress resources come in the following two types:

- Ingress for external HTTP(S) load balancer deploys the Google Cloud external HTTP(S) load balancer. This internet-facing load balancer is deployed globally across Google's edge network as a managed and scalable pool of load-balancing resources.
- Ingress for Internal HTTP(S) load balancing deploys the Google Cloud internal HTTP(S) load balancer. This internal HTTP(S) load balancer is powered by Envoy proxy systems outside of your GKE cluster, but within your VPC network.

HTTP(S) load balancing, configured by Ingress, includes the following features:

- Flexible configuration for Services. An Ingress defines how traffic reaches your Services and how the traffic is routed to your application. In addition, an Ingress can provide a single IP address for multiple Services in your cluster.
- Integration with Google Cloud network services.
- Support for multiple TLS certificates. An Ingress can specify the use of multiple TLS certificates for request termination.

When you create the Ingress resource, GKE provisions an HTTP(S) load balancer in the Google Cloud project according to the rules in the manifest and the associated Service manifests. The load balancer sends a request to a node's IP address at the NodePort. After the request reaches the node, the chosen GKE Dataplane routes the traffic to the appropriate Pod (for the desired Service). For Dataplane v1, the node uses its iptables NAT table to choose a Pod. kube-proxy manages the iptables rules on the node. For Dataplane v2, GKE provides this functionality using eBPF and Cilium agents.

In the following example, the Ingress definition routes traffic for demo.example.com to a Service named frontend on port 80, and demo-backend.example.com to a Service named users on port 8080:

```
apiVersion: networking.k8s.io/v1beta1
kind: Ingress
metadata:
  name: demo
spec:
  rules:
  - host: demo.example.com
    http:
      paths:
      - backend:
          serviceName: frontend
          servicePort: 80
  - host: demo-backend.example.com
    http:
      paths:
      - backend:
          serviceName: users
          servicePort: 8080
```

Requests to host demo.example.com are forwarded to the Service frontend on port 80.

Requests to host demo-backend.example.com are forwarded to the Service users on port 8080.

Container-native load balancing

Container-native load balancing is the practice of load balancing directly to Pod endpoints in GKE using network endpoint groups (NEGs). With Ingress, Service-bound traffic is sent from the HTTP load balancer to any of the node IPs on the node port. After the request reaches the node, the GKE Dataplane routes the traffic to the desired Pod, a process that results in extra hops. In some cases, the Pod may not even be running on the node, and thus, the node sends the request to the node where the desired Pod is running. Additional hops add latency and make the traffic path more complex.

With NEGs, traffic is load balanced from the load balancer directly to the Pod IP, as opposed to traversing the nodes. In addition, Pod readiness gates are implemented to determine the health of Pods from the perspective of the load balancer and not just the Kubernetes in-cluster health probes. This improves overall traffic stability by making the load balancer infrastructure aware of life cycle events such as Pod startup, Pod loss, or VM loss. These capabilities resolve the previously described limitations and result in more performant and stable networking.

Container-native load balancing is enabled by default for Services when all the following conditions are true:

- For Services created in GKE clusters 1.17.6-gke.7 and up
- Using VPC-native clusters
- Not using a shared VPC
- Not using GKE network policy

For clusters where NEGs are not the default, it is still strongly recommended to use container-native load balancing, but it must be enabled explicitly on a per-Service basis. The annotation should be applied to Services in the following manner:

```
kind: Service
...
  annotations:
    cloud.google.com/neg: `{"ingress": true}'
...
```

The annotation creates a network endpoint group for Pods in the service.

In the Service manifest, you must use `type: NodePort` unless you're using container-native load balancing. If you're using container-native load balancing, use `type: ClusterIP`.

Shared VPC considerations and best practices

The GKE Ingress controllers use a Google Cloud service account to deploy and manage Google Cloud resources. When a GKE cluster resides in a service project of a shared VPC, this service account may not have the rights to manage network resources owned by the host project. The Ingress controller actively manages firewall rules to provide access between load balancers and Pods as well as between centralized health checkers and Pods. You can manage this in the following ways:

- *Manual firewall rule provisioning*—If your security policies allow firewall management only from the host project, you can provision these firewall rules manually.

When deploying Ingress in a shared VPC, the Ingress resource event provides the specific firewall rule you need to provide access. To manually provision a firewall rule, view the Ingress resource using the `describe` command:

```
kubectl describe ingress INGRESS_NAME
```

The output of this command, shown next, should have the required firewall rule that can be implemented in the host network project:

```
Events:
Type      Reason  Age                       From                       Message
----      ------  ----                      ----                       -------
Normal    Sync    9m34s (x237 over 38h)     loadbalancer-controller
Firewall change required by network admin: `gcloud compute firewall-
rules update k8s-fw-l7--6048d433d4280f11 --description "GCE L7 firewall
rule" --allow tcp:30000-32767,tcp:8080 --source-ranges
130.211.0.0/22,209.85.152.0/22,209.85.204.0/22,35.191.0.0/16 --target-
tags gke-l7-ilb-test-b3a7e0e5-node --project <project>`
```

- *Automatic firewall rule provisioning*—An automated approach is to provide the GKE Ingress controller service account the permissions to update firewall rules. You do this by creating a custom IAM role, providing the ability to manage firewall rules in the host network project and then granting this role to the GKE Ingress service account.

  First, create a custom IAM role with the required permissions:

```
gcloud iam roles create ROLE_NAME \
    --project PROJECT_ID \
    --title ROLE_TITLE \
    --description ROLE_DESCRIPTION \
    --permissions=compute.networks.updatePolicy, compute.firewalls.*\
    --stage GA
```

Then, grant the custom role to the GKE Ingress controller service account:

```
gcloud projects add-iam-policy-binding my-project \
    --member=user:SERVICE_ACCOUNT \
    --role=roles/gke-ingress-fw-management
```

Multicluster Ingress

In some cases, you have to run the same service on multiple GKE clusters. Many factors drive multicluster topologies, including close user proximity for apps, cluster and regional high availability, security and organizational separation, cluster migration, and data locality. Multicluster Ingress (MCI), shown in figure 10.8, is a cloud-hosted multicluster Ingress controller for Anthos GKE clusters. It's a Google-hosted service that supports deploying shared load-balancing resources across clusters and across regions. Multicluster Ingress is designed to meet the load-balancing needs of multicluster, multiregional environments. It's a controller for the external HTTP(S) load balancer to provide Ingress for traffic coming from the internet across one or more clusters. Multicluster Ingress's multicluster support satisfies many use cases, including the following:

- A single, consistent VIP for an app, independent of where the app is deployed globally
- Multiregional, multicluster availability through health checking and traffic failover
- Proximity-based routing through public Anycast VIPs for low client latency
- Transparent cluster migration for upgrades or cluster rebuilds

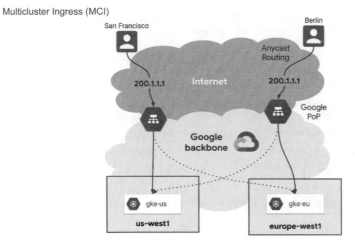

Figure 10.8   Multicluster Ingress to multiple GKE clusters in GCP

Multicluster Ingress is an Ingress controller that programs the external HTTP(S) load balancer using NEGs. When you create a `MultiClusterIngress` resource, GKE deploys the Compute Engine load balancer resources and configures the appropriate Pods across clusters as backends. The NEGs are used to track Pod endpoints dynamically, so the Google load balancer has the right set of healthy backends.

Multicluster Ingress uses a centralized Kubernetes API server to deploy Ingress across multiple clusters. This centralized API server is called the *config cluster*. Any GKE cluster can act as the config cluster. The config cluster uses two custom resource types: `MultiClusterIngress` and `MultiClusterService`. By deploying these resources on the config cluster, the Anthos Ingress controller deploys load balancers across multiple clusters. The following concepts and components make up Multicluster Ingress:

- *Anthos Ingress controller*—A globally distributed control plane that runs as a service outside of your clusters. This allows the life cycle and operations of the controller to be independent of GKE clusters.

- *Config cluster*—A chosen GKE cluster running on Google Cloud where the `MultiClusterIngress` and `MultiClusterService` resources are deployed. This is a centralized point of control for these multicluster resources, which exist in and are accessible from a single logical API to retain consistency across all clusters. The Ingress controller watches the config cluster and reconciles the load-balancing infrastructure.
- *Fleet*—A concept that groups clusters and infrastructure, manages resources, and keeps a consistent policy across them (for more details about fleets, see chapter 2). MCI uses the concept of fleets for how Ingress is applied across different clusters. Clusters that you register to a fleet become visible to MCI, so they can be used as backends for Ingress. Fleets possess a characteristic known as *namespace sameness*, which assumes that resources with identical names and the same namespace across clusters are instances of the same resource. In effect, this means that Pods in the `ns1` namespace with the label `app: foo` across different clusters are all considered part of the same pool of application backends from the perspective of Multicluster Ingress. Figure 10.9 shows an example of two services, `foo` and `bar`, running on two clusters being load balanced by MCI.

Multicluster Ingress (MCI): Environ and namespace sameness

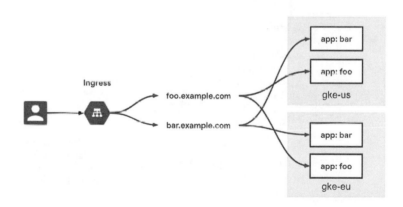

Figure 10.9   Multicluster Ingress: Fleet and namespace sameness

- *Member cluster*—Clusters registered to a fleet are called member clusters. Member clusters in the fleet comprise the full scope of backends that MCI is aware of.

After the config cluster has been configured, you create the two custom resources, `MultiClusterIngress` and `MultiClusterService`, for your multicluster Service. Note that the resource names are comparatively similar to `Service` and `Ingress`, required for Ingress in a single cluster. Examples of these resources deployed to the config cluster follow:

```
# MulticlusterService with cluster selector
apiVersion: networking.gke.io/v1beta1
kind: MultiClusterService
metadata:
  name: foo
  namespace: blue
spec:
  template:
    spec:
      selector:
        app: foo
      ports:
      - name: web
        protocol: TCP
        port: 80
        targetPort: 80
  clusters:
  - link: "europe-west1-c/gke-eu"
  - link: "asia-northeast1-a/gke-asia-1"
```

The MultiClusterService spec looks similar to the Service spec, with a clusters section added to define Service in multiple clusters.

The GKE Cluster URI links for Service running in multiple clusters

```
# MulticlusterIngress
apiVersion: networkin.g.gke.io/v1alpha1
kind: MultiClusterIngress
metadata:
  name: foobar-ingress
  namespace: blue
spec:
  template:
    spec:
      backend:
        serviceName: default-backend
        servicePort: 80
      rules:
      - host: foo.example.com
        backend:
          serviceName: foo
          servicePort: 80
      - host: bar.example.com
        backend:
          serviceName: bar
          servicePort: 80
```

The MultiClusterIngress spec is similar to the Ingress spec, except that it points to a MultiClusterService (instead of a Service).

Note that `MulticlusterService` includes a cluster selector stanza at the bottom. Removing this sends Ingress traffic to all member clusters. Adding a cluster selector may be useful if you want to remove MCI traffic from a specific cluster (or clusters)—for example, if you are performing upgrades or maintenance to a cluster. If the clusters stanza is present in the `MulticlusterService` resource, Ingress traffic is sent to only the clusters available in the list. Clusters are explicitly referenced by <region | zone>/<name>. Member clusters within the same fleet and region should have unique names so that there are no naming collisions. Like a Service, `MulticlusterService` is a selector for Pods, but it is also capable of selecting labels and clusters. The pool of clusters that it selects across are called member clusters, and these are all the clusters registered to the fleet. This `MulticlusterService` deploys a derived Service in all member clusters with the selector app: foo. If app: foo Pods exist in that cluster, then those Pod IPs will be added as backends for the `MulticlusterService`.

ANTHOS ON-PREM (ON VMWARE)

Anthos on-prem clusters on VMware automatically create an island mode configuration in which Pods can directly talk to each other within a cluster but cannot be reached from outside the cluster. This configuration forms an "island" within the network that is not connected to the external network. Clusters form a full node-to-node mesh across the cluster nodes, allowing a Pod to reach other Pods within the cluster directly.

Networking requirements

Anthos on-prem clusters are installed using an admin workstation VM, which contains all the tools and configurations required to deploy Anthos on-prem clusters. The admin workstation VM deploys an admin cluster. The admin cluster deploys one or more user clusters. Your applications run on user clusters. The admin cluster manages the deployment and life cycle of multiple user clusters. You do not run your applications on the admin cluster. In your initial installation of Anthos on-prem, you create the following virtual machines (VMs):

- One VM for an admin workstation
- Four VMs for an admin cluster
- Three VMs for a user cluster (you can create additional user clusters as well as larger user clusters if needed)

In your vSphere environment, you must have a network that can support the creation of these VMs. Your network must also be able to support a vCenter Server and a load balancer. Your network needs to support outbound traffic to the internet so that your admin workstation and your cluster nodes can fetch GKE on-prem components and call certain Google services. If you want external clients to call services in your GKE on-prem clusters, your network must support inbound traffic from the internet. IP address architecture and allocation is discussed in the next section.

Anthos on-prem cluster IP allocation

The following IP addresses are required for Anthos on-prem on a VMware cluster:

- *Node IP*—Dynamic Host Configuration Protocol (DHCP) or statically assigned IP addresses for the nodes (virtual machines or VMs). Must be routable within the data center. You can manually assign static IPs. Node IP addressing depends on the implementation of a load balancer in the Anthos on-prem cluster. If the cluster is configured with integrated mode load balancing or bundled mode load balancing, you can use DHCP or statically assigned IP addresses for the nodes. If the cluster is configured with manual mode load balancing, you must use static IP addresses for nodes. In this case, ensure enough IP addresses are set aside to account for cluster growth. Load-balancing modes are discussed in detail in the next section.

- *Pod IP CIDR*—Non-routable CIDR block for all Pods in the cluster. From this range, smaller /24 ranges are assigned per node. If you need an *N* node cluster, ensure this block is large enough to support *N* x /24 blocks.

- *Services IP*—In island mode, like Pod CIDR block, so this is used only within the cluster and is any private CIDR block that does not overlap with the nodes, VIPs, or Pod CIDR block. You can share the same block among multiple clusters. The size of the block determines the number of services. In addition to your Services, a block of Service IP addresses is used for cluster control plane Services. One Service IP is needed for the Ingress service, and 10 or more IPs for Kubernetes services like cluster DNS.

Egress traffic and controls

All egress traffic from the Pod to targets outside the cluster is run through NAT by the node IP. You can use NetworkPolicy to further control the flow of traffic between Pods within a cluster as well as traffic egressing Pods. These policies are enforced by Calico running inside each cluster. At the Service layer, you can use `EgressPolicy` through ASM to control what traffic exits the clusters. In this case, an Envoy proxy called the `istio-egressgateway` exists at the perimeter of the service mesh through which all egress traffic flows.

Load balancers

Anthos on-prem clusters provide two ways to access Services from outside of the cluster: load balancers and Ingress. This section addresses load balancers and different modes of implementations.

Anthos on-prem clusters can run in one of three load-balancing modes: integrated, manual, or bundled:

- *Integrated mode*—With integrated mode, Anthos on-prem uses an F5 BIG-IP load balancer. The customer provides the F5 BIG-IP load balancer with the appropriate licensing. You need to have a user role with sufficient permissions to set up and manage the F5 load balancer. Either the administrator role or the resource administrator role is sufficient. For more information, see http://mng.bz/ oJnN. You set aside multiple VIP addresses to be used for Services, which are configured to be type `Loadbalancer`. Each Service requires one VIP. The number of VIPs required depends on the number of Services of type `Loadbalancer`. You specify these VIPs in your cluster configuration file, and Anthos on-prem automatically configures the F5 BIG-IP load balancer to use the VIPs.

    The advantages of integrated mode are you get to use an enterprise-grade load balancer and its configuration is mostly automated. This mode is also opinionated in that it requires an F5 load balancer, which may incur additional licensing and support cost.

- *Manual mode*—With manual mode, Anthos on-prem uses a load balancer of your choice. Manual load-balancing mode requires additional configuration compared to integrated mode. You need to manually configure the VIPs to be used for Services. With manual load balancing, you cannot run Services of type `Loadbalancer`. Instead, you can create Services of type `NodePort` and manually configure your load balancer to use them as backends. You must specify the `NodePort` values to be used for these Services. You can choose values in the 30000–32767 range. For more information, see http://mng.bz/nJov.

  The advantage of manual mode is you get absolute freedom in terms of what load balancer you choose. On the other hand, the configuration is manual, which may result in increased operational overhead.

- *Bundled mode*—In bundled load-balancing mode, Anthos on-prem provides and manages the load balancer. Unlike integrated mode, no license is required for a load balancer, and the amount of setup that you must do is minimal. The bundled load balancer that GKE on-prem provides is the Seesaw load balancer (https://github.com/google/seesaw). Seesaw load balancers run as VMs inside VMware. We recommend that you use vSphere 6.7+ and Virtual Distributed Switch 6.6+ for bundled load-balancing mode. You can run Seesaw load balancer in high availability (HA) and non-HA mode. In HA mode, two Seesaw VMs are configured. In non-HA mode, a single Seesaw VM is configured.

  The advantage of bundled mode is a single team can oversee both cluster creation and load balancer configuration. For example, a cluster administration team would not have to rely on a separate networking team to acquire, run, and configure the load balancer ahead of time. Another advantage is that the configuration is completely automated. Anthos on-prem configures the Service VIPs automatically on the load balancer.

Anthos on VMware clusters can run Services of type `Loadbalancer` as long as a `loadBalancerIP` field is configured in the Service's specification. In the `loadBalancerIP` field, you need to provide the VIP that you want to use. This will be configured on F5, pointing to the NodePorts of the Service.

An example of a Service manifest follows. You can access a Service running inside an Anthos on-prem cluster called `frontend` via the `SERVICE VIP`:

```
apiVersion: v1
kind: Service
metadata:
  labels:
    app: guestbook
  name: frontend
spec:
  ports:
  - port: 80
    protocol: TCP
    targetPort: 80
```

```
selector:
  app: guestbook
type: LoadBalancer
loadBalancerIP: [SERVICE VIP]  ◁────
```

The load balancer IP address is defined in the Service spec.

In addition to Service VIPs, a control plane VIP for the Kubernetes API server is required by the load balancer. And last, an Ingress controller runs inside each Anthos on-prem cluster. The Ingress controller Service also has a VIP called the Ingress VIP. Services exposed via Ingress use the Ingress VIP to access Kubernetes Services.

The Anthos on-prem high-level load-balancing architecture is shown in figure 10.10.

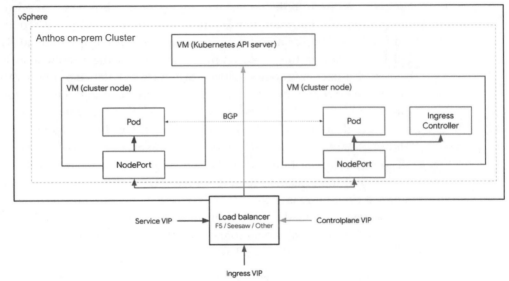

Figure 10.10   Anthos on-prem: load balancer network architecture

Table 10.2 summarizes what you must do to prepare for load balancing in various modes.

Table 10.2   How to prepare for load balancing

	Integrated/bundled mode	Manual mode
Choose VIPs before you create your clusters.	Yes	Yes
Choose node IP addresses before you create your clusters.	No, if using DHCP Yes, if using static IP addresses	Yes
Choose nodePort values before you create your clusters.	No	Yes
Manually configure your load balancer	No	Yes

Ingress

Anthos on-prem includes an L7 load balancer with an Envoy-based Ingress controller that handles Ingress object rules for `ClusterIP` Services deployed within the cluster. The Ingress controller itself is exposed as a NodePort Service in the cluster. The Ingress NodePort Service can be reached through a L3/L4 F5 load balancer. The installation configures a VIP address (Ingress VIP) (with port 80 and 443) on the load balancer. The VIP points to the ports in the NodePort Service for the Ingress controller. This is how external clients can access services in the cluster.

To expose a Service via Ingress, you must create a DNS A record to point the DNS name to the Ingress VIP. Then you can create a Service and an Ingress resource for the Service. For example, let's say you want to expose a `frontend` Service of a sample guestbook application. First, create a DNS A record for the guestbook application pointing to the Ingress VIP as follows:

```
*.guestbook.com    A    [INGRESS_VIP]
```

Next, create a Service for the `frontend` Deployment. Note that the Service is of type `ClusterIP`:

```
apiVersion: v1
kind: Service
metadata:
  labels:
    app: guestbook
  name: frontend
spec:
  ports:
  - port: 80
    protocol: TCP
    targetPort: 80
  selector:
    app: guestbook
  type: ClusterIP        ⏴──┐ For Ingress, the Service
                              type is ClusterIP (instead
                              of Loadbalancer).
```

Finally, create the Ingress rule:

```
apiVersion: extensions/v1beta1
kind: Ingress
metadata:
  name: frontend
  labels:
    app: guestbook
spec:
  rules:
    - host: www.guestbook.com
      http:
        paths:
          - backend:
              serviceName: frontend        The Ingress rule points to
              servicePort: 80              the Service name and port.
```

ANTHOS ON BARE METAL

Anthos on bare metal is a GCP-supported Anthos GKE implementation deployed on bare metal servers. Anthos on bare metal eliminates the need for a virtualization layer or a hypervisor. All cluster nodes and API servers run directly on bare metal servers.

Anthos on bare metal deployment models and networking architecture are described in detail in chapter 17.

ANTHOS ON AWS

Anthos clusters on AWS (GKE on AWS) is hybrid cloud software that extends Google Kubernetes Engine to Amazon Web Services. Anthos on AWS uses AWS resources such as Elastic Compute Cloud (EC2), Elastic Block Storage (EBS), and Elastic Load Balancer (ELB). Anthos clusters on AWS have the following two components:

- *Management service*—An environment that can install and update your user clusters, uses the AWS API to provision resources
- *User clusters*—Anthos on AWS clusters where you run your containerized applications

Networking requirements

Both the management service and the user clusters are deployed inside an AWS VPC on EC2 instances. You can create your management service in a dedicated AWS VPC (http://mng.bz/v1ax) or an existing AWS VPC (http://mng.bz/41GB). You need a management service in every AWS VPC where you run Anthos on AWS user clusters. The management service is installed in one AWS Availability Zone. You only need one management service per VPC; a management service can manage multiple user clusters.

A user cluster consists of two components: a control plane or the Kubernetes API server and node pools where your applications run. The management service's primary component is a cluster operator. The cluster operator is a Kubernetes operator that creates and manages your `AWSClusters` and `AWSNodePools`. The cluster operator stores configuration in an etcd database with storage persisted on an AWS EBS volume. An `AWSClusters` resource creates and manages the user clusters' control plane, and an `AWSNodePools` resource creates and manages the user clusters' node pools.

When you install a management cluster into a dedicated VPC, Anthos on AWS creates control plane replicas in every zone you specify in `dedicatedVPC.availabilityZones`. When you install a management cluster into existing infrastructure, Anthos on AWS creates an `AWSCluster` with three control plane replicas in the same Availability Zones. Each replica belongs to its own AWS Auto Scaling group, which restarts instances when they are terminated. The management service places the control planes in a private subnet behind an AWS Network Load Balancer (NLB). The management service interacts with the control plane using NLB.

As shown in figure 10.11, each control plane stores configuration in a local etcd database. These databases are replicated and set up in a stacked, high-availability topology (http://mng.bz/wPKW). One control plane manages one or more `AWSNodePools`.

Anthos on AWS Arch

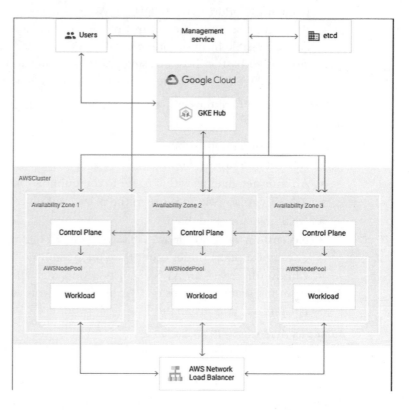

Figure 10.11   Anthos on AWS architecture

The following VPC resources are required when creating Anthos on AWS clusters in a dedicated VPC:

- *VPC CIDR range*—The total CIDR range of IP addresses for the AWS VPC that anthos-gke creates, for example, 10.0.0.0/16.
- *Availability Zones*—The AWS EC2 Availability Zones where you want to create nodes and control planes.
- *Private CIDR block*—The CIDR block for your private subnet. Anthos on AWS components, such as the management service, run in the private subnet. This subnet must be within the VPC's CIDR range specified in vpcCIDRBlock. You need one subnet for each Availability Zone.
- *Public CIDR block*—The CIDR blocks for your public subnet. You need one subnet for each Availability Zone. The public subnet exposes cluster services such as load balancers to the security groups and address ranges specified in AWS network ACLs and security groups.
- *SSH CIDR block*—The CIDR block that allows inbound SSH to your bastion host. You can use IP ranges, for example, 203.0.113.0/24. If you want to allow SSH

from any IP address, use 0.0.0.0/0. When you create a management service using the default settings, the control plane has a private IP address. This IP address isn't accessible from outside the AWS VPC. You can access the management service with a bastion host or using another connection to the AWS VPC such as a VPN or AWS Direct Connect (https://aws.amazon.com/directconnect/).

The following VPC resources are required when creating Anthos on AWS clusters in an existing VPC:

- At least one public subnet.
- At least one private subnet.
- An internet gateway with a route to the public subnet.
- A NAT gateway with a route to the private subnet.
- DNS hostnames enabled.
- No custom value for domain-name in your DHCP options sets. Anthos on AWS does not support values other than the default EC2 domain names.
- Choose or create an AWS security group that allows SSH (port 22) inbound from the security groups or IP ranges where you will be managing your Anthos clusters on AWS installation.

Anthos on AWS cluster IP allocation

The management service creates user clusters and uses a cluster operator with the resources AWSClusters and AWSNodePools to create the user clusters' control planes and node pools, respectively. The IP address per user cluster is defined in the AWSCluster resource. An example of an AWSCluster resource follows:

```
apiVersion: multicloud.cluster.gke.io/v1
kind: AWSCluster
metadata:
  name: CLUSTER_NAME
spec:                                        Anthos on AWS
  region: AWS_REGION                          cluster networking
  networking:                                 values are defined.
    vpcID: VPC_ID
    podAddressCIDRBlocks: POD_ADDRESS_CIDR_BLOCKS
    serviceAddressCIDRBlocks: SERVICE_ADDRESS_CIDR_BLOCKS
    ServiceLoadBalancerSubnetIDs: SERVICE_LOAD_BALANCER_SUBNETS
  controlPlane:                                     Anthos on AWS cluster
    version:  CLUSTER_VERSION                        control plane values
    instanceType: AWS_INSTANCE_TYPE                  are defined.
    keyName: SSH_KEY_NAME
    subnetIDs:
    - CONTROL_PLANE_SUBNET_IDS
    securityGroupIDs:
    - CONTROL_PLANE_SECURITY_GROUPS
    iamInstanceProfile: CONTROL_PLANE_IAM_ROLE
    rootVolume:
      sizeGiB: ROOT_VOLUME_SIZE
    etcd:
      mainVolume.sizeGIB: ETCD_VOLUME_SIZE
```

```
databaseEncryption:
  kmsKeyARN: ARN_OF_KMS_KEY
hub: # Optional
  membershipName: ANTHOS_CONNECT_NAME
workloadIdentity: # Optional
  oidcDiscoveryGCSBucket: WORKLOAD_IDENTITY_BUCKET
```

You define the required IP addresses in the `networking` section.

An Anthos on AWS cluster requires the following IP addresses:

- *Node IP*—Node IPs are assigned to the EC2 instances as they are created. Each EC2 instance is assigned a single IP from the private subnet in its availability zone. These addresses are defined in the management service spec.
- *Pod IP CIDR*—The CIDR range of IPv4 addresses used by the cluster's Pods. The range must be within your VPC CIDR address range but not part of a subnet.
- *Services IP*—The range of IPv4 addresses used by the cluster's Services. The range must be within your VPC CIDR address range but not part of a subnet.

Egress traffic and controls

All egress traffic from the Pod to targets outside the cluster is run through NAT by the node IP. You can use `NetworkPolicy` to further control the flow of traffic between Pods within a cluster as well as traffic egressing Pods. These policies are enforced by Calico running inside each cluster. At the Service layer, you can use `EgressPolicy` through ASM to control what traffic exits the clusters. In this case, an Envoy proxy called the `istio-egressgateway` exists at the perimeter of the service mesh through which all egress traffic flows.

In addition, you can control the traffic flow at the `AWSNodePools` security group layer. With security groups, you can further allow or deny traffic for both Ingress and egress.

Load balancers

When you create a Service of type `Loadbalancer`, a Anthos on AWS controller configures a classic or network ELB on AWS. Anthos on AWS requires tags on subnets that contain load balancer endpoints. Anthos on AWS automatically tags all subnets specified in the `spec.Networking.ServiceLoadBalancerSubnetIDs` field (http://mng.bz/X5mY) of the `AWSCluster` resource.

To create the tag, get the subnet ID of the load balancer subnets. Use the aws command-line utility to create the tag on the subnets as follows. For multiple subnets, make sure the subnet IDs are separated by spaces:

```
aws ec2 create-tags \
--resources [SUBNET_IDs] \
--tags Key=kubernetes.io/cluster/$CLUSTER_ID,Value=shared
```

You need a tag for every user cluster on the subnet.

You can create internal and external load balancers. Internal load balancers are created on the private subnets whereas external load balancers are created on the public subnets. You can create either type of load balancer using either a classic or a network load balancer. For more information on the differences between load balancer types, see the AWS documentation (http://mng.bz/ydpJ).

Different types of load balancers are created using annotations. Consider the following Service spec:

```
apiVersion: v1
kind: Service
metadata:
  name: my-lb-service
spec:
  type: LoadBalancer
  selector:
    app: products
    department: sales
  ports:
  - protocol: TCP
    port: 60000
    targetPort: 50001
```

This resource creates a classic public load balancer for the Service. To create a public network load balancer, add the following annotation to the previous spec:

```
...
metadata:
  name: my-lb-service
  annotations:
    service.beta.kubernetes.io/aws-load-balancer-type: nlb
...
```

The annotation creates a classic public load balancer in AWS, exposing a Service.

To create a private classic load balancer, add the following annotation to the Service spec:

```
...
metadata:
  name: my-lb-service
  annotations:
    service.beta.kubernetes.io/aws-load-balancer-internal: "true"
...
```

The annotation creates an internal load balancer in AWS, exposing a Service.

Finally, to create a private network load balancer, add both annotations to the Service spec:

```
...
metadata:
  name: my-lb-service
  annotations:
    service.beta.kubernetes.io/aws-load-balancer-type: nlb
    service.beta.kubernetes.io/aws-load-balancer-internal: "true"
...
```

Both annotations together create an internal network load balancer in AWS.

Ingress

You can use Ingress on Anthos on AWS clusters in the following two ways:

- *Application Load Balancer*—Application Load Balancer (ALB) (http://mng.bz/ Mlr2) is an AWS-managed L7 HTTP load balancer. After the load balancer receives a request, it evaluates the listener rules in priority order to determine which rule to apply and then selects a target from the target group for the rule action. This method uses an `alb-ingress-controller` installed in the Anthos on AWS cluster with proper permissions to create ALBs for Ingress.
- *ASM Ingress*—You can install Anthos Service Mesh on an Anthos on AWS cluster and use ASM Ingress. ASM Ingress, a Service called `istio-ingressgateway`, in an L7 Envoy proxy that lives at the perimeter of the service mesh. The `istio-ingressgateway` Service itself is exposed using ELB, as described in the previous section. All L7 load balancing and routing is handled by the `istio-ingressgateway`.

Exposing Services using Ingress

To use the ALB method, follow the instructions at http://mng.bz/aMpJ and deploy the `alb-ingress-controller` to the Anthos on AWS cluster. The `alb-ingress-controller` is a Deployment that runs on the Anthos on AWS cluster with proper AWS credentials and Kubernetes RBAC permission to create the rules and resources required to create an ALB for Ingress.

You can now create an Ingress resource with proper annotations to create an ALB and the required resources for your Service. An example of a Service spec follows. Note that the type of the Service must be `NodePort`:

```
apiVersion: v1
kind: Service
metadata:
  name: "service-2048"
  namespace: "2048-game"
spec:
  ports:
    - port: 80
      targetPort: 80
      protocol: TCP
  type: NodePort
  selector:
    app: "2048"
```

And the Ingress resource to expose this Service using an ALB is shown next. Note the two annotations that configures an internet-facing ALB:

```
apiVersion: extensions/v1beta1
kind: Ingress
metadata:
  name: "2048-ingress"
  namespace: "2048-game"
```

```
    annotations:
      kubernetes.io/ingress.class: alb
      alb.ingress.kubernetes.io/scheme: internet-facing
    labels:
      app: 2048-ingress
spec:
  rules:
    - http:
        paths:
          - path: /*
            backend:
                serviceName: "service-2048"
                servicePort: 80
```

These annotations create an internet-facing Application Load Balancer in AWS.

You can also use ASM Ingress to expose your Services. To use ASM, follow the steps at http://mng.bz/gJKR to install ASM on your Anthos on AWS cluster. Once ASM is installed, you should see the istio-ingressgateway Deployment and Service in the istio-system namespace.

An example of the Service spec looks like the following. Note that the Service type is ClusterIP instead of NodePort, used in the ALB method. The reason is that in the case of ASM, the L7 proxy runs inside the cluster, whereas the ALB is a managed HTTP load balancer that runs outside of the cluster:

```
apiVersion: v1
kind: Service
metadata:
  labels:
    app: hello-app
  name: hello-app
spec:
  type: ClusterIP
  selector:
    app: hello-app
  ports:
  - protocol: TCP
    port: 8080
    targetPort: 8080
```

And the Ingress resource looks like the following. Note the annotation that uses ASM for Ingress:

```
apiVersion: networking.k8s.io/v1beta1
kind: Ingress
metadata:
  annotations:
    kubernetes.io/ingress.class: istio
  labels:
    app: hello-app
  name: hello-app
spec:
  rules:
```

The annotation uses the Istio Ingress controller.

```
- host:
  http:
    paths:
    - backend:
        serviceName: hello-app
        servicePort: 8080
```

ANTHOS ATTACHED CLUSTERS

The final type of Anthos clusters is Anthos attached clusters. Attaching clusters lets you view your existing Kubernetes clusters in the Google Cloud console along with your Anthos clusters and enable a subset of Anthos features on them, including configuration with Anthos Config Management. You can attach any conformant Kubernetes cluster to Anthos and view it in the Cloud console with your Anthos clusters.

Regardless of where your clusters are, you need to register any clusters that you want to use with Anthos with your project's fleet by using Connect. A fleet provides a unified way to view and manage multiple clusters and their workloads as part of Anthos. We previously discussed fleets in regard to Anthos GKE on GCP, but on-prem clusters can join a fleet as well. Any Anthos cluster can be part of any one fleet, though not all features are available, based on where the cluster is located.

Networking requirements

To successfully register your cluster, you need to ensure that the following domains are reachable from your Kubernetes cluster:

- cloudresourcemanager.googleapis.com—Resolves metadata regarding the Google Cloud project the connecting cluster
- oauth2.googleapis.com—To obtain short-lived OAuth tokens for agent operations against gkeconnect.googleapis.com
- gkeconnect.googleapis.com—To establish the channel used to receive requests from Google Cloud and issue responses
- gkehub.googleapis.com—To create Google Cloud–side hub membership resources that correspond to the cluster you're connecting with Google Cloud
- www.googleapis.com—To authenticate service tokens from incoming Google Cloud service requests
- gcr.io—To pull a GKE Connect Agent image

If you're using a proxy for Connect, you must also update the proxy's allow list with these domains. If you use gcloud to register your Kubernetes cluster, these domains also need to be reachable in the fleet where you run the gcloud commands.

You only need outbound connectivity on port 443 to these domains. No inbound connections are required to register Anthos attached clusters. You can also use VPC Service Controls for additional TE security.

Using VPC Service Controls

If you use VPC Service Controls (http://mng.bz/51z1) for additional data security in your application, ensure that the following services are in your service perimeter:

1   Resource Manager API (`cloudresourcemanager.googleapis.com`)
2   GKE Connect API (`gkeconnect.googleapis.com`)
3   GKE Hub API (`gkehub.googleapis.com`)

You also need to set up private connectivity for access to the relevant APIs. You can find out how to do this at http://mng.bz/610D.

10.2.2 *Anthos GKE IP address management*

Except for Anthos GKE on GCP, all other Anthos clusters operate in an island mode configuration in which Pods can directly talk to each other within a cluster but cannot be reached from outside the cluster. This configuration forms an "island" within the network that is not connected to the external network. This allows you to create multiple Anthos clusters using the same IP addressing.

For Anthos clusters in island mode, IP address management and IP exhaustion is not an problem. You can standardize on an IP schema and use the same schema for all clusters.

GCP recommends running Anthos GKE on GCP clusters in VPC-native mode. In VPC-native mode, any IP address used by any cluster is a real VPC IP address. This means with VPC-native clusters, you cannot use overlapping IP addresses, and you must use unique subnets for every cluster. Recall that each Anthos GKE on GCP cluster requires the following three IP ranges:

- *Node IP*—Assigned to GCE instances or nodes belonging to clusters. One IP is required per node. These IP addresses are automatically assigned using the primary subnet.
- *Pod IP CIDR*—Assigned to every Pod that runs inside the cluster. A large subnet is assigned to the cluster. The cluster control plane divides this large subnet into smaller subnets, and each subnet (of equal size) is assigned to every node. For example, you can have a Pod IP CIDR of 10.0.0.0/16, and the cluster control plane assigns subnets of size /24 (from the Pod IP CIDR block) to each node, starting with 10.0.0.0/24 for the first node, 10.0.1.0/24 for the second node, and so on.
- *Service IP CIDR*—Assigned to Services running inside the cluster. Every Service of type `ClusterIP` requires one IP address.

Let's address these one at a time in a bit more detail.

NODE IP

To determine the size of the node IP pool, you must know the following:

- Number of clusters in a GCP region
- Number of maximum nodes per cluster

If you have equal-sized clusters, you can simply multiply the two numbers to get the total number of maximum nodes required to run in that region:

```
total number of nodes = number of clusters x max number of nodes per cluster
```

You can then determine the host bits you need for the node IP subnet from table 10.3.

Table 10.3   Determining the required host bits

Nodes required	Host bits for nodes
1–4	3 (or /29)
5–12	4 (or /28)
13–28	5 (or /27)
29 60	6 (or /26)
61–124	7 (or /25)
125–252	8 (or /24)
253–508	9 (or /23)
509–1020	10 (or /22)
1021–2044	11 (or /21)
2045–4092	12 (or /20)
4093–8188	13 (or /19)

You can use a single subnet for multiple GKE clusters.

POD IP CIDR

To determine the Pod IP CIDR, determine the maximum number of Pods per node you need in your cluster over its lifetime. If you cannot determine the maximum number you need, use the quota limit of 110 Pods per node as the maximum. Use table 10.4 to determine the host bits needed for the required number of Pods.

Table 10.4   Determining the host bits required for the Pods

Pods-per-node count	Host bits for Pods
1–8	4
9–16	5
17–32	6
33–64	7
65–110	8

To calculate the Pod IP CIDR block, you need the host bits for nodes and pods, and use the following formula:

```
Pod IP CIDR block netmask = 32 - (host bits for Nodes + host bits for Pods)
```

For example, let's assume that you need 110 pods per node, and the total number of nodes across all GKE clusters in the region is 5,000. First, determine the host bits for nodes using table 10.3; this would be 13. Then, determine the host bits for Pods using table 10.4; this would be 8. Then, using the formula, your Pod IP CIDR block netmask needs to be the following:

```
Pod IP CIDR block netmask = 32 - (13 + 8) = 11
```

You would need a subnet with a mask of /11.

SERVICE IP CIDR

To calculate the Service IP CIDR, determine the maximum number of cluster IP addresses you need in your cluster over its lifetime. Every Service requires one cluster IP. You cannot share Service IP subnets between clusters. This means you need a different Service IP subnet per cluster.

Once you know the maximum number of Services in a cluster, you can use table 10.5 to get the subnet mask you need.

Table 10.5   Determining the required subnet mask

Number of cluster IP addresses	Netmask
1–32	/27
33–64	/26
65–128	/25
129–256	/24
257–512	/23
513–1,024	/22
1,025–2,048	/21
2,049–4,096	/20
4,097–8,192	/19
8,193–16,384	/18
16,385–32,768	/17
32,769–65,536	/16

CONFIGURING PRIVATELY USED PUBLIC IPS FOR ANTHOS GKE

From the previous section, you can see that in very large GKE environments, you may run into IP exhaustion. The biggest source of IP exhaustion in large GKE environments is the Pod IP CIDR block. GCP VPCs use the RFC1918 address space for networking resources. In large environments, the RFC1918 space might not be sufficient to configure Anthos. This is especially a concern for managed service providers that deliver their managed services to many tenants on Anthos.

One way to mitigate address exhaustion is to use privately used public IP (PUPI) addresses for the GKE Pod CIDR block. PUPIs are any public IP addresses not owned by Google that a customer can use privately on Google Cloud. The customer doesn't necessarily own these addresses.

Figure 10.12 shows a company (producer) that offers a managed service to a customer (consumer).

Anthos GKE using PUPI Addressing

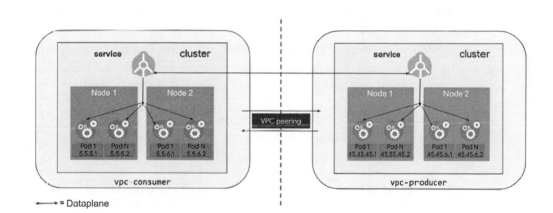

Figure 10.12 Anthos GKE using privately used public IP (PUPI) addressing

This setup involves the following considerations:

- *Primary CIDR block*—A non-PUPI CIDR block used for nodes and internal load balancing (ILB) and must be nonoverlapping across VPCs
- *Producer secondary CIDR block*—A PUPI CIDR block used for Pods (e.g., 45.45.0.0/16)
- *Consumer secondary CIDR block*—Any other PUPI CIDR block on the customer side (e.g., 5.5/16)

The company's managed service is in the producer VPC (`vpc-producer`) and is built on an Anthos GKE Deployment. The company's GKE cluster uses the PUPI 45.0.0.0/8 CIDR block for Pod addresses. The customer's applications are in the consumer VPC

(vpc-consumer). The customer also has an Anthos GKE installation. The GKE cluster in the consumer VPC uses the PUPI 5.0.0.0/8 CIDR block for Pod addresses. The two VPCs are peered with one another. Both VPCs use the RFC1918 address space for node, service, and load balancing addresses.

By default, the consumer VPC (vpc-consumer) exports all RFC1918 address spaces to the producer VPC (vpc-producer). Unlike RFC1918 private addresses and extended private addresses (CGN, Class E), PUPIs aren't automatically advertised to VPC peers by default. If the vpc-consumer Pods must communicate with vpc-producer, the consumer must enable the VPC peering connection to export PUPI addresses. Likewise, the producer must configure the producer VPC to import PUPI routes over the VPC peering connection.

The vpc-consumer address space that is exported into vpc-producer must not overlap with any RFC1918 or PUPI address used in vpc-producer. The producer must inform the consumer which PUPI CIDR blocks the managed service uses and ensure that the consumer isn't using these blocks. The producer and consumer must also agree and assign nonoverlapping address space for ILB and node addresses in vpc-producer.

PUPIs don't support service networking. In most cases, resources in vpc-consumer communicate with services in vpc-producer through ILB addresses in the producer cluster. If the producer Pods are required to initiate communication directly with resources in vpc-consumer, and PUPI addressing doesn't overlap, then the producer must configure the producer VPC to export the PUPI routes over the VPC peering connection. Likewise, the consumer must configure the VPC peering connection to import routes into vpc-consumer. If the consumer VPC already uses the PUPI address, then the producer should instead configure the IP masquerade feature and hide the Pod IP addresses behind the producer node IP addresses.

The previous example shows a more complex producer/consumer model. You can simply use this in a single project model. This would free up RFC1918 space that may otherwise be used for Pod IP CIDR.

10.3   *Anthos multicluster networking*

This section addresses mechanisms for connecting Services running across multiple clusters. Every hybrid and multicloud Anthos architecture, by definition, has more than one cluster. For example, you have Anthos GKE clusters running in GCP and Anthos GKE on-prem clusters running in on-prem data centers. The Services running on Anthos clusters often require network connectivity to Services running in other Anthos clusters. For multicluster Service networking, let's look at the following scenarios:

- *Multicluster networking on GCP*—In this architecture, all Services run on multiple Anthos GKE clusters in GCP.
- *Multicluster networking in hybrid and multicloud environments*—In this architecture, Services run on multiple Anthos GKE clusters in hybrid and multicloud environments.

10.3.1 *Multicluster networking on GCP*

Cloud native enterprises can run the Anthos platform on GCP. This can be on a single cluster in a single region. Often, an Anthos platform consists of multiple clusters in multiple regions for resiliency.

In GCP, Google recommends using a shared VPC model with multiple Service projects. One of these Service projects belongs to the `platform_admins` group and contains all the Anthos GKE clusters that form the Anthos platform. Resources on these clusters are shared by multiple tenants. We also recommend using VPC-native clusters. VPC-native clusters use VPC IP addresses for Pod IPs, which allow direct Pod-to-Pod connectivity across multiple clusters. A typical Anthos platform architecture on GCP looks like the one shown in figure 10.13.

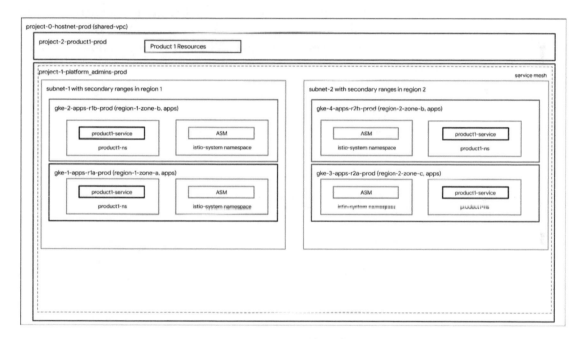

Figure 10.13   Anthos architecture: single environment

This architecture represents a single environment, for example, production in this case. A single network host project called project-0-nethost-prod manages the shared VPC. Two service projects exist, one for platform admins called `project-1-platform_admins-prod`, where the Anthos platform is deployed and managed by the platform administrator, and one for a product called project-2-product1-prod, where resources pertaining to `product1` reside. In this example, the Anthos platform is deployed across two GCP regions to provide regional redundancy. You can create the same architecture with more than two regions or even a single region. Inside each region is a single subnet with secondary ranges. Two zonal Anthos GKE clusters exist per region.

Multiple clusters per region provide cluster- and zone-level resiliency. You can use the same design for more than two clusters per region. All clusters are VPC-native clusters allowing Pod-to-Pod connectivity between clusters. ASM is installed on all clusters, forming a multicluster service mesh. ASM control planes discover Services and endpoints running in all clusters and configure the Envoy sidecar proxy running inside each Pod with routing information pertaining to all Services running inside the mesh.

Every tenant or product gets a landing zone in the form of a Kubernetes namespace (in all clusters inside the mesh) and a set of policies. Tenants can deploy their Services inside their own namespaces only. You can run the same Service in multiple Anthos GKE clusters for resiliency. These Services are called *distributed services*. Distributed services act as a single logical Service from the perspective of all other entities. In figure 10.13, `product1-service` is a distributed service with four endpoints, where each endpoint runs in a different cluster. As shown in figure 10.14, ASM takes care of Service discovery, and VPC-native clusters allow for L3/L4 Pod-to-Pod connectivity.

Anthos GKE Multicluster Networking

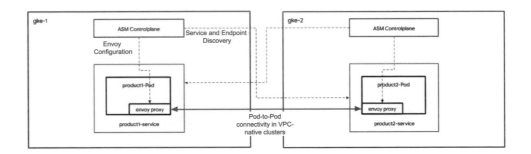

Figure 10.14   Anthos GKE multicluster networking

10.3.2 *Multicluster networking in hybrid and multicloud environments*

Apart from Anthos GKE on GCP, all other Anthos GKE clusters run in island mode. This means that the IP addressing used for Pods and Services inside the cluster is not routable outside of the cluster. In this scenario, you can still connect Services running on multiple clusters either in the same environment—for example, multiple Anthos GKE clusters running in an on-prem data center—or across multiple infrastructure environments—for example, Services running in Anthos GKE in GCP and in on-prem data center environments.

You should consider the following three aspects when connecting multiple Anthos GKE clusters in hybrid or multicloud environments:

- Network connectivity between Pods running on multiple clusters
- Service discovery across multiple clusters
- In the case of hybrid and multicloud architectures, connectivity between infrastructure environments

NETWORK CONNECTIVITY

Every Anthos GKE cluster has a load balancer. The load balancer either comes bundled during installation or can be configured manually. These load balancers allow Services to be exposed via NodePort to resources running outside the cluster. Each Service gets a VIP address (Service VIP), which is routable and reachable inside the network. The load balancer routes the traffic to the node IP on the Service NodePort, which gets forwarded to the Pod IP on the desired port.

Services (and Pods) running in one cluster can access the Service VIP for a Service running in another cluster, which gets routed to the desired Pod via the load balancer, as shown in figure 10.15.

Anthos GKE Hybrid Multicluster Networking

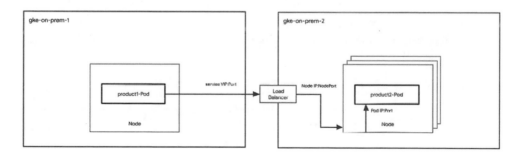

Figure 10.15   Anthos GKE hybrid multicluster networking

Anthos clusters can also be configured with Ingress controllers. Ingress controllers are L7/HTTP load balancers that typically reside inside the cluster. The Ingress controllers themselves are exposed via an L3/L4 load balancer. This way you can use one VIP (the Ingress VIP) for multiple Services running on the same cluster, as shown in figure 10.16. Ingress controllers act upon Ingress rules, which dictate how the traffic is to be routed inside the cluster.

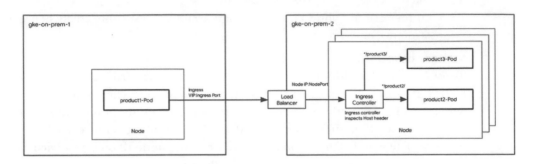

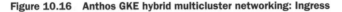

Figure 10.16   Anthos GKE hybrid multicluster networking: Ingress

MULTICLUSTER SERVICE DISCOVERY

Anthos Service Mesh is used for multicluster Service discovery, as illustrated in figure 10.17. An ASM control plane is installed in each cluster. The ASM control plane discovers Services and endpoints from all clusters. This is also known as the Service Mesh. The ASM control plane must have network access to the Kubernetes API server of all Anthos clusters inside the Service Mesh. ASM creates its own service registry, which is a list of Services and their associated endpoints (or Pods).

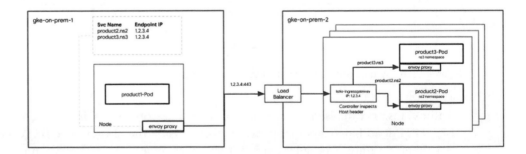

Figure 10.17   Anthos GKE hybrid multicluster networking: Anthos Service Mesh

In Anthos GKE on GCP, the endpoints are the actual Pod IP addresses if using VPC-native clusters. Traffic flows from Pod to Pod using VPC routing. In non-GCP Anthos clusters, traffic between clusters flows through an L7 Envoy proxy. This proxy runs as a

Service in every Anthos cluster called the `istio-ingressgateway`. Traffic bound for all Services inside a cluster flows through the `istio-ingressgateway`, which is configured to inspect the host header and route the traffic to the appropriate Service inside the cluster.

For distributed Services, we recommend using ASM, which provides Service discovery and traffic routing functionality across multiple clusters.

HYBRID AND MULTICLOUD CONNECTIVITY

You can connect Services running in multiple Anthos clusters across multiple infrastructure environments as long as you can reach the Kubernetes API server and the external public load balancer of the target Anthos cluster. You can connect infrastructure environments in the following three ways:

- *Cloud Interconnect*—Cloud Interconnect extends the on-prem network to Google's network through a highly available, low-latency connection. You can use Dedicated Interconnect to connect directly to Google or use Partner Interconnect to connect to Google through a supported service provider. Dedicated Interconnect provides direct physical connections between your on-prem network and Google's network.
- *Cloud VPN*—Cloud VPN securely connects your peer network to your VPC network through an IPsec VPN connection. Traffic traveling between the two networks is encrypted by one VPN gateway and then decrypted by the other VPN gateway.
- *Public internet*—An Anthos platform on multiple environments can be connected over the public internet without using Cloud Interconnect or VPN. Services running on the platform connect over the public internet using TLS/mTLS. This type of connectivity is done at a per-service level using ASM and not at the network level.

These connectivity models are explained in detail in section 10.1.2, "Multi/hybrid cloud deployment."

10.4 Services and client connectivity

This section addresses services and client connectivity in the Anthos platform, which can be divided into the following three categories:

- *Client-to-Service connectivity*—This is also sometimes referred to as north-south traffic, suggesting traffic originates from outside of the platform (north) and travels into the platform (south).
- *Service-to-Service connectivity*—This is also sometimes referred to as east-west traffic, suggesting traffic traverses the platform laterally (hence east-west). All traffic originates and terminates inside the Anthos platform.
- *Service-to–external service connectivity*—This is traffic egressing the platform.

10.4.1 *Client-to-Service connectivity*

In this context, a client refers to an entity that resides outside of the Anthos platform and a Service that runs inside the Anthos platform. You can access Services inside the Anthos platform in the following two ways:

- *With ASM*—With ASM, you can use ASM Ingress for HTTP(S) and TCP traffic. ASM provides additional L7 functionality, for example, the ability to perform authentication and authorization at Ingress. ASM is the recommended way of accessing web-based Services in the Anthos platform. ASM can also be used for TCP-based Services.
- *Without ASM*—All Anthos clusters support the option to configure a load balancer. The load balancer either comes integrated/bundled when you deploy the Anthos cluster or it can be configured manually. Any TCP-based service can be exposed using a service of type `Loadbalancer`, which creates a Service VIP that can be accessed by the client. In addition, all Anthos clusters can be configured with Ingress. Ingress controllers typically run inside the cluster as L7 proxies (with the exception of Anthos GKE on GCP and Anthos on AWS using ALB). The Ingress controllers themselves are exposed using the L3/L4 load balancer. Ingress is the recommended way to expose web-based Services. Ingress rules are implemented as part of the Service deploy pipeline, and Ingress controllers enforce these rules, which include listening and routing traffic to the appropriate service.

10.4.2 *Service-to-Service connectivity*

Services that run inside the cluster require network connectivity. This is accomplished in two ways:

- *With ASM*—We recommend using ASM, especially in a multicluster Anthos platform. ASM provides Service discovery as well as routing logic between Services. ASM can also handle authentication and authorization between Services. For example, you can enable mTLS at the service mesh level, encrypting all Service-to-Service traffic. You can also configure security policies at an individual Service layer. Besides Service discovery and networking, ASM provides additional features such as telemetry, quotas, rate limiting, and circuit breaker. For more on the features and benefits of ASM, please see chapter 4.
- *Without ASM*—If you choose to not use ASM, you can still configure Service-to-Service connectivity. From a networking standpoint, you can use either the load balancer or the Ingress pattern to access Services running inside clusters. You would have to configure Service discovery yourself. You can use DNS to provide this functionality.

In either case, you can also use NetworkPolicy inside the cluster to control/limit the traffic between Pods and Services.

10.4.3 *Service-to-external Services connectivity*

You can control egress traffic from any Anthos cluster in the following two ways:

- *With ASM*—ASM provides both an Ingress and an egress gateway. We have previously discussed how Ingress works with ASM. Similarly, you can configure a second proxy at the perimeter of the Service Mesh called the `istio-egressgateway`. You can then configure `ServiceEntries` for only the Services that are allowed to be accessed from inside the cluster. You can set the `outboundTrafficPolicy` mode to `REGISTRY_ONLY`. This blocks all outbound traffic that is not destined for a Service inside the mesh. You can then create individual `ServiceEntries` for access to Services running outside the platform. An example of `ServiceEntry` may look like the following:

```
apiVersion: networking.istio.io/v1alpha3
kind: ServiceEntry
metadata:
  name: httpbin-ext
spec:
  hosts:
  - httpbin.org
  ports:
  - number: 80
    name: http
    protocol: HTTP
  resolution: DNS
  location: MESH_EXTERNAL   <──┐  The location MESH_EXTERNAL
                                signifies that the Service is
                                external to the Service Mesh,
                                and a DNS entry is manually
                                added to the mesh registry.
```

This rule allows traffic destined for httpbin.org on port 80. Note the location of the Service is `MESH_EXTERNAL`, signifying this service is outside of the Service Mesh and the Anthos platform.

- *Without ASM*—You can use `NetworkPolicies` inside the cluster to control Ingress and egress traffic to Pods based on label selectors. Because all Pod egress traffic exits via the node IP, you can further control egress traffic through firewall rules by limiting what destinations the node IP subnets can access.

Summary

Anthos networking can be divided into the following four layers:

- *Cloud networking and hybrid connectivity*—The lowest layer of Anthos networking. This layer describes how to set up networking within each cloud environment as well as options to securely connect multiple cloud environments together. Inside GCP, you can set up a single network (or VPC), a shared VPC, or multiple VPCs, depending on the organizational and functional requirements. In non-GCP environments, all Anthos clusters are treated as isolated networks (or in "island mode"). Multiple hybrid connectivity options follow:
  - *Dedicated Interconnect*—Provides direct physical connections between your on-prem network and Google's network. Dedicated Interconnect enables you to

transfer large amounts of data between networks, which can be more cost effective than purchasing additional bandwidth over the public internet.

– *Cloud VPN*—Securely extends your peer network to Google's network through an IPsec VPN tunnel. Traffic is encrypted and travels between the two networks over the public internet. Cloud VPN is useful for low-volume data connections.

– *Public internet*—Does not require any special software or hardware to connect disparate networks together. Instead, TLS/mTLS connection is used to secure Service-to-Service connections.

■ *Anthos GKE networking*—The Kubernetes networking layer. Anthos GKE clusters can be deployed to a variety of environments, for example, GCP, on VMware in an on-prem data center, on bare metal servers, and on AWS. In addition to the supported Anthos clusters, you can also register any conformant Kubernetes cluster to the Anthos platform. For example, you can register EKS clusters running in AWS and AKS clusters running in Azure to the Anthos platform. The following six types of Anthos clusters are currently available:

– Anthos clusters on GCP(GKE)

– Anthos clusters on VMware (GKE on-prem)

– Anthos clusters on bare metal

– Anthos clusters on AWS (GKE on AWS)

– Anthos clusters on Azure (GKE on Azure)

– Anthos attached clusters (conformant Kubernetes clusters)

■ *Anthos multicluster networking*—Deals with environments with multiple clusters where services need to communicate across cluster boundaries. This section can be divided into the following two subsections:

– *Anthos multicluster networking with GKE on GCP*—In GKE on GCP, you can either have a flat network architecture (using a single or shared VPC) or a multiple-network (multiple-VPC) model. In a flat network architecture using VPC-native GKE clusters, VPC networking automatically allows for Pod-to-Pod connectivity between multiple clusters. Clusters can be in any region. No additional configuration is required for Pod-to-Pod connectivity between clusters. In a multiple VPC architecture, you need additional configuration to connect Pods and Services between multiple clusters. For example, you can use special gateways or Ingress model to communicate between clusters.

– *Anthos multicluster networking in non-GCP environments*—In all non-GCP clusters, a cluster and its address range are isolated from other clusters. This means that no direct connectivity exists between Pods in multiple clusters. To connect multiple clusters, you must use special gateways or Ingress. Anthos Service Mesh can be used to deploy such gateways. Often called "east-west gateways," these are deployed in all clusters participating in a multicluster mesh. In addition, ASM also provides multicluster Service discovery.

- *Service layer networking*—The top layer of Anthos networking is Service layer networking. This layer addresses how Services discover and communicate with one another. In the previous section, we mentioned Anthos Service Mesh, which can enable you to do the following tasks:
  - ASM allows you to create a Service Mesh atop multiple Anthos clusters running in multicloud environments. This layer abstracts the complexity of lower-layer networking and allows you to focus on the Service layer.
  - ASM uses sidecar-per-workload and specialized gateways to connect multiple clusters across multiple environments and networks.
  - By using ASM, you can focus on Service layer functions—for example, authentication, encryption, and authorization—instead of managing individual workloads at the cluster level. This allows operators and administrators to operate at scale where there may be multiple clusters, in multiple environments, in multiple networks running numerous services.

11
Config Management architecture

Michael Madison

This chapter covers

- Why configuration at scale is a challenge
- An overview of Anthos Config Management
- Examples and case studies of ACM implementations showing the utility and versatility of the solution.

In the world of application development, we always desire more speed and more capability as well as more applications that fulfill more tasks, automate more minutiae, run faster, and operate in locations closer to where they are actually used. The proliferation of smartphones, tablets, and IoT devices, as well as the continued advancement of computers into every part of our daily lives, drives the need for more compute power. Environmental factors, the availability of high-speed internet and other utilities, and government regulations are changing the way companies deploy resources. Depending on the circumstances, this could result in a concentration of compute resources in a few data centers, a move to mostly cloud-based compute, fragmenting to lots of "mini" data centers, or a combination of these solutions.

Organizations rarely decide to reduce the total resources they manage. Although short-term reductions, consolidations, or even eliminations of applications might occur, most companies will be managing more tomorrow than today. This has been the path that application development has followed for the past 40 years or longer.

But the expanding use of Kubernetes has brought this problem into focus for many organizations as they come to grips with moving and managing thousands of VMs and applications in the Kubernetes landscape. Although many legacy tools would still work, using them in the same way would negate most of the advantages available with Kubernetes. On top of that, legacy toolsets are often disconnected from one another, forcing managers to make firewall changes in one tool, granting VM access in another, and setting up routing through a third. These challenges fall largely on the shoulders of IT operations teams who are charged with implementing and maintaining all of this infrastructure.

As more companies move to Kubernetes for their daily operations, the need for security professionals and managers to be confident in their ability to configure, administer, and audit Kubernetes clusters has become critical for business success. IT security groups are responsible for developing and implementing security controls around and within the IT infrastructure, including software, hardware, and physical limitations, policies, procedures, and guidance. Many companies adopt a tiered permissions model, allowing super users a greater subset of abilities without becoming full administrators. Because much of the work in Kubernetes is driven by a common definition language, expressed in JSON or YAML, the security framework should also be familiar to IT security teams who regularly work with Kubernetes.

To help organizations address this need, Google has created Anthos Config Management (ACM) to simplify the development, deployment, and maintenance of Kubernetes policies, resources, and configuration. In the next section, you'll examine the full scope of challenges that ACM helps solve and the opportunities ACM provides to drive efficiencies within an organization.

11.1 What are we trying to solve?

Over time, businesses have moved processes to digital formats. Even without the internet as an engagement platform, companies have shifted their internal operations to rely on digital applications and communications. When that's added to the massive drive to engage digital customers, companies' need for compute power becomes greater than ever before, and it shows no signs of slowing. One of the newest aspects of computing, edge computing, is expected to be an over $155 billion market alone by 2030, according to Grandview Research (http://mng.bz/oJnr).

Additionally, many businesses see greater efficiency by having these systems communicate with each other to automate their processes. The proliferation of, for example, ticket-based self-service software such as ServiceNow, personnel management solutions like Workday, and combined authentication and authorization services such as Okta encourage companies to expand their capabilities on-site and in the cloud. As companies pivot to depend more heavily on their staff's development capabilities for mission-critical solutions, the complexity involved in the deployment of these applications increases with each new vendor they bring into their ecosystem.

The needs of any company diverge from their closest competitor as they design their unique value to customers, but most businesses have a digital presence both on-prem and in the cloud. Although some companies have used multiple data centers or colocation facilities to provide their redundant and reliable infrastructure, many have turned to cloud providers. But cloud providers' best practices and user experiences can vary widely. Each cloud brought online by an operations team greatly increases their technical burden and operational overhead, as shown in figure 11.1. Even in the case of data centers designed to be identical, security controls and physical separation still impose barriers to their operation and maintainability.

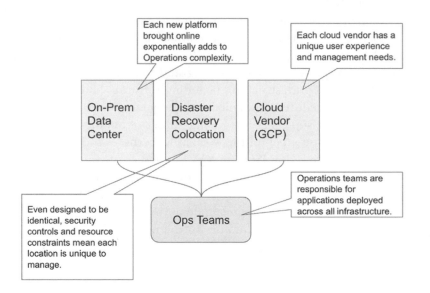

Figure 11.1   Bringing multiple infrastructure platforms online adds considerable operations overhead.

The size of a company's digital footprint also adds complexity to the configuration and operation of their systems. Multiple working locations, more data centers, and a corresponding increase of the number of people involved in the management of these systems all add their own challenges. As an organization grows, introducing and using systemic security and configuration controls becomes vital. ACM addresses these challenges using the following central capabilities:

- Managing complexity
- Workload observability and inspection
- Remediating and preventing problems when they do occur

Next, you'll examine how ACM manages complexity in modern infrastructure.

11.1.1 Managing complexity

You can configure compute infrastructure in innumerable ways, but most solutions do follow some general patterns. These solutions can generally be grouped by whether the system scales horizontally or vertically. For a company adopting or using a Kubernetes-based infrastructure, a similar decision must be made about the overall design of all the Kubernetes clusters at a company. A company using multiple, smaller clusters for different purposes (e.g., one or more per team) is implementing a horizontal scaling solution. A company using a smaller number of larger clusters (e.g., one each for Dev, Test, and Prod) is building vertical scalability into their Kubernetes infrastructure. Neither approach is better than the other, but a company should determine what fits best with their approach to deployments and software design.

Geographic limitations, edge-processing needs, and telecommunications operations also impose restrictions on how clusters are delineated. Government regulations in certain countries prevent the egress of data from those regions, requiring the databases and application layers to be located inside the country. Even without government regulation, the operations of certain types of businesses, such as restaurants, retail stores, or even banks, might prefer a local processing system running a subset of applications that would benefit from, or require, a shorter communications loop.

In addition, large businesses require more staff to efficiently organize and operate the IT infrastructure. To mitigate single points of failure among IT personnel, developing simple processes that can be scaled out to multiple people is critical to long-term success.

11.1.2 Transparency and inspection

Visibility and inspection of workloads and overall health of a Kubernetes cluster is outside the purview of this chapter (it is primarily covered in chapter 5). However, the plaintext representation of policies and configurations for all clusters afforded by Anthos Config Management can do a great deal on the frontend to ensure that appropriate policies are adhered to.

The goal of Anthos Config Management is to maintain a cluster in a state specified by a policy directory stored in a Git repository. This policy directory exists separate from the clusters being managed and is stored in a text-based format. Thus, the policy directory itself can be used as a source of information about the configuration of the cluster. By using the features of the Git repo itself, the IT operations team can determine when a cluster is out of compliance and can easily track changes to a cluster's configuration.

ACM provides a command-line utility, via the nomos command, to interrogate clusters directly and determine their current state. Operations teams can use nomos to diagnose the rollout of a change and determine whether an error or lag occurs that would be causing problems. Much of the information that is provided via nomos is visible in the Anthos UI[1] within the Google Cloud console, showing what configuration version each cluster is currently running, as well as the overall state of the ACM

---

[1] The Anthos UI is covered primarily in chapter 1.

installation. Also, the Kubernetes operator for the system logs events and information in the same manner as other containers and, thus, can be viewed in Cloud Logging and used in Cloud Monitoring alerts and metrics.

11.1.3 *Remediating and preventing problems*

One of the major responsibilities of an IT operations team is to maintain system reliability and uptime. Knowing that a change has caused a disruption and being able to quickly isolate the problem and rapidly apply a remediation are critical tools in the team's arsenal. On all three of these points, ACM brings unique features that enable the team to respond to situations as they occur.

Because ACM is driven from a Git repository, you can easily add guardrails and policy enforcement through existing pull request mechanisms or tie activity on one or many branches into a monitoring suite and bring additional alerting to bear after a change to the policies. Using the repo as the source of truth, the team can investigate what changes were applied at what times to narrow down any problematic configurations. Existing Git tooling can then be used to revert or fix the configuration. Due to ACM's design, these changes normally take effect within a minute or two of the change being pushed to the policy repo.

In addition to fixing problems that have already been deployed, you can use existing CI/CD tooling and processes to verify configurations before they are allowed to take effect. Other tooling around Git, such as pull and merge requests, branching, and more, can also serve to allow multiple users to develop new policies, while permitting the organization the ability to approve those changes prior to deployment.

ACM includes the ability to apply a configuration to a subset of clusters. Although we use this in our examples to deploy different versions of an application to clusters by region, the same functionality can be used to deploy changes in a controlled fashion, or to apply different roles per cluster. For example, a retail chain running a cluster in each store can deploy a new version of an application to a specific set of test stores before rolling it out to the entire chain. A company using different clusters for Dev, Test, and Prod environments can grant users different permissions based on the cluster while still taking advantage of a single policy repository.

11.1.4 *Bringing it together*

All three of these problems are well handled with Anthos Config Management. By providing tools familiar to IT professionals and with a design that thrives in a highly distributed ecosystem, ACM can help teams manage large systems easily. In the next section, we will give a brief overview of how ACM works and the components that can be included with an installation.

11.2 *Overview of ACM*

Now that we have a good idea of the problems we are trying to solve with Anthos Config Management, let's take a deeper look at the technical implementation of

ACM. ACM works by way of a Kubernetes operator[2] deployed onto each cluster to be managed. A configuration file containing the canonical name of the cluster, a Git configuration, and a set of feature flags are also applied to the cluster. The operator uses the Git configuration to connect to a Git repository hosted in any accessible Git service containing the full configuration information for the cluster. The feature flags are switches to activate Config Sync, Policy Controller, or Hierarchy Controller, which will be covered later in this chapter. ACM uses the name of the cluster, along with the policy configurations in the Git repo, to add ephemeral tags to the cluster. These tags can then be used within the policy repo to modify which resources are deployed to each cluster.

ACM works on a minimum-footprint mentality: it does not try to take over the entire Kubernetes cluster. Rather, the operator knows what objects are defined in the policy configuration and works to manage only those specific objects. This allows multiple deployment mechanisms to work in parallel on a single Kubernetes cluster without stepping on each other. However, using multiple tools does add the additional burden of needing to know which tools have deployed each object. ACM includes a specific annotation on objects it manages,[3] but that may not look the same for all tools. As we will see later, ACM repos can be configured in an unstructured mode that allows an organization to continue using existing tools that support outputting to YAML or JSON while still using ACM to perform the actual deployment and management processes.

The operator syncs every few minutes, and this frequency can be adjusted in the configuration, depending on the needs of the organization. ACM can use both public and private repos, with appropriate credentials, as the policy repository. In addition, the Git configuration can be pointed at a directory below the top level of the repository. This can be useful if the Git repository uses a templating engine or even application code where a subdirectory can be used to store the policies.

You can deploy Anthos Config Management in three primary ways, depending on the type of Kubernetes cluster you are using: a Google Kubernetes Engine (GKE) cluster deployed on GCP, a GKE on VMware cluster, or another flavor of Kubernetes. For GKE on GCP, enabling ACM is a simple matter of selecting a checkbox on the cluster configuration page. For GKE on VMware, ACM is enabled by default and cannot be disabled. Only clusters that do not fit into either category require manual configuration to install the operator: retrieve the most recent version of the operator's custom resource definition file, provided by Google, and apply it to the cluster.

At this point, all flavors of Kubernetes have the operator installed and running, but ACM still needs to be enabled and told where to pull policies from. This is done by creating an operator configuration object and applying it to the cluster, along with whatever Git credentials are required. Multiple methods of Git authentication are supported, including public repos with no authentication, SSH key pairs, personal access

---

[2] For more information on the Kubernetes operator pattern, see http://mng.bz/nJog.

[3] The annotation is `configmanagement.gke.io/managed: enabled`.

tokens, and Google service accounts. Some of these methods require specific information to be loaded into a Kubernetes Secret for the operator to load it properly. The configuration object allows specifying proxies for the Git repository, if needed. In addition to the Git connection information, the configuration object can contain settings to enable or disable the individual components named earlier, as well as name the cluster for use within ACM policy rules. Note that the `ConfigManagement` object created on the cluster and the configuration YAML used by gcloud to initially install ACM are similar but are not the same. As ACM's capabilities expand, more options will be added to this configuration object, but the current structure of the initial deployment YAML follows:

```
applySpecVersion: 1
spec:
  clusterName: <name of cluster>
  enableMultiRepo: <true/false, enables multiple repository mode>
  enableLegacyFields: <true/false, used with multi repo, see below>
  policyController:
    enabled: <true/false>
    templateLibraryInstalled: <true/false, installs the Google-provided
      template library for policy controller>
  sourceFormat: <hierarchy or unstructured. Sets the type of policy
      organization>
  preventDrift: <if set to true, rejects changes to the cluster that conflict
      with managed resources>
  git:
    syncRepo: <url of the git repository>
    syncBranch: <branch of the git repository to sync from>
    policyDir: <relative path in the git repository to the policy directory>
    syncWait: <number of seconds between sync attempts>
    syncRev: <git revision to sync from. Used if a specific commit or tag
      should be used instead of a branch>
    secretType: <ssh, cookiefile, token, gcenode, gcpserviceaccount or none.
      Specifies the type of authentication to perform>
    gcpServiceAccountEmail: <email of the service account to use for git
      access. Only used when secretType is gcpserviceaccount>
    proxy:
      httpProxy: <proxy information for http connection, styled similarly to
      the HTTP_PROXY environment variable>
      httpsProxy: <proxy information for https connection, styled similarly
      to the HTTPS_PROXY environment variable>
```

The operator on the individual clusters is the mechanism ACM uses to update the objects on each cluster. Although ACM uses a central Git repository, because the individual clusters reach out to fetch the configuration, this greatly simplifies connectivity between the cluster and the repository. The repository does not push out the configs, so we do not need to introduce additional complexity or security ingress holes, nor does the central repository need to know about every individual cluster beforehand.

11.2.1 *ACM policy structure*

The ACM policy directory must be in one of two supported formats, either hierarchy or unstructured, with hierarchy as the default. This setting is also reflected in the operator configuration object referenced earlier, in the `spec.sourceFormat` key. In both cases, the policy directory defines Kubernetes objects, which are then examined and applied by the ACM operator on each of the clusters connected to the Git repository. ACM itself uses some of these objects internally to determine which resources to apply to the current cluster.

In addition to the overall format of the repository, you can use multiple repositories to configure clusters. When using the `enableMultiRepo` functionality, a single repository is used as the root repository (and may be hierarchy or unstructured), whereas all other repositories are used to configure objects in a single namespace.

HIERARCHY

In a hierarchy repository, top-level directories in the policy directory separate configuration files based on purpose and scope—system, clusterregistry, cluster, and namespaces—as shown in table 11.1.

Table 11.1 Top-level directories in a hierarchy repository

Directory	Purpose
System	Configs related to the policy repository itself, such as the version of the deployed configuration.
Clusterregistry	Stores `Cluster` and `ClusterSelector` objects, which are used together to select subsets of clusters to restrict where a specific object is applied to. `Cluster` definitions attach specific tags to a cluster by name; `ClusterSelectors` can then use these tags to select a set of clusters meeting a certain set of requirements.
Cluster	Contains objects that are defined for the entire cluster, except for namespaces.
Namespaces	Contains objects that are assigned to one or more specific namespaces, as well the `Namespace` and `NamespaceSelector` definitions.

ACM in hierarchy mode uses a concept of "abstract" namespaces, a grouping of one or more actual namespaces, which should share a set of Kubernetes objects. For instance, you might define a Role or ConfigMap in each namespace that a team uses. When ACM analyzes the repository, any object defined in an abstract namespace is automatically copied into every namespace beneath it. These abstract namespaces can also be nested within each other to have multiple layers of abstraction. For example, you may place all application development teams under an `app-dev` abstract namespace, and then each team in a separate abstract namespace within `app-dev`.

Although ACM will copy an object in an abstract namespace to all child namespaces, you can use a `NamespaceSelector` to restrict what namespaces the object is applied to. Using the `app-dev` example, we want to deploy a `ConfigMap` to multiple namespaces across multiple teams, but only to the namespaces that contain finance-related applications. By applying a label to those namespaces, we can then define a `NamespaceSelector` to select only those namespaces, and then link the `ConfigMap` config object to the `NamespaceSelector`. Although these selectors do have their purpose in a hierarchy repo, their primary use is in an unstructured repo. Further, in a hierarchy repo, a specific namespace must be a child of the folder containing the object, as well as matching the selector. A full example in an unstructured repo with the configuration objects defined can be found in the Evermore Industries example at the end of the chapter.

Once you have a specific namespace name to be created, you also should decide on which abstract namespace to inherit from. This may mean that certain objects must be defined at a higher level than you would normally do, simply to have them inherited by the individual namespaces. Once you have the name and the abstract namespaces, you create a folder with that name at the bottom of that set of namespace directories. Inside the newly created directory, you must also create the Kubernetes `Namespace` object with the same name. All the objects defined in the abstract namespaces are also created inside the leaf namespace. Let's look at an example with the following folder structure:

```
namespaces
├── staging
│   ├── qa-rbac.yaml
│   └── weather-app-staging
│       └── namespace.yaml
└── production
    ├── developer-rbac.yaml
    ├── app-service-account.yaml
    ├── weather-app-prod
    │   ├── namespace.yaml
    │   └── application.yaml
    ├── front-office-prod
    │   ├── namespace.yaml
    │   └── application.yaml
    └── marketing
        └── namespace.yaml
```

For the `production` abstract namespace, we are defining a role and binding for developers in the developer-rbac.yaml and a Kubernetes service account for the applications in the app-service-account.yaml. Because the `weather-app-prod`, `front-office-prod`, and `marketing` namespaces are under the `production` abstract namespace, the role, role binding, and Kubernetes service account will be created in all three namespaces. Due to how ACM analyzes the policy repository, actual namespaces cannot have subdirectories in their folder, and every leaf directory must be an actual namespace with the corresponding namespace declaration in the directory. Failing to adhere to this restriction will cause a configuration error when ACM is deployed.

In addition to abstract namespaces, objects can use `NamespaceSelectors` (which are declared in a manner similar to `ClusterSelectors`, covered later in this chapter), to affect only a subset of namespaces within the object's scope. In the previous example, the `app-service-account` can use a selector to deploy only to the `weather-app-prod` and `front-office-prod` namespaces, and not the `marketing` namespace. However, `NamespaceSelectors` in hierarchy repositories operate only on namespaces in the current folder tree. For example, even if the namespace selector included `weather-app-staging` in its criteria, the `app-service-account` defined under the `production` abstract namespace would never be applied to the `staging` namespace because the `weather-app-staging` directory is not a child of the directory that contains the `app-service-account`.

Pros and cons

A hierarchy repository simplifies the deployment of objects to a subset of namespaces, because an object can be deployed only to the namespaces at or below the level of the configuration file in the repository. With the use of `NamespaceSelectors`, an organization can further restrict what namespaces an object can be deployed to. This can be especially useful if there are multiple ways to group namespaces. For example, a development team might group namespaces, but they may also need to be grouped by function (e.g., frontend, middleware) or business unit. Using a hierarchy repo, you must choose one "primary" grouping strategy; if an object needs to be deployed to multiple namespaces that are not grouped together, the object would be placed at a higher level in the repo and restricted using a `NamespaceSelector`. This organization makes it very simple to start determining which namespaces an object deploys to, because it can be only those defined at or below the object's definition file. Cluster level resources and resources that are primarily used to deliver ACM also have dedicated folders where they must be located, making it easier to find a given object.

However, this rigid structure can cause difficulties when implementing ACM at your organization. Many organizations already have at least a basic familiarity with Kubernetes and use existing toolsets and processes to deploy Kubernetes resources and applications. Because cross-namespace objects must be configured in different folders in a hierarchy repository, this can complicate the integration of ACM into an existing CI/CD pipeline. An organization should weigh the benefits of the automatic duplication of objects afforded by a hierarchy repository with the restrictions it imposes.

UNSTRUCTURED

Unlike a hierarchy repo, an unstructured repo has no special directory structure. Teams are free to use whatever style of organization they wish, such as grouping files and objects by application or team. Using an unstructured repo, however, prevents ACM from using the concept of an abstract namespace to automatically create a single object in multiple namespaces. To compensate for this restriction, an object must declare either a namespace, or a `NamespaceSelector`. Though `NamespaceSelectors` behave in the same manner as in a hierarchy repository, without the restriction of only operating on namespaces in the same folder tree, greater care must be taken to make sure only the desired namespace(s) actually matches the selector.

Pros and cons

When an organization is already using a templating engine to deploy objects to Kubernetes, an unstructured repo becomes even more favorable. Because most templating engines, including Helm, include the ability to export the completed Kubernetes objects to a local directory, you can use the output from those commands and simply place the generated configurations directly into the ACM policy directory. An unstructured ACM repo does not care about the exact placement of configurations under the policy directory, so this can provide a less-stressful upgrade path when implementing ACM.

However, unstructured repositories have a couple of wrinkles when it comes to namespace assignment. Configurations in an unstructured repository cannot infer the namespace they should be assigned to, so users must explicitly assign all objects. This can result in the deployment of an object to an unintended namespace if the selector is defined or used improperly. In addition, finding a resource becomes more complicated because no implicit relationship exists between the location of the configuration file and the deployment namespace.

MULTIPLE REPOSITORY MODE

Configuring ACM to pull from multiple repositories allows organizations to permit individual teams to manage their own namespaces while still taking advantage of many of the benefits of ACM. When the cluster configuration object is set to enable multiple repository mode (http://mng.bz/zmB6), using the `enableMultiRepo` flag, the `spec.git` set of fields is not supported. Instead, you create a separate `RootSync` object to hold the configuration details for the root repository.

With `enableMultiRepo` set, an organization can define the repository to be used for each individual namespace. As with the `RootSync` object, these individual `RepoSync` objects contain the configuration for fetching from a Git repository as well as the directory in that repository for the top of the policy tree. Even when using multiple repository mode, the root repository can still define objects to be managed in any namespace. In the case of a conflict between the root repository and the individual namespace repositories, the root repository's version is the one used.

The root repository of a multiple repository setup functions identically to a configuration that is not in multiple repository mode; only the configuration of how to fetch the repository changes. Therefore, multiple repository mode is an ideal solution to allow operations and security teams to impose policies, RBAC rules, and Istio rules, configure namespaces, and so on while enabling application teams to manage and deploy their own applications into individual namespaces. The team managing the root repository also needs to add the appropriate policies to define which objects the individual repositories can modify. This is done by defining a custom Role or ClusterRole, or using one of the built-in roles, and then using a RoleBinding to attach the namespace's worker service account to that role. This allows the operations team to offload much of the work of configuring a given application to the teams and defining custom permissions per team if needed, rather than requiring the central team to validate or perform the work themselves.

11.2.2 ACM-specific objects

Although ACM can manage any valid Kubernetes object, custom objects can adjust how the system operates and applies new configurations.

CONFIGMANAGEMENT

ACM uses this object to determine how and where to fetch the policy configurations to be used for the cluster. Deploying a `ConfigManagement` object to the cluster activates ACM for that cluster. This object also defines the name of the cluster, as used inside ACM, and determines which plug-ins (Config Sync, Policy Controller, and Hierarchy Controller) are active for the cluster.

ROOTSYNC/REPOSYNC

When the cluster is running in multiple repository mode, the configuration for fetching policies, including Git URLs and Secrets, are not stored in the `ConfigManagement` object but rather in either the `RootSync` object (for the core repository) or in `RepoSync` objects in each namespace.

CLUSTER

A cluster config is created in the ACM policy repo and allows users to attach labels to a specific cluster by cluster name. These labels are then used in `ClusterSelectors` to select specific types of clusters. In a hierarchy repo, the `Cluster` definitions must be in the clusterregistry directory.

CLUSTERSELECTOR

This object uses the common Kubernetes `labelSelectors` pattern[4] to select a subset of clusters. The `ClusterSelector` can then be used by an object, such as a `Deployment`, `ConfigMap`, or `Secret`, to deploy only that object in clusters matching the selector. In a hierarchy repo, these must be in the clusterregistry directory.

NAMESPACESELECTOR

Similar to the `ClusterSelector`, this selector also uses `labelSelectors`, but it is used to select namespaces instead. It is primarily used in unstructured repos or in a hierarchy repo as an additional method to limit to which namespaces an object is deployed.

HIERARCHYCONFIGURATION

These objects are declared in individual namespaces and point to their parent. This sets up the hierarchical namespace relationship that the Hierarchy Controller uses. Note that using the Hierarchy Controller is not the same as a hierarchy repository; the Hierarchy Controller will be explored further later in the chapter.

---

[4] This is the same pattern Deployments and Jobs use and is detailed at http://mng.bz/41Ga.

11.2.3 *Additional components*

Although not strictly part of ACM itself, Config Connector, Policy Controller, and Hierarchy Controller greatly enhance the functionality of ACM and your Kubernetes environments. This section gives only a short introduction to each component, but all three are demonstrated in the examples at the end of the chapter. Google is also integrating additional components as development on Anthos continues. Please refer to the online documentation at http://mng.bz/Q8rw for the most up-to-date information on available add-ons.

CONFIG CONNECTOR

Config Connector (https://cloud.google.com/config-connector/docs) is an add-on to Kubernetes that allows you to configure GCP resources, such as SQL instances, storage buckets, and Compute Engine VMs, using Kubernetes objects. A full example of the structure of one of these objects is provided in the Evermore Industries case study in this chapter. With proper permissioning, this add-on allows a developer proficient with Kubernetes to create several types of GCP resources, including SQL databases, networks, BigQuery datasets and tables, Compute Instances, Pub/Sub topics and subscriptions, and storage buckets. In addition, these configurations can reference each other, simplifying configuration and allowing for a single source of truth.

Users can also use Kubernetes Secrets to store sensitive information, such as passwords, and then use that information in Config Connector resources. Each of the Config Connector objects also includes a status section, describing the current state of the resource as it is created or updated in GCP.

POLICY CONTROLLER

Although the Kubernetes role-based access control system can finely control what a specific user is permitted to do at the namespace and object-type level, it does not enforce arbitrary policies, or policies on specific objects. For example, we may want all Pods deployed in a specific namespace to declare CPU limits for the containers, or require that all namespaces include a custom label that indicates the cost center that should be billed for the resource usage. We may also want to protect a specific deployment and prevent modifications to that specific resource, while still allowing other resources in the same namespace to be modified. This is where Policy Controller comes into play.

Built from the open source OPA Gatekeeper project (http://mng.bz/ydpG), Policy Controller (http://mng.bz/X5mG) is an admission controller that checks and verifies any creation of, or update to, an object against the policies that have been declared and loaded to the cluster. Each policy consists of a constraint template, which is written using Rego to perform the test needed, and a constraint, which provides the arguments to the template for the specific policy. A set of existing templates, known as a template library, is provided by default when Policy Controller is enabled, though users can create customized constraint templates as well. Users can then create constraints that use these policy templates to enforce specific restrictions on the cluster.

Because we are utilizing ACM, we can pair the policy constraints with `Cluster-Selectors` to restrict which clusters a particular policy applies to, locking some down while allowing a more relaxed set of rules on others.

HIERARCHY CONTROLLER

Hierarchy Controller (http://mng.bz/Mlr7) is the newest add-on to fall under the ACM umbrella and is still in open beta at the time of writing. This controller substantially changes how namespaces work within Kubernetes by allowing for inheritance between namespaces and is driven from the Kubernetes Working Group for Multitenancy (https://github.com/kubernetes-sigs/multi-tenancy). Though similar to how abstract namespaces work in a hierarchy ACM repo, this component takes it a step further by allowing objects to be actively replicated from a parent namespace to a child. This is especially useful when using an ACM repo that does omit Secrets as part of the repo (due to the security considerations involved). By configuring the Hierarchy Controller to replicate a Secret from a parent to a child or children, a single Secret can be replicated to multiple namespaces, simplifying the amount of rework or manual intervention required.

One other useful feature of Hierarchy Controller is the synergy between the controller and Cloud Logging. When the `enablePodTreeLabels` flag is set on the ACM config file, Hierarchy Controller sets flags on all pods, including those in child namespaces. This also indicates how far down the hierarchy tree the pod is located. Figure 11.2 contains an example.

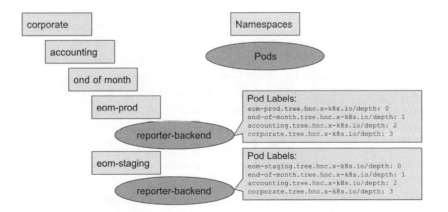

Figure 11.2 Namespaces and Pods with hierarchy-related labels when `enablePodTreeLabels` is enabled

As you can see in this example, we have the `eom-prod` and `eom-staging` namespaces as children of the `end-of-month` namespace. The `end-of-month` namespace is a child of `accounting`, which is a child of the `corporate` namespace. As you can see in figure 11.2, the hierarchy labels applied to the `reporter-backend` Pods correspond to the namespace hierarchy. In Kubernetes, you can query by the presence of a label, as well as by the value. So, if we wanted to see all Pods under the `accounting` and child namespaces, we can run `kubectl --all-namespaces get pods -l accounting.tree .hnc.x-k8s.io/depth`, and it would fetch both instances of the reporter backend. These labels also appear in Cloud Logging and can be used to fetch Pods in multiple namespaces there.

11.3 *Examples and case studies*

ACM is built on top of Kubernetes objects, operating within the cluster life cycle to efficiently manage the state of the cluster. So far, we have seen the components of ACM; in the next section, let's examine three case studies in detail. Each of these fictional companies is either using Kubernetes currently and wants to optimize their deployment or is moving to Kubernetes for the first time; each will use ACM to perform slightly different functions.

Our first company, Evermore Industries, has decided to use a single, large cluster with many nodes. All their application teams will run their Dev, QA, and production environments in parallel namespaces. Evermore wants to take advantage of GCP resources whenever possible, but their application developers do not have a lot of experience with infrastructure as code (IaC) tools. The core infrastructure team does have experience in IaC but lacks sufficient members to provision everything the application teams desire. Management has decided to allow the application teams to manage portions of their own cloud infrastructure but still wants to impose certain guidelines and policy rails to prevent out-of-control expenditures. Finally, due to the multitude of applications in the company and the variable permission levels involved, a service mesh is needed to isolate and control traffic.

Village Linen, LLC, was founded approximately two decades ago and previously ran all their infrastructure locally in two data centers near their headquarters. Partially due to a change in ownership at one of their data centers, but also due to bad results on past high-traffic shopping days, the company has decided to use the cloud to enable rapid scalability, while keeping several core functions in their one remaining data center. However, corporate leadership wishes to retain the ability to run their entire application stack solely from the local data center and has mandated that the two environments be as close to identical as possible and that failover should be as simple and quick as possible. Village Linen also wants to allow developers the freedom to manage their own namespaces, without accidentally affecting other applications and without creating a lot of overhead to approve each change.

Our final company, Ambiguous Rock Feasting, runs several hundred restaurants across the United States and Canada and has started expanding into Europe and Asia. Currently, their onsite applications (including inventory control, payroll, FOH systems, scheduling, and accounting) are updated via a monthly patch process that pushes the changes to the individual stores. This requires specialized networking and can be temperamental at times. The company wishes to pivot to a solution that does not require their central IT network to maintain persistent connections to the individual stores. They have also had problems in the past modifying their deployment processes and technology when adding a new application to the suite, as well as when trying to deploy targeted versions of the software to different regions.

11.3.1 Evermore Industries

For Evermore Industries, the simplicity of only having one large cluster to manage was key. However, managing the large number of namespaces, users, permissions, and GCP resources was proving too much for their IT operations. Thus, they turned to ACM, Policy Controller, and Config Connector to take some of the heavy load.

During a short proof of concept at the beginning of their migration, the IT operations team realized that an unstructured repo would allow them to more easily attach specific policies to individual namespaces (such as applying consistent rules to production namespaces) while also allowing the use of team-based rules without requiring a large amount of duplication. The unstructured repository also permitted the IT security team to easily restrict which users had permission to modify specific folders in the repo. Thus, a developer on Team Griffins could not accidentally delete something from Team Unicorns, and no application team members were allowed to modify the global policies. This reduced, but did not eliminate, the amount of configuration review needed for each change.

Although Evermore has been using Kubernetes for a few years, their CI/CD process[5] uses a templating engine (Helm) to deploy directly to the cluster. This setup has caused a few problems in the past, and management has decided to move away from users having direct access to make changes to the `prod` namespace directly, including the CI/CD service accounts. Because an unstructured repo does not mandate any particular organization for the config elements in the directory, Evermore has decided to continue to use their templating engine but write the configs directly to the ACM repo and create pull requests when a new version is to be deployed. Because these actions can quickly be validated by the operations team administrators, they can be quickly deployed to the active repo.

In addition, several application teams have expressed interest in using GCP resources to offload some of the workloads for their applications. Primarily, these teams are interested in Cloud SQL, Pub/Sub, and storage buckets. Because the application teams have almost no one with experience using IaC tools, or with GCP in general, Evermore will be using Config Connector to allow the teams to remain in the Kubernetes space for all deployment needs, as well as removing the need to configure and train users to access both Kubernetes and GCP itself. Let's take a look at the repo outline, shown here:

```
<Git Repo Parent>
├── bin
└── policies
```

---

[5] For more information on CI/CD and Anthos, see chapter 12.

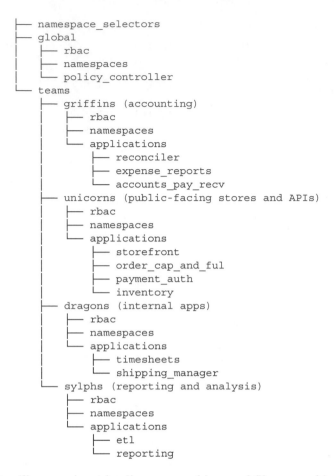

```
├── namespace_selectors
├── global
│   ├── rbac
│   ├── namespaces
│   └── policy_controller
└── teams
    ├── griffins (accounting)
    │   ├── rbac
    │   ├── namespaces
    │   └── applications
    │       ├── reconciler
    │       ├── expense_reports
    │       └── accounts_pay_recv
    ├── unicorns (public-facing stores and APIs)
    │   ├── rbac
    │   ├── namespaces
    │   └── applications
    │       ├── storefront
    │       ├── order_cap_and_ful
    │       ├── payment_auth
    │       └── inventory
    ├── dragons (internal apps)
    │   ├── rbac
    │   ├── namespaces
    │   └── applications
    │       ├── timesheets
    │       └── shipping_manager
    └── sylphs (reporting and analysis)
        ├── rbac
        ├── namespaces
        └── applications
            ├── etl
            └── reporting
```

We will not go into detail on every object and file created in this repo, but this outline gives us a place to start with the structure Evermore has chosen.

In an unstructured repo, the policy directory is not permitted to be at the top level of the Git repository, so the company has chosen to place it in a policies directory one level down. Within that directory, objects can be placed at any level, so the IT operations team has placed a set of common namespace selectors in the namespace_selectors directory. One of these is the production selector, as shown next:

```
kind: NamespaceSelector
apiVersion: configmanagement.gke.io/v1
metadata:
  name: production
spec:
  selector:
    matchLabels:
      env: production
```

To simplify the work for the application teams, IT operations also defined a selector that would normally only reference one namespace as follows:

```
kind: NamespaceSelector
apiVersion: configmanagement.gke.io/v1
metadata:
  name: cc-project-ns
spec:
  selector:
    matchLabels:
      evermore.com/is-active-project: true
```

To prevent massive changes in the event a new project is created, all Config Connector objects defined by the teams use the namespace selector method to choose the appropriate namespace to deploy their objects to. For example:

```
apiVersion: storagebuckets.storage.cnrm.cloud.google.com/v1beta1
kind: StorageBucket
metadata:
  name: evermore-shipping-pk-list-archive
  annotations:
    configmanagement.gke.io/namespace-selector: cc-project-ns
spec:
  versioning:
    enabled: true
  storageClass: ARCHIVE
```

In the global directory are policies defined by the IT operations team that apply across the cluster for both RBAC and Policy Controller. In the RBAC directory, the namespace-scoped roles for Dev/QA and production are defined separately. The roles use `NamespaceSelectors` to apply to multiple namespaces with one configuration. `NamespaceSelectors` are used via an annotation, and all namespace-scoped objects in an unstructured repo must declare either a namespace directly (via `metadata.namespace`) or use a `NamespaceSelector`. Here is the basic production role most developers will receive:

```
apiVersion: rbac.authorization.k8s.io/v1
kind: Role
metadata:
  name: prod-developer
  annotations:
    configmanagement.gke.io/namespace-selector: production
rules:
- apiGroups: [""]
  resources: ["pods", "configmaps"]
  verbs: ["get", "watch", "list"]
- apiGroups: ["apps", "extensions"]
  resources: ["deployments", "replicasets"]
  verbs: ["get", "watch", "list"]
- apiGroups: [""]
  resources: ["secrets"]
  verbs: ["list"]
```

The policy_controller directory is where Evermore has decided to put all their Policy Controller constraints. In addition to constraints requiring the definition of container limits and restrictions on the Istio[6] Service Mesh, the IT operations team has also added the following constraint to force teams to define the environment and team for a given namespace:

```
apiVersion: constraints.gatekeeper.sh/v1beta1
kind: K8sRequiredLabels
metadata:
  name: ns-must-have-env-and-team
spec:
  match:
    kinds:
    - apiGroups: [""]
      kinds: ["Namespace"]
  parameters:
    labels:
    - key: "env"
      expectedRegex: "^(production|development|qa)$"
    - key: "team"
      expectedRegex: "^(griffins|unicorns|dragons|sylphs)$"
```

In addition to requiring the labels to be set on namespaces, this constraint also limits what the valid values are. The Policy Controller infrastructure allows for the creation of custom constraint templates, but Evermore has been able to implement all their desired policies with those from the provided library.

The namespaces directory in the global folder holds configurations that are managed by IT operations and are either not used by any application team or are used by most or all teams. For example, this includes the Istio namespace and the Config Connector project namespace. In addition, subfolders underneath this folder contain Secrets, ConfigMaps, and Deployments that would be used across the system. The IT operations staff has placed some of the general Istio configs as well as configs that should be replicated to multiple namespaces (including a contact information `ConfigMap` that can be mounted via environment variables in each application) in this structure.

For each team's folder, the rbac and namespaces directories are handled by the individual application teams, though the changes must still be approved by a member of IT operations via a pull request. The namespace directory holds the namespace declarations for each application and environment, whereas the rbac directory holds the RoleBindings and ClusterRoleBindings for each user.

Inside each of the application folders (reconciler, storefront, etl, etc.), three folders exist for each environment. These folders are tied into the CI/CD processes that already exist for each application. The CI/CD pipelines were already configured to generate the Kubernetes objects to be loaded onto a cluster, so the teams changed the

---

[6] Istio is explored in detail in chapter 4.

destination to output to a set of files in the appropriate environment's directory. This CI/CD process also triggers an automatic pull request with the change, which can then be quickly approved and processed by a member of the IT operations staff.

Evermore chose this configuration for their repo because it best suits their needs at the present time. However, they are using an unstructured repo, so changing the directory structure is a low-cost option, if needed. Other companies might choose to concentrate all RBAC-related objects into a single directory, or to eliminate the concept of a "team" altogether and organize everything based on the individual applications. The unstructured repo allows the freedom to organize your policies in a manner that makes the most sense for your organization, instead of being restricted to a namespace-centered structure.

11.3.2 Village Linen, LLC

Village Linen has decided to go forward with a hierarchy repo, but they are going to use Hierarchy Controller to help with automatic replication of some of their Secrets and ConfigMaps. They are running GKE on GCP, as well as a GKE on VMware in their existing data center and want both to operate almost identically inside the cluster.

Disaster recovery is an important problem for corporate management, but management understands that data replication can sometimes be a problem when handling failover. Therefore, the architects have developed a system that allows for users to use both the cloud and the on-prem application layer but uses a single database cluster in the cloud. The database is replicated locally (the configuration of the replication is not included or covered here), and a configuration change directs the applications to use the standby database located in the data center. The repo generally looks as follows:

```
<Git Repo Parent>
├── bin
└── policy_directory
    ├── namespaces
    │   ├── rbac.yaml
    │   ├── central
    │   │   ├── namespace.yaml
    │   │   └── database_location_config.yaml
    │   ├── applications
    │   │   ├── service_account.yaml
    │   │   ├── website
    │   │   │   ├── namespace.yaml
    │   │   │   ├── hierarchy.yaml
    │   │   │   └── repo-sync.yaml
    │   │   └── inventory
    │   │       ├── namespace.yaml
    │   │       ├── hierarchy.yaml
    │   │       └── repo-sync.yaml
    │   └── village-linen-ac15e6
    │       ├── namespace.yaml
    │       ├── hierarchy.yaml
    │       └── repo-sync.yaml
```

```
├── cluster
│   ├── rbac.yaml
│   ├── hierarchy.yaml
│   └── constraints.yaml
├── clusterregistry
│   ├── data center.yaml
│   ├── cloud.yaml
│   └── selectors.yaml
└── system
    └── repo.yaml
```

Starting from the bottom, we have a definition for the repo that contains the current version of the policies. In the clusterregistry directory, we have cluster definitions for the cluster in the local data center, as well as the cluster in GCP. We also have selectors defined for each of these clusters so that we can restrict resources in the namespaces directory. The cloud cluster declaration and selector, for example, are as follows:

```
kind: Cluster
apiVersion: clusterregistry.k8s.io/v1alpha1
metadata:
  name: vili-cloud
  labels:
    locality: cloud
---
kind: ClusterSelector
apiVersion: configmanagement.gke.io/v1
metadata:
  name: sel-clu-cloud
spec:
  selector:
    matchLabels:
      locality: cloud
```

In the cluster directory, we have configurations that apply to the cluster as a whole. These include ClusterRoles and ClusterRoleBindings and Policy Controller constraints. By default, Hierarchy Controller only propagates RBAC Roles and RoleBindings from parent to child namespaces. However, Village Linen wants to use Hierarchy Controller to synchronize Secrets and config maps from the central namespace to the application and project namespaces. This way, Secrets can be applied directly to the central namespace and replicated automatically without needing to be checked into a Git repository. The modified HNCConfiguration follows:

```
apiVersion: hnc.x-k8s.io/v1alpha1
kind: HNCConfiguration
metadata:
  name: config
spec:
  types:
    - apiVersion: v1
      kind: ConfigMap
      mode: propagate
```

```
- apiVersion: v1
  kind: Secret
  mode: propagate
```

Moving up to the namespaces directory, we have a top-level file to define a set of RBAC roles to be created in each namespace. Village Linen can then bind these roles at either the `applications` abstract namespace (which would apply the bindings to the `website` and `inventory` namespaces), or to the explicitly defined namespaces to control who has access to these roles.

The directory here defines a total of four namespaces: `central`, `website`, `inventory`, and `village-linen-ac15e6`. The last namespace matches the project ID used to deploy resources for use with these clusters (also the location where the cloud GKE cluster is deployed). The two application namespaces share a service account definition, though this will create two separate service accounts, one in each namespace. In the central namespace, we declare a `ConfigMap`, which tells the applications which database to use, either the Cloud SQL or the on-prem cluster.

In each of the "child" namespaces (`website`, `inventory`, and `village-linen-ac15e6`), the repository has a `HierarchyConfiguration` object that enables the Hierarchy Controller to propagate objects from parent to child:

```
apiVersion: hnc.x-k8s.io/v1alpha2
kind: HierarchyConfiguration
metadata:
  name: hierarchy
spec:
  parent: central
```

In this case, all the "child" namespaces inherit from a common parent, but it is possible to "stack" these namespaces into a chain. For example, we could introduce another namespace—applications—which inherits from `central` and modify `inventory` and `website` to inherit from `applications` instead. Performing this type of stacked hierarchy allows for a finer control of what is replicated, as well as adds additional tagging to the logs, if enabled.

When enabling Hierarchy Controller for a given cluster, an additional option can be selected, which includes the tree labels on Pods. These labels indicate the hierarchy relationship for the Pod and can be used both with command-line tools and in Cloud Logging, to filter for logs that descend from a given namespace.

Because Village Linen is using a hierarchy repo, explicitly defining the `metadata` `.namespace` field is not required for objects in the namespaces directory. However, the namespace itself is required to be explicitly defined; Village Linen has chosen to place these definitions in the namespace.yaml files, though that is not required. The objects defined in the `website` and `inventory` namespaces are used to enable the multiple repository functionality covered next. However, the Cloud SQL cluster is defined in the final folder of the namespaces directory. The cloud_sql.yaml defines the SQL database, instance, and user as follows:

```
---
apiVersion: sql.cnrm.cloud.google.com/v1beta1
kind: SQLInstance
metadata:
  name: village-linen
  annotations:
    configmanagement.gke.io/cluster-selector: sel-clu-cloud
spec:
  region: us-central1
  databaseVersion: POSTGRES_9_6
  settings:
    tier: db-custom-16-61440
---
apiVersion: sql.cnrm.cloud.google.com/v1beta1
kind: SQLDatabase
metadata:
  name: village-linen-primary
  annotations:
    configmanagement.gke.io/cluster-selector: sel-clu-cloud
spec:
  charset: UTF8
  collation: en_US.UTF8
  instanceRef:
    name: village-linen
---
apiVersion: sql.cnrm.cloud.google.com/v1beta1
kind: SQLUser
metadata:
  name: village-linen-dbuser
  annotations:
    configmanagement.gke.io/cluster-selector: sel-clu-cloud
spec:
  instanceRef:
    name: village-linen
  password:
    valueFrom:
      secretKeyRef:
        name: db-creds
        key: password
```

As you can see, Config Connector allows references both to other Config Connector objects (the `instanceRef` declarations in the previous code snippet) and Secrets. Config Connector can also pull information from ConfigMaps. For security reasons, the `db-creds` Secret is not stored in the ACM repo. However, because the Hierarchy Controller is configured to replicate Secrets and ConfigMaps, we can manually create or update the Secret in the central namespace, and the Hierarchy Controller will handle the replication to the application and project namespaces. When Config Connector reconciles the next time, the new password will be used for the user.

All the Config Connector configurations include an annotation with a cluster selector. This references the cluster selector defined in the clusterregistry directory for the cloud installation of GKE. Because Config Connector works to create GCP resources from Kubernetes objects, it is active only on GKE in GCP clusters. The company did not enable Config Connector in the local cluster, so trying to deploy these resources would fail. Even if Config Connector were enabled on the local cluster, deploying the resources there should not have any effect and would probably cause more troubleshooting problems, so we only deploy them to the cloud cluster.

With this configuration, if Village Linen needs to switch from the cloud database back to a local database, a simple change to the `database_location_config` should be made. After deploying and pushing the updated configuration, the individual applications would need to be restarted.

In the directory structure outlined earlier, each application namespace contains a repo-sync file. These objects are used to implement multiple repository mode:

```
apiVersion: configsync.gke.io/v1alpha1
kind: RepoSync
metadata:
  name: repo-sync
  namespace: website
spec:
  git:
    repo: https://source.developers.google.com/p/village-linen-
      ac15e6/r/website
    branch: master
    auth: gcenode
    secretRef:
      name: acm-website-repo
```

By using multiple repository mode, Village Linen can create separate repositories for each namespace, allowing application teams a simpler experience when modifying Kubernetes objects (including the Deployment, Services, and persistent volumes) for their application. This arrangement also restricts the teams from accidentally deploying something outside of their namespace. The operations team is still able to add items to each namespace using the core repository, and these exist in parallel with the namespace-specific objects. In the event of a conflict, the core repository's version is the one used, preventing the application teams from overriding policies, service accounts, Secrets, and so on that the operations team has already defined. In addition, because the operations team has restricted which objects the namespace's worker can modify using RBAC, the individual repositories are sandboxed to control only a limited set of objects and cannot grant themselves permissions unless the operations team allows it.

For Village Linen, ACM provides a convenient location for all core configurations to be centrally located and updated, while freeing the application teams to control their own namespaces. It also provides a convenient audit trail when configurations change. When either the local data center cluster or the cloud cluster fails for any reason, a new cluster can be spun up and connected to the ACM repo, rapidly and automatically deploying the full operational stack.

11.3.3 *Ambiguous Rock Feasting*

For Ambiguous Rock Feasting (A.R. Feasting), managing their expanding set of restaurants and the technology deployed within has become increasingly difficult over the past few years. The company now feels that the implementation time for the technology pieces along with the additional operational overhead each new location places on their IT operations team have become unsustainable. Therefore, they are moving to a more flexible model that will scale better.

The restaurants already ran Kubernetes clusters on their local servers, but updating the deployed applications or troubleshooting problems caused a significant time loss for each location. Therefore, A.R. Feasting has pivoted to using ACM to manage the individual clusters. In general, the repository layout matches that of Village Linen, except A.R. Feasting is not using Hierarchy Controller.

When deploying the ACM operators, each location's cluster was given a dedicated name, such as `arf-043-01a`. The IT operations team then labeled these clusters using Cluster definitions in the policy repo like so:

```
kind: Cluster
apiVersion: clusterregistry.k8s.io/v1alpha1
metadata:
  name: arf-043-01a
  labels:
    sales-area: us-midwest
    country: us
    region: texas
    city: austin
    location-code: alpha
```

Or like this one for `arf-101-01a`:

```
kind: Cluster
apiVersion: clusterregistry.k8s.io/v1alpha1
metadata:
  name: arf-101-01a
  labels:
    sales-area: emea
    country: uk
    region: england
    city: london
    location-code: alpha
    is-rollout-tester: true
```

The IT operations team then define selectors based on these labels, some of which are included here:

```
---
kind: ClusterSelector
apiVersion: configmanagement.gke.io/v1
metadata:
  name: rollout-testers
```

```
spec:
  selector:
    matchLabels:
      is-rollout-tester: true
---
kind: ClusterSelector
apiVersion: configmanagement.gke.io/v1
metadata:
  name: non-testers
spec:
  selector:
    matchExpressions:
    - key: is-rollout-tester
      operator: DoesNotExist
---
kind: ClusterSelector
apiVersion: configmanagement.gke.io/v1
metadata:
  name: country-us
spec:
  selector:
    matchLabels:
      country: us
```

These selectors are then used to control deployments of new versions of applications,
or to deploy only certain applications in certain regions. For example, only restaurants in the United States have drive-throughs. Therefore, the drive-through management application needs to be deployed only to the country-us clusters. The company
has also decided to have certain selected stores be test beds of new software, as indicated by the is-rollout-tester flag on their cluster. An example deployment for an
application is included here. However, some portions of the template have been
removed because they are identical between the two examples:

```
---
apiVersion: apps/v1
kind: Deployment
metadata:
  name: foh-engine
  annotations:
    configmanagement.gke.io/cluster-selector: rollout-testers
spec:
  template:
    spec:
      containers:
      - name: engine
        image: gcr.io/ambiguous-rock/foh/engine:v2.1.0
        imagePullPolicy: IfNotPresent
---
apiVersion: apps/v1
kind: Deployment
metadata:
  name: foh-engine
```

```
    annotations:
      configmanagement.gke.io/cluster-selector: non-testers
spec:
  template:
    spec:
      containers:
      - name: engine
        image: gcr.io/ambiguous-rock/foh/engine:v2.0.3
        imagePullPolicy: IfNotPresent
```

The differences between these two deployments are the cluster selector used and the version of the engine image. Looking back at the cluster selectors defined, `rollout-testers` and `non-testers` do not overlap. If we had not defined a `non-testers` group and left the annotation off the second deployment earlier, we would have had a collision for the `rollout-testers` because both deployments would have been valid.

Because ACM logs the changes it makes using the same logging standards as Kubernetes, and with A.R. Feasting restaurants forwarding their logs to Cloud Logging, the IT operations team can set up monitoring using Cloud Monitoring to determine the status of specific applications and versions on the various clusters. Using this dashboard, they can quickly diagnose where potential problems might be (such as a power outage at a store) and work more efficiently.

11.4 Conclusions

Organizations face increasing complexity managing their IT environments. Using Anthos Config Management with Kubernetes clusters, whether on-prem, in Google Cloud, or in another cloud provider, provides administrators with a familiar, declarative method to control the foundations of their clusters. This chapter has provided a broad overview of the service, some of the reasons to adopt a strategy incorporating ACM, and a couple of examples to illustrate the power of Anthos Config Management.

However, we have not fully explored the capabilities and possibilities of Anthos Config Management: doing so would take a book all its own. Ultimately, ACM is intended to make your business more efficient and to reduce the complexity of managing your clusters. This chapter should have provided you with ideas on how to use ACM in your own organization, as well as some examples of how to drive adoption.

For more information and examples on various topics touched on in this chapter, see the corresponding section of this book:

- Policy Controller: chapter 13
- Cloud Logging: chapter 5

Summary

- As the number of clusters an organization manages increases, enforcing best practices or providing core functionality becomes exponentially more difficult.
- Modern development practices and the security landscape encourage organizations to adopt technologies that can rapidly adapt and deploy changes.

- Anthos Config Management is a core component of the Anthos platform, intended to provide the security and transparency that infrastructure, security, and operations teams desire, while also giving development teams the ability to deploy their applications with minimal additional hurdles.
- ACM can be deployed in the following two modes, both offering distinct advantages:
  - Hierarchical mode allows for easy deployment of a single resource across multiple namespaces and requires a logical collection of namespaces to be effective.
  - Unstructured mode allows for developers and administrators to more easily pick and choose which namespaces to deploy components to, with the drawback of needing to be explicit about which namespace(s) to use. This mode is also compatible with many templating frameworks that may not function properly in hierarchical mode.
- ACM includes custom resources allowing for greater control over which namespaces and which clusters to apply configuration elements to.
- ACM also brings in the following additional components based on open source tools:
  - Config Connector provides infrastructure-as-data capability to a Kubernetes cluster, allowing for the provisioning of Google Cloud resources by declaring a Kubernetes resource.
  - Policy Controller gives administrators a convenient tool to create and enforce policies across their clusters.
  - Hierarchy Controller is the result of an initiative to provide an alternative method of replicating resources between namespaces in a cluster. Because storing Secrets in a Git repo is an antipattern, Hierarchy Controller definitions allow an organization to define a Secret or configuration once and have it replicated to the descendant namespaces automatically.
- The following three case studies explored different reasons for using and implementing ACM:
  - Evermore Industries wants to reduce the number of users directly working in their production environment and allow development teams to provision certain Google Cloud resources directly. They are currently using, and will continue to use, a templating engine for generating their Kubernetes configurations.
  - Village Linen, LLC, is using ACM both on- and off-prem, as well as Hierarchy Controller to manage the replication of ConfigMaps and Secrets within both sets of clusters.
  - Ambiguous Rock Feasting is well versed in Kubernetes but is making specific use of the `ClusterSelector` feature of ACM to more precisely control where their applications are deployed.

Integrations with CI/CD

Konrad Cłapa and Jarosław Gajewski

This chapter covers

- Understanding CI/CD concepts
- Automating a continuous development workflow
- Introducing continuous integration for your Anthos application
- Using Cloud Deploy to manage continuous deployment
- Understanding modern CI/CD platforms

In this chapter, we will guide you in developing and deploying Anthos applications. To simplify this task, we will use a simple Hello World application. We will go through the entire workflow, shown in figure 12.1, using examples in both Python and Go. We'll start with continuous development, where we will learn how we can start developing an Anthos application and preview it even before we commit the code to the Git repository. We'll then look at continuous integration, and finally, we will discuss continuous deployment and delivery.

The following three personas interact with CI/CD pipelines:

- *Developers*—Develop the application code
- *Operators*—Configure the application deployments using Kubernetes manifests
- *Security*—Configures the policies to make the Kubernetes Deployments secure

In this chapter, we will concentrate on the first two personas. If you want to learn more about the Security persona, refer to chapter 13.

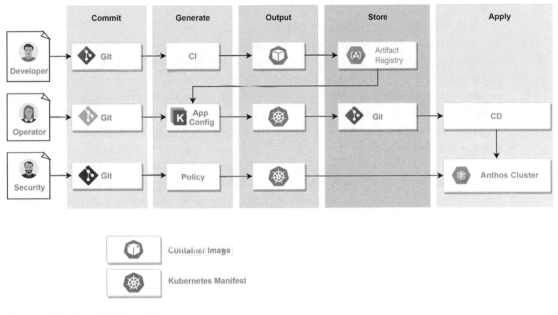

Figure 12.1 The CI/CD workflow

Looking at the workflow of developers, we see that they develop the application code and want to see the preview of the application immediately. Then, if they are finished with their changes, they commit the code to the source code repository. This is where CI kicks in with code reviews, testing, and builds of container images.

When we think about the operators, we see that they are responsible for both configuring the Kubernetes infrastructure and deploying the application. They need to be able to configure the application for multiple environments, including development, test, and production. Once the configuration is ready, the application can be deployed using CD tools.

Now that we understand the use case, let's start with a brief introduction to CI/CD concepts.

12.1 Introduction to CI/CD

Modern software development processes are complex. Producing high-quality software at a consistent pace and in a sustainable manner involves several processes and tools. The implementation of a CI/CD pipeline is one of the best practices to achieve this. *Continuous integration (CI)* is the practice of software development where developers check in their code frequently, integrating regularly—at least once a day—and each integration is followed by validation, which is an automated process to build and test integrated change (http://mng.bz/aMpz). This process allows us to achieve reliable, repeatable, and reusable builds with constant speed and at a proper level while preventing chaos and improving efficiency.

Continuous integration is only one aspect of the software delivery process. For a successful pipeline-driven development, CI must be followed by continuous delivery. *Continuous delivery (CD)* (https://continuousdelivery.com/) is the ability to get changes of all types, including new features, configuration changes, bug fixes, and experiments, into production safely and quickly in a sustainable way. It applies to infrastructure configurations, application deployment, and mobile app publishing, and database and static resource modifications. Continuous delivery can be used in any environment, regardless of the regulatory requirements for a particular organization. A CD pipeline improves delivery of software from source to production by making this process more automated, thus improving reliability, predictability, and visibility of the pipeline, which reduces risks.[1]

Let's look at some features that characterize modern CI/CD platforms.

12.1.1 Repeatability

Repeatability allows for automation of requirements and processes around created code and artifacts. Build processes should be deterministic, so developers have confidence in produced artifacts. Repeatable builds and testing allow developers to run the same processes in their local environments as well. Automation of deployment and configuration management helps to provide consistency across environments.

12.1.2 Reliability

Reliability improves confidence of the development and operational teams in the processes and systems that guarantee availability and suitability of the tools as well as the completeness and sufficiency of integration, testing, and operational requirements. Automated testing via defined workflows is key to capture and track components' final success and failure states, increasing team confidence and knowledge during development and release cycles.

---

[1] Jez Humble and David Farley, *Continuous Delivery: Reliable Software Releases Through Build, Test, and Deployment Automation* (Addison-Wesley Professional, 2010).

12.1.3 *Reusability*

Reusability enables teams to scale up, simplify, and speed up development workflows. A CI/CD pipeline should be implemented in such a way that allows for reusing components of the pipeline for similar applications. This not only reduces the cost of setting up new pipelines but also improves developer efficiency when working with multiple applications across the enterprise.

12.1.4 *Automated tests*

In a high-quality delivery process, it is critical to validate developed systems' architecture and functionality. This can be achieved via the implementation of a robust automated testing flow as an integral part of the CD pipeline. Modern delivery pipelines should have as many automated tests as possible, including not only unit, component, and system functional tests but also nonfunctional ones that check capability, availability, and security compliance. Automated tests provide almost immediate feedback to developers, decreasing the number of bugs and the error rate for production deployments.

12.1.5 *Trunk-based development*

Continuous delivery can be significantly slowed down when developers work in "split-brain" environments, where feature or bug-fix code branches have a very long lifetime. As a result, in big teams, code changes can cause conflicts when integrating long live branches. This may require manual activities, grinding CI processes to a halt.

12.1.6 *Environment parity*

Environmental consistency is one of the key aspects of reducing risk in production deployments. Deployments to the development and production environment must rely on the same processes, architectural principles, and configuration policies. Fully automated deployments are essential to enable automated testing and feedback in the CD pipeline. It allows easy reproduction of the entire state of the environment based on the code and data stored in the version control systems.

12.1.7 *Deployment automation*

It's important to acknowledge that deployment automation can be a journey that should be realized in small steps. You should start with components that are easy to automate, reduce the number of manual steps, and slowly progress to automate more complex components. Looking at deployment automation and testing, one factor plays an important role: architecture. The best processes and tools used for CD cannot help us if our architecture introduces significant limitations and is a tightly coupled design.

12.1.8   Team culture

Full cooperation between operations and development teams is required to automate build, testing, deployment, and infrastructure. This ensures the entire process is fully understood by all parties and does not introduce unnecessary complexity. It is not an easy process, and it often requires long hours spent together to rework architecture for existing processes.

12.1.9   Built-in security/DevSecOps

Prevention is better than cure. The same applies for software delivery and challenges related to security. Shortening the feedback loop for teams during software delivery is known as the *shifting-left approach*. The same approach is used to introduce security processes early in the development process and across the entire continuous delivery flow. This approach enables teams to build a development stack that is based on pre-approved, standardized tools and policies (http://mng.bz/gJKl). This tooling helps teams address security requirements as part of their regular development and delivery activities. Standardization enables additional testing capabilities, where automated tests can be extended to meet security and regulatory requirements in the production setups. Like automated deployment, automation for security measures can be implemented in small steps, reducing the need for manual reviews and tests over time. As a result, developers don't need to care about it anymore.

12.1.10 Version control

Version control must be applied to every single artifact of our delivery and integration pipelines, starting from application code, configuration, and system configuration, and closing on scripts used for automated build and configuration of environments. It supports developers during application development via auditability or scalability of "as a code"–based environments. It also reacts to demand for immediate changes or disasters in production caused by vulnerability or defects discovered in the system or environment, allowing them to be released in a controlled way with an easy way for automated rollback.

It is quite simple to maintain a small version control system, but when teams are growing, code maintainability becomes more and more challenging. In such cases, it is key to allow all team members easy access to code. Due to this, they will reuse existing code instead of creating duplicate copies and extend the code for new capabilities or to fix bugs globally. Version control promotes quick software delivery because knowledge can be passed between teams easily. It results in a higher quality of code and, consequently, increases scalability and availability.

12.1.11 Artifact versioning

Build artifacts need to be idempotent and immutable for teams to trust the integrity of the build system. Systems that create artifacts from the same source multiple times risk generating slightly different artifacts in each step due to config drifts. Managing build artifacts and their versions is important to prevent storing different versions of the same artifact in multiple places. Immutable versioned artifacts provide full visibility into history and references in a single place. This also helps manage dependencies and improves reuse.

12.1.12 Monitoring

The final capability to highlight is *monitoring*. Understanding and monitoring the health of a system are critical to mitigate possible problems before they occur. Proactive failure notifications based on threshold or rate-of-change warnings build operational knowledge about the system's status. Extended by logging and monitoring, failure alerts routed to teams or systems introduce a chance to react to these events in a timely manner and prevent outages and downtime.

Full-stack monitoring allows support teams to debug systems and measure their behaviors against defined patterns or changes. *Historical monitoring data* allows us to introduce continuous improvements fast, which improves efficiency of the CI/CD pipelines.

12.2 Continuous delivery vs. continuous deployment

We talked a lot about continuous delivery, which often is mixed with continuous deployment. Even though they are hidden behind the same CD abbreviation, a subtle difference exists between the concepts. Continuous deployment extends continuous delivery by adding autodeployment of delivered artifacts to user environments without manual intervention. Though continuous delivery is applied to all kinds of software, business applications, mobile apps, and firmware, continuous deployment is applicable mostly when code changes can be immediately applied to production.

As we have familiarized ourselves with the CI/CD concept and capabilities, we can now move into detailed description of implementation options, practices, and tools.

12.3 Continuous development

Developing cloud native applications is very exciting but comes with some challenges. Figure 12.2 shows the flow that developers need to follow to get the preview of a Kubernetes application.

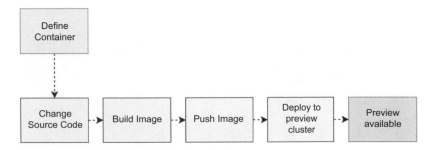

Figure 12.2 Continuous development workflow

As we see, once the code is developed, an image needs to be built and pushed to the container registry, following predefined steps. Next, the application needs to be deployed to the target cluster. This means that for every change committed by the developer, the same workflow is triggered. Imagine a full day of running multiple commands just to get your application previewed! This is becoming a developer's nightmare.

In this section, we will look at some tools that will allow us to both deploy the Anthos application locally without the need to have a running Anthos cluster and automate the entire flow we identified.

Let's start by setting our local execution environment based on minikube. Next, we will look at how to automate the repeatable and laborious tasks needed to preview the application after code changes. Finally, we will discuss how we can use an integrated development environment (IDE) to deliver a complete Anthos application development experience (DX).

12.3.1 *Setting up a local preview minikube cluster*

minikube (https://minikube.sigs.k8s.io/docs/start/) is a popular software application that allows you to run Kubernetes applications locally on your laptop. It runs on Windows, Linux, and macOS. Instead of deploying your application to an Anthos cluster, you can deploy it locally and preview your application before pushing the code to the Git repository. This will save you time and reduce development environment cost. Even though minikube is not designed to host production workloads, it supports most of the features supported by Kubernetes.

You can interact with it like with a regular cluster using the kubectl command-line interface. You can Minikube on any laptop that fulfills the following minimum requirements:

- 2 CPUs
- 2 GB of free memory
- 20 GB of free disk space
- Internet connectivity
- Virtualization software like Virtual Box

Figure 12.3 shows the tools that you can use to interact with minikube. We will review Skaffold and Cloud Code in the following sections of this chapter. They provide a great alternative for a development Anthos cluster.

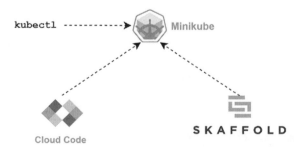

Figure 12.3   minikube integrations

The installation process is fairly simple but depends on the OS you use. This might change with new version releases, so it is recommended you refer to the official page at https://minikube.sigs.k8s.io/docs/start/ for the installation procedure. Let's look at how we can deploy our example application using minikube.

Once minikube is successfully installed, you can start it by running the following command:

```
minikube start
```

Now you can create a simple hello-minikube Deployment and expose it using the NodePort service. We will use an already existing container image, echoserver:1.4, but you can also build your own image:

1 Create a Deployment by running the following:

```
kubectl create deployment hello-minikube --image=k8s.gcr.io/echoserver:1.4
```

2 Expose the Deployment by creating a service:

```
kubectl expose deployment hello-minikube --type=NodePort --port=8080
```

3 Check the service exists:

```
kubectl get services hello-minikube
```

4 You should see the following prompt:

```
NAME             TYPE       CLUSTER-IP      EXTERNAL-IP   PORT(S)          AGE
hello-minikube   NodePort   10.102.94.116   <none>        8080:31029/TCP   8s
```

5 Configure port forwarding for the service to your local machine port:

```
kubectl port-forward service/hello-minikube 8080:8080
```

The following prompt will appear indicating the port is forwarded:

```
Forwarding from 127.0.0.1:8080 -> 8080
Forwarding from [::1]:8080 -> 8080
```

6 Now we can open the browser and see that the service is responding on the address http://localhost:8080, as shown in figure 12.4.

We have now seen how to preview our application. As you may have noticed, it still requires us to build the images and use kubectl to update the preview of the application followed by a change in code. This process is not very efficient, and, ideally, we need a tool to automate these steps. A common tool to achieve that is Skaffold.

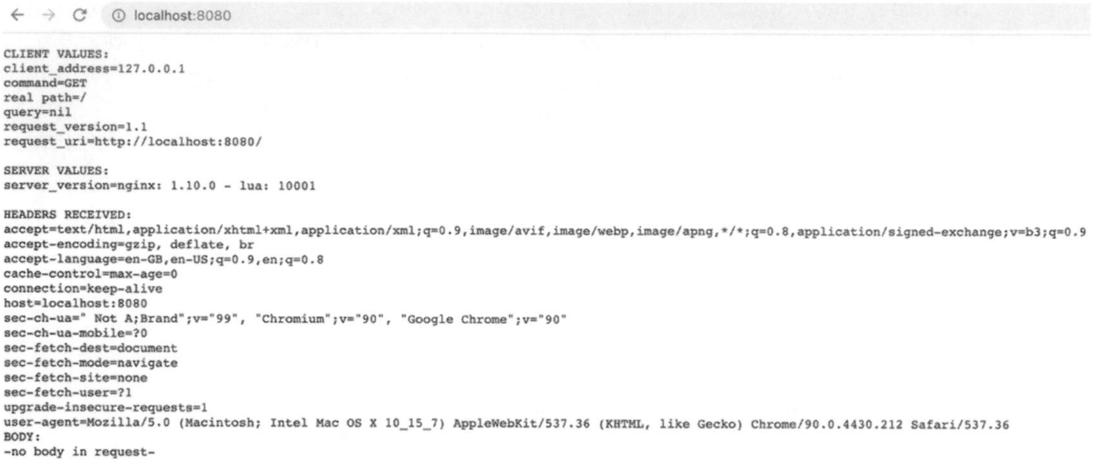

← → C   ⓘ localhost:8080

CLIENT VALUES:
client_address=127.0.0.1
command=GET
real path=/
query=nil
request_version=1.1
request_uri=http://localhost:8080/

SERVER VALUES:
server_version=nginx: 1.10.0 - lua: 10001

HEADERS RECEIVED:
accept=text/html,application/xhtml+xml,application/xml;q=0.9,image/avif,image/webp,image/apng,*/*;q=0.8,application/signed-exchange;v=b3;q=0.9
accept-encoding=gzip, deflate, br
accept-language=en-GB,en-US;q=0.9,en;q=0.8
cache-control=max-age=0
connection=keep-alive
host=localhost:8080
sec-ch-ua=" Not A;Brand";v="99", "Chromium";v="90", "Google Chrome";v="90"
sec-ch-ua-mobile=?0
sec-fetch-dest=document
sec-fetch-mode=navigate
sec-fetch-site=none
sec-fetch-user=?1
upgrade-insecure-requests=1
user-agent=Mozilla/5.0 (Macintosh; Intel Mac OS X 10_15_7) AppleWebKit/537.36 (KHTML, like Gecko) Chrome/90.0.4430.212 Safari/537.36
BODY:
-no body in request-

Figure 12.4   The browser results page

12.3.2   *Continuous development with Skaffold*

Skaffold (https://skaffold.dev/) is an open source project sponsored by Google. It was started to address the needs for continuous development for Kubernetes applications. As we learned in the previous section, for a developer to deploy an application, they must write the necessary steps to create the container image, push the created image to a repo, and finally, get it deployed to a cluster.

Skaffold achieves this by handling all those steps automatically. It continuously watches the source files and triggers the previously mentioned steps to create a preview of the Kubernetes application on a local minikube or remote Anthos cluster. The application resources are cleaned up automatically when the developer stops Skaffold by simply pressing Ctrl+C.

On top of continuous development capabilities, Skaffold offers building blocks for CI/CD pipelines. It supports deployments using kubectl, Helm (https://helm.sh/), and Kustomize (https://kustomize.io/). Let's look at figure 12.5, which visualizes a flow for how development with Skaffold looks.

In this figure, you can see a simple pipeline visualization. Skaffold is watching for source file changes in an indicated folder. When it detects a change, Skaffold automatically builds images and pushes them to the registry. Once containers are built, Skaffold deploys the container image to a predefined Kubernetes endpoint. In an upcoming section, we will explain how Skaffold is integrated with Cloud Code (https://cloud.google.com/code) for an even better developer experience.

WORKING WITH SKAFFOLD

The user interacts with Skaffold using a command-line interface (CLI). A complete guide for Skaffold can be found here: https://skaffold.dev/docs/references/cli/. For

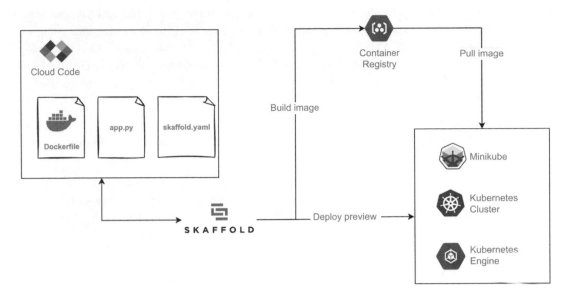

Figure 12.5   Skaffold functionalities

a quick overview of how to work with Skaffold, let's look at the basic steps. We will see how we can deploy the Hello World application written in Go.

INSTALLING SKAFFOLD

The process for installing Skaffold varies, depending on the underlying operating system. Skaffold can be installed as a component of gcloud. It is also available as a container image, gcr.io/k8s-skaffold/skaffold:latest, which can be used directly in cloud native CI/CD tools. All installation options are explained at the official site (https://skaffold.dev/docs/install/). For a local preview, you can use minikube, which will allow you to deploy your application on your laptop.

SKAFFOLD CONFIGURATION FILE

Skaffold uses a single configuration YAML file, skaffold.yaml, to define the steps in a CD pipeline. It resembles a Kubernetes resource manifest. Let's look at a very basic sample config file here:

```
apiVersion: skaffold/v2beta8
kind: Config
build:
  artifacts:
  - image: skaffold-example
deploy:
  kubectl:
    manifests:
      - k8s-*
```

Two phases are defined in the previous pipeline: build and deploy. In the build phase, Skaffold looks for a Dockerfile definition and uses it to build a container image with the name `skaffold-example`. In the deploy phase, Skaffold uses kubectl to deploy all objects defined in the YAML files starting with the `k8s-` prefix. A comprehensive explanation of the configuration file structure can be found on the Skaffold site (https://skaffold.dev/docs/references/yaml/).

INITIATING SKAFFOLD

You can generate a skaffold.yaml configuration automatically by running the following:

```
skaffold init
```

This will detect the source files in the current folder and create a very simple configuration file with build and deploy sections. Let's create the following three files, as shown in the next code snippet:

- *Dockerfile*—Container image definition
- *main.go*—Simple Hello World Go application
- *k8s-pod.yaml*—Kubernetes pod definition

Dockerfile content:

```
FROM golang:1.12.9-alpine3.10 as builder
COPY main.go .
ARG SKAFFOLD_GO_GCFLAGS
RUN go build -x -gcflags="${SKAFFOLD_GO_GCFLAGS}" -o /app main.go
FROM alpine:3.10
runtime
ENV GOTRACEBACK=single
CMD ["./app"]
COPY --from=builder /app .
Main.go content:
package main
import (
  "fmt"
  "time"
)

func main() {
  for {
    fmt.Println("Hello world!")
    time.Sleep(time.Second * 1)
  }
}
k8s-pod.yaml content:
apiVersion: v1
kind: Pod
metadata:
  name: getting-started
spec:
  containers:
  - name: getting-started
    image: skaffold-example
```

This will generate a skaffold.yaml file, which we have already seen in the previous section, with two phases:

```
apiVersion: skaffold/v2beta3
kind: Config
metadata:
  name: getting-started
build:
  artifacts:
  - image: skaffold-example
deploy:
  kubectl:
    manifests:
    - k8s-pod.yaml
```

You can take it from here and expand the file as per your needs, using the Skaffold documentation.

DEVELOPING WITH SKAFFOLD

We ended up having four files in the folder, including the Skaffold config file. Now we can start to do continuous development, where Skaffold will be watching the source folder for changes and perform all the steps defined in the skaffold.yaml file. To start the development, run the next command:

```
skaffold dev
```

Skaffold will automatically tail the logs from the deployed container to the console. Now if you change the source file main.go to print hello from Skaffold instead of hello world, Skaffold will automatically detect the change, rebuild the image, push it to the registry, and deploy it. As the logs tail to the console, you should see the message hello from Skaffold.

SINGLE RUN WITH SKAFFOLD

Although skaffold dev has been continuously watching the source files, you can also perform a single execution of the workflow by running the skaffold run command. This is useful when you want to run the execution only once and not trigger the flow every time your code is modified.

SUPPORTED FEATURES

By now you should have a basic understanding of how to start development with Skaffold, so let's look at other useful features available.

Pipelines stages

Up to now, we have looked only at the basic functionalities of Skaffold. However, the tool has more capabilities that can address advanced pipeline stages. For example, a developer might not want to rebuild the images after every code change. In such a case, Skaffold can synchronize the files into the container main.go source file. To achieve this, you would use the file sync feature. Figure 12.6 shows all the steps in the workflow.

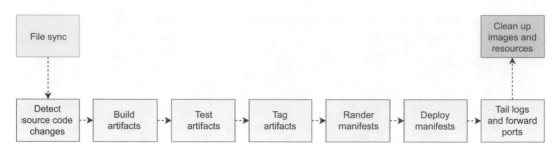

Figure 12.6   Skaffold workflow

The following list shows all the Skaffold pipeline stages that can be used to execute these steps:

- *Init*—Generates basic Skaffold configuration
- *Build*—Builds images with builders of choice
- *Test*—Tests images with structure tests[2]
- *Tag*—Tags images based on different policies
- *Deploy*—Deploys the application with kubectl, Kustomize, or Helm
- *File sync*—Synchronizes the changed files directly to running containers
- *Log tailing*—Tails logs from containers
- *Port forwarding*—Forwards ports from services to localhost
- *Cleanup*—Cleans up manifests and images

As you can see, we have a complete pipeline that allows us to deploy and preview Anthos applications.

Supported environments

Skaffold supports both local and remote Kubernetes clusters. You can use a local development cluster like minikube or an Anthos/Kubernetes cluster deployed in a remote location.

To connect to a remote Kubernetes cluster, you need to set a context in the kubeconfig file as if connecting to any Kubernetes cluster. The default context can be overwritten by running

```
skaffold dev --kube-context <myrepo>
```

or by updating the skaffold.yaml file deploy.kubeContext attribute:

```
deploy:
  kubeContext: minikube
```

---

[2] Structure tests are a Google-developed mechanism of testing containers; for details consult http://mng.bz/eJzz.

Supported build tools

If you need to use another tool to build container images, the build section of the skaffold.yaml configuration file can be configured for custom builders. To use a custom builder, define the proper options for using that builder to the build section. Details about customer builders are at http://mng.bz/pdvG. The following tools are currently supported:

- Docker
- Jib (http://mng.bz/Oprn)
- Bazel (http://mng.bz/Y64N)
- Buildpacks (http://mng.bz/GRAq)

You can also use custom scripts that are in line with the Skaffold defined standard.

USING SKAFFOLD IN CI/CD PIPELINES

You can also use Skaffold as a tool in your CI/CD pipelines. An existing community-maintained builder (http://mng.bz/zmOa) can be directly used with Cloud Build, which is a native CI Google Cloud tool (we will have a look at it in detail in the next section). Some of the most useful Skaffold commands in CI/CD workflows follow:

- `skaffold build`—Builds and tags your image(s)
- `skaffold deploy`—Deploys the given image(s)
- `skaffold delete`—Cleans up the deployed artifacts
- `skaffold render`—Builds and tags images and outputs templated Kubernetes manifests

SKAFFOLD SUMMARY

In this section, we have learned how to install Skaffold and use it in a continuous development workflow. Follow the Skaffold Quickstart guide at https://skaffold.dev/docs/quickstart/ for more information on using Skaffold with development workflows.

12.3.3 Cloud Code: Developing with a local IDE

We have learned how we can preview the Anthos application, but now let's look at how we can elevate this experience. One of the unaddressed challenges so far is maintaining the configuration for the development environment. Developers want to develop their applications without leaving their favorite IDE. Cloud Code improves the developer experience by integrating the already known set of tools to provide containerization and deployment of applications, including the following:

- kubectl
- Skaffold
- Google Cloud SDK (gcloud)

Cloud Code is a plug-in for IDEs like Visual Studio Code (https://code.visualstudio.com/) and IntelliJ (https://www.jetbrains.com/idea/). It integrates with minikube and Kubernetes clusters, including Anthos clusters. It comes with the Google Cloud platform API explorer and Kubernetes objects explorer. You can use it to view your Kubernetes resources directly from IDE without running a single kubectl command.

Figures 12.7 and 12.8 show the collection of prebuilt application templates that can run and debug an Anthos application (both Kubernetes and Cloud Run). The first figure allows you to generate all the files you need to deploy simple applications. The second automatically detects changes to source files, builds container images, and deploys to the selected Kubernetes endpoint. All these tasks are deployed by Skaffold.

Figure 12.7 also shows the flow for an Anthos/Kubernetes application, which is very similar to the Skaffold flow. The difference is that the developer uses an IDE to perform these steps.

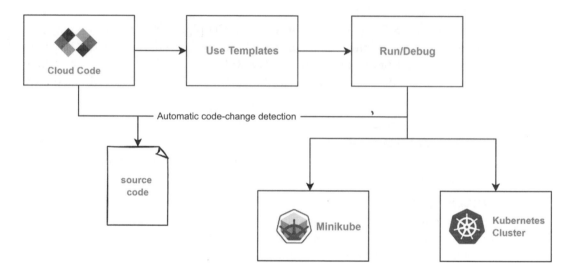

Figure 12.7   Running and debugging a Kubernetes application with Cloud Code

As shown in figure 12.8, Cloud Code helps us by setting up an emulator based on minikube. It runs locally and enables the developer to run and test the Cloud Run applications. It is also possible to deploy to GCP-managed services like Cloud Run or Cloud Run for Anthos.

For both options, you can debug your code running on the local and remote endpoint by creating breakpoints in your code. In the next section, you'll start working on our Hello World Anthos application with Cloud Code.

STARTING DEVELOPING WITH CLOUD CODE

You can kick-start development of your application by using prebuilt templates for both Kubernetes and Knative (Cloud Run) applications. This includes both simple single-service applications and multiservice apps for a variety of languages.

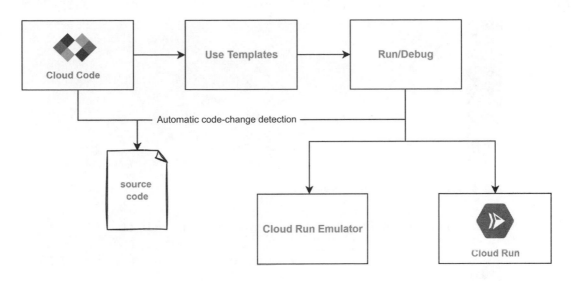

Figure 12.8   Running and debugging a Cloud Run application with Cloud Code

Let's look how we can start developing with Cloud Code. This time we will be using Visual Studio Code to work on an example Python Hello World application using the following steps:

1 Start by installing the Cloud Code from the Visual Studio Code Marketplace.
2 Open Visual Studio Code.
3 Find and click </> Cloud Code on the bottom blue bar in the main window, shown in figure 12.9.

Figure 12.9   Visual Studio Code: starting a new application

4 From the drop-down list that appears on the top of the screen, choose the New Application option, shown in figure 12.10. Note: This is also the starting point for other actions, such as the following:
  – Running the application on Kubernetes
  – Debugging the application on Kubernetes
  – Running the application on a Cloud Run emulator
  – Debugging the application on a Cloud Run emulator
  – Deploy the application to Cloud Run

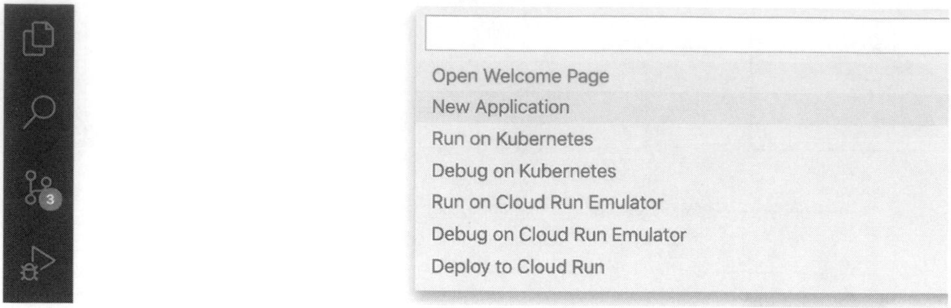

Open Welcome Page
New Application
Run on Kubernetes
Debug on Kubernetes
Run on Cloud Run Emulator
Debug on Cloud Run Emulator
Deploy to Cloud Run

Figure 12.10   Cloud Code New Application

5   Now choose Kubernetes Application, shown in figure 12.11.

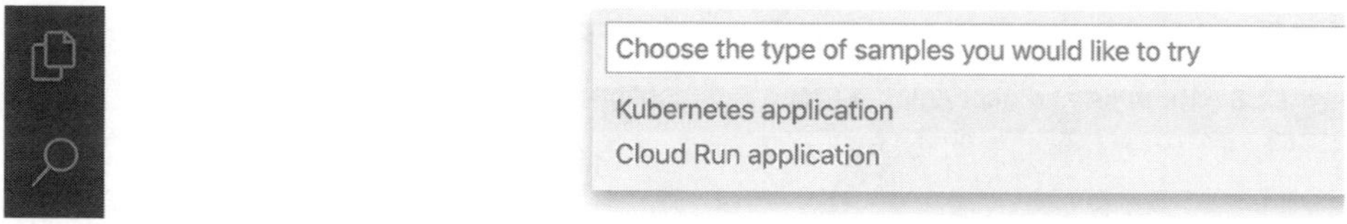

Choose the type of samples you would like to try

Kubernetes application
Cloud Run application

Figure 12.11   Cloud Code Kubernetes Application

6   For simplicity, we will use the Python (Flask) Hello World application, as shown in figure 12.12.

Choose a Template.

Python (Flask): Hello World
Python (Flask): Guestbook
Python (Django): Hello World
Python (Django): Guestbook
Go: Hello World
Go: Guestbook
Node.js: Hello World
Node.js: Guestbook
Java: Hello World
Java: Guestbook
.NET: Hello World
.NET: Guestbook

Figure 12.12   Cloud Code Python (Flask): Hello World

7   Wait a couple of seconds for Cloud Code to pull the templates with all the files, including vscode configuration files, Kubernetes manifests, source code, and the Skaffold config file, as illustrated in figure 12.13.

Figure 12.13   The Cloud Code skaffold.yaml

8   When all the files are ready, you can run the application by clicking </> Cloud
    Code again and choosing Run on Kubernetes from the drop-down menu, as
    shown in figure 12.14.

Figure 12.14   The Cloud Code option to run on Kubernetes

9   Cloud Code will ask if you want to use the default context. In this case, it is
    pointing to minikube. Confirm with Yes or choose a different context to deploy
    to different clusters, as shown in figure 12.15.

Figure 12.15   Cloud Code: setting the context to minikube

10 In the console, you should see the output shown in figure 12.16 with the URL to access the application.

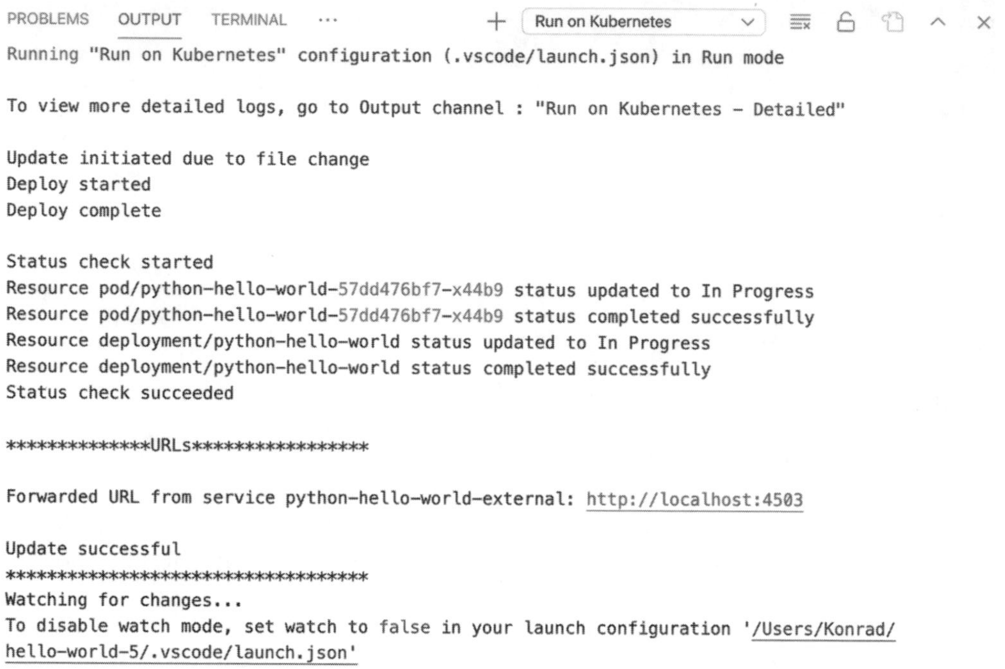

```
PROBLEMS   OUTPUT   TERMINAL   ...          +   [ Run on Kubernetes    ∨ ]   ≣ₓ  🔒  🗍  ∧  ✕
Running "Run on Kubernetes" configuration (.vscode/launch.json) in Run mode

To view more detailed logs, go to Output channel : "Run on Kubernetes - Detailed"

Update initiated due to file change
Deploy started
Deploy complete

Status check started
Resource pod/python-hello-world-57dd476bf7-x44b9 status updated to In Progress
Resource pod/python-hello-world-57dd476bf7-x44b9 status completed successfully
Resource deployment/python-hello-world status updated to In Progress
Resource deployment/python-hello-world status completed successfully
Status check succeeded

*************URLs*****************

Forwarded URL from service python-hello-world-external: http://localhost:4503

Update successful
*********************************
Watching for changes...
To disable watch mode, set watch to false in your launch configuration '/Users/Konrad/
hello-world-5/.vscode/launch.json'
```

Figure 12.16   Cloud Code console output

11 If you go to the URL, you will see the application is running, as shown in figure 12.17.

Figure 12.17   Cloud Code application output

12 Now you can make a small change to the source code. In the app.py file, find the Hello World message, shown in figure 12.18.

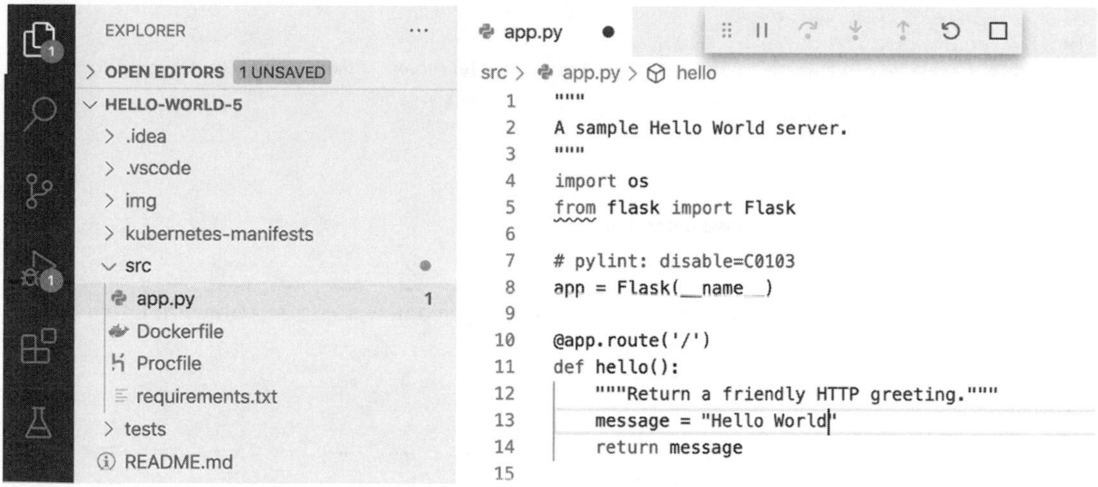

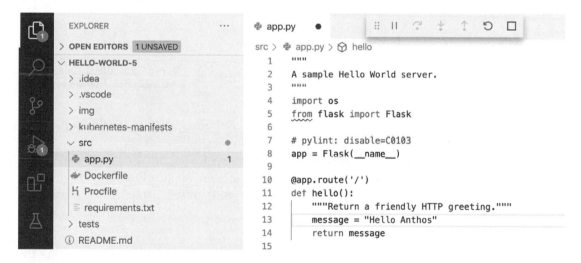

Figure 12.18   Cloud Code: browse the app.yaml.

13 Change the message to "Hello Anthos" and save the file, as shown in figure 12.19.

Figure 12.19   Cloud Code: change the message to "Hello Anthos."

14 You will notice, as shown in figure 12.20, that Cloud Code has detected the change and deployed the app to minikube.

```
************************************
Watching for changes...
To disable watch mode, set watch to false in your launch configuration '/Users/Konrad/hello-world-5/.vscode/
launch.json'
Update initiated due to file change
Deploy started
Deploy complete
```

Figure 12.20   Cloud Code: code change detection

15   Now when we access the application, we see a new message, shown in figure 12.21.

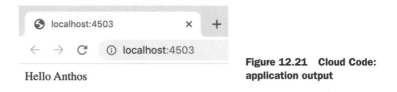

**Figure 12.21   Cloud Code:
application output**

Any changes in the source code will be picked up automatically. Note that you can pause or stop the application using the control bar, shown in figure 12.22, on the top of the screen.

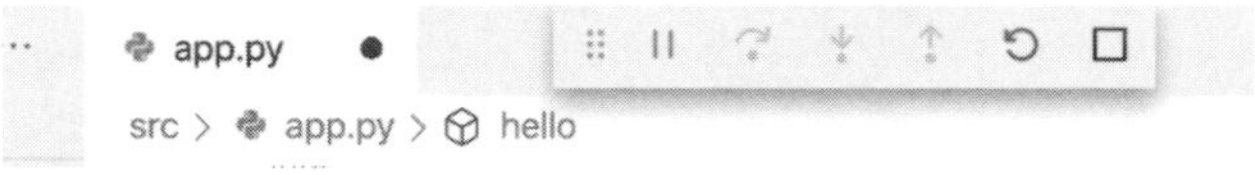

**Figure 12.22   Cloud Code:
continuous development menu**

You have successfully created a preview of the Kubernetes Hello World application. Now you can try more complex application examples.

As you have seen in the drop-down menu in step 4, you can also create and deploy applications to Cloud Run. You can also debug your applications by putting break points in your source code. Follow the how-to guide to see a step-by-step tutorial on how to do it at http://mng.bz/0yex.

SUMMARY OF CLOUD CODE

Cloud Code is a tool that not only seamlessly integrates with GCP but also makes the development, containerization, and preview of your Anthos application easy. It bundles the already discussed Skaffold functionality into your IDE to automate continuous development workflows.

Previewing Kubernetes applications requires a number of steps, like building a container image and deploying it to the preview environment every time you make changes to the code. With Cloud Code, you can concentrate on your source code and let the Cloud Code integrations take care of all those steps. In this section, we have used already existing templates to show you what the setup looks like. You can take it from there and start developing your own Anthos applications, and Cloud Code will make sure the preview will be updated for you.

12.3.4 *Anthos Developer Sandbox: Development with a cloud native IDE*

Anthos Developer Sandbox is a free tool for developers that gives you the feeling of what it looks like to develop on Anthos. It allows performing the same tasks described in the previous section but using Google Cloud Shell instead of locally. It is built of the following components:

- *Cloud Shell*—A computing environment with the best of Google Cloud Platform tooling preinstalled
- *Cloud Code*—The IDE plug-in, which we've already seen
- *Minikube*—A single-node Kubernetes cluster, which we've already discussed
- *Cloud Build Local Builder*—Runs continuous integration locally in the Cloud Shell

You don't need to perform any up-front configuration to use Anthos Developer Sandbox. You can access it from http://mng.bz/KlrK and start developing your first Anthos application. The most important thing is that it is available for free for anyone with a Google account. With Anthos Developer Sandbox, you can perform the following day-to-day development tasks:

- Run applications locally on an emulated Anthos cluster or Cloud Run emulator
- Use Cloud Build for testing locally
- Iterate on your application with automated live updates as you develop
- Use buildpacks to create your images

If you just started developing Anthos applications, using Sandbox will help you to kick-start your development journey because it comes with tutorials that are accessible directly from the interface.

STARTING WITH ANTHOS DEVELOPER SANDBOX

Let's have a quick look at the tool using the next steps:

1 Access the tool by opening the link we mentioned earlier in the browser. You will be informed that the Anthos Developer Sandbox will be cloned, as shown in figure 12.23.

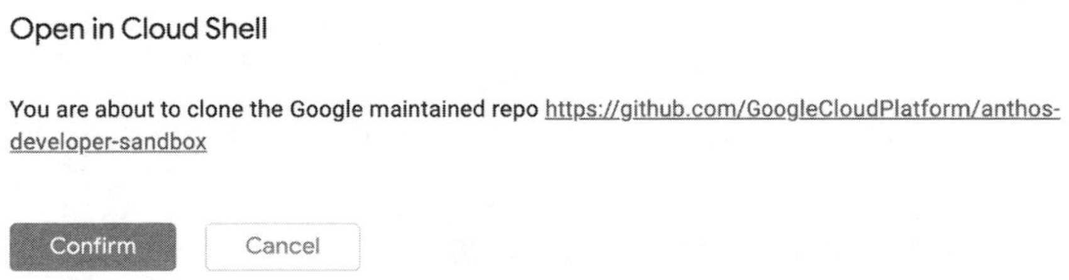

Open in Cloud Shell

You are about to clone the Google maintained repo https://github.com/GoogleCloudPlatform/anthos-developer-sandbox

Confirm   Cancel

Figure 12.23 Anthos Developer Sandbox: Welcome screen

2 Click Confirm and wait for the environment to be set up. You can see all the components being configured for you, as shown in figure 12.24.

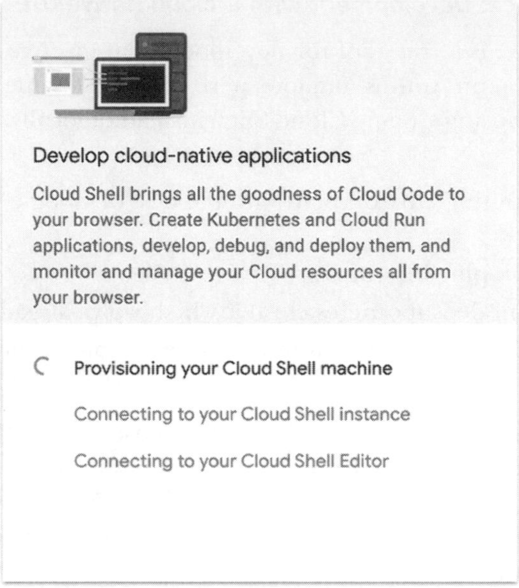

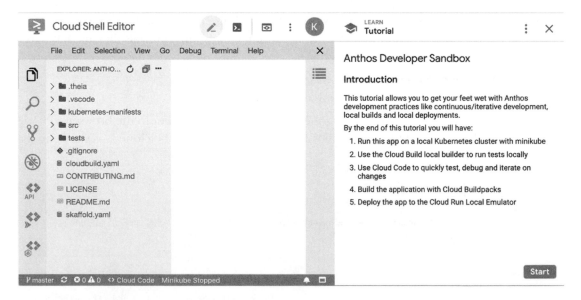

Figure 12.24   Anthos Developer Sandbox: preparation of the environment

3 Once it is finished, you should see the IDE loaded and the workspace ready with the cloned repo, as shown in figure 12.25. In the right pane, you can see the tutorial.

Figure 12.25   Anthos Developer Sandbox: main screen

4 Click Start to begin the tutorial. It will walk you through the same flow we had with Cloud Code.

As you have seen, you can start continuous development on Anthos with a few clicks and no special configuration.

12.4 Continuous integration

In this section, we will look at continuous integration. We will first walk through the GCP native tools and then see what the third-party alternatives are. To introduce continuous integration for your Anthos application, you will need the following components:

- Git source repository
- Container registry
- CI server

Let's start by creating a Git repository that will store and version the Anthos application code.

12.4.1 Cloud Source Repositories

Cloud Source Repositories (https://cloud.google.com/source-repositories) are fully featured, private Git repositories hosted on Google Cloud. The service helps developers to privately host, track, and manage changes to large codebases on Google Cloud Platform. It's designed to integrate easily with GCP services like Anthos, GKE, Cloud Run, App Engine, and Cloud Functions, as shown in figure 12.26. You can configure an unlimited number of repositories and also mirror Bitbucket and GitHub repositories. Changes in Cloud Source Repositories are monitored and can trigger event notifications to Cloud Pub/Sub or a Cloud Function. One of the differentiators of Code Source Repositories is that you can use regex expression to search for phrases in your repository (http://mng.bz/91jl). Cloud Source Repository audit logs are available in Cloud Operations, so you always know who has accessed your repository, and when.

As you see in figure 12.26, the integration for Cloud Run is particularly interesting. You can use a combination of Cloud Source Repositories and Cloud Build to create a CD pipeline to trigger an automated deploy pipeline of your application whenever there is code merge in your code repository. Cloud Run makes the operations more streamlined by taking care of your traffic shaping (blue/green, canary, rolling updates) based on your configuration under the hood. Refer to chapter 9 for details on how to configure it.

CREATING A REPOSITORY

To start working with Cloud Source Repositories, you first need to create the repository by running the following command:

```
gcloud init
```

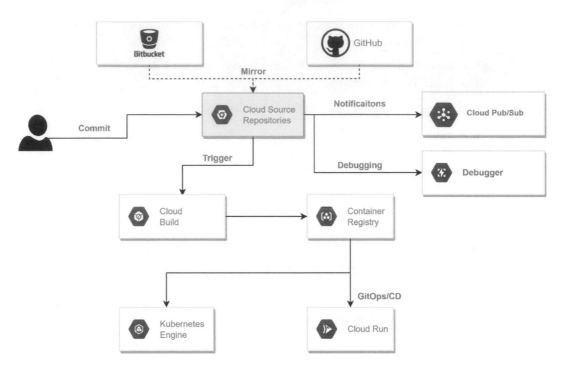

Figure 12.26   Cloud Source Repositories integrations

The next snippet will initialize your gcloud command-line tool:

```
gcloud source repos create [REPO_NAME]
```

This will create a repository of the name `REPO_NAME`.

Now that the repository is ready to use, you need to choose one of the following three authentication methods:

- SSH
- Cloud SDK
- Manually generated credentials

Refer to the following link to see a step-by-step guide on how to do it: http://mng .bz/jmWx.

Once the repository is set up and you have successfully authenticated, you can interact with it using Git commands like `git clone`, `git pull`, and `git push`.

12.4.2   *Artifact Registry*

Artifact Registry is the next iteration of the Google Container Registry service. On top of being able to store container images, Artifact Registry can store other packages like Maven (https://maven.apache.org/), npm (https://www.npmjs.com/), and Python, with more capabilities to come soon. The services are fully integrated with the Google Cloud Platform ecosystem, so you can control access to your artifacts using IAM policies, access Cloud Source Repositories, trigger automatic builds using Cloud Build, and deploy to Google Kubernetes Engine, App Engine, and Cloud Functions. You can create Artifact Repositories in regions closest to your workloads so you can take advantage of the high-speed Google network to pull your artifacts.

From a security standpoint, you can scan your containers for vulnerabilities, and Binary Authorization can be used to approve the images that can be pushed to production. You can use native tools to interact with Artifact Registry so it is easy to integrate them into CI/CD pipelines.

USING ARTIFACT REGISTRY WITH DOCKER

Let's see how you can interact with the Artifact Registry to store container images, using the next procedure:

1 Start by creating an artifact repository:

```
gcloud artifacts repositories create quickstart-docker-repo --
repository-format=docker \
--location=us-central1 [--description="Docker repository"]
```

2 You can list your repositories by running the next command:

```
gcloud artifacts repositories list
```

3 Before pushing images, you should authenticate to the repository:

```
gcloud auth configure-docker us-central1-docker.pkg.dev
```

4 Now, for demo purposes, just pull the official alpine image from Docker Hub instead of building a new image:

```
docker pull alpine
```

5 Tag the image with the repository name:

```
docker tag alpine us-central1-docker.pkg.dev/PROJECT/quickstart-docker-
repo/quickstart-image:tag1
```

6 You can finally push the image to the Artifact Registry:

```
docker push us-central1-docker.pkg.dev/PROJECT/quickstart-docker-
repo/quickstart-image:tag1
```

Now you are ready to pull your container images from the registry.

At the time of writing, the Artifact Registry is generally available, though some of the features might be in preview. As a successor of Container Registry, it will eventually be the only container registry available in GCP, so all your new projects should be already using Artifact Registry. The step-by-step tutorial on how to transition to Artifact Registry for existing projects can be found here: http://mng.bz/WAn0.

12.4.3   *Cloud Build*

We have already seen how we can version the Anthos application code and build container images. Now let's look at how we can create a CI pipeline.

Cloud Build is a managed, GCP-native CI/CD platform and is an alternative for tools like GitLab CI/CD, Jenkins, or CircleCI. It allows you to deploy, test, and build your application on all Google compute services including Anthos GKE and Cloud Run for Anthos. The Cloud Build pipeline steps are run as containers, as shown in figure 12.27.

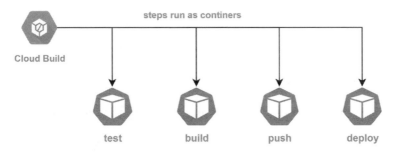

Figure 12.27   Cloud Build steps run as containers.

The pipeline steps are defined in a simple-to-understand cloudbuild.yaml file presented here. These steps are read by Cloud Build and executed. Each step defines a container to run as a task. The containers used in pipelines are specially built for Cloud Build and are called *cloud builders*. We will learn more about them in the following section.

```
# cloudbuild.yaml
steps:
# This step runs the unit tests on the app
- name: 'python:3.7-slim'
  id: Test
…
# This step builds the container image.
- name: 'gcr.io/cloud-builders/docker'
  id: Build
…
# This step pushes the image to a container registry
- name: 'gcr.io/cloud-builders/docker'
  id: Push
```

```
...
# This step deploys the new version of our container image
- name: 'gcr.io/cloud-builders/kubectl'
  id: Deploy
```

Cloud Build is completely serverless and can scale up and down based on the load. You pay only for the execution time. It does not require you to install any plug-ins and can support a variety of tools with custom cloud builders. Because it is connected to the GCP network, it can significantly reduce build and deployment time via direct access to repositories, registries, and workloads. You can also combine Cloud Build with tools like Spinnaker (https://spinnaker.io/) to execute even more complex pipelines that include various deployment scenarios. Cloud Build pipelines can be triggered either manually or by code repository pull requests.

Now that we understand the basis of how Cloud Build works, let's look at cloud builders.

CLOUD BUILDERS

As we have already learned, Cloud Build runs a series of steps defined in the cloud-build.yaml file that are executed within containers. The containers are deployed using container images defined in the name attribute of each step. Those container images are called cloud builders, which are specially packaged images that run a specific tool like Docker, Git, or kubectl with a set of user-defined attributes. Three types of builders follow:

- Google-supported builders
- Community-supported builders
- Custom-developed builders

Let's look at each type.

Google-supported builders

You can find a full list of Google-supported builders on GitHub at http://mng.bz/819P. All the images are available in a container registry under gcr.io/cloud-builders/<builder name>. Some of the most important builders in the context of Anthos follow:

- docker
- git
- gcloud
- gke-deploy
- kubectl

Community-supported builders

If no official builder exists that fits your requirements, you can use one of the community builders, which are available with tools like Helm, Packer, Skaffold, Terraform, and Vault. The complete list of the community cloud builders can be found here: http://mng.bz/ElrJ.

Custom-developed builders

You can create your own custom builder for use in your builds. A custom builder is a container image that Cloud Build pulls and runs with your source. Your custom builder can execute any script or binary inside the container. As such, it can do anything a container can do. For instructions on creating a custom builder, see http://mng.bz/NmrD.

BUILDING CONTAINER IMAGES

You can build containers with Cloud Build either using config files or by using Dockerfile only. Let's look at each of the options.

Building container images using a configuration file

The first method of building the container requires you to provide the cloudbuild.yaml config file as an input, as shown in figure 12.28.

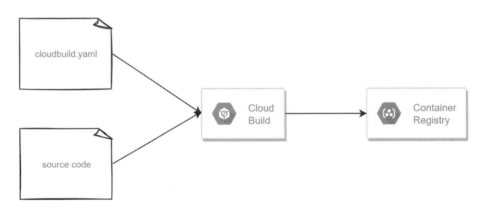

Figure 12.28   Building container images with Cloud Build config files

To build your image from the configuration file, you need to specify the build steps in the cloudbuild.yaml file using the Docker cloud builder as follows:

```
steps:
- name: 'gcr.io/cloud-builders/docker'
  args: [ 'build', '-t', 'us-central1-
     docker.pkg.dev/$PROJECT_ID/${_REPOSITORY}/${_IMAGE}', '.' ]
images:
- 'us-central1-docker.pkg.dev/$PROJECT_ID/${_REPOSITORY}/${_IMAGE}'
```

Next, run the following command to submit the build:

```
gcloud builds submit --config [CONFIG_FILE_PATH] [SOURCE_DIRECTORY]
```

This builds the image and stores it in Google Artifact Registry as indicated in the configuration file. If you don't specify the [CONFIG_FILE_PATH] and [SOURCE_DIRECTORY] parameters, the current directory will be used.

Using a Dockerfile to build a container image

You can create container images without using the configuration file because your Dockerfile contains all information needed to build a Docker image using Cloud Build, as shown in figure 12.29.

Figure 12.29 Building an image from a Dockerfile

To run a build request using your Dockerfile, run the following command from the directory containing your application code, Dockerfile, and any other assets:

```
gcloud builds submit --tag us-central1-docker.pkg.dev//[PROJECT_ID]/[IMAGE_NAME]
```

This builds the image and stores it in Google Artifact Registry.

Cloud Build notifications

You have multiple ways of getting notifications from Cloud Build. You can get notified about any changes in the build state, including start, transition, and completion of the build.

Cloud Build is well integrated with Pub/Sub and publishes messages to Pub/Sub topics. Both push and pull subscription models are supported. Having the message in the Pub/Sub queue gives you endless options for sending the notifications to the next step.

In addition to Pub/Sub, you can also get notifications from Cloud Build using one of the following notifications channels:

- *Slack*—Posts notifications to a Slack channel
- *SMTP*—Emails notifications via SMTP protocol
- *HTTP*—Sends notifications in JSON format to an HTTP endpoint

All three types of notifications use containers running as a Cloud Run service. An example of how to create such notifications can be found at http://mng.bz/DZrE.

DEPLOYING TO ANTHOS GOOGLE KUBERNETES ENGINE

Deployment to Google Kubernetes Engine can be done using either kubectl or the gke-deploy builder. Note that gke-deploy (https://github.com/GoogleCloudPlatform/cloud-builders/tree/master/gke-deploy) is basically a wrapper around kubectl that incorporates Google best practices to deploy Kubernetes resources. For example, it adds the label `app.kubernetes.io/name` to the deployed Kubernetes resources.

Next, you can see an example use of the gke-deploy builder to deploy to a GKE cluster:

```
steps:
...
# deploy container image to GKE
- name: "gcr.io/cloud-builders/gke-deploy"
  args:
  - run
  - --filename=[kubernetes-config-file]
  - --location=[location]
  - --cluster=[cluster]
```

In the future, we can expect other cloud builders like AnthosCLI that will make the experience even more unified.

DEPLOYING TO CLOUD RUN AND CLOUD RUN FOR ANTHOS

Cloud Build allows you to build your Cloud Run container image and then deploy it to either Cloud Run or Cloud Run for Anthos. In both cases, you would first build and push the image using a standard Docker builder:

```
steps:
# Build the container image
- name: 'gcr.io/cloud-builders/docker'
  args: ['build', '-t', 'us-central1-docker.pkg.dev/$PROJECT_ID/${_IMAGE}',
    '.']
# Push the container image to a registry
- name: 'gcr.io/cloud-builders/docker'
  args: ['push', 'us-central1-docker.pkg.dev/$PROJECT_ID/${_IMAGE}']
```

Then use the `cloud-sdk` builder to run the `gcloud run` command. For Cloud Run, set the `--platform` flag to 'managed':

```
# Deploy container image to Cloud Run
- name: 'gcr.io/google.com/cloudsdktool/cloud-sdk'
  entrypoint: gcloud
  args: ['run', 'deploy', 'SERVICE-NAME', '--image', 'us-central1-
    docker.pkg.dev/$PROJECT_ID/${_IMAGE}', '--region', 'REGION', '--platform',
    'managed']
images:
- 'us-central1-docker.pkg.dev/$PROJECT_ID/${_IMAGE}'
```

For Cloud Run for Anthos, set the `--platform` flag to 'gke' and indicate which cluster to deploy to by setting the `--cluster` and `--cluster-location` flags:

```
# Deploy container image to Cloud Run on Anthos
- name: 'gcr.io/google.com/cloudsdktool/cloud-sdk'
  entrypoint: gcloud
  args: ['run', 'deploy', 'SERVICE-NAME', '--image', 'us-central1-
    docker.pkg.dev/$PROJECT_ID/${_IMAGE}', '--cluster', 'CLUSTER',
    '--cluster-location', 'CLUSTER_LOCATION', '--platform', 'gke']
images:
- 'us-central1-docker.pkg.dev/$PROJECT_ID/${_IMAGE}'
```

DEPLOYING TO ANTHOS USING THE CONNECT GATEWAY WITH CLOUD BUILD

The Connect gateway, shown in figure 12.30, allows users to connect to registered clusters outside Google Cloud with their Google Cloud identity in the Cloud console. You don't need to have direct connectivity from the Cloud Build to the Anthos cluster API. Anthos Hub acts as a proxy for the kubectl command run in the cloud builder.

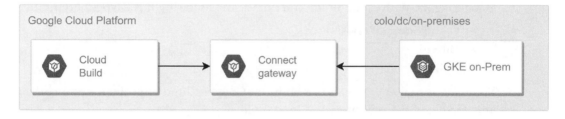

Figure 12.30 Connect gateway

To configure the Connect gateway and connect your Anthos cluster, follow the steps described in the Google documentation at http://mng.bz/lJ5y.

Once the Connect gateway is configured and the Anthos servers are registered, check whether they are visible in the fleet by running the following:

```
gcloud container fleet memberships list
```

In this case, we see two clusters are registered—one is a GKE on VMware, and the other is a GCP GKE cluster:

```
NAME                 EXTERNAL_ID
my-vmware-cluster    0192893d-ee0d-11e9-9c03-42010a8001c1
my-gke-cluster       f0e2ea35-ee0c-11e9-be79-42010a8400c2
```

Let's define the following step to deploy an application defined in the myapp.yaml manifest:

```
steps:
- name: 'gcr.io/cloud-builders/gcloud'
  entrypoint: /bin/sh
  id: Deploy to Anthos cluster on VMware
  args:
  - '-c'
  - |
    set -x && \
    export KUBECONFIG="$(pwd)/gateway-kubeconfig" && \
    gcloud beta container fleet memberships get-credentials my-vmware-cluster && \
    kubectl --kubeconfig gateway-kubeconfig apply -f myapp.yaml
```

As we see, in this case, the gateway kubeconfig is used rather than the cluster kubeconfig itself. The request will be sent to the gateway, and then the gateway will forward it to the `my-vmware-cluster`. This means that no hybrid connectivity like Cloud VPN or Interconnect is required to deploy your Anthos cluster outside of GCP.

TRIGGERING CLOUD BUILD

In the previous section, we learned how to deploy the application to any Anthos clusters. Now let's look at how we can trigger a Cloud Build pipeline by using either the `gcloud` command (which we have already looked at in the previous section) or automatic triggers. With Cloud Build, you can use the following three types of repositories:

- Cloud Source Repositories
- GitHub
- Bitbucket

To create a trigger, you can use both the Google Cloud console and the command line. First, add the repository to Cloud Build:

```
gcloud beta builds triggers create cloud-source-repositories \
--repo=[REPO_NAME] \
--branch-pattern=".*" \
--build-config=[BUILD_CONFIG_FILE] \
```

Then, add the trigger:

```
gcloud beta builds triggers create github \
--repo-name=[REPO_NAME] \
--repo-owner=[REPO_OWNER] \
--branch-pattern=".*" \
--build-config=[BUILD_CONFIG_FILE] \
```

With the `--branch-pattern`, you can specify which branch will trigger the build. In this case, it will be all branches.

If you would like know how to create triggers from the other repositories, consult the documentation at http://mng.bz/BlrJ.

SUMMARY OF CLOUD BUILD

Cloud Build, though simple to use, can provide an E2E CI/CD experience for delivering your Anthos applications, as shown in figure 12.31. If you want to get more hands-on experience with E2E pipelines, we encourage you to follow a tutorial at your own pace: http://mng.bz/dJGQ. In this tutorial, you will develop a pipeline that will support the following:

- Test of the committed code
- Build container image
- Push image to the registry
- Update the Kubernetes manifest and push it to the environment repository
- Detect changes on the branch
- Apply the manifest to an Anthos GKE cluster
- Update the production branch with the Kubernetes manifest applied

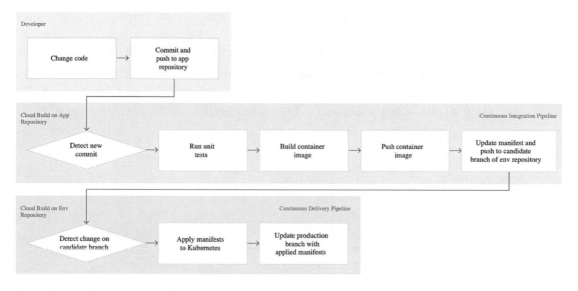

Figure 12.31   Steps in the CI/CD pipeline based on Cloud Build

This tutorial will give you a good idea of how to perform advanced tasks with Cloud Build. Note that you can deliver the same result with third-party tools like GitHub, GitLab, or Bitbucket, but Cloud Build is a native GCP tool that integrates nicely with Anthos.

12.4.4 *Kustomize for generating environment-specific configuration*

In real-life scenarios, you will deploy your application to multiple environments. In the CI/CD pipeline, you need a tool that will adjust the configuration of your app for each environment without changing the actual code base.

Kustomize is a standalone tool to customize Kubernetes resources by using a kustomization.yaml file. The good news is that since version 1.14 of Kubernetes, Kustomize has been merged into the kubectl tool, as shown in figure 12.32.

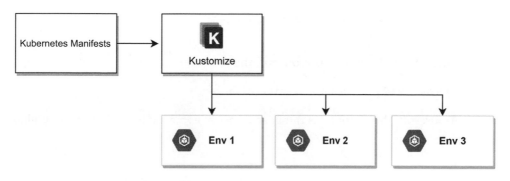

Figure 12.32   Customizing a Kubernetes manifest

As we see in figure 12.32, the basic manifest is patched and applied to each of the environments.

In figure 12.33, we see the following three files residing in a single folder:

- *Definition of the Deployment*—deployment.yaml
- *Kustomize file*—kustomization.yaml
- *Patch file*—patch.yaml, which defines which attributes should be changed in the Deployment

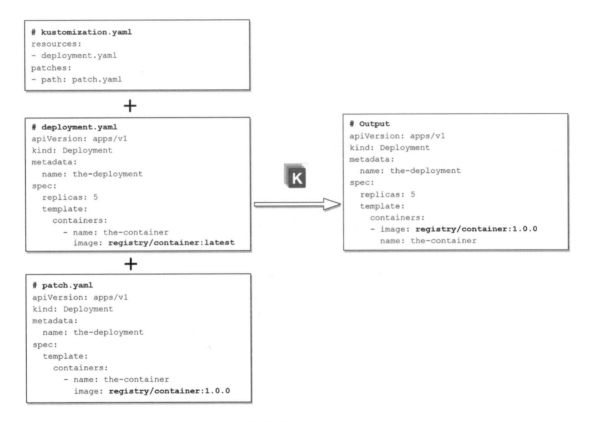

Figure 12.33   Patching deployment images with Kustomize

To perform the customization, run the next command:

```
kubectl apply -k <kustomization_directory>
```

As a result, the output has the `spec.template.containers.image` attribute updated.

KUSTOMIZE FEATURE LIST

Kustomize comes with all the features needed to customize your Kubernetes deployment, including the following, as shown in figure 12.34:

- Generating resources (ConfigMaps and Secrets)
- Setting cross-cutting fields
- Composing and customizing resources

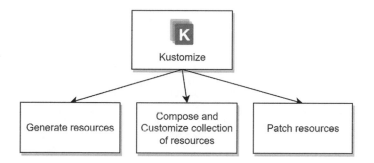

Figure 12.34   Kustomize features

Let's look at each of them in detail.

Composing

You can use the `resources` attribute to define which resource definitions you want to customize. If you don't include any other customization feature in the file, the resources will be simply composed into one definition. In the following example, we compose the deployment.yaml and service.yaml definitions:

```
# kustomization.yaml

resources:
- deployment.yaml
- service.yaml
```

To run the customization, execute the next command:

```
kubectl kustomize ./
```

Customizing

Customization allows you to patch your resources with specific values using the following methods:

- `patchesStrategicMerge` (http://mng.bz/rdQX)
- `patchesJson6902` (http://mng.bz/Vpo5)

For example, you can patch the `my-deployment` Deployment defined in the deployment.yaml file with the number of replicas by creating the following files:

```
# increase_replicas.yaml

apiVersion: apps/v1
kind: Deployment
metadata:
  name: my-deployment
spec:
  replicas: 3
```

```
# kustomization.yaml

resources:
- deployment.yaml
patchesStrategicMerge:
- increase_replicas.yaml
```

And run the following code:

```
kubectl kustomize ./
```

In addition to this customize feature, you can also change container images in your Deployment by defining the `image` attribute.

Setting cross-cutting fields

Using cross-cutting fields, you can set the following attributes for your Kubernetes resources:

- `namespace`
- `namePrefix`
- `nameSuffix`
- `commonLabels`
- `commonAnnotation`

In the next example, we set the namespace to `my-namespace` for the deployment.yaml definition. Note: You can use the `resources` attribute to define the resources you want to be affected.

```
# kustomization.yaml

apiVersion: kustomize.config.k8s.io/v1beta1
kind: Kustomization
namespace: my-namespace
resources:
- deployment.yaml
```

Generating resources

With Kustomize, you can generate ConfigMaps and Secrets resources. As we have already learned, they are used for feeding configuration and credentials to your application. You can generate objects either from a literal or a file. The following generators are supported:

- configMapGenerator
- secretGenerator

For example, to generate a ConfigMap with the key-value pair, you can use the following file:

```
# kustomization.yaml

configMapGenerator:
- name: example-configmap
  literals:
  - FOO=Bar
```

And run the next code:

```
kubectl kustomize ./
```

Using variables

Variables are useful when you want to capture an attribute of one resource and pass it to other resources. For example, you might want to use the service name to pass it to a container command to be executed. Note that this currently supports string types. You can see an example of this usage at http://mng.bz/xdEB.

BASES AND OVERLAYS

Now that we have a good understanding of what features Kustomize offers, we can look at how we can use them to prepare Kubernetes for different environments in your CI/CD pipeline. Kustomize comes with the concepts of *bases* and *overlays*. A base is a root directory with Kubernetes resource definitions and the main kustomization.yaml file. It performs a first layer of customization. Note that you can also set your base in a Git repository. Overlay is a directory that stores the kustomization.yaml that customizes resources already customized in the base layer. You can create multiple overlays to represent each of your environments, as shown in figure 12.35.

Next, you can see an example of file structure for a single base with three overlays for the dev, test, and prod environments:

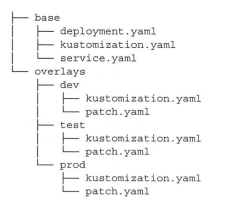

```
├── base
│   ├── deployment.yaml
│   ├── kustomization.yaml
│   └── service.yaml
└── overlays
    ├── dev
    │   ├── kustomization.yaml
    │   └── patch.yaml
    ├── test
    │   ├── kustomization.yaml
    │   └── patch.yaml
    └── prod
        ├── kustomization.yaml
        └── patch.yaml
```

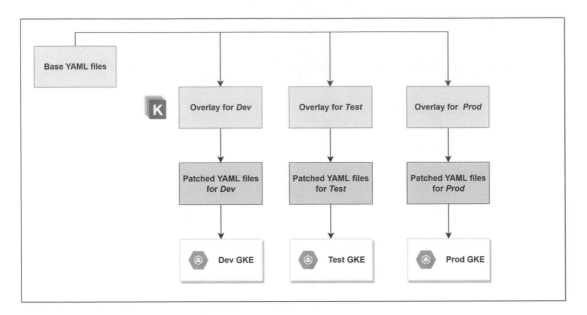

Figure 12.35   Kustomize base and overlays

You could use this file structure to set the number of replicas to be different for each environment. For example, maybe for development, you don't need to consume as many resources as for tests, where you might want to run performance testing.

SUMMARY OF KUSTOMIZE

As we have seen, Kustomize can be a powerful tool in your CI/CD pipeline to generate and patch Kubernetes resources for each of your environments. If you want to learn more about how to use Kustomize, check out the Kustomize examples at http://mng .bz/AlKW and the API references at https://kubectl.docs.kubernetes.io/references/.

12.5   *Continuous deployment with Cloud Deploy*

Cloud deploy is a fully managed CD service that allows you to deliver your applications to a defined series of target environments according to a promotion sequence. The life cycle of your applications is managed using releases and is controlled by delivery pipelines.

12.5.1   *Cloud Deploy in the Anthos CI/CD*

Google Cloud Deploy integrates with the Google Cloud Platform ecosystem of services that we have already learned about, as shown in figure 12.36, to complete the end-to-end CI/CD solution for GKE and Anthos clusters.

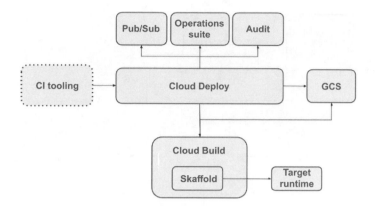

Figure 12.36   The Cloud Deploy CI/CD ecosystem

Figure 12.36 shows the Google Cloud Deploy interface with the following services:

- *CI tooling*—Calls the Google Cloud Deploy API or CLI to create a release. Hence, most of the CI tools are supported, including Cloud Build.
- *Cloud Build*—Used to render the manifests and to deploy to the target runtime.
- *Skaffold*—Used by Cloud Build to render and deploy the manifests. As a result, the application is deployed.
- *Cloud Storage*—Stores the rendering source and rendered manifests.
- *Google Cloud's operations suite*—Collects and stores the audit logs of the Cloud Deploy service.
- *Pub/Sub*—Allows publishing Cloud Deploy messages to Pub/Sub topics. This can be used to integrate with external systems.
- *GKE and Anthos clusters*—The target runtimes to which Google Cloud Deploy deploys the applications using Skaffold, through Cloud Build, to your target runtime.

Now that we know how Cloud Deploy interacts with the other Anthos CI/CD tools, let's see how we can configure it for CD of Anthos applications.

12.5.2   Google Cloud Deploy delivery pipeline for Anthos

Cloud Deploy uses delivery pipeline manifests that define the promotion sequence to describe the order in which to deploy to targets. The targets are described in the pipelines' definition or in separate files. The Skaffold configuration file is used to render and deploy the Kubernetes resource manifest. Figure 12.37 defines the components and the flow that Cloud Deploy uses.

Let's look at the sequences of action needed to configure continuous delivery with Cloud Build, shown in the next set of steps. As a prerequisite, we should already have

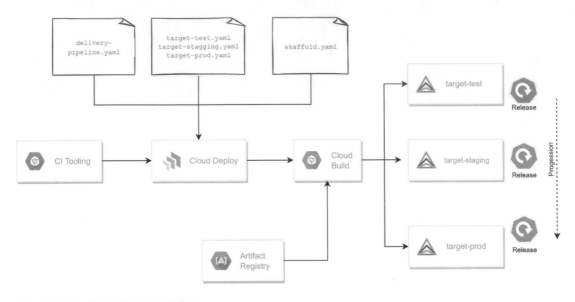

Figure 12.37   Cloud Deploy workflow

three GKE/Anthos clusters deployed for each of your environments, as shown in figure 12.38:

1   The first step is to define the delivery pipeline with the progressions (the promotion sequence) and, optionally, the runtime targets. In this example, we will create separate target files, so we can define the following pipeline:

```
delivery-pipeline.yaml
apiVersion: deploy.cloud.google.com/v1
kind: DeliveryPipeline
metadata:
  name: web-app
description: web-app delivery pipeline
serialPipeline:
 stages:
 - targetId: test
 - targetId: staging
 - targetId: prod
```

2   The targets can be defined as separate files. You can define a separate file per target and will end up with the following three files:

   – target_test.yaml
   – target_staging.yaml
   – target_prod.yaml

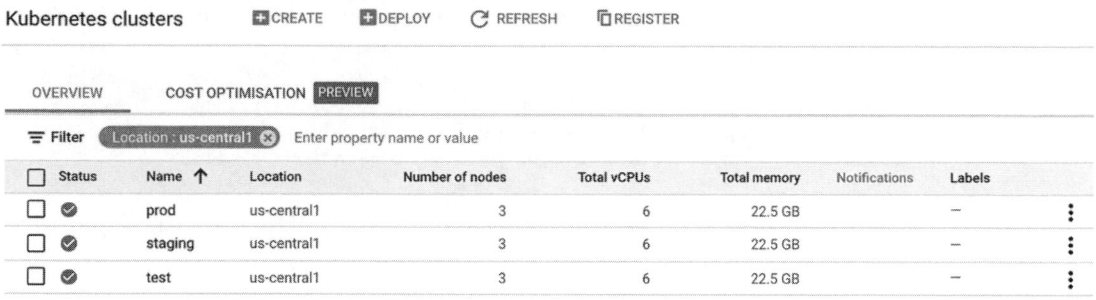

Kubernetes clusters   ⊞ CREATE   ⊞ DEPLOY   ↻ REFRESH   🗇 REGISTER

OVERVIEW	COST OPTIMISATION PREVIEW

⛃ Filter   (Location : us-central1 ⊗)   Enter property name or value

	Status	Name ↑	Location	Number of nodes	Total vCPUs	Total memory	Notifications	Labels	
☐	✓	prod	us-central1	3	6	22.5 GB	—	—	⋮
☐	✓	staging	us-central1	3	6	22.5 GB	—	—	⋮
☐	✓	test	us-central1	3	6	22.5 GB	—	—	⋮

Figure 12.38   Target GKE/Anthos clusters

In each of the files, you define the name of the target and the target cluster. Here you can see an example for the test target:

```
target-test.yaml
apiVersion: deploy.cloud.google.com/v1
kind: Target
metadata:
  name: test
description: test cluster
gke:
  cluster: projects/${PROJECT_ID}/locations/${REGION}/clusters/test
```

3   In the next step, you define the Skaffold configuration file needed for the rendering and deployment of the application manifest. At this stage, you should already have a container image to deploy and a Kubernetes manifest that identifies the container image—these should be generated in your CI process. For more information on how to use Skaffold with Cloud Deploy, check out section 12.3.2, "Continuous development with Skaffold."

Your Skaffold configuration might look like the following:

```
skaffold.yaml
apiVersion: skaffold/v2beta29
kind: Config
build:
  artifacts:
    - image: example-image
      context: example-app
  googleCloudBuild:
    projectId: ${PROJECT_ID}
deploy:
  kubectl:
    manifests:
      - kubernetes/*
portForward:
  - resourceType: deployment
    resourceName: example-app
    port: 8080
    localPort: 9000
```

4 Next, register the pipeline and the target by running the following commands:

```
gcloud deploy apply --file=delivery-pipeline.yaml --region=us-central1 && \
gcloud deploy apply --file=target_test.yaml --region=us-central1 && \
gcloud deploy apply --file=target_staging.yaml --region=us-central1 && \
gcloud deploy apply --file=target_prod.yaml --region=us-central1
```

Now Cloud Deploy knows your application, and it will manage the deployment to targets according to your defined promotion sequence.

5 Now you can initiate the delivery pipeline by creating a release either from the command line or from your CI tooling. Google Cloud Deploy creates a rollout resource, which associates the release with the first target environment. Based on that rollout, your application is deployed to the first target. Run the following command from the directory containing your Skaffold config:

```
gcloud deploy releases create RELEASE_NAME --delivery-pipeline=PIPELINE_NAME
```

6 If you want to use Cloud Build as your CI tool, the following YAML file shows an example Cloud Build configuration, which includes a call to Google Cloud Deploy to create a release, with a release name based on the date and Skaffold used for the build:

```
- name: gcr.io/k8s-skaffold/skaffold
  args:
    - skaffold
    - build
    - '--interactive=false'
    - '--file-output=/workspace/artifacts.json'
- name: gcr.io/google.com/cloudsdktool/cloud-sdk
  entrypoint: gcloud
  args:
    [
      "deploy", "releases", "create", "rel-${SHORT_SHA}",
      "--delivery-pipeline", "PIPELINE_NAME",
      "--region", "us-central1",
      "--annotations", "commitId=${REVISION_ID}",
      "--build-artifacts", "/workspace/artifacts.json"
```

7 Once you are ready to deploy the application to the next target of the sequence, you can promote it. Make a call to Google Cloud Deploy and create a new rollout:

```
gcloud deploy releases promote --release=RELEASE_NAME --delivery-
pipeline=PIPELINE_NAME
```

8 You can continue the promotion to the last environment. In the example sequence, shown in figure 12.39, it is production.

Figure 12.39   Promotion sequence

9   If you want to introduce approvals into the progression process, you can do it in
    the target definitions. For example, we might want to approve all promotions in
    testing to staging and production as shown in figure 12.40.

Figure 12.40   Manual approvals

You can define approvals in each of the target definitions as follows:

```
apiVersion: deploy.cloud.google.com/v1
kind: Target
metadata:
 name:
 annotations:
 labels:
description:
requireApproval: true
gke:
 cluster: projects/[project_name]/locations/[location]/clusters/[cluster_name]
```

The parameter `requireApproval: true` indicates whether promotion to this target
requires manual approval. The value can be `true` or `false` and is optional; the default
is `false`.

Now you can either approve or reject the rollout. To approve the rollout, run the
next command:

```
gcloud deploy rollouts approve rollout-name --delivery-pipeline=pipeline-name
```

Or reject the approval by running the following:

```
gcloud deploy rollouts reject rollout-name --delivery-pipeline=pipeline-name
```

As you can see, this gives you full control over your application rollouts.

SUMMARY OF CLOUD DEPLOY

In this section, we have learned how Cloud Deploy can be used for CD of your application. It comes with many important features like approvals, logging, and integrations with third-party tools, making it an enterprise-grade solution. It seamlessly integrates with the end-to-end CI/CD pipeline for Anthos. To learn more about Cloud Deploy, see https://cloud.google.com/deploy.

If you want to get hands-on experience with Cloud Build, we encourage you to look at the example tutorials that cover even more features and integrations: http://mng.bz/ZoKZ.

12.6 *Modern CI/CD platform*

Modern CI/CD platforms must allow sustainable software development and operation of the entire application delivery pipeline. No single way to achieve that goal exists, and it is always dependent on application and organization specifics. All of them should follow the same pattern when addressing tree key layers, as shown here and in figure 12.41:

- *Infrastructure*—Used for hosting
- *Platforms*—Used by developers to create, maintain, and consume continuous integration capabilities
- *Applications*—Consumption layers for end users

Figure 12.41   CI/CD platform layers

Each layer is under the responsibility of at least the following three types of personas:

- *Developers*—Mostly focused on application development, automated testing, and releases
- *Operators*—Focused on keeping the application, the underlying platform, and the infrastructure working to deliver agreed performance and availability indicators
- *Security officers*—Guarantee that agreed policies and security standards are applied, regardless of environment type, structure, or layer

Depending on the organization, more personas could exist. Each of them not only must have different responsibilities and roles and different constraints and restrictions applied on them, but they also must share the same methodologies across entire teams, which leads to a shared responsibility for delivery, as illustrated in figure 12.42.

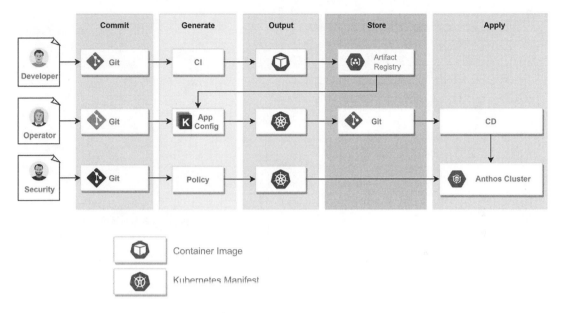

Figure 12.42 Personas vs. code repositories

Anthos introduced the capabilities to centralize management and unify toolsets while maintaining the flexibility to integrate external tools into the pipeline. The goal for modern CI/CD platforms is to support enterprise-ready and secure GitOps implementations. That means every component must be described as a set of configuration files and definitions stored in the version control system. Each set is managed and maintained by a separate team. It was already mentioned that the modern CI/CD platform relies on shared responsibility. In such models, there are always touch points for all parties via common interfaces like the code repository, the image build, and the Kubernetes manifest definition stage.

Modern application delivery relies on Kubernetes orchestration and microservices-based architecture. In such, there must be separation between developers and the operator playground. Implementation depends on defined requirements. We can use single cluster with multiple namespaces for single-site or nonproduction setups. If services we are delivering must be highly available or deliver high latency across a globe or we must limit infrastructure life cycle activity impact, consider using multiple Anthos clusters. Multicluster setup allows us to roll out applications in small steps to individual clusters before they are fully released.

Let's define an example application: a simple microservices-based voting system capable of visualizing voting results, as presented in figure 12.43.

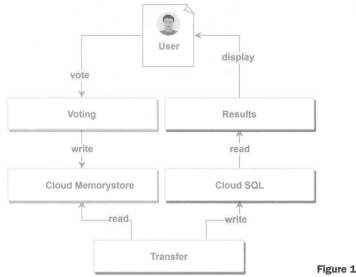

Figure 12.43   **Application schema**

The underlying infrastructure consumes Anthos GKE cluster on GCP. Three namespaces are created, one for each service:

- `Voting`
- `Transfer`
- `Results`

It also uses the following three Google-managed services:

- Cloud Memorystore as managed Redis
- Cloud SQL as a central database for all votes delivered as managed Postgres
- Secret Manager as a secure Secrets management system to store credentials for Memorystore and Cloud SQL

Developers consume infrastructure and do not care how it is delivered. It must meet their requirements related to namespaces and managed services. A responsible team must create a CI/CD pipeline that can be used for application-hosting purposes and have full flexibility to test any changes.

To achieve this goal, we can use multiple different tools. If our teams are familiar with Terraform, we can use already available knowledge and integrate it into our CI/CD pipeline. Such an approach is fully in line with DORA's State of DevOps research program (https://www.devops-research.com/research.html). It defines one of the key success factors for implementation of DevOps in organizations: the freedom to choose the tools developers and operation people are using. One more question exists: can we deliver such infrastructure even more simply? Because we are using GCP-managed resources instead of using external tools, we can take advantage of the Anthos Config Connector capability to deliver Secret Manager, Cloud Memorystore, and Cloud SQL as declared objects in our code repository.

If we are required to deliver services for other sources like Anthos on-prem, it is important to introduce infrastructure changes starting from day one in an automated way, as shown in figure 12.44. Every Anthos on VMware or Anthos on bare metal must rely on predefined practices and security policies that can be constantly reused if needed.

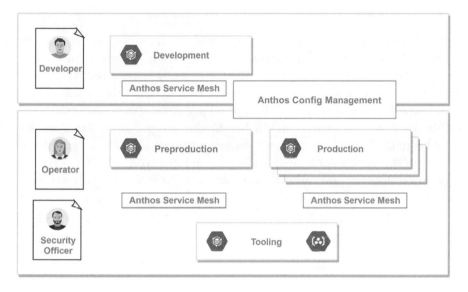

Figure 12.44   Infrastructure resources

Going deeper into our modern platform infrastructure, it must deliver the following elements to enable successful application delivery:

- *High performance, high availability, and a stable shared tooling infrastructure*—It is used as a central repository for CI/CD, container images, and application and infrastructure code and configuration. It can be expanded for additional business support tools mandated by your company.
- *Separate preproduction and multiple production environments with coherent configuration*— Consistent security policies, RBAC, or networking configuration improves testing quality and efficiency, reduces error rate, and increases production software delivery.
- *Development infrastructure*—Used for extensive unit testing and delivering freedom to our developers to work in their own namespaces.

That moves us into the target CI/CD platform. It is important that platform choice is multidimensional and must be driven by the following factors:

- *The platform must be known to the teams that are operating it.* It is not necessary that the platform is already used, but proper training must be delivered, and teams must have time to get familiar with it.

- *The platform must fit into the desired state of application and infrastructure delivery model.* That includes operational models and business logic implemented in enterprise.
- *The availability and health of the application must be properly measured and monitored on all levels.* This means starting from infrastructure, through tooling platform, and closing at application level itself.
- *As described in the introduction section, the platform must be DevOps ready.*

When choosing a code repository, consider what capabilities are mandatory for you. For simple code version management at a small scale, Google Cloud Source Repository can be enough. When additional functionality is required, you must consider other Git providers. Common patterns for GitLab, GitHub, or Bitbucket adoption would be a demand to keep code in your on-prem data center or to introduce responsibility for particular folders in Git by implementing code owners. Similar choices must be made for integration and deployment tools. Driven by additional requirements, we can have already on-prem implementation of GitLab CI/CD. For complex application delivery, you can use Spinnaker as a CD tool. The Anthos-based platform is flexible in that area. We can use Google Cloud Platform tools or easily integrate into external tools and still benefit from out-of-the-box Anthos automation and features, as shown in figure 12.45.

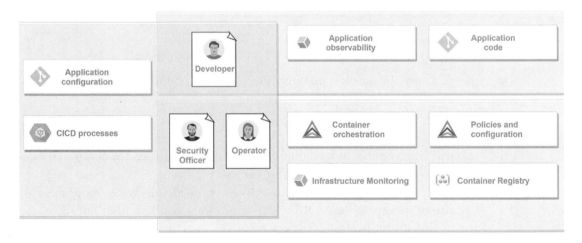

Figure 12.45   Software resources

As soon as we have our infrastructure and CI/CD platform ready, we can enable them for development activities. We defined personas and what interfaces they use to cooperate with each other. Let's look at the end-to-end workflow for that cooperation, presented in figure 12.46.

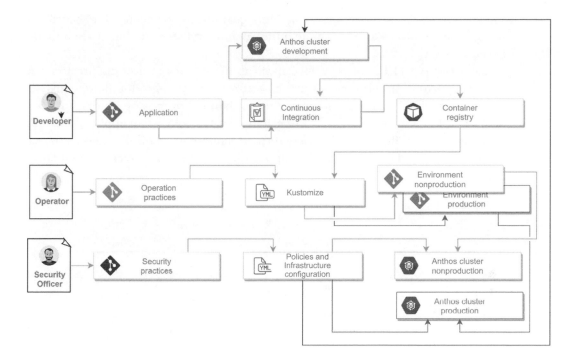

Figure 12.46   Application delivery workflow

As soon as code is ready, it must be shipped into a production-like environment to guarantee quality in the new code update's validation process. As already described, code can be pushed to Cloud Code or any other Git repository, where quality and sanity checks are performed. When it passes, you can produce container images and push them into the container registry. After the image is acknowledged by operators, they apply to them best practices, applications, and company standards from an operational practices Git repository. Operators define pipelines using tools like Kustomize, creating environment-specific repositories that become the source of truth for environment-specific manifests. Moreover, because all environments rely on the same application and operational practices code repositories, they are guaranteed to be consistent. As a result, nonproduction environments are as close to production environments as possible.

   We already mentioned the importance of shifting security adaptation left as much as possible in the development life cycle. Kubernetes cluster consistency between development and production environments plays an important role in application delivery speed. In chapter 13, we will learn how Anthos Policy Controller works, whereas in chapter 11, we already learned how Anthos Config Management helps to keep the configuration consistent. We can apply both policy and infrastructure controllers to the final version of our CI/CD pipeline. Similar to application consistency, a single source of truth for all environments guarantees consistency for security measures, which allows us to incorporate infrastructure and security changes in a modern, declarative way.

Let's come back to our reference application and look at how the previous workflow applies to it. In our case, we can have three separate development teams. Each of them is producing a separate image that is handed over to operators responsible for the end-to-end application. A Kubernetes cluster delivers an application landing zone, as shown in figure 12.47, as a dedicated namespace. This provides us the capability for workload isolation between applications on resource, security, and connectivity levels.

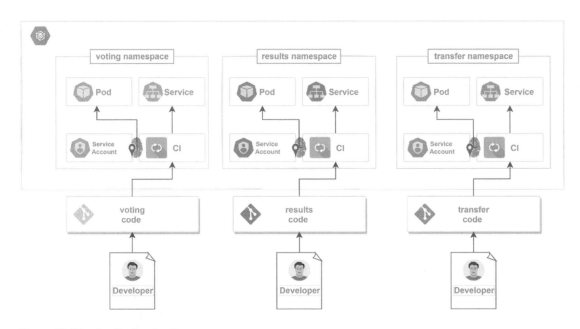

Figure 12.47   Application landing zones

Summary

- Modern application delivery CI/CD platforms play a significant role in the modern enterprise application delivery process.
- Developers can focus on applications, which increases the performance and efficiency of development teams.
- The same applies to operators that can control application delivery on early stages, offload daily routines, and minimize configuration overhead.
- Automated pipelines unify the ways of working with an application and infrastructure.
- Security teams become an inseparable part of the integration and delivery process.

- Modern CI/CD platforms introduced unified tools. They built knowledge, awareness of expectations, and a way of working across all involved parties.
- Unified toolsets improve cooperation in the shared responsibility model that the platform introduced into organization.
- Processes, operating models, learning, and communication paths must be adapted to fit that new model. Its benefits include reduced lead time for changes, increased deployment frequency, and a significant drop in service recovery time.

Security and policies

13

Scott Surovich

This chapter covers

- Kubernetes security overview
- Anthos security features
- Understanding root versus privileged containers
- Using ACM to secure a cluster

Google has made deploying Anthos clusters an easy, automated process. Because the process is automated, administrators may not consider anything past the initial simple cluster creation. When you deploy a cluster without considering postinstallation tasks like security, the likelihood is high that an attacker will be able to take control of your cluster with little effort.

Like many base installations of a product, a new Kubernetes cluster will include few, if any, enhanced security settings. For most enterprise systems, this setup is by design. Rather than force a rigid security model on an organization, potentially enabling features that may not be usable in some organizations, Kubernetes designers opt to make security a post-cluster-installation process that is designed and implemented by the organization.

In today's connected world, it seems that not a day goes by without news of a new hacking attack. Ransomware, botnets, distributed denial-of-service attacks, and countless others are becoming a daily cat-and-mouse game between organizations and hackers. Regardless of the placement of your cluster, on-prem or off-prem, you need to secure all areas that could be exploited. Failure to sufficiently plan for these attacks can lead to data leaks, service interruptions, fines, brand change, or loss of revenue.

In this chapter, we will discuss the features that Anthos provides to secure your Kubernetes clusters. Utilities like Anthos Config Management (ACM) and the Anthos Service Mesh (ASM) offer features to secure a cluster, limiting or blocking the effects from bad actors and honest user mistakes.

For example, a default installation of Kubernetes may allow a user to deploy a container that mounts host volumes, uses the host PID and host networking, runs as root, or runs in privileged mode. All of these can lead to different problems, but let's look at one of the most dangerous: privileged containers. A privileged container allows a user to mount the host's root filesystem into a mount point in the running container. Once the filesystem is mounted, a user can get into the running container and browse the entire filesystem of the worker node. With the host filesystem mounted, the attacker could go one step further and remount the root filesystem, allowing them to halt a running container, start a new rogue container, or destroy the host operating system filesystem.

Running a privileged container is a commonly used example that shows why you need to add additional security to a cluster. Although security policies are usually the first type of policy created for a cluster, you can't forget about other settings that can have an effect on the cluster and your services. To secure a cluster, you need to understand what an attacker may do that will lead not only to a security breach but service interruptions and data loss as well.

13.1 Technical requirements

The hands-on portion of this chapter will require you to have access to a Google Kubernetes Engine cluster running in GCP with ACM and Policy Controller enabled.

13.2 Hypervisors vs. container runtimes

When a new technology is released, it's commonly deployed without the appropriate knowledge required to run it securely. This often causes people to consider the new technology as less secure than a more mature technology, like containers versus virtual machines. Until recently, it was common for people to say that containers are not as secure as a virtual machine, with many pointing out that the containers sharing the host's kernel is the primary security concern.

This shared kernel opens an avenue of attack for malicious actors, possibly allowing them to hack into a less-than-secure container and, from there, break out into the host itself. If an attacker breaks out of a container, they could, potentially, gain complete control of the host operating system. This is commonly contrasted with a virtual machine running on a hypervisor, where there's no way a breakout could happen. Or could it?

Over the years, different hypervisors have had common vulnerabilities and exposures (CVEs) that have led to varying levels of security problems, including privileged escalations, allowing an attacker access to the hypervisor with administrative permissions. (More information about CVEs can be found at https://cve.mitre.org/.) Once they have compromised the hypervisor, an attacker would have access to every virtual machine on the host, including the virtual disks used to run the virtual machine.

This section is not intended to spark a debate about container security versus virtual machine security. Our intention is to call out that no system is completely secure, and when a system, like Kubernetes, is deployed without understanding basic security, you put yourself and your organization at risk.

Let's look at some common Kubernetes security concerns that need to be examined before a cluster should be considered "production ready."

13.3   *Kubernetes security overview*

A basic Kubernetes cluster usually enables limited security settings, if any at all, which leaves organizations to address security on their own as follows:

- Configuring any base Kubernetes security features
- Finding add-on products to address any missing security not included with a base cluster
- Educating staff on the installation and support of each component
- Scanning images for vulnerabilities
- Enabling network security to encrypt traffic between workloads

These tasks may not sound like large obstacles to overcome in some organizations. You may already know about various open source packages that add security to clusters, like admission controllers such as OPA (Open Policy Agent) or Gatekeeper (https://github.com/open-policy-agent/gatekeeper). An organization can decide to deploy Gatekeeper using the open source project release, but doing so would leave them to handle support internally or by submitting an issue on the GitHub repository for Gatekeeper. Problems with an admission controller can have detrimental effects on the cluster, potentially causing obstacles with every deployment request. Until you have been on the receiving end of an admission controller problem, you may not fully understand the effect and how having a support contact can be a cluster lifesaver.

Throughout this book, we have discussed how Anthos brings Kubernetes clusters to the next level by providing add-ons to a cluster backed by full Google support. Security is one of the key areas that Anthos excels in, as you read in chapter 11, where you learned about some of the features of ACM, including configuration syncing and Config Connector. ACM can also be used to configure the base aspects of Kubernetes security, including Roles and RoleBindings, but also provides additional security by including the Gatekeeper policy engine.

Before taking a deeper look at Policy Controller and the policies that can be implemented with it, let's quickly go over the security mechanisms that are provided as part of a base Kubernetes installation.

13.3.1   Understanding Kubernetes security objects

As a cluster administrator, you need to understand the included security options and how they address, or don't address, your organization's security policies. Fully covering the base security objects included with Kubernetes is beyond the scope of this chapter. They are presented here to provide an overview that you can further look into using the reference links provided. Some commonly used security objects follow:

- *NetworkPolicies*—Defines conditions to control Ingress and egress traffic to services (http://mng.bz/61vy)
- *Role-based access control (RBAC)*—Provides granular access to Kubernetes objects using user and group membership (http://mng.bz/oJMM)

A once common Kubernetes security concept, pod security policies (PSPs), is deprecated with the current release of Kubernetes. However, Policy Controller addresses the conditions previously provided by PSPs.

Because this chapter and book are intended to highlight the advantages Anthos itself brings to your Kubernetes experience, we will not be covering RBAC policies or NetworkPolicies, which are explained in more detail on the kubernetes.io pages referred to earlier and in several other Kubernetes books. This chapter is not intended to provide an exhaustive tutorial for securing Kubernetes clusters and workloads. Rather, we will focus on the additional tooling that Anthos provides to streamline, implement, and monitor the solutions for common security concerns. We will use specific vulnerabilities to demonstrate solutions, but in no way is this coverage exhaustive.

13.3.2   Types of security

Securing any digital service must include several avenues of attack: physical, internal (either malicious or accidental by employees or contractors), and external. In addition, the purpose of such attacks takes several forms. Is the intent to steal data or code, disrupt the service, or hold the system hostage? No solution is ever 100% secure—the very fact that it needs to be usable means it will always be susceptible to some form of attack. However, as an industry, we should work to make our services as difficult to disrupt as possible.

Part of the driving force behind Kubernetes is to reduce the barriers to deploying functional workloads. This reduces the support overhead on the team that runs the cluster itself, with the tradeoff that more people have access to deploy workloads and configurations that may cause service disruption. Therefore, from the cluster security perspective, we need to put specific policies in place to minimize the possibility of a vulnerability being exploited. Although some organizations can do this entirely with people-oriented policies, the best security policies are those where the enforcement mechanism is automatic and does not rely on manual intervention.

As with any compute-abstraction platform, Kubernetes contains multiple avenues of attack, especially in the default configuration. Some of these will always be present, to one degree or another, to deliver the value of the workloads in the cluster. For example, a middleware service that stores and retrieves data from a database is always going to need access to the database server, leaving an opening between the two components.

Every organization should reduce the possible avenues of attack on their systems. However, no organization is exactly like another. Therefore, most Kubernetes flavors are distributed with intentionally less-restrictive security settings. The first task of a Kubernetes administrator should be to apply a more rigorous set of security policies, in keeping with their organization's directives and needs. We can't provide an exhaustive list of every possible policy for every organization.[1] However, we will cover a couple of basic policies that apply to most clusters.

PRIVILEGED CONTAINERS AND THE ROOT USER

One of the great advantages of container-based orchestration systems is the reduction of resource usage by sharing the system's kernel (and typically, a portion of the filesystem) with the underlying containers; Kubernetes is no different. These orchestrators, including Kubernetes, include safeguards to prevent processes inside containers from accessing the host machine's resources directly. However, certain components of the orchestration system may need access to specific portions of the host infrastructure, either as a user or root. Before the development of in-container image builders, this was a common way to build images while running in a clean environment within a container.

In Kubernetes, the ability for a container to "break out" and issue commands to the host system is governed through the `privileged` flag on a container or Pod spec. Running commands on the host system as an individual user may be of limited use in most cases, unless the container is running as a superuser or assumes the identity of one. For simplicity, many container images available publicly run internally as the root user, to avoid permissions issues within the container. However, if the `privileged` flag is set to `true`, this would allow processes inside the container to break out and affect the host system as the superuser.

Two safeguards must be put in place to prevent a container from running as a superuser account: force containers to prevent privilege escalation, and prevent images from running as the root user by default.

Previously, Kubernetes included the `PodSecurityPolicy` object type to enforce specific policies for deployed Pods. However, PSPs have been deprecated starting in

---

[1] Kubernetes.io does provide an initial set of recommendations: http://mng.bz/nJyK.

Kubernetes 1.21 and will be removed, in their current form, in the 1.25 release. The Kubernetes SIG decided to deprecate PSPs for many reasons, including these:

- Difficulty in troubleshooting policies due to how they are applied. PSPs are bound to either the Pod's Service Account or the user that submitted the request.
- Cannot limit the type of `PersistentVolumeClaims`, which means a user could create a PersistentVolumeClaim using a `HostPath`.
- Failing closed, which means that if a policy has not been defined, the action will fail. Due to this behavior, you cannot enable PSPs at the start of rolling out a cluster—you need to have all your policies created before enabling PSPs for the entire cluster.

Even before the deprecation of PSPs, many organizations skipped using them due to the limitations mentioned. Instead, they decided to implement an admission controller like Gatekeeper (previously known as OPA, or Gatekeeper 1.0).

To secure a cluster, you need to think about what a malicious actor would attempt to execute before you can mitigate the risk. Let's discuss some of the common security concerns that you need to consider before a new cluster goes live.

13.4 Common security concerns

The Kubernetes API and configuration design provides for a large amount of flexibility to support a wide range of deployment scenarios and applications. However, most organizations do not need, nor do they want, the more security-sensitive configuration options to be enabled. Some of these sensitive fields that are permitted by default are included in table 13.1.

Table 13.1 Manifest fields that may lead to a security incident

`pod.spec` **fields**	
Field	**Description**
`hostPID`	Allows containers to share the host's process namespace
`hostIPC`	Allows containers to share the host's IPC namespace
`hostNetwork`	Allows container to share the host's network namespace
`pod.spec.containers.securityContext` **fields**	
Field	**Description**
`privileged`	Allows containers to access all the host's devices
`allowPrivilegeEscalation`	Allows a process to have more access than its parent process

One vulnerability occurs in Kubernetes if containers are set to run as root and the `privileged` field is set to `true`. Many widely distributed images use the root user as the default user—developers and administrators can, and should, change this to use a nonroot user. However, just running as a root user does not give the container access to the host system, because the container daemon will prevent access. But, if users can set the `privileged` field to `true`, then a run-as-root container *will* be able to access the host system and make changes or extract data they should not have access to. To prevent this from occurring, we need to create a new Gatekeeper policy instance.

These fields represent only a small list of items that may be used to compromise a host. Later in the chapter, we will use these options to demonstrate how an attacker can use them to gain full access to a Kubernetes host in a cluster.

Attackers don't always want to take over a host system. They may be content simply disrupting services and causing general havoc. Unfortunately, this type of incident can also be triggered by an innocent user who may not have full knowledge of the system, leading to a system outage or degradation. Your security standards need to consider all actions that may lead to a service interruption initiated from outside entities, such as permitted but malicious users or potential misconfigurations from well-meaning users.

The following list outlines some often overlooked settings that, if not addressed, may have an effect that could lead to revenue losses, fines, service outages, or negative company brand consequence:

- Duplicate Ingress controller URLs
  - Could lead to service interruption for the Ingress rules that conflict
- An application, or namespace, that consumes all a node's resources
  - Leads to host resource problems, affecting all applications on the host
- Rogue container images that have not been pulled from an approved registry
  - May lead to malware or ransomware
- An Istio policy that uses "*"
  - Leads to service interruption for all Istio services
- Unencrypted traffic between Pods in a cluster
  - Could lead to data leaks

This is just a small list of common concerns that need to be considered to increase the security and availability of a cluster. If you had to think about every scenario that could affect a Kubernetes application, it could take you months to create policies that address each task, and they would not cover scenarios you did not think of. Far too often, you will learn about an action that you didn't consider only after an event has occurred.

Anthos includes products that provide configuration management and enhanced security to your cluster, including a set of policies developed by the community and Google. But, before getting into the Anthos security and policy features, let's review general container security, so we can understand the need for the tools Anthos provides.

13.4.1 *Understanding the Policy Controller*

The ACM Policy Controller provides an admission controller to a cluster. An admission controller is a component that validates or mutates requests to the Kubernetes API Server, executing the logic of the controller before allowing or denying the request.

When you enable the policy engine, a `ValidatingWebHook` configuration is created, which registers the engine as an admission controller with the API server. Once registered, the API server will send object requests to the admission controller to be evaluated, as shown in figure 13.1.

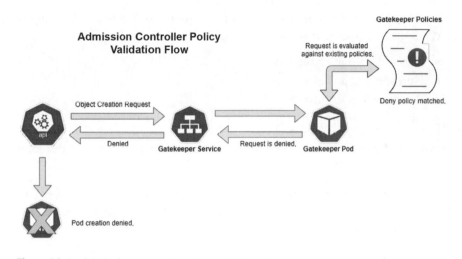

Figure 13.1 Admission controller policy validation flow

In the workflow shown in figure 13.1, the API server has received a request to create a new Pod. Because the cluster has ACM installed with the Policy Controller enabled, the request is sent to the Gatekeeper service. The service then forwards the request to the Gatekeeper Pod, which checks the configured policies for any violations.

At this point, you may be wondering what kind of latency or performance effects a cluster may experience once Gatekeeper has been deployed. On average, policy evaluation takes about one millisecond, even when larger policies are evaluated. Like any system that allows you to create your own objects, you can create a policy that will affect the performance of the policy engine, resulting in overall system latency. Creating policies is beyond the scope of this chapter. If you want to learn more about policies and performance, you can find additional details on the Open Policy Agent website at http://mng.bz/v1GM.

In the example shown in figure 13.1, a policy was found that denied the request, resulting in the admission controller sending the denial to the API server. Because the admission controller returned a denial, the API server will not create the object and will update the status of the object with the error provided by the policy engine.

A policy engine is a simple evaluation system that checks a request and decides whether the request will be allowed. Policy engines have an easy flow to them, but the real power in them is the policies themselves, which provide the logic for the decision process. In ACM we use constraint templates and constraints to implement security policies in our clusters. In the next sections, we will explain what constraint templates are and how they are implemented in a cluster by creating constraints.

INTRODUCING GATEKEEPER CONSTRAINT TEMPLATES

Think of constraint templates as the logic that is used by the policy engine to make decisions about requests. When Gatekeeper is enabled on a cluster, it will create a set of default policies that contain rules for common use cases. At the time of writing, ACM's policy controller includes 32 templates, including these:

- Allowed container registries
- Istio-specific policies
- Resource constraints
- Alternative security that provides security similar to PSPs

> **NOTE** You can find a complete list of each template and a description of what each does by visiting http://mng.bz/41oV.

Each policy is a custom resource type known as a `ConstraintTemplate`. You can view all the templates in a cluster by executing `kubectl get constrainttemplates`. An abbreviated list is shown in figure 13.2.

```
NAME                                    AGE
allowedserviceportname                  50m
destinationruletlsenabled               49m
disallowedauthzprefix                   49m
k8sallowedrepos                         49m
k8sblockprocessnamespacesharing         49m
k8scontainerlimits                      49m
k8sdisallowedrolebindingsubjects        49m
k8semptydirhassizelimit                 49m
k8shttponly                             49m
k8slocalstoragerequiresafetoevict       49m
k8smemoryrequestequalslimit             49m
k8snoexternalservices                   49m
k8spspallowedusers                      49m
```

Figure 13.2   Constraint template list

Constraint templates, by themselves, are only a definition of a policy—the logic that will be used for the evaluation. In the next section, we will explain how to use constraint templates to create a constraint, which will enable a selected policy on the cluster.

ENABLING A POLICY

To enable the enforcement of a policy, you need to create a YAML file that defines a constraint, which will be evaluated when a new object is created. This is a key behavior to remember: because the policy engine is an admission controller, it evaluates objects only when they are created or admitted to the cluster. It will not enforce the policy against any existing objects until they are recreated, but it will show violations of the policy running in the cluster. This aspect is often overlooked by users who are newer to Gatekeeper and is a key point to remember when you implement a new policy in your cluster.

Earlier we explained how a container that is started as a privileged container could be used to compromise the host and, ultimately, the cluster. Because of this potential, you may want to deny the creation of privileged Pods. Because this is a common use case, ACM includes a template to deny privileged containers. The example manifest that follows creates an object called `deny-privileged`, using the custom resource kind `K8sPSPPrivilegedContainer`:

```
apiVersion: constraints.gatekeeper.sh/v1beta1
kind: K8sPSPPrivilegedContainer
metadata:
  name: deny-privileged
spec:
  match:
    kinds:
      - apiGroups: [""]
        kinds: ["Pod"]
```

Notice that, in the spec section of the manifest, we define a `match` parameter. This parameter defines which object(s) the policy engine will evaluate against the constraint. In the example, the policy will be evaluated against all `apiGroups` for the object type `pod`. This means that any time a Pod request is received, it will be checked to see whether it is attempting to start as a privileged container.

You might be wondering why we are matching only Pods, and not Deployments or ReplicaSets. The Pods match will evaluate any attempts to create a Pod, which includes a manifest that uses a type of Pod, or when any other object like a Deployment tries to create a Pod. When a Deployment is submitted, the API server will create a `Deployment` object, which creates a `ReplicaSet` object, which creates the Pods. No matter how the Pod is created, it will be checked against the policy.

By default, once a constraint has been created, it will be enforced for every object defined in the match list. This includes Anthos system namespaces like `kube-system`, `gke-system`, and `gke-connect`. If you were to add the constraint in the previous example, Pods like `kube-proxy` and CNI Pods like Calico or Cilium would be blocked from starting up. If CNI Pods are denied startup, the cluster nodes will not have any network connectivity, causing all Pods to fail. Because constraints have a clusterwide effect, you need to carefully plan and understand how the policy will affect the entire cluster, including existing objects.

It may seem that a policy will affect every namespace, and by default, that it is true of a new policy. Luckily, ACM allows you to exclude a namespace by adding a constraint that includes the namespace in the `spec.match.excludedNamespaces`, or you can configure the Policy Controller to have exemptableNamespaces as documented here: http://mng.bz/Q84j.

Because policies can have unintended consequences, the Anthos policy manager has an option that allows you to audit the results of a constraint without actually enforcing it. In the next section, we'll discuss auditing a constraint.

AUDITING A CONSTRAINT

Before enforcing a new constraint, you should test it against the cluster to avoid any unexpected results. As mentioned in the previous section, when you create a new constraint, it will be enforced by default. You can change this default behavior from enforcement to auditing by adding the enforcementAction: dryrun option to the constraint manifest. Using the psp-privileged-container example, we can add the dryrun option to change the default enforcement behavior from enforcement to auditing as follows:

```
apiVersion: constraints.gatekeeper.sh/v1beta1
kind: K8sPSPPrivilegedContainer
metadata:
  name: psp-privileged-container
spec:
  enforcementAction: dryrun
  match:
    kinds:
      - apiGroups: [""]
        kinds: ["Pod"]
```

Now that the enforcement has been changed to auditing, any Pod that violates the constraint will only be logged as a violation, but it will still be allowed to start up. Also, unlike the default enforcement behavior, setting the constraint to dryrun will evaluate not only new requests but all running Pods as well. This allows you to verify the effects of a constraint on every Pod, rather than just new requests, so you will know how it would affect any Pods that are restarted.

Once set to dryrun, you can view the results of the audit using kubectl get <constraint kind> <constraint name> -o yaml. For our example, we can view the affected Pods by executing kubectl get K8sPSPPrivilegedContainer psp-privileged-container -o yaml. Depending on how many violations there are, you may receive a lengthy list of affected containers. The next output is an abbreviated list from a default cluster running Anthos on bare metal:

```
violations:
- enforcementAction: dryrun
  kind: Pod
  message: 'Privileged container is not allowed: cilium-agent, securityContext:
    {"capabilities": {"add": ["NET_ADMIN", "SYS_MODULE"]}, "privileged": true}'
  name: anetd-4nldm
  namespace: kube-system
- enforcementAction: dryrun
  kind: Pod
```

```
message: 'Privileged container is not allowed: kube-proxy, securityContext:
  {"privileged":
   true}'
name: kube-proxy-4z8qh
namespace: kube-system
```

The output shows that if we were to enforce this policy, the kube-proxy and Cilium Pods would be denied startup. This presents a catch-22: we want to deny privileged containers from running, but we need to have privileged containers to allow the system container to run. It is not uncommon for certain containers to go against a policy that would deny the container starting. Because this is a common scenario, the policy engine allows you to exempt namespaces from being evaluated from either all policies or only certain policies.

CREATING A NAMESPACE EXEMPTION

Once a constraint is created, it will affect every container that is started, without any regard for the type of Pod that is being started. Many common system containers, like networking or logging agents, require privileges that may be denied by a cluster policy. Because policies secure a cluster, they are enforced at the cluster level, across all namespaces. This may work for certain policies, but others may block a legitimate container from being scheduled. To allow exemptions, the admission controller includes controls that allow namespaces to be exempt from either all policies or just select policies.

Exempting a namespace from specific processing

To exempt namespaces from all Gatekeeper policies, you can create a config object that contains the namespace(s) that you want to exempt. You can exempt each namespace from all Gatekeeper functions or only certain processes, like auditing, by adding one or more processing options. Table 13.2 shows the four processing options that can be set.

Table 13.2 Namespace exemption options

Process option	Results of exemption
Audit	Namespace(s) will not report audit results but will still be part of the webhook and sync processes.
Webhook	Namespace(s) will be exempt from the admission controller but will still be part of the audit and sync processes.
Sync	Namespace(s) resources will not be reported into Gatekeeper but will still be part of the audit and webhook processes.
*	Exempts the namespace(s) from all Gatekeeper processes.

For example, we may want to exempt a few namespaces from all Gatekeeper processing. To exempt all processes, we can create a new config that contains the namespaces, with an * in the processes field. The manifest shown next creates a config that exempts the `kube-system` *and* `gatekeeper-system` namespaces from *all* Gatekeeper processes:

```
apiVersion: config.gatekeeper.sh/v1alpha1
kind: Config
metadata:
  name: config
  namespace: "gatekeeper-system"
spec:
  match:
    - excludedNamespaces: ["kube-system", "gatekeeper-system"]
      processes: ["*"]
```

You can add different process exemptions for different namespaces by adding additional matches. For example, you can create a match that exempts a namespace only from the webhook process, whereas another namespace may be exempt only from Gatekeeper's auditing process.

Exempting a namespace from all policies

In some organizations, creating an exemption for all Gatekeeper policies might violate a security standard. Creating a namespace exemption is quick and easy, but it will exempt every deployment in that namespace from *all* Gatekeeper policies, without exception.

To exclude a namespace from all policies is a two-step process. The first step is to add a list of namespaces that the policy engine will allow to ignore policies, and the second is to label the namespace(s) that you want to exempt with `admission.gatekeeper.sh/ignore=true`.

If you attempt to skip the first step and you only label a namespace to exempt it, you will receive the following error from the API server that only exempt namespaces can have the ignore label:

```
Error from server (Only exempt namespace can have the
    admission.gatekeeper.sh/ignore label): admission webhook "check-ignore-
    label.gatekeeper.sh" denied the request: Only exempt namespace can have
    the admission.gatekeeper.sh/ignore label
```

Before labeling any namespaces, you must first add the namespaces by editing the installed `configManagement` object and adding a list of namespaces in the `exemptable-Namespaces` field, which is added using the GCP console.

To allow a namespace to be added as an exemption using the Anthos console, you need to edit the config management settings for the cluster. In the GCP console, open Anthos > Config Management to see the list of clusters that are available. Select the button next to the cluster you want to configure and click Configure at the top of the GCP console page. If you expand the settings and scroll to the bottom, you will see the Policy Controller section. Click on the ACM settings for your clusters to open a list of exempt namespaces, as shown in figure 13.3.

> **NOTE** You must be careful when adding a new namespace. The console does not verify whether a namespace already exists or if it is misspelled.

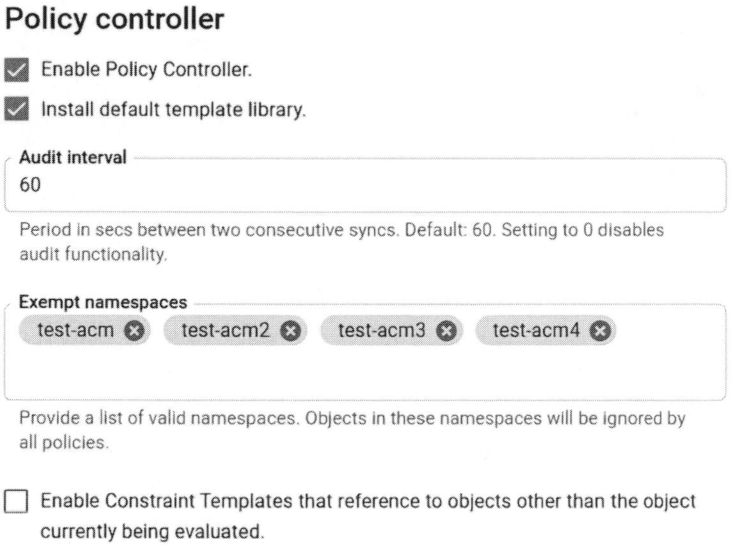

Policy controller

☑ Enable Policy Controller.

☑ Install default template library.

Audit interval

60

Period in secs between two consecutive syncs. Default: 60. Setting to 0 disables audit functionality.

Exempt namespaces

test-acm ⊗   test-acm2 ⊗   test-acm3 ⊗   test-acm4 ⊗

Provide a list of valid namespaces. Objects in these namespaces will be ignored by all policies.

☐ Enable Constraint Templates that reference to objects other than the object currently being evaluated.

Figure 13.3   Adding an exemption using the GCP console

In figure 13.3, you can see that we have created the ability to exempt four namespaces. To add another namespace, you only need to click in the Exempt Namespaces box, type the name of the namespace, and click Done. Always double-check that the namespaces you enter are spelled correctly. The system does not validate the list against the cluster, so any errors in spelling will fail to add the namespace to the exemption list. Once the namespaces have been added to the exemption list, you must label the namespace with the `admission.gatekeeper.sh/ignore=true` label, exempting the namespace from all Gatekeeper policies.

Labeling the namespace to ignore Gatekeeper will cause the admission controller to ignore *every* policy for any object that is created in the namespace. Rather than exempting a namespace from every policy, you may want to consider exempting the namespace from individual policies, allowing you to enforce some policies, while exempting only the required policies for object creation in the namespace.

Exempting a namespace from a constraint template

If you find yourself in a situation where you need to exempt a certain namespace from a policy, but you cannot exempt the namespace from *all* policies, you can add an exemption to the constraint itself. For example, suppose we have a policy that requires all namespaces to have a billing code assigned to them. However, we want to exempt the `kube-system` namespace and a new namespace that will be created called `web-frontend`. We can do this by adding the `excludedNamespaces` field to our constraint as follows:

```
apiVersion: constraints.gatekeeper.sh/v1beta1
kind: K8sRequiredLabels
metadata:
  name: ns-billing
```

```
spec:
  match:
    kinds:
    - apiGroups: [""]
      kinds: ["Namespace"]
    excludedNamespaces:
    - kube-system
    - web-frontend
  parameters:
    labels:
    - key: "billing"
```

If we attempt to create a new namespace called `test-fail` without a label, Gatekeeper will deny the request with the following error:

```
Error from server ([denied by ns-billing] you must provide labels:
    {"billing"}): admission webhook "validation.gatekeeper.sh" denied the
    request: [denied by ns-billing] you must provide labels: {"billing"}
```

However, if we try to create the `web-frontend` namespace without a label, as shown next, Gatekeeper will allow it, because it is included in the `excludedNamespaces` for the constraint:

```
[root@localhost gke-bm]# kubectl create ns web-frontend
namespace/web-frontend created
```

ACM provides granular controls to exempt namespaces by providing the ability to exempt a namespace from either all policies or only certain policies. You can use a mix of each type for different namespaces, exempting one namespace for all policies, whereas other namespaces may be exempt from only certain policies. Try to avoid exempting namespaces from all policies, unless you have strong justification to do so. Once exempt, no policies will ever be enforced for a fully exempted namespace.

Although Anthos includes several constraint templates, some scenarios may exist where you need to create a custom constraint. In the next section, we will explain how to create a custom constraint template, allowing you to extend the included set of policies.

CREATING A CONSTRAINT TEMPLATE

The default template library included with ACM has grown from a handful of policies in the early releases to more than 32 with the most current release. Google and the community continue to add policies to the default library, but you may have a unique policy requirement for your clusters that Google does not provide.

If you find yourself needing to create a policy, you can create a custom constraint template by creating your own policy using a language called Rego. Covering Rego in depth is beyond the scope of this book, but you can read more about Rego and how to use it to create policies at http://mng.bz/X5e6.

To create a new template, you need to create a new `ConstraintTemplate` object, which will contain the Rego code to evaluate the policy. Google offers documentation to assist you in creating a template at http://mng.bz/ydKq.

The next example creates a new template that will check for an image digest when a new container is created:

```
apiVersion: templates.gatekeeper.sh/v1
kind: ConstraintTemplate
metadata:
  name: k8simagedigests
  annotations:
    metadata.gatekeeper.sh/title: "Image Digests"
    description: >-
      Requires container images to contain a digest.

      https://kubernetes.io/docs/concepts/containers/images/
spec:
  crd:
    spec:
      names:
        kind: K8sImageDigests
      validation:
        openAPIV3Schema:
          type: object
          description: >-
            Requires container images to contain a digest.

            https://kubernetes.io/docs/concepts/containers/images/
          properties:
            exemptImages:
              description: >-
                Any container that uses an image that matches an entry in
    this list will be excluded
                from enforcement. Prefix-matching can be signified with '*'.
    For example: 'my-image-*'.

                It is recommended that users use the fully-qualified Docker
    image name (e.g. start with a domain name)
                in order to avoid unexpectedly exempting images from an
    untrusted repository.
              type: array
              items:
                type: string
  targets:
    - target: admission.k8s.gatekeeper.sh
      rego: |
        package k8simagedigests

        import data.lib.exempt_container.is_exempt

        violation[{"msg": msg}] {
          container := input.review.object.spec.containers[_]
          not is_exempt(container)
          satisfied := [re_match("@[a-z0-9]+([+._-][a-z0-9]+)*:[a-zA-Z0-9=_-
    ]+", container.image)]
          not all(satisfied)
```

```
        msg := sprintf("container <%v> uses an image without a digest
<%v>", [container.name, container.image])
    }

  violation[{"msg": msg}] {
    container := input.review.object.spec.initContainers[_]
    not is_exempt(container)
    satisfied := [re_match("@[a-z0-9]+([+._-][a-z0-9]+)*:[a-zA-Z0-9=_-
]+", container.image)]
    not all(satisfied)
    msg := sprintf("initContainer <%v> uses an image without a digest
<%v>", [container.name, container.image])
    }

  violation[{"msg": msg}] {
    container := input.review.object.spec.ephemeralContainers[_]
    not is_exempt(container)
    satisfied := [re_match("@[a-z0-9]+([+._-][a-z0-9]+)*:[a-zA-Z0-9=_-
]+", container.image)]
    not all(satisfied)
    msg := sprintf("ephemeralContainer <%v> uses an image without a
digest <%v>", [container.name, container.image])
    }
 libs:
   - |
     package lib.exempt_container

     is_exempt(container) {
         exempt_images := object.get(object.get(input, "parameters",
{}), "exemptImages", [])
         img := container.image
         exemption := exempt_images[_]
         _matches_exemption(img, exemption)
     }

     _matches_exemption(img, exemption) {
         not endswith(exemption, "*")
         exemption == img
     }

     _matches_exemption(img, exemption) {
         endswith(exemption, "*")
         prefix := trim_suffix(exemption, "*")
         startswith(img, prefix)
     }
```

It's important to note that the Rego code contains multiple violation sections. At first glance, it may appear that the code is the same for each, but on closer inspection, you will notice one minor difference on the container := lines. The first violation block checks all containers for a digest, whereas the second violation block checks all init-Containers for a digest, and the third checks any ephemeralContainers. Because they are all unique objects, we need to include each object in our code, or it will not be checked by the policy engine.

Finally, to activate the constraint, we apply a manifest that uses the new custom resource created by the previous template, `K8sImageDigests`:

```
apiVersion: constraints.gatekeeper.sh/v1beta1
kind: K8sImageDigests
metadata:
  name: container-image-must-have-digest
spec:
  match:
    kinds:
      - apiGroups: [""]
        kinds: ["Pod"]
```

Once applied to the cluster, any new Pod request that does not supply a digest will be denied by the admission controller.

13.4.2 *Using Binary Authorization to secure the supply chain*

Since the SolarWinds security breach, there has been a spotlight on how you need to secure your software supply chain. You should always consider and implement this, but it often takes an event like the SolarWinds breach to capture the attention of the public. Securing the supply chain is a large topic, and to give it the coverage it deserves would require a dedicated chapter, but we wanted to provide an overview of the tools Google provides to help you secure your supply chain.

You may have recently heard the phrase "Shifting left on security." This term refers to the practice of considering security earlier in the software development process. You should consider a number of topics when shifting left, and if you want to read an independent report sponsored by companies including Google, CloudBees, Deloitte, and more, read the State of DevOps from 2019, which covers key findings from multiple companies and their DevOps practices, located at https://cloud.google.com/devops/state-of-devops.

Anthos includes a powerful tool that centralizes software supply chain security for workloads on both Anthos on GCP and Anthos on-prem, called Binary Authorization (BinAuth). At a high level, BinAuth adds security to your clusters by requiring a trusted authority signature on your deployed images, which is attested when a container is deployed. If the deployed container does not contain a signature that matches the trusted authority, it will be denied scheduling and fail to deploy. Google's BinAuth provides you several features, including the following:

- Policy creation
- Policy enforcement and verification
- Cloud security command center integration
- Audit logging
- Cloud KMS support
- Uses the open source tool, Kritis, for signature verification
- Dry-run support

- Break-glass support
- Third-party support, including support for Twistlock, Terraform, and CloudBees

Along with the features provided, you can integrate BinAuth with Google's Cloud Build and Container registry scanning, allowing you to secure your supply chain based on build metadata and vulnerability scans. Google has several integrations docs that will step you through integrating BinAuth with several systems like CircleCI, Black Duck, Terraform, and Cloud Build on the Binary Authorization page, located at https:// cloud.google.com/binary-authorization/.

13.4.3   Using Gatekeeper to replace PSPs

As Kubernetes deprecates PSPs, you may want to start moving away from using PSPs to secure your clusters. One way to move away from PSPs as your main security mechanism is to migrate to using Gatekeeper policies instead. The Gatekeeper project has a GitHub repository dedicated to policies that are designed to replace PSPs at http:// mng.bz/Ml6n.

In the next section, we will close out the chapter by learning about securing your images using Google container Scanning.

13.5   Understanding container scanning

Like any standard operating system or application, containers may contain binaries that have known vulnerabilities. To keep your cluster secure, you need to verify the integrity of your containers by continuously scanning each one.

Many solutions on the market today, including Aqua Security, Twistlock, Harbor, and Google's Container Registry, scan containers for vulnerabilities. Each of these tools offers different levels of scanning abilities—in most cases, for an additional cost. At a minimum, you will want to scan your images for any vulnerabilities from the common vulnerabilities and exposures (CVE) list.

The CVE list (http://cve.mitre.org/cve) is a publicly disclosed list of security vulnerabilities for various software components, including operating systems and libraries. Entries in the list contain only a brief overview of the vulnerability—they do not contain any detailed information like consequences, risks, or how to remediate the problem. To retrieve the details for the CVE, each entry has a link that will take you to the National Vulnerability Database, which will provide additional details about the CVE, including a description, the severity, references, and a change history.

Although Anthos does not include a vulnerability scanner, Google does provide scanning if you store your images in the Google Container Registry. In this section, we will explain how to enable scanning on your repository and how to view the scanning results.

13.5.1   Enabling container scanning

The first requirement to enable scanning in your registry is to enable two APIs on your GCP project: the Container Analysis API and the Container Scanning API. The

Container Analysis API enables metadata storage in your project and is free, whereas the Container Scanning API will enable vulnerability scanning and is charged per scanned image. You can view the pricing details for the scanning API at http://mng .bz/aMjB.

To enable the required APIs using the gcloud CLI, use the following steps:

1 Set your default project as follows. Our example is using a project called test1-236415:

```
gcloud config set project test1-236415
```

2 Next, enable the Container Analysis API:

```
gcloud services enable containeranalysis.googleapis.com
```

3 Finally, enable the Container Scanning API:

```
gcloud services enable containerscanning.googleapis.com
```

Once the APIs are enabled on the project, you will need to create a repository in which to store your images. The next example creates a Docker registry called docker-registry in the us-east4 location with a description of the registry:

```
gcloud artifacts repositories create docker-registry --repository-format=docker
    --location=us-east4 --description="Docker Registry"
```

To push images to your repository, you need to configure Docker on your client to use your GCP credentials. Authentication to repositories in GCP is configured on a per-region basis. In the previous step, we created a registry in the us-east4 zone, so to configure authentication, we would execute the gcloud command here:

```
gcloud auth configure-docker us-east4-docker.pkg.dev
```

Now that your registry and Docker have been configured, you can start to use your registry to store images. In the next section, we will explain how to tag images and push them to your new repository.

13.5.2 *Adding images to your repository*

To add an image to a GCP registry, you follow the same steps that you would use for any other Docker registry, but the tag may be different from what you are used to:

1 If you do not have the image locally, you must either build a new image using Docker or pull the image from another registry.
2 Tag the image with your GCP registry.
3 Push the new image to the registry.

For example, to add a CentOS 8 image to a registry, follow these steps:

1 Download the CentOS 8 image from Docker Hub:

```
docker pull centos:8
```

2 Next, tag the newly pulled image with the Google registry information. When you tag an image that will be stored in a GCP registry, you must follow a specific naming convention. The image tag will use the convention LOCATIONdocker .pkg.dev/<project_ID>/<repository>/<image_name>. In the next example, the region is us-east4, the project is test-236415, and the registry is named docker-registry:

```
docker tag centos:8 us-east4-docker.pkg.dev/test1-236415/docker-
registry/centos:8
```

3 Finally, push the new image to the registry:

```
docker push  us-east4-docker.pkg.dev/test1-236415/docker-registry/centos:8
```

In the next section, we will explain how to look at your images and any vulnerabilities that have been found in them.

13.5.3   *Reviewing image vulnerabilities*

Because our project has the required APIs enabled, each image will be scanned when it is pushed to the registry. To review the vulnerabilities, open the GCP console and click Artifact Registry > Repositories, as shown in figure 13.4.

Figure 13.4   **Navigating to your registries**

This will bring up all the registries in your project. Continuing with our example, we created a registry called docker-registry, as shown in figure 13.5.

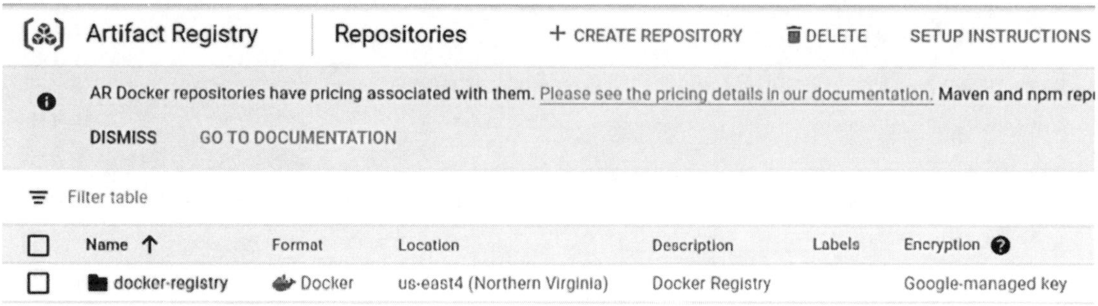

Figure 13.5   Project registries

Open the repository that you pushed the image to and click the image to view it. Previously, we pushed the CentOS image to our registry, as shown in figure 13.6.

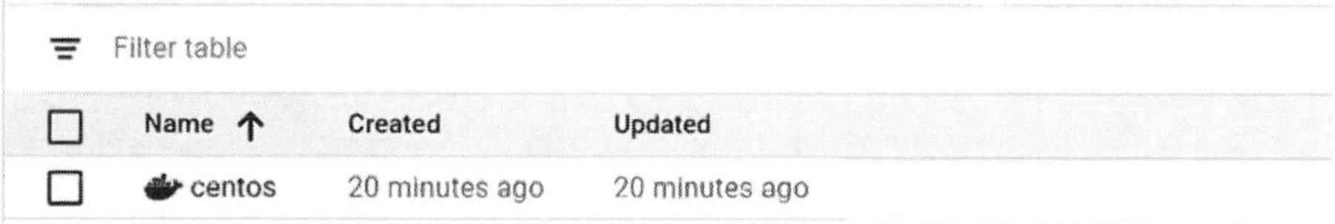

Figure 13.6   Images list

Clicking the image displays the digests for the image and the number of vulnerabilities that the image contains. Our example is shown in figure 13.7.

Figure 13.7   Image hash list

To view each of the vulnerabilities, click the number in the Vulnerabilities column. A new window opens, listing all CVEs for the image. Depending on the image and the scan results, you may see different links or options for the CVEs. Using our CentOS image example, shown in figure 13.8, we can see that the results have a link to view fixes for each CVE.

In another example, an Ubuntu image, no fixes are listed in the CVEs, so the results screen will contain different options, as shown in figure 13.9.

⇥ Filter vulnerabilities

Name	Effective severity ❓ ↓	CVSS ❓	Fix available	Package	
CVE-2020-14352	● High	8.5	Yes	librepo	**VIEW FIX**
CVE-2020-13631	● Medium	2.1	Yes	sqlite-libs	**VIEW FIX**
CVE-2020-8619	● Medium	4	Yes	bind-export-libs	**VIEW FIX**
CVE-2019-5018	● Medium	6.8	Yes	sqlite-libs	**VIEW FIX**
CVE-2019-19906	● Medium	5	Yes	cyrus-sasl-lib	**VIEW FIX**
CVE-2019-20907	● Medium	5	Yes	platform-python	**VIEW FIX**
CVE-2018-20843	● Medium	7.8	Yes	expat	**VIEW FIX**
CVE-2020-10029	● Medium	2.1	Yes	glibc	**VIEW FIX**

Figure 13.8   CVE example list with fixes

⇥ Filter vulnerabilities

Name	Effective severity ❓ ↓	CVSS ❓	Fix available	Package	
CVE-2018-20839 ⧉	● Medium	5	–	systemd	**VIEW**
CVE-2019-13050 ⧉	● Low	5	–	gnupg2	**VIEW**
CVE-2018-1000654 ⧉	● Low	7.1	–	libtasn1-6	**VIEW**
CVE-2019-12904 ⧉	● Low	4.3	–	libgcrypt20	**VIEW**

Figure 13.9   CVE example without fixes

You can view additional details for each CVE by clicking the CVE in the name column, or you can click View on the right-hand side. Clicking the CVE name will take you to the vendor's site, whereas clicking View will provide additional details about the vulnerability.

In this section, we introduced Google's container registry scanning, how to enable it, and how to view the scanning results. This was only an introduction to the service, but you can expand the functionality by integrating with Pub/Sub, adding access controls, and more. To see additional documentation, you can visit Google's how-to guides at http://mng.bz/gJ6E.

13.6   *Understanding container security*

You should consider two main concepts when you are creating a security policy: the user the container will run as and whether the container can run in privileged mode. Both ultimately decide what access, if any, a potential container breakout will have on the host.

When a container is started, it will run as the user that was set at the time of image creation, which is often the root user. However, even if you run a container as root, it doesn't mean that the processes inside the container will have root access on the worker node because the Docker daemon itself will restrict host-level access, depending on the policy regarding privileged containers. To help explain this, table 13.3 shows each setting and the resulting permissions.

Table 13.3   Root and privileged container permissions

Running container user	Privileged value	Host permissions
Running as root	False	None
Running as root	True	Root access
Running as nonroot	False	None
Running as nonroot	True	Limited; only permissions that have been granted to the same user on the host system

Both values determine what permissions a running container will be granted on the host. Simply running an image as root does not allow that container to run as root on the host itself. To explain the effect in greater detail, we will show what happens when you run a container as root and how allowing users to deploy privileged containers can enable someone to take over the host.

13.6.1   Running containers as root

Over the years, container security has received a somewhat bad reputation. Many of the examples that have been used as evidence to support this are, in fact, not container problems but configuration problems on the cluster. Not too long ago, many developers created new images running as root, rather than creating a new user and running as the new user, which limited any security consequences. This is a good time to mention that if you commonly download images from third-party registries, you should always run them in a sandboxed environment before using them in production. You don't know how the image was created, who it runs as, or whether it contains any malicious code. *Always inspect images before running them in production.* In the last section of this chapter, we will cover Google Container Scanning, which will scan your images for known security concerns.

You can use multiple tools to limit deployments of malicious containers, including

- *Container scanning*—Included in the Google Container Registry with scanning
- *Allowing only trusted container repositories*—Either internal or trusted partner registries
- *Requiring images to be signed*

One of the most dangerous, and commonly overlooked, security concerns is allowing a container to run as root. To explain why this is a bad practice, let's use a virtual machine example: would you allow an application to run as root or as administrator? Of course you wouldn't. If you had a web server running its processes as an administrator, any application breakout would be granted the permissions of the user that was running the process. In this case, that would be an account with root or administrator privileges, which would provide full access to the entire system.

To mitigate any problems from a breakout, all applications should be run with their least-required set of permissions. Unfortunately, it is far too common for developers to run their container as root. If we ran a container as root, any container breakout would grant the intruder access to any resources on the host. Many images on Docker Hub and GitHub are distributed using root as the default user, including the common busybox image.

To avoid running an image as root, you need to create and set a user account in your image or supply a user account when you start the container. Because busybox is normally pulled from Docker Hub, we can run it with a nonroot account by configuring a security context in the deployment.

As part of a Pod definition, the container can be forced to run as a user by adding the securityContext field, which allows you to set the context for the user, group, and fsGroup:

```
spec:
  securityContext:
    runAsUser: 1500
    runAsGroup: 1000
    fsGroup: 1200
```

Deploying the image with the additional securityContext will execute the container as user 1500. We also set the group to 1000 and the fsGroup to 1200. We can confirm all these values using the whoami and groups command, as shown in figure 13.10.

The UID and group IDs that were used are unknown in the image because it was pulled from Docker Hub and it contains only the users and groups that were included when the image was created. In an image that you or someone in your organization created, you would have added the required groups during the Docker build and would not receive the unknown ID warnings.

In this section, we explained how you can set a security context to run an image as a nonroot user or group at deployment time. This covers only the first half of securing our hosts from malicious containers. The next section will explain how privileged containers can affect our security and how they work together to provide access to the host.

13.6.2 *Running privileged containers*

By default, containers execute without any host privileges. Even when you start a container as root, any attempts to edit any host settings will be denied, as shown in figure 13.11.

```
busybox-example $ kubectl exec deploy/busybox-example -- whoami
root
busybox-example $ kubectl patch deployment busybox-example -p '
{
  "spec": {
    "template": {
      "spec": {
        "securityContext": {
          "runAsUser": 1500,
          "runAsGroup": 1000,
          "fsGroup": 1200
        }
      }
    }
  }
}'
deployment.apps/busybox-example patched
busybox-example $ kubectl exec deploy/busybox-example -- whoami
whoami: unknown uid 1500
command terminated with exit code 1
busybox-example $ kubectl exec deploy/busybox-example -- groups
1000groups: unknown ID 1000
groups: unknown ID 1200
 1200
command terminated with exit code 1
busybox-example $ █
```

Figure 13.10   A Pod running as the root user and using `securityContext` to change the defined user and user groups

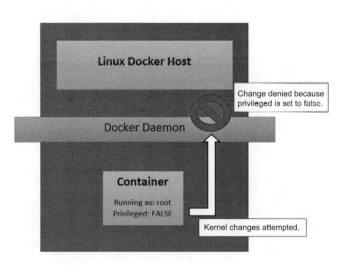

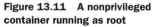

Figure 13.11   A nonprivileged container running as root

For example, we can try to set a kernel value from a container that is running as root, but not as a privileged container, as illustrated in figure 13.12.

```
[root@localhost ~]# kubectl exec -it root-demo sh
/ $ sysctl kernel.domainname=test.com
sysctl: error setting key 'kernel.domainname': Read-only file system
```

Figure 13.12   An attempted kernel change from a container without privileges

The kernel change is denied because the running image does not have elevated privileges on the host system. If there was a reason to allow this operation from a container, the image could be started as a privileged container. To run a privileged container, you need to allow it in the securityContext of the Pod:

```
apiVersion: v1
kind: Pod
metadata:
  name: root-demo
spec:
  containers:
  - name: root-demo
    image: busybox
    command: [ "sh", "-c", "sleep 1h" ]
    securityContext:
      privileged: true
```

Now that the Pod has been allowed to run as a privileged container, and it is running as root, it will be allowed to change kernel parameters, as shown in figure 13.13.

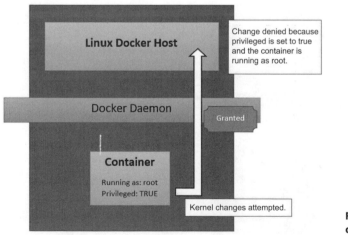

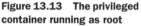

Figure 13.13   The privileged container running as root

In figure 13.14, notice that the domain name change does not return an error, which verifies that the container can modify host-level settings.

This time, the kernel change worked for two reasons: the container is running as the *root* user, and the container was allowed to start up as a *privileged container.*

```
[root@localhost ~]# kubectl exec -it root-demo sh
/ # sysctl kernel.domainname=test.com
kernel.domainname = test.com
```

Figure 13.14 The host kernel change allowed from a running container

For the last scenario, the manifest has been edited to run as user 1000, who does not have root privileges, and to start as a privileged container:

```
apiVersion: v1
kind: Pod
metadata:
  name: root-demo
spec:
  containers:
  - name: root-demo
    image: busybox
    command: [ "sh", "-c", "sleep 1h" ]
    securityContext:
      privileged: true
      runAsUser: 1000
```

Even though the container is running as a privileged container, the user is a standard user, so any kernel changes will be denied, as shown in figure 13.15.

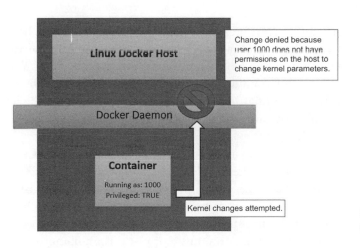

Figure 13.15 The privileged container running as nonroot

In summary, securing the actions that a container can take on the host is controlled by the user running in the container and whether the container is allowed to run as a privileged container. To secure a cluster, you need to create a policy that defines controls for each of these values.

Right now, you know why containers should not be allowed to run as root and why you should limit Pods that are allowed to run as a privileged container, but we haven't explained how to stop either of these actions from occurring on a cluster. This is an area that Anthos excels in! By providing Anthos Config Manager, Google has included all the tools you need to secure your cluster with these and many other common security settings.

In the next section, we will explain how to use ACM to secure a cluster using the included policy manager, Gatekeeper.

13.7   *Using ACM to secure your service mesh*

As you have seen throughout this book, Anthos goes beyond simply providing a basic Kubernetes cluster. It also provides additional components like Anthos Service Mesh (ASM) to provide a service mesh, Binary Authorization, serverless workloads, and ACM to handle infrastructure as code.

In chapter 11, you learned about designing and configuring ACM to enforce deployments and objects on an Anthos cluster. In this section, we will use ACM to secure communication between services in a cluster by using a policy. We will then move on to an additional component included with ACM, the Policy Controller, which provides an admission controller based on the open source project Gatekeeper.

> **NOTE**   When enabling mTLS using an ACM policy, remember that the policy will be applied to all clusters that are managed by the external repository, unless you use a `ClusterSelector` to limit the clusters that will be configured.

13.7.1   *Using ACM to enforce mutual TLS*

In chapter 4, you learned that ASM includes the ability to encrypt traffic between services using mutual TLS (mTLS). Mutual TLS is the process of verifying service identities before allowing communication between the services, via Istio's sidecar. Once the identities have been verified, the communication between the services will be encrypted. However, by default, Istio is configured to use permissive mTLS. Permissive mTLS allows a workload that does not have a sidecar running to communicate with a sidecar-enabled service using HTTP (plaintext).

Developers or administrators who are new to service meshes generally use the permissive setting. Although this is beneficial for learning Istio, allowing HTTP traffic into a service running a sidecar makes it insecure, nullifying the advantages of Istio and the sidecar. Once you are comfortable with Istio, you may want to consider changing the permissive policy to the more secure strict setting.

You can force strict mTLS for the entire mesh or just certain namespaces by creating a Kubernetes object called `PeerAuthentication`. Deciding on the correct scope for mTLS is different for each organization and cluster. You should always test any mTLS policy changes in a development environment before implementing them in production, to avoid any unexpected application failures.

Because this is an important policy, it's a perfect example to demonstrate the importance of using ACM as a configuration management tool. Remember that once an object is managed by ACM, the configuration manager will control it. This means that the manager will recreate any managed object that is edited or deleted for any reason. For the mTLS use case, you should see the importance of using ACM to make sure that the policy is set and, if edited, remediated to the configured strict value.

To enable a strict mTLS meshwide policy, you need to create a new `Peer-Authentication` object that sets the mTLS mode to strict. An example manifest is shown next:

```
apiVersion: security.istio.io/v1beta1
kind: PeerAuthentication
metadata:
  name: default
  namespace: istio-system
spec:
  mtls:
    mode: STRICT
```

The manifest assumes that Istio has been installed in the `istio-system` namespace. Because the namespace selector is the `istio-system` namespace, it will enforce a strict mTLS policy for all namespaces in the cluster.

> **NOTE** To enforce a strict mTLS policy for every namespace in the cluster, the `PeerAuthentication` object must be created in the same namespace that Istio was installed in. By default, this is the `istio-system` namespace.

If you have decided to implement per-namespace enforcement, the manifest requires a single modification, the namespace value. For example, if we wanted to enable mTLS on a namespace called `webfront`, we would use the following manifest:

```
apiVersion: security.istio.io/v1beta1
kind: PeerAuthentication
metadata:
  name: default
  namespace: webfront
spec:
  mtls:
    mode: STRICT
```

To use either of these manifests with ACM to enforce a strict mTLS mesh policy, you simply need to store it in your ACM repository. Because the policy is stored in the ACM repository, it will be managed by the controller, and any changes or deletion will result in the object being recreated using the strict setting. The mTLS policy is just an example of how we can use ACM and ASM together to enforce a security policy for a cluster.

13.8 Conclusion

ACM's policy engine is a powerful add-on included with all Anthos clusters. Gatekeeper allows an organization to create granular policies to secure a cluster against potential attackers by providing additional security and stability. Google provides a collection of default policies that address some of the most common security concerns that have been collected from the community and Google's own experiences. If the included policy library doesn't address a security problem in your organization, you can create your own policies by using Gatekeeper's policy language, Rego.

13.9   *Examples and case study*

Using the knowledge from the chapter, address each of the requirements in the following case study.

13.9.1   *Evermore Industries*

Evermore Industries has asked you to evaluate the security of their Anthos Kubernetes cluster. The cluster has been configured as follows:

- Multiple control plane nodes
- Multiple worker nodes
- ASM to provide Istio, configured with permissive mTLS
- ACM configured with the policy engine enabled, including the default template library

They have asked you to document any current security concerns and remediation steps to meet the following requirements:

- Audit for any security concerns, and provide proof of any exploit covered by policies.
- All containers must only be allowed to pull from an approved list of registries, including these:
  - gcr.io
  - hub.evermore.local
- All policies, other than the approved registry policy, must be tested to assess their consequences before being enforced.
- Containers must deny any privilege escalation attempts, without affecting any Anthos namespaces, including these:
  - kube-system
  - gke-system
  - config-management-system
  - gatekeeper-system
  - gke-connect
- Containers must not be able to use hostPID, hostNetwork, or hostIPC in any namespace other than the kube-system namespace.
- All requirements must be addressed using only existing Anthos tools.

The next section contains the solution to address Evermore's requirements. You can follow along with the solution or, if you are comfortable, configure your cluster to address the requirements and use the solution to verify your results.

EVERMORE INDUSTRIES SOLUTION: TESTING THE CURRENT SECURITY

Meets requirement 1

The first requirement necessitates you document any security concerns with the current cluster. To test the first three security requirements, you can deploy a manifest that attempts to elevate the privileges of a container. The test manifest should pull an image from a registry that is not on the approved list and set the fields to elevate privileges and the various host values. We have provided an example manifest here:

```
apiVersion: v1
kind: Pod
metadata:
  labels:
    run: hack-example
  name: hack-example
spec:
  hostPID: true
  hostIPC: true
  hostNetwork: true
  volumes:
  - name: host-fs
    hostPath:
      path: /
  containers:
  - image: docker.io/busybox
    name: hack-example
    command: ["/bin/sh", "-c", "sleep infinity"]
    securityContext:
      privileged: true
      allowPrivilegeEscalation: true
    volumeMounts:
    - name: host-fs
      mountPath: /host
```

This manifest will test all the security requirements in a single deployment. The image tag that is being pulled is from docker.io, which is not on the approved registry list. It also maps the host's root filesystem into the container at mount /host, and it is starting as a privileged container.

Because the container started successfully, we can document that the cluster can pull images from registries that are not in the accepted list. A successful start also shows that the Pod started as a privileged container and that the mount to `hostPath` also succeeded. To document that the container does have access to the host filesystem, we can access the image and list the /host directory. Figure 13.16 shows that we can successfully list the host's root filesystem.

After capturing the output and adding it to the documentation, you can delete the Pod because we will need to test the same deployment with the policies enabled in the next test. You can delete it by executing `kubectl delete -f use-case1.yaml`.

```
[root@localhost gke-bm]# kubectl exec -it hack-example sh
/ # ls -la /host
total 24
dr-xr-xr-x    17 root      root          224 Nov  1 00:04 .
drwxr-xr-x     1 root      root           41 Nov  1 23:16 ..
lrwxrwxrwx     1 root      root            7 May 11  2019 bin -> usr/bin
dr-xr-xr-x     6 root      root         4096 Nov  1 00:21 boot
drwxr-xr-x    19 root      root         3120 Nov  1 20:59 dev
drwxr-xr-x   100 root      root         8192 Nov  1 20:58 etc
drwxr-xr-x     2 root      root            6 May 11  2019 home
lrwxrwxrwx     1 root      root            7 May 11  2019 lib -> usr/lib
lrwxrwxrwx     1 root      root            9 May 11  2019 lib64 -> usr/lib64
drwxr-xr-x     2 root      root            6 May 11  2019 media
drwxr-xr-x     4 root      root           47 Nov  1 19:20 mnt
drwxr-xr-x     4 root      root           35 Nov  1 19:18 opt
dr-xr-xr-x   411 root      root            0 Nov  1 20:58 proc
dr-xr-x---     7 root      root          214 Nov  1 19:16 root
drwxr-xr-x    33 root      root         1020 Nov  1 20:59 run
lrwxrwxrwx     1 root      root            8 May 11  2019 sbin -> usr/sbin
drwxr-xr-x     2 root      root            6 May 11  2019 srv
dr-xr-xr-x    13 root      root            0 Nov  1 20:58 sys
drwxrwxrwt    12 root      root         4096 Nov  1 23:26 tmp
drwxr-xr-x    12 root      root          144 Nov  1 00:04 usr
drwxr-xr-x    21 root      root         4096 Nov  1 00:21 var
```

Figure 13.16   Accessing the host filesystem in a container

EVERMORE INDUSTRIES SOLUTION: ADDING REPO CONSTRAINTS
Meets requirement 2

Evermore's second requirement is that containers can be pulled only from trusted registries. In the requirements, only images pulled from gcr.io and hub.evermore.local are allowed to be deployed in the cluster.

To limit images to only the two registries, we need to create a new Constraint-Template that uses the k8sallowedrepos.constraints.gatekeeper.sh object. An example ConstraintTemplate is provided next:

```
apiVersion: constraints.gatekeeper.sh/v1beta1
kind: K8sAllowedRepos
metadata:
  name: allowed-registries
spec:
  match:
    kinds:
      - apiGroups: [""]
        kinds: ["Pod"]
  parameters:
    repos:
      - "gcr.io"
      - "hub.evermore.local"
```

Once this manifest is deployed, any attempts to pull an image from a registry other than gcr.io and hub.evermore.local will result in the admission controller denying the Pod creation with the following error that an invalid image repo was used:

```
Error creating: admission webhook "validation.gatekeeper.sh" denied the
    request: [denied by allowed-registries] container <nginx2> has an
    invalid image repo <bitnami/nginx>, allowed repos are ["gcr.io",
    ""hub.evermore.local""]
```

Now that we have addressed requirement 2, we can move on to address requirements 3 and 4.

EVERMORE INDUSTRIES SOLUTION: ADDING PRIVILEGED CONSTRAINTS

Meets requirements 3 and 4

We need to address the security requirements for Evermore's cluster. To secure the cluster from running privileged Pods in the cluster, but not affect Pods in any Anthos system namespaces, we need to enable a constraint with exemptions. However, before enabling a constraint, Evermore has required that all constraints be tested and the output of affected Pods be supplied as part of the documentation.

The first step is to create a manifest to create the constraint. The manifest shown next creates a constraint called `privileged-containers` in auditing mode only. It also excludes all of the system namespaces that Evermore has supplied in the requirements document:

```
apiVersion: constraints.gatekeeper.sh/v1beta1
kind: K8sPSPPrivilegedContainer
metadata:
  name: privileged-containers
spec:
  enforcementAction: dryrun
  excludedNamespaces:
    - kube-system
    - gke-system
    - config-management-system
    - gatekeeper-system
    - gke-connect
  match:
    kinds:
      - apiGroups: [""]
        kinds: ["Pod"]
```

To add the audit output to the documentation, you must describe the constraint and direct the output to a file by executing the following kubectl command:

```
kubectl get K8sPSPPrivilegedContainer psp-privileged-container -o yaml > privtest
```

This will create a file called privtest in the current folder, containing the audit results for the `psp-privileged-container` constraint. You should check the file to verify that it contains the expected audit results under the violations section. An abbreviated output from our audit follows:

```
  violations:
  - enforcementAction: dryrun
    kind: Pod
```

```
      message: 'Privileged container is not allowed: cilium-agent, securityContext:
        {"capabilities": {"add": ["NET_ADMIN", "SYS_MODULE"]}, "privileged": true}'
      name: anetd-4qbw5
      namespace: kube-system
    - enforcementAction: dryrun
      kind: Pod
      message: 'Privileged container is not allowed: clean-cilium-state,
        securityContext:
        {"capabilities": {"add": ["NET_ADMIN"]}, "privileged": true}'
      name: anetd-4qbw5
```

You may have noticed that the audit output contains Pods running in namespaces that were added as an exclusion. Remember that when you exclude a namespace in a constraint, the namespace will still be audited—the exclusion only stops the policy from being enforced.

Because the output looks correct, we can enforce the policy to meet the security requirements to deny privileged containers. To remove the existing constraint, delete it using the manifest file executing kubectl delete -f <manifest file>.

Next, update the manifest file and remove the enforcementAction: dryrun line from the manifest and redeploy the constraint.

EVERMORE INDUSTRIES SOLUTION: ADDING HOST CONSTRAINTS

Meets requirement 5

The fifth requirement from Evermore is to deny hostPID, hostNetwork, and hostIPC in all namespaces, except kube-system. We also need to test the policy before implementation, as stated in the requirements.

To meet the set requirements, we need to implement two new policies. The first, k8spsphostnamespace, will block access to host namespaces including hostPID and hostIPC. Finally, to address blocking hostNetwork, we need to implement the k8sps-phostnetworkingports policy.

To block access to host namespaces from all namespaces except kube-system, you need to create a new constraint that exempts kube-system. We also need to test the constraint before it's implemented, so we need to set the enforcementAction to dryrun. An example manifest follows:

```
apiVersion: constraints.gatekeeper.sh/v1beta1
kind: K8sPSPHostNamespace
metadata:
  name: psp-host-namespace
spec:
  enforcementAction: dryrun
  excludedNamespaces:
    - kube-system
  match:
    kinds:
      - apiGroups: [""]
        kinds: ["Pod"]
```

After this manifest has been deployed, any attempts by a Pod to use a host name-space like hostPID will be denied startup by the admission controller. Setting the dryrun option will only audit the policy, without enforcing it. Once it's tested, you can remove enforcementAction: dryrun from the manifest and deploy it to enforce the policy.

To block hostNetworking, we will need to create another constraint that will use the k8spsphostnetworkingports policy:

```
apiVersion: constraints.gatekeeper.sh/v1beta1
kind: K8sPSPHostNetworkingPorts
metadata:
  name: psp-host-network-ports
spec:
  enforcementAction: dryrun
  excludedNamespaces:
    - kube-system

  match:
    kinds:
      - apiGroups: [""]
        kinds: ["Pod"]
  parameters:
    hostNetwork: false
```

Just like the previous constraint, we have included the dryrun option to test the constraint before being enforced. Once tested and deployed, any Pod that attempts to set hostNetwork to true will be denied by the admission controller with the following error stating that only hostNetwork=false is allowed:

```
Error creating: admission webhook "validation.gatekeeper.sh" denied the
request: [denied by psp-host-network-ports] The specified hostNetwork and
hostPort are not allowed, pod: privileged-test-7694b64776-qmp47. Allowed
values: {"hostNetwork": false}
```

Congratulations! By deploying the last two constraints, we have met all Evermore's requirements.

Summary

- Root and privileged containers can be used to take over an unprotected host.
- Anthos can secure a cluster by deploying built-in policies or custom policies that are deployed using Anthos Configuration Management.
- Virtual machines provide better security than containers. Both patterns have unique security concerns and must be deployed correctly, keeping security in mind from the beginning of their deployments.
- We covered an overview of Kubernetes security and features included with Anthos to help remediate security concerns in clusters, including ACM and ASM.

- Security problems with containers running as root or as a privileged container can be used to compromise a host.
- You can use ACM features to secure a cluster by using Gatekeeper and the included constraint template libraries provided by Anthos.
- Google's container vulnerability scanning engine can identify container vulnerabilities.

14

Marketplace

Antonio Gulli

This chapter covers
- The public Google Marketplace
- The private Google Marketplace
- Deploying a Marketplace solution
- Real-world scenarios

Google Cloud Marketplace is a one-stop solution to try, buy, configure, manage, and deploy software products. Frequently, multiple vendors offer the same package, providing an array of options for your specific use case and industry in terms of operative systems, VMs, containers, storage costs, execution environment, and SaaS services. Google Cloud offers new users an initial credit that can also be used in the Marketplace. As of January 2023, this credit is $300, but it might change in the future. In this chapter, we will discuss how you can use Google Cloud Marketplace to deploy packages automatically in different Kubernetes environments, including Anthos, GKE, and GKE on-prem. When it comes to simplifying the developer experience, Marketplaces add value by making it as easy as possible for users to install components, while making use of the maintainers'/providers' opinionated, best practice configuration.

14.1   The Google Marketplace

The Google Cloud Platform (GCP) Marketplace website (http://cloud.google.com/marketplace) offers a single place for GCP customers to find free and fee-based applications, provided either by Google or third-party partners, who extend what is offered in the platform. Deployments can use either default configurations or be specialized for specific needs, such as increased memory, storage, or more computational power with larger vCPUs. Each package has specific instructions for getting assistance after installation. Note that the Marketplace team keeps each image updated to fix critical problems and bugs. However, it is your responsibility to update the solutions that are already deployed in your environments.

14.1.1   Public Marketplace

Currently, more than two thousand solutions are available across GCP, including proper application packages and datasets. You can access the GCP Marketplace by clicking the Marketplace link in the Cloud console. To select a package, either search for a package name or browse using the left-hand pane of the Marketplace screen, as shown in figure 14.1. The solutions from the Marketplace makes it easy to deploy new

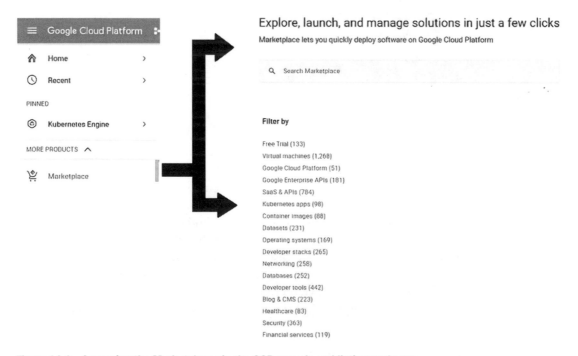

Figure 14.1   Accessing the Marketplace via the GCP console and listing packages

applications with a simple "point-and-click" operation, which is the same across multiple environments, either in public clouds or on-prem.

For the scope of this book, we are interested in applications running on Kubernetes. From the Google Cloud Marketplace website, choose Explore the Marketplace, and you will reach the Marketplace offerings (http://mng.bz/41Nv). In the Type pane on the left, choose Kubernetes Apps. Currently, about 100 solutions are available for GKE in different areas such as networking, databases, analytics, machine learning, monitoring, storage, and more, as shown in figure 14.2.

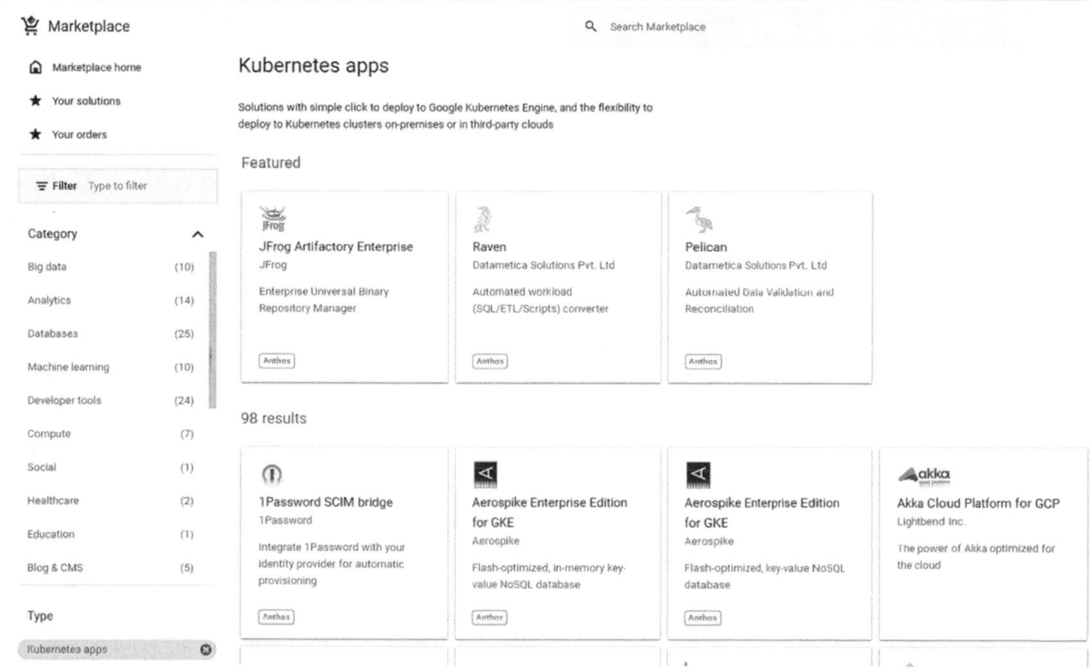

Figure 14.2 Solutions available for the Anthos GKE environment

Solutions are categorized according to the license model: either open source, paid, or "bring your own license" (BYOL). BYOL is a licensing model that allows enterprises to use their licenses flexibly, whether on-prem or in the cloud.

As of March 2023, about 70 solutions have been tested against the GKE on-prem environment. We can view the solutions for on-prem by adding the appropriate filter `deployment-env:gke-on-prem`, as shown in figure 14.3, to the search options. As of March 2023, 93 solutions have been tested against Anthos environments.

While browsing the solutions in the marketplace, you can identify third-party solutions that are compatible with Anthos by looking for the "Works with Anthos" logo

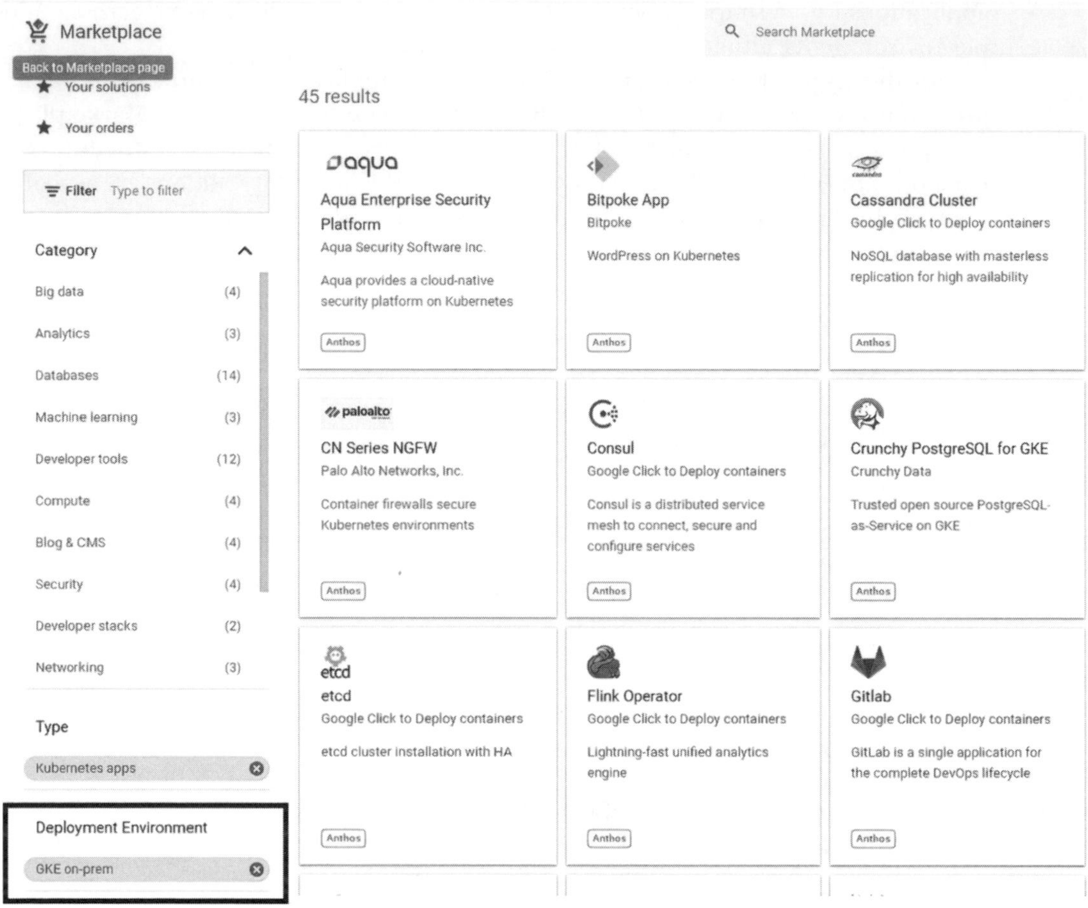

Figure 14.3   Solutions available for Anthos GKE-on-prem environment

attached to the listing. In figure 14.4, you can see solutions that have a small Anthos button. This button showcases the solutions that have been certified to work with Anthos. These listings conform to the requirements of the Anthos Ready program (https://cloud.google.com/anthos/docs/resources/anthos-ready-partners), which identifies partner solutions that adhere to Google Cloud's interoperability requirements and have been validated to work with the Anthos platform to meet the infrastructure and application development needs of enterprise customers. To qualify, partner-provided solutions must complete, pass, and maintain integration requirements to earn the Works with Anthos badge.

If you select one of the offerings that are certified for Anthos, you will see the "Works with Anthos" logo in the details screen for the selected offering, as shown in figure 14.5.

The public Marketplace provides enterprises with a quick deployment for several applications provided by various vendors, including NetApp, Aqua, JFrog, and Citrix.

★ Your solutions

★ Your orders

☰ Filter   Type to filter

Category   ⌃

Blog & CMS   (5)

Security   (15)

Developer stacks   (4)

Networking   (9)

Storage   (4)

Monitoring   (8)

Mobile   (1)

Security Command Center
Services   (2)

Financial services   (2)

Other   (3)

Type

Kubernetes apps   ⊗

Deployment Environment

Anthos   ⊗

---

78 results

1Password SCIM bridge
1Password

Integrate 1Password with your identity provider for automatic provisioning

[Anthos]

Aerospike Enterprise Edition for GKE
Aerospike

Flash-optimized, in-memory key-value NoSQL database

[Anthos]

Aerospike Enterprise Edition for GKE
Aerospike

Flash-optimized, key-value NoSQL database

[Anthos]

Avantra
Avantra

Avantra is the industry-leading AIOps platform for SAP

[Anthos]

Bitpod Survey
Bitpod

Create survey and start collecting data in minutes

[Anthos]

Bitpoke App
Bitpoke

WordPress on Kubernetes

[Anthos]

citrix
Citrix Ingress Controller
Citrix Systems, Inc

Kubernetes Ingress Controller for Citrix ADC

[Anthos]

Cloud Vision OCR On-Prem
Google

OCR service from Google Cloud Vision

[Anthos]

paloalto
CN Series NGFW
Palo Alto Networks, Inc.

Container firewalls secure Kubernetes environments

[Anthos]

Figure 14.4   Solutions available for the Anthos environment

Figure 14.5   An example solution, certified "Works with Anthos"

But what if you want to add your own solution for your developers? Of course, you probably wouldn't want this included in the public Marketplace, and Google accommodates this by offering a private Marketplace, which we will discuss in the next section.

14.1.2   Service Catalog

Service Catalog offers Marketplace capabilities to private enterprises to be used internally without exposing their internals to the rest of the world. Administrators can manage the visibility of applications and deployment rights at organization, folder, and project levels. The deployment manager can be used to define preset configurations, such as deploy regions, types of servers used for deployment, deployments rights, and other parameters, according to enterprise policy.

Service Catalog Admin	Catalogs	+ CREATE CATALOG	🗑 DELETE	⬏ SHARE
Catalogs				
Solutions	☰ Filter Enter property name or value			
Deployments	☐ Name ↑ Description Solutions Last modified Shared with			

Figure 14.6   Accessing the Service Catalog

You can access the Service Catalog via the Cloud console Navigation menu under Tools (see figure 14.6). From there, you can create new private Marketplaces, add applications, and configure access rights. Each Service Catalog should be hosted by a GCP project, and you can add catalog IAM permissions at the folder and project level. Sharing a catalog with a GCP organization, folder, or project allows customers to share their solutions with their end users. The steps are very intuitive, and the interested reader can find more information online (https://cloud.google.com/service-catalog).

14.1.3   Deploying on a GKE on-prem cluster

If you intend to deploy solutions from the Marketplace to an Anthos GKE on-prem cluster, then you need to define one or more namespaces on the target clusters and annotate them with a Secret, which will allow you to deploy the chosen solutions. The following steps are required:

1   If your cluster runs Istio, any external connections to third-party services are blocked by default, so it's important to configure Istio egress traffic to allow connection to the external OS package repository (see chapter 4).

2   You need to allow the downloading of images from the Google Container Registry by creating a firewall or proxy rule that allows access to marketplace.gcr.io.

3   In your GKE on-prem cluster, you might need to create a Google Cloud service account. This can be done via a cloud shell like this:

```
gcloud iam service-accounts create sa-name \
    --description="sa-description" \
    --display-name="sa-display-name"
```

4 Sign in to your Anthos GKE on-prem cluster using a token or credentials for a Kubernetes Service Account with a Kubernetes cluster-admin role. (Roles were discussed in chapter 3.) This would allow you to have superuser access to perform any action on any resource.

From the console, you can generate a new public/private key-pair downloaded to your machine by running the following command:

```
gcloud iam service-accounts keys create ~/key.json \
  --iam-account sa-name@project-id.iam.gserviceaccount.com
```

5 If you are deploying from the Cloud Marketplace for the first time, create an application-system namespace in your cluster by running the next command:

```
kubectl create namespace application-system
```

6 Then, create the Kubernetes Secret that contains an imagePullSecret for application-system:

```
JSON_KEY_FILENAME=path_to/service_account_key.json
IMAGEPULLSECRET_NAME=gcr-json-key
kubectl create secret docker-registry $IMAGEPULLSECRET_NAME \
  --namespace="application-system" \
  --docker-server=gcr.io \
  --docker-username=_json_key \
  --docker-password="$(cat $JSON_KEY_FILENAME)"
```

7 The next step is to apply imagePullSecret to the default service account in the application-system namespace:

```
kubectl patch sa default -n application-system -p '"imagePullSecrets":
[{"name": "gcr-json-key" }]'
```

8 Finally, for each namespace to which you want to deploy an application, you must create a new Secret and annotate the namespace with that Secret with the following command:

```
JSON_KEY_FILENAME=path_to/service_account_key.json
IMAGEPULLSECRET_NAME=gcr-json-key
kubectl create secret docker-registry $IMAGEPULLSECRET_NAME \
  --namespace=$NAMESPACE_NAME \
  --docker-server=gcr.io \
  --docker-username=_json_key \
  --docker-password="$(cat ~/$JSON_KEY_FILENAME)"

kubectl annotate namespace $NAMESPACE_NAME
marketplace.cloud.google.com/imagePullSecret=$IMAGEPULLSECRET_NAME
```

9 Once $NAMESPACE_NAME is defined as explained in the previous step, this namespace can be used to install on your on-prem cluster.

In other words, deploying on Anthos, whether on GCP or on-prem, is just a matter of defining the appropriate namespace on your target Kubernetes clusters and annotating the namespace with the Secret keys needed to pull images for your solutions.

In the next section, we describe how to install several predefined solutions belonging to different categories, including modernization tools, databases, monitoring and logging, CI/CD, productivity, and machine learning.

14.2   Real-world scenarios

In this section, we briefly describe how to deploy Marketplace solutions available for Anthos. Our examples are intentionally heterogeneous and belong to different categories. Note that after you launch deployments from Cloud Marketplace, you can use Google Cloud tools to view, modify, and monitor your deployment. For example, you can use Cloud Deployment Manager to add resources to a deployment or remove software deployments that you no longer need.

14.2.1   Example 1: Elasticsearch

Elasticsearch is an open source solution for searching and analyzing your data in real time. This solution can be deployed on-prem, but this example shows deployment on GKE. The solution (see figure 14.7) is available at http://mng.bz/Q8OQ.

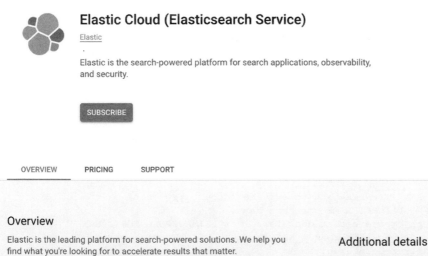

Figure 14.7   **Deploying an Elasticsearch solution**

After selecting the solution, you can choose the cluster and the namespace where it should be deployed (see figure 14.8). In this case, we leave the default choices, which will install on a cluster in us-central-1 region with the instance name `elasticsearch-1` and two replicas.

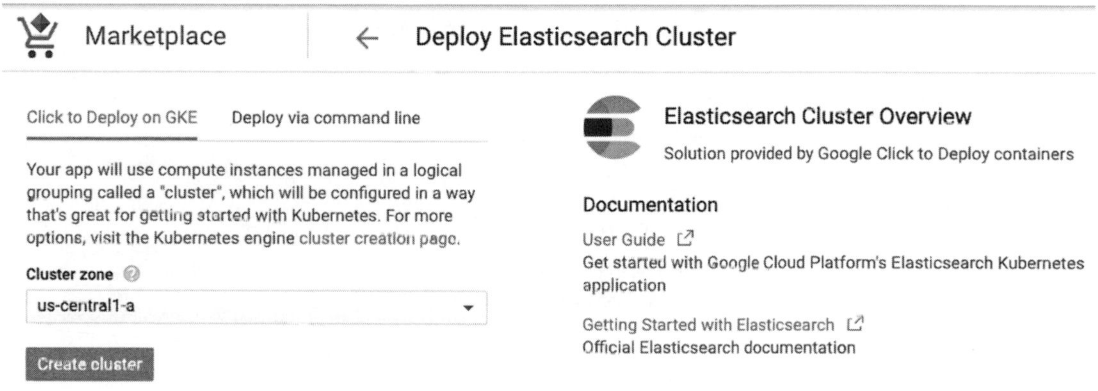

Figure 14.8   Deploying an Elasticsearch solution

Creating the clusters might take a few minutes (see figure 14.9), which is always a good reason to have a coffee break and let Marketplace do all the work.

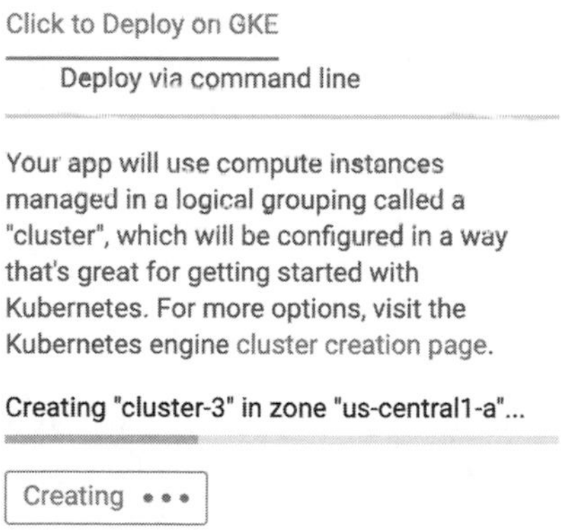

Figure 14.9   Creating a cluster for the new Elasticsearch solution

Once the cluster is created, Marketplace will start deploying the solution (see figure 14.10).

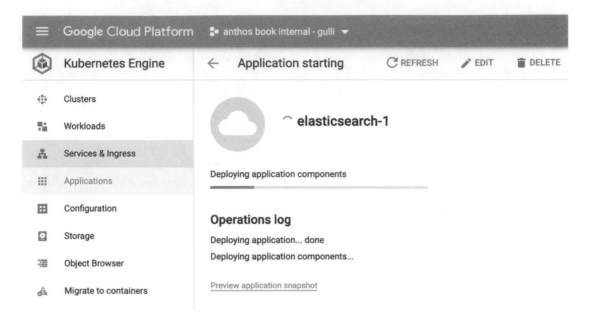

Figure 14.10   Deploying application components for the Elasticsearch solution

When the deployment is successfully executed, you can see the deployed solution on your chosen cluster, as shown in figure 14.11—easy, indeed. Marketplace saves you a lot of time and speeds up the administrative tasks needed to maintain your Anthos applications.

Figure 14.11   The Elasticsearch solution deployed

Once Elasticsearch is deployed from the Marketplace, you can use Anthos to manage the cluster. In figure 4.12, you will see CPU, memory, and disk details.

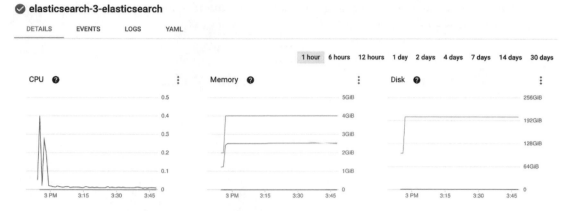

Figure 14.12   CPU, memory, and disk monitoring for Elasticsearch deployed from Marketplace

14.2.2   *Example 2: MariaDB*

Let's now focus on how to deploy MariaDB, a popular open source database, which was forked from the more popular MySQL relational database management system after being acquired by Oracle in 2009. The solution (see figure 14.13) is available at https://console.cloud.google.com/marketplace/details/google/mariadb.

Figure 14.13   Deploying a MariaDB solution

In this case, we decide to change the default parameters and require a higher number of replicas—two (see figure 14.14).

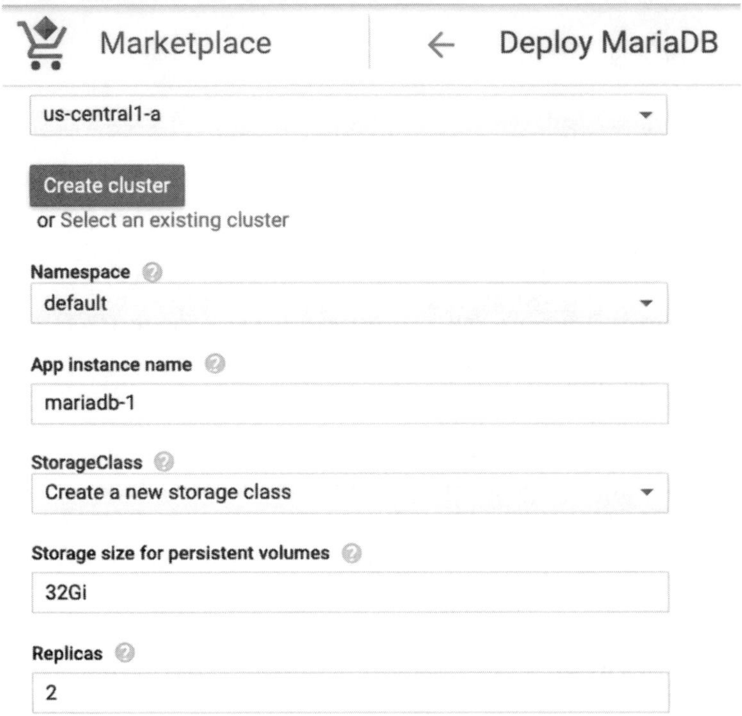

Marketplace   ←   Deploy MariaDB

us-central1-a   ▼

Create cluster
or Select an existing cluster

Namespace ?
default   ▼

App instance name ?
mariadb-1

StorageClass ?
Create a new storage class   ▼

Storage size for persistent volumes ?
32Gi

Replicas ?
2

Figure 14.14   Deploying a MariaDB solution with a higher number of replicas

The result of our deployment is straightforward (see figure 14.15). Once again, Marketplace allows us to save time while administering our Anthos clusters.

| ☐ | mariadb-1-mariadb | ✅ OK | Stateful Set | 1/1 | default | **cluster-5** |
| ☐ | mariadb-1-mariadb-secondary | ✅ OK | Stateful Set | 2/2 | default | **cluster-5** |

Figure 14.15   MariaDB deployed solution

Once MariaDB is deployed from the Marketplace, you can use Anthos to manage the cluster. Figure 14.16 shows an example of inspecting the cluster and the running Pods.

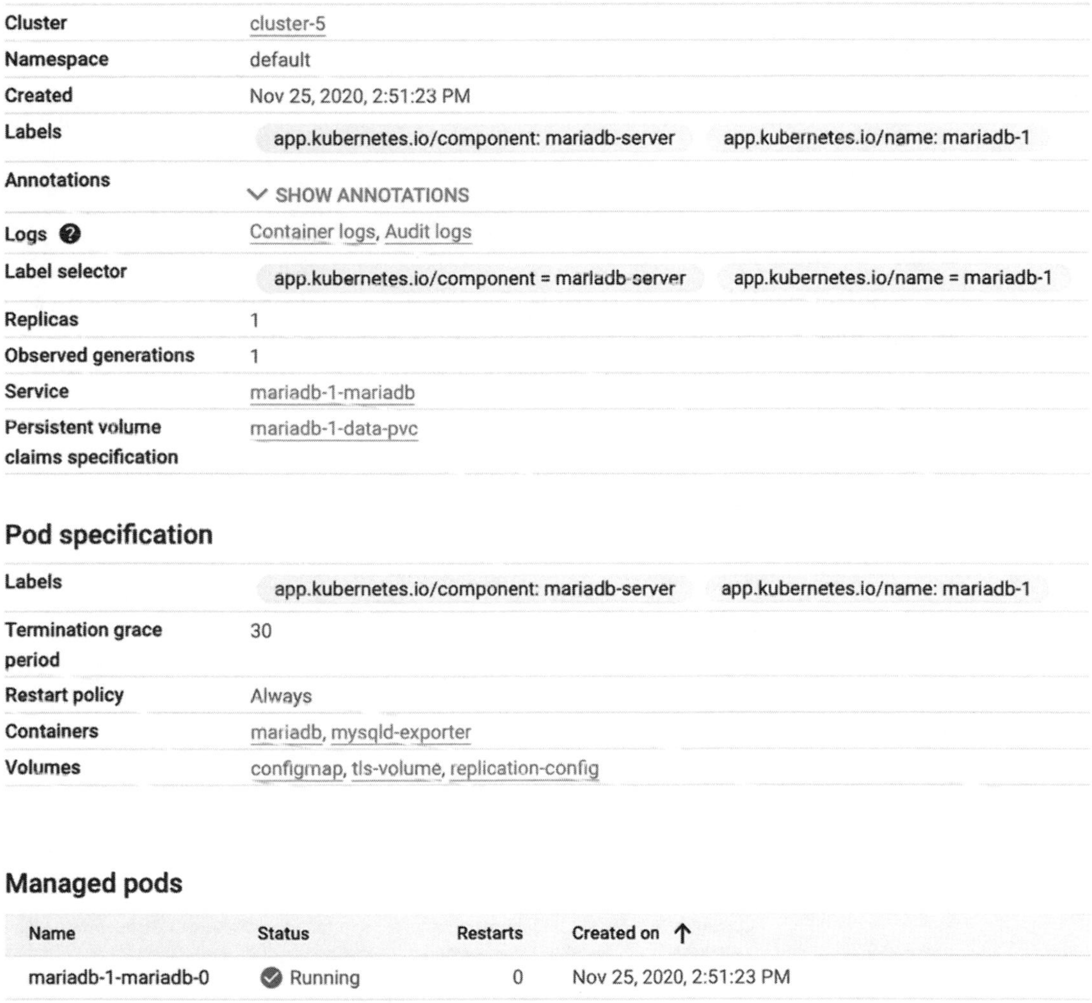

Cluster	cluster-5
Namespace	default
Created	Nov 25, 2020, 2:51:23 PM
Labels	app.kubernetes.io/component: mariadb-server app.kubernetes.io/name: mariadb-1
Annotations	∨ SHOW ANNOTATIONS
Logs ❓	Container logs, Audit logs
Label selector	app.kubernetes.io/component = mariadb-server app.kubernetes.io/name = mariadb-1
Replicas	1
Observed generations	1
Service	mariadb-1-mariadb
Persistent volume claims specification	mariadb-1-data-pvc

Pod specification

Labels	app.kubernetes.io/component: mariadb-server app.kubernetes.io/name: mariadb-1
Termination grace period	30
Restart policy	Always
Containers	mariadb, mysqld-exporter
Volumes	configmap, tls-volume, replication-config

Managed pods

Name	Status	Restarts	Created on ↑
mariadb-1-mariadb-0	✅ Running	0	Nov 25, 2020, 2:51:23 PM

Figure 14.16   MariaDB inspecting the solution deployed from the Marketplace

14.2.3   *What we have done so far*

So far, we have installed two applications on Anthos cluster on GKE. If we want to check their status, we can access our GKE under Applications, as shown in figure 14.17.

Filter applications

Name	Status	Namespace	Cluster	Software	Version	Updates
elasticsearch-1 Elasticsearch by Google Click to Deploy	OK	default	cluster-3	Elasticsearch	6.3.2-20201025-144515	
mariadb-1 MariaDB by Google Click to Deploy	OK	default	cluster-3	MariaDB	10.3.25-20201025-150334	

Figure 14.17 Solutions deployed via Marketplace

14.2.4 Example 3: Cassandra

Cassandra is a NoSQL, highly scalable, high-performance distributed database with high availability. Deploying a Cassandra cluster is easy. You can access the solution at https://console.cloud.google.com/marketplace/details/google/cassandra?q=anthos (figure 14.18).

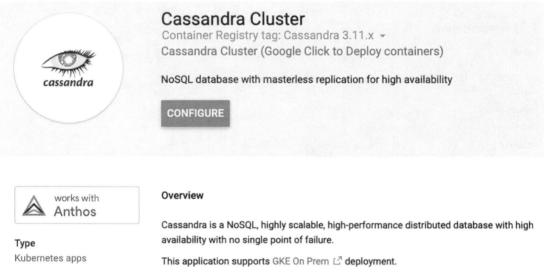

Figure 14.18 Deploying a Cassandra solution

After installation, you can access and manage your deployed solutions. For instance, you might be interested in monitoring CPU, memory, and disk usage for a given period, as shown in figure 14.19.

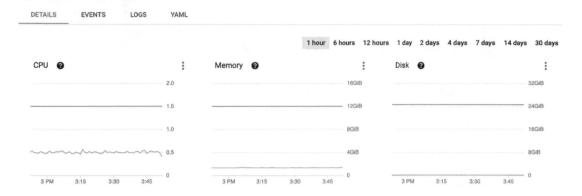

Figure 14.19 Managing a Cassandra solution

14.2.5 *Example 4: Prometheus and Grafana*

Once you understand the mechanism, installing a new solution is a streamlined process. For instance, suppose we want to install a more complex set of applications that work together. A classic example is Prometheus and Grafana. Prometheus is an open source monitoring and alerting platform adopted by many companies as a monitoring tool, and Grafana provides several dashboards, which visualize the metrics collected by the Prometheus server. The solution can be accessed at https://console.cloud.google .com/marketplace/details/google/prometheus?q=anthos and is shown in figure 14.20.

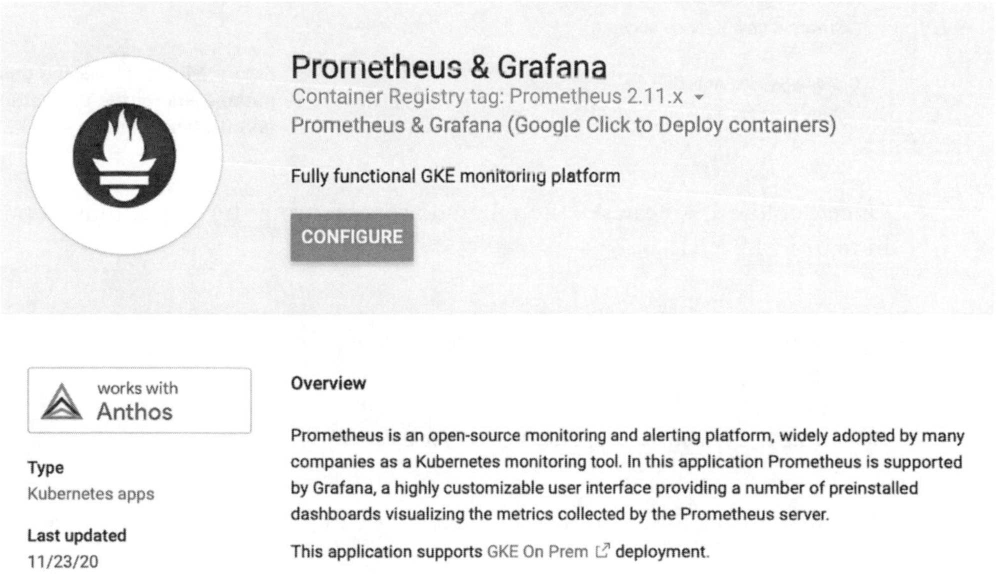

Prometheus & Grafana
Container Registry tag: Prometheus 2.11.x ▾
Prometheus & Grafana (Google Click to Deploy containers)

Fully functional GKE monitoring platform

CONFIGURE

works with
Anthos

Type
Kubernetes apps

Last updated
11/23/20

Overview

Prometheus is an open-source monitoring and alerting platform, widely adopted by many companies as a Kubernetes monitoring tool. In this application Prometheus is supported by Grafana, a highly customizable user interface providing a number of preinstalled dashboards visualizing the metrics collected by the Prometheus server.

This application supports GKE On Prem ⤴ deployment.

Figure 14.20 Deploying a Prometheus and Grafana solution

Let's use the default parameters, shown in figure 14.21, for deploying the solution.

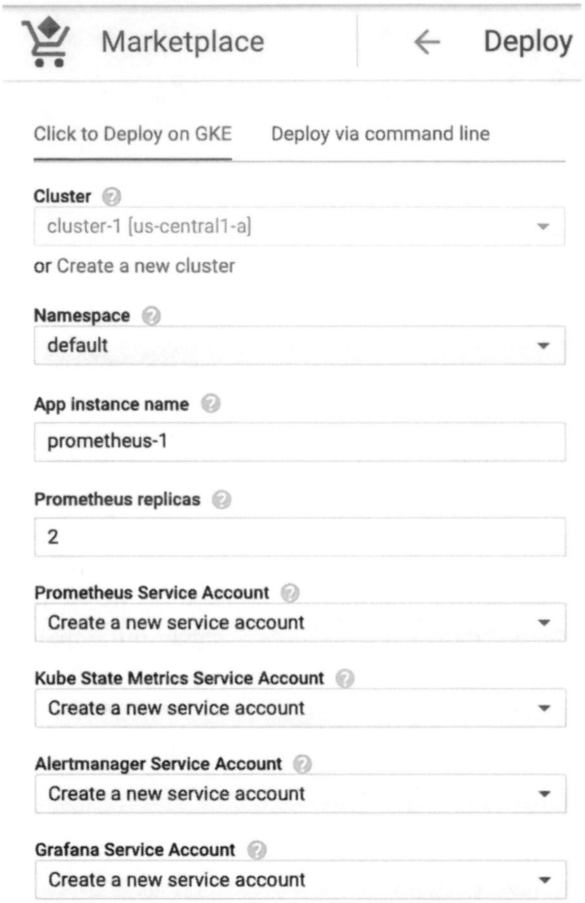

Figure 14.21   **Using the default parameters for the Prometheus and Grafana solution**

Once deployed, we can see the solution available from the Application details, shown in figure 14.22.

Figure 14.22   Prometheus and Grafana deployed solution

Of course, you can use Anthos to manage the deployed solution, as illustrated in figure 14.23.

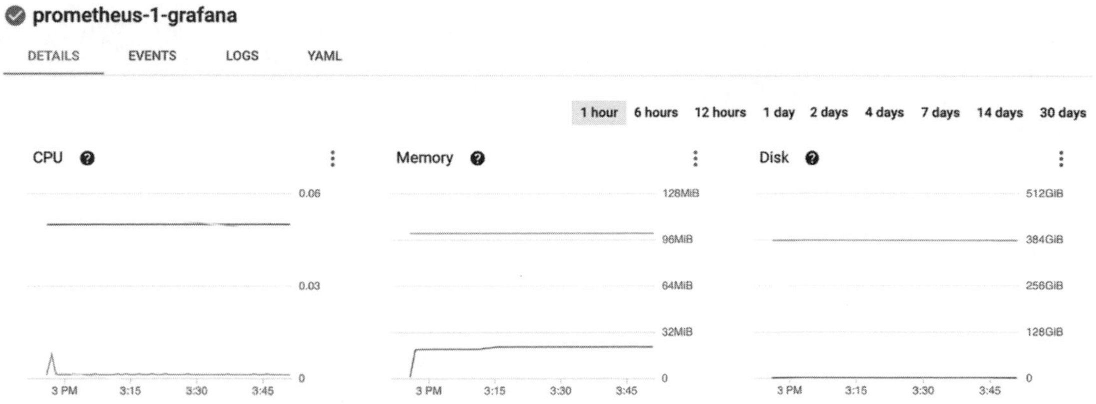
prometheus-1-grafana
DETAILS
EVENTS
LOGS
YAML
1 hour
6 hours
12 hours
1 day
2 days
4 days
7 days
14 days
30 days
CPU
0.06
0.03
0
Memory
128MiB
96MiB
64MiB
32MiB
0
Disk
512GiB
384GiB
256GiB
128GiB
0
3 PM
3:15
3:30
3:45

Figure 14.23 Managing the Prometheus and Grafana solution

Once the solution is deployed, you can start recording real-time metrics in the Prometheus time-series database. Then you can use Grafana to create dashboards and monitor your system performance.

This example concludes the section. It might be worth noticing that Grafana can be deployed via the Marketplace separately and is supported in Anthos, so it can be compatible with managed Prometheus.

Summary

- Both the public and private Marketplaces can be used to deploy simple and complex workloads for developers.
- The public Google Marketplace is a service provided by Google that contains several vendor solutions, including solutions specific for Kubernetes, both in GCP and on-prem.
- The private Google Marketplace allows a company to offer private solutions for their internal developers, enabling companies to provide the same deployment simplicity that Google offers in the public Marketplace.
- Consuming Marketplace solutions on-prem requires additional setup steps that a GCP cluster does not require.
- We deployed a few Marketplace solutions to demonstrate how easy it is to deploy a workload in the real world, using a provided solution.

15

Migrate

Antonio Gulli

This chapter covers

- The benefits of using Migrate for Anthos
- Recommended workloads for migration
- Migrate for Anthos architecture
- Using Migrate for Anthos to migrate a workload
- Best practices for Migrate for Anthos

Containers provide developers multiple advantages, including increased speed when deploying and provisioning workloads, higher resource utilization, portability, and cost efficiency compared to virtual machines (VMs).

However, many customers have several thousands of applications written over multiple years running on VM infrastructure using heritage frameworks. For these customers, it would be too time consuming and expensive to rewrite their applications. Therefore, they need tools to modernize workloads and to provide the benefits of modern cloud native environments without incurring the cost of rewriting applications from scratch. The whole value proposition is to decrease customers' time to market during transformation projects and to augment and optimize traditional workloads with modern cloud infrastructure and services.

Google believes that modernization doesn't have to be all or nothing. Microservices architectures structure an application as a collection of services that are highly maintainable and testable, loosely coupled via APIs, and independently deployable. However, even if you don't use a microservice architecture from the beginning, you can convert your applications into containers and still take advantage of many of the benefits typically obtained by cloud native applications. This is what we'll see in this chapter.

Migrate for Anthos (in short, M4A) is a tool that helps extract your legacy workloads from your VMs and transform them into containers, including all you need for execution—the runtime, system tools, libraries, code, configurations, and settings. Once your application is migrated, you can run it on Anthos, either on Google's Kubernetes Engine (GKE), on-prem, or in other clouds. In this way, the management of infrastructure, hardware, and the OS/kernel are "abstracted away" and delegated to your cloud provider(s).

Furthermore, M4A generates the artifacts that enable you to switch to modern software development using CI/CD pipelines and shifting from package management to container-/image-based management. You can think about M4A as an accclerator to the ultimate goal of modernization, and this acceleration can happen at scale, with many legacy applications migrated together in bulk. M4A can let you operate thousands of legacy applications at scale by modernizing the underlying compute infrastructure, network, storage, and management.

M4A supports both Linux and Windows migration to containers. Source environments can include either a GCP Compute Engine environment, a VMware vSphere environment, a Microsoft Azure VM environment, or an Amazon Elastic Compute Cloud (Amazon EC2) environment. All workloads are directly migrated with no need for access to the original source code, rewriting your workloads, or manually containerizing your workloads.

Most of the migration work is done automatically, and you can modify the generated migration plans to fine tune the desired modernization. While the migration process executes, the application can continue to run uninterrupted, and you can be up and running with the containerized app in minutes. If you want to go back to the initial state, you can roll back with no data lost. Migrated workload container images that are generated by M4A are automatically deployed into Google Container Registry (GCR) or other local repositories and can run in any environment without you having to install an M4A component on target workload clusters. Of course, the whole M4A process can be performed and monitored via the Google Cloud console UI.

Now that we have set up the context, let's look at M4A's benefits in detail.

15.1 *Migrate for Anthos benefits*

M4A allows us to unbundle more and more infrastructure from inside VMs and manage it with Kubernetes. This modernization unifies app management with modern IT skills. Indeed, in the numerous cases described in detail in this chapter, it is possible to promote legacy applications to first-class objects in a cloud native environment with no need to change or access the code. The unlocked improvements at scale follow:

- Define the infrastructure with declarative APIs, dynamic scaling, self-healing, and programmatic rollout.
- Take advantage of improved workload density on the data center, allowing for better resource utilization.
- Maintain the infrastructure metrics, business metrics, network policies, and project access control.
- Integrate CI/CD pipelines and build systems.

M4A benefits are transparently gained in different areas: density, cost, security, infrastructure, automation, service management, and Day 2 operations. Let's discuss each class in more detail.

15.1.1 *Density*

VMs are abstracted from the underlying physical hardware. Whereas legacy bare metal servers can support only a single application, hypervisor[1] virtualization allows the applications of multiple VMs to run on a single bare metal server, sharing the underlying resources. Bare metal use is described here:

- Typically, bare metal utilization is at 5%–15%, and virtual machines can increase it up to 30%.
- Containers enhance workload density, because multiple containers are typically run on the same VM or bare metal server. In addition, the density is increased because things like OS/kernels, networking, and storage are abstracted away, as discussed earlier in the chapter.

The actual utilization gains will depend on several specific factors in your environment. Frequently, many organizations report significant gains as they move from physical servers, to VMs, to containers. For instance, the *Financial Times* content platform team reported an 80% reduction of server costs by adopting containers (see http:// mng.bz/mJ0P).

15.1.2 *Cost*

An increase in density results in immediate cost savings for infrastructure. As discussed earlier, density increase is a result of two facts: multiple containers can be packed on the

---

[1] A hypervisor is software, firmware, or hardware that creates and runs virtual machines.

same physical machine, and many software layers are abstracted away, which results in better usage of the available resources, requiring fewer servers, leading to an overall cost savings. Cost is a by-product of being able to elastically scale. If demand is low, then resources can be reduced, thus saving on the operating cost.

Moreover, after migration, legacy applications are promoted to first-class citizens together with cloud native applications. As a side effect, you don't need to maintain two working environments (both the legacy and the modern one), so, the unified management of workloads allows further cost reduction at scale.

If you want to know more about cost reduction, check the Google Cloud pricing calculator at https://cloud.google.com/products/calculator to estimate your monthly charges, including cluster management fees and worker node pricing for GKE.

15.1.3 *Infrastructure*

After moving the application to containers, you can see the whole infrastructure as code, knowing how the applications, processes, and dependencies work together. Any change in infrastructure can be stored in a repository (in short, repo) with operations such as commit, push, pull, merging, and branching applied to any part of your infrastructure, including config files. Traditionally, maintaining an infrastructure is a considerable cost for enterprise. Moving to infrastructure as code allows teams to implement DevOps/SRE methodologies, which leads to further cost savings at scale due to enhanced agility and reliability.

15.1.4 *Automation*

Managing virtual machines is an expensive, time-consuming, and error-prone process due to the need to patch and upgrade infrastructure either manually or with a plethora of third-party tools, which might increase the level of complexity. Anthos is an enabler for modernization and facilitates the move to containers for legacy workloads, which has an indirect effect on cost. For instance, on GKE for Anthos many operations are run automatically on the customer's behalf, including the following:

- *Node autorepair*—Keeps the nodes in your Kubernetes cluster in a healthy, running state.
- *Node autoupgrade*—Keeps the nodes in your Kubernetes cluster up to date with the cluster master version when your master is updated on your behalf.
- *Node autosecurity*—Security patches can be automatically deployed in a transparent way.
- *Node autoscale*—Dynamically scales your Kubernetes nodes up and down according to instantaneous load increase/decrease.
- *Node autoprovisioning*—Automatically manages a set of Kubernetes node pools on the user's behalf.
- *Progressive rollout/canary/A/B testing*—Programmatically rolls out applications on Kubernetes clusters, with rollbacks in case of problems.

As a rule of thumb, increasing the automation in your infrastructure will reduce the risk of accidental errors, enhance the reliability of the whole system, and reduce the cost.

15.1.5 Security

Once you move into containers, several security operations are facilitated. On Anthos, these operations include the following:

- *Security-optimized node kernel and OS updates*—Anthos offers automatic operating system upgrades and kernel patches for the worker nodes, freeing you from the burden of maintaining the OS, which is a substantial cost if your server fleet is large. VMs must run a full guest operating system, even if they host only a single app. Instead, containers reduce operational cost because there is no need to run an OS.
- *Binary authorization and container analysis*—Anthos offers a deploy-time security control that ensures only trusted container images are deployed in your environment.
- *Zero-trust security model*—Anthos Service Mesh (ASM), covered in chapter 4, and the core capabilities of Kubernetes allow us to provide network isolation and TLS security without changing the application code.
- *Identity-based security model*—With ASM, you can get security insights, security policies, and policy-driven security. These cases are discussed in detail in chapter 4.

Transparently increasing security will reduce the risk of an incident and the associated high cost.

15.1.6 Service management

After moving to the containers, you can use Anthos Service Mesh (see chapter 4) to determine where your services are connected and get telemetry and visibility into your application without changing code. Some of the benefits transparently gained on Anthos follow:

- *Encryption*—Applications can communicate with end-to-end encryption with no need for changing the code.
- *Integrated logging and monitoring*—You can get uniform metrics and traffic flow logs across your application.
- *Uniform observability*—You can observe service dependencies and understand the critical customer journey and how they affect your service-level agreement (SLA[2]) from end to end. You do this by setting up service-level objectives (SLOs[3]) on your applications.

---

[2] The SLA is the agreement that specifies what service is to be provided, how it is supported, times, locations, costs, performance, and responsibilities of the parties involved.

[3] SLOs are specific measurable metrics of an SLA such as availability, throughput, frequency, response time, or quality.

- *Operational agility*—You can dynamically migrate traffic and perform circuit breaking,[4] retries within your environment, canaries,[5] and A/B testing. Taking a canary as an example, you can move, based on a weighting, a certain amount of traffic from one service to a newer version of that service.
- *Bridging*—You can use service meshes to bridge traffic between on-prem and multiple clouds.

In general, adopting a service mesh will enhance your understanding of your infrastructure, which might become quite complex over time.

15.1.7 Day 2 operations

Anthos relieves the burden of Day 2 operations. Once your application is migrated, you can benefit from many Google Cloud Platform (GCP) capabilities, such as the following:

- *Cloud Logging and Cloud Monitoring*—Cloud Logging allows you to store, search, analyze, monitor, and alert on log data and events from Google Cloud, whereas Cloud Monitoring provides visibility into the performance, uptime, and overall health of cloud-powered applications. After migration, both services are available via configuration change only.
- *Unified policy and integrated resource management*—Anthos offers a declarative desired-state management via Anthos Config Management, which is covered in chapter 11. *Declarative* means that the user defines only the desired end state, leaving Anthos the definition of optimized steps to implement the changes. Anthos Config Management allows you to automate and standardize security policies and best practices across all your environments with advanced tagging strategies and selector policies. As users, you will have a single UI for defining unified policy creation and enforcement (chapter 13).
- *Cloud Build to implement Day 2 maintenance procedures*—Cloud Build offers control over defining custom workflows for building, testing, and deploying across multiple environments and multiple languages.
- *CI/CD pipelines*—Anthos integrates CI/CD pipelines for enhancing the agility of your environment. This allows you to have smaller code changes, faster turnaround on feature changes, shorter release cycles, and quicker fault isolation.
- *GCP Marketplace*—Anthos is integrated within GCP Marketplace, including a Service Catalog for deploying new applications with a single click. This is covered in detail in chapter 14.

---

[4] Circuit breakers are a design pattern used in modern software development to detect failures and to prevent a failure from constantly reappearing, during maintenance, external failures, or unforeseen problems.
[5] Canary deployments are a pattern for rolling out releases to a subset of users or servers. The idea is to first deploy the change to a small subset of servers/users, test it, and then roll the change out to the remaining servers/users.

One of the most important benefits of M4A is that legacy applications are promoted to first-class objects with the same benefits in terms of Day 2 operations as those typically expected in a cloud native environment.

In this section, we have discussed the benefits of using Migrate for Anthos to modernize VM workloads in place and containerize your application automatically with no need to rewrite it. As discussed, containerized applications increase agility and efficiency because they require less management time compared to VMs. In addition, they offer an increase of infrastructure density and a related reduction in cost. Finally, containerized applications can benefit from the service mesh in terms of observability, Day 2 operation streamlining, and uniform policy management and enforcement across environments.

In the next section, we will take a deep dive into what workloads are best suited for migration.

15.2   *Recommended workloads for migration*

Modernizing applications for the cloud can be difficult. Complex apps are often multitiered and typically have multiple dependencies. Data has gravity, and migration might depend on large volumes of data, either in files or in databases. Legacy applications might have been written in outdated code with legacy frameworks, and in many situations, the code itself might not be available for recompiling in a modern environment. In this section, we discuss the following types of applications that are particularly suitable for automatic migration:

- *Stateless web frontend*—A suitable class consists of stateless applications such as web servers and similar applications serving customer traffic. Containers are generally more lightweight than virtual machines, and it is, consequently, easier to scale them up and down according to various load situations.
- *Multi-VM, multitier stacks, and business logic middleware*—In this class are multitier web service stacks such as LAMP (Linux, Apache, MySQL, PHP/Perl/Python) or WordPress, because they can be broken down into multiple independent containers. Also in this class are J2EE Middleware such as Java Tomcat and other COTS (commercial off-the-shelf) apps. In M4A jargon, we typically say that the sweet-spot application categories include multitier web-based enterprise applications.
- *Medium to large-sized databases*—Databases such as MySQL, Postgres, and Redis are supported; the data layer can be typically separated from the compute layer, and containers can, therefore, help to manage lightweight computation.
- *Low duty cycle and bursty workloads*—Containers are the preferred solution in any situation where intermittent rises and decreases in compute activity occur because they are more lightweight than virtual machines. So, M4A should be considered any time we need to rapidly set up Dev/Test environments, training environments, or labs.

Overall, we can say that *ideal migration candidates* include the following:

- Workloads where modernization through a complete rewrite is either impossible or too expensive
- Workloads with unknown dependencies that could break something if touched
- Workloads that are maintained but not actively developed
- Workloads that aren't maintained anymore
- Workloads without source code access

Sometimes it might be difficult to have automatic migration. This is true if dependencies exist on specific kernel drivers or specific hardware, or if software licenses need to be tied to certain hardware or virtual machines. Another relevant case is VM-based workloads that require the whole Kubernetes node capacity, including high-performance and high-memory databases (such as SAP HANA). Except for these specific cases, all the other workloads should be considered for a migration from VMs to containers.

In this section, we have rapidly reviewed relevant workloads suitable for migration. In the next few paragraphs, we will discuss the migration architecture and some real examples of migration.

15.3 M4A architecture

In this section, we will discuss a typical migration workflow and how a virtual machine is transformed into several different containers. Once the migration is finished, the generated artifacts can run anywhere. In the case of failure, tools report detailed motivations for debugging and inspection.

> **NOTE** You no longer need to install the migration components on target clusters.

15.3.1 Migration workflow

Migration consists of three phases: the setup, actual migration, and optimization (see figure 15.1). Let's take a closer look at each step.

During the setup phase, a processing cluster is created, and the migration sources are defined. Among the supported migration sources we have VMware, AWS EC2, Azure VM, GCE VM, bare metal, and local VMware. As of version 1.9 of Anthos Migrate, the operating systems supported for migrations are RHEL, CentOS, SUSE, Ubuntu, Debian, and Windows. The list is always expanding, however, and it is good to check online for the latest list (see http://mng.bz/51Gz).

During the setup phase, we need to set up the cloud landing zone, considering identity, network configuration, security, and billing. Several tools can help make an infrastructure as code task more automatic, including Cloud Foundation Toolkit (https://cloud.google.com/foundation-toolkit) and Terraform (https://www.terraform.io/). These templates can be used off the shelf to rapidly build a repeatable, enterprise-ready foundation, depending on your specific needs. Furthermore, during setup, you

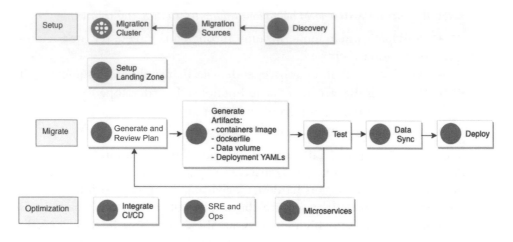

Figure 15.1   Setup and Migrate for Anthos

need to discover the workloads that you want to migrate. The desired workloads can be identified either manually or via discovery tools such as StratoZone (https://www .stratozone.com/; now acquired by Google), modelizeIT (https://www.modelizeit.com/), Cloudamize (https://www.cloudamize.com/en/home/), or CloudPhysics (https:// www.cloudphysics.com/). Since version 1.5 of M4A, native discovery tools are included, which will be covered in the next section.

During the migration phase, M4A is run and new container images are automatically generated, together with a Dockerfile, data volumes, and new YAML files for deployment. We will see the details in the next sections, where we will cover both the command-line interface (CLI) and graphical user interface (GUI) processes. Once these artifacts are automatically generated, you can test them on GKE/Anthos or in another cloud, and if everything looks good, you can deploy them to GKE/Anthos. It's also important to note that data is automatically moved and synchronized as part of the migration process.

Anthos supports live migrations, which means that applications can be migrated to modern environments without any interruptions. Behind the scenes, M4A creates a snapshot for the source VM, and this source VM is left running and operational with no need for downtime. In the meantime, all the storage operations are done on that snapshot of the VM. All workloads are directly migrated without requiring the original source code.

During the optimization phase, deployed artifacts can be integrated with CI/CD platforms such as Cloud Build, GitHub, Jenkins (https://www.jenkins.io/), Spinnaker (https://spinnaker.io/), GitLab CI/CD (https://docs.gitlab.com/ee/ci/), and others according to your specific preferences (see chapter 12).

15.3.2 *From virtual machines to containers*

A typical VM consists of multiple layers (see figure 15.2, left side). At the top are the applications run by users, together with cron jobs, config files, and user data. Just below are multiple services, including services running in the user space and SysV or Systemd[6] service. Then, a logging and monitoring layer sits on the top of the OS kernel and OS drivers. At the very bottom is the virtual hardware, including networking, storage with logical volumes on various filesystems, CPUs, and memory.

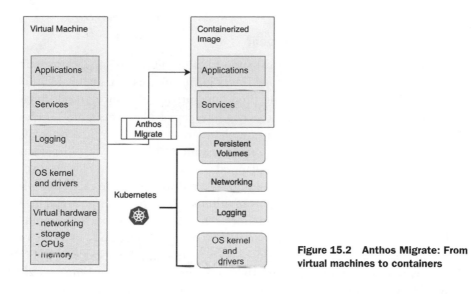

Figure 15.2   Anthos Migrate: From virtual machines to containers

For each application, M4A produces CI/CD artifacts in the form of a Docker Image, a Dockerfile, and deployment YAML files, including the applications, the user services, and the persistent volumes (see figure 15.2, right side). In particular, storage is refactored into a Kubernetes-supported persistent volume. Common functions such as networking, logging and monitoring, and OS kernel and drivers are abstracted away and delegated to Kubernetes management. A persistent volume is mounted using the Migrate for Anthos Container Storage Interface (CSI) driver (see appendix D). Then data is streamed directly from the source VM filesystem. Internally, Migrate also takes care of generating command-line input and Customer Resource Definitions (CRD[7]). Logically, the migration produces two layers in the containerized image: the first layer is the captured user-mode system, whereas the second layer is the runtime environment for migration, together with all the necessary CRDs. However, after migration, you

---

[6] Two common Unix service layers; see https://fossbytes.com/systemd-vs-sys-v-vs-upstart/.
[7] CRD is an extension of the Kubernetes API, which is not necessarily available in a default Kubernetess installation. CRD is a standard mechanism to customize Kubernetes in a modular way. See http://mng.bz/61zy.

don't need to maintain the second layer and the generated artifacts can run on any Kubernetes-conformant distribution.[8]

VM-related files and components that are not essential for the application in the Kubernetes environment are explicitly left out. In fact, this exclusion implies benefits. As discussed, containers allow higher density and cost reduction due to their lightweight nature when compared to virtual machines. The application life cycle stays within the system container. Once ported, applications can run on either any Anthos environment (on-prem, on GCP, etc.) or any Kubernetes-conformant distribution independently of M4A deployment.

15.3.3   *A look at the Windows environment*

Version 1.4+ of Migrate for Anthos supports the migration of workloads from Windows servers to GKE/Windows. Like Linux environments, the goal is to automate the replatforming of the workload and then integrate it with a more modern cloud environment. At the end of 2021, all the Windows server platforms from Windows Server 2008r2 to Windows Server 2019 are available as targets. Currently, only GCE is supported as a source for Windows applications modernization, with direct support for on-prem VMware, AWS, and Azure planned for the next version. However, you can use Migrate for Compute Engine (sometime referred to as Migrate to Virtual Machines[9]) to migrate or clone a Windows VM from other sources into Compute Engine and then migrate the resulting VM into a container. The good news is that a migrated Windows VM does not have to be configured to run on Compute Engine.

Behind the scenes, the migration works by extracting the ASP.NET application and the IIS configuration and applying them on top of the official Windows 2019 server image. M4A for Windows works well with applications developed with IIS 7+, ASP.NET, especially with web and business logic middleware. Sweet spots for migration are stateless tiers of Windows web applications, application servers, and web frontends.

15.3.4   *A complete view of the modernization journey*

Now that we have discussed the modernization journey with both Linux and Windows workloads, we provide a comprehensive view, which also includes mainframes (see figure 15.3).

If the source application is a modern app, then it is containerized, integrated with CI/CD, and can run on Anthos where integration with the whole ecosystem can facilitate further refactoring into a microservice environment. If the source application is a traditional monolithic application in either Linux or Windows, then we can use M4A to containerize it.

If the source application is a Linux/Window application with particular needs either for specific drivers or legacy support, then it is still possible to directly migrate

---

[8] As of 2023, there are 90 certified Kubernetes-conformant distributions. See http://mng.bz/oJ9M.

[9] See https://cloud.google.com/migrate/compute-engine.

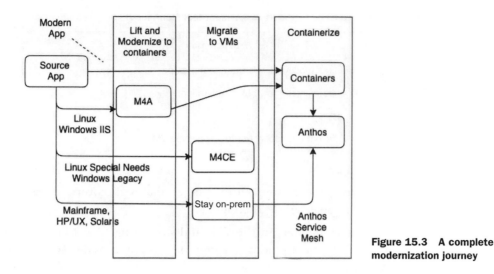

Figure 15.3 A complete modernization journey

the VM to GCP either in bare metal (BMS; https://cloud.google.com/bare-metal) or in GCVE (Google Cloud VMware Engine; https://cloud.google.com/vmware-engine) and manually refactor the application into microservices later.

15.4 Real-world scenarios

In this section, we will review real examples of migration with M4A. First, we'll introduce the migration fit assessment tool (http://mng.bz/v1VM). Then, we'll provide a hands-on session on how to migrate for both Linux and Windows.

15.4.1 Using the fit assessment tool

In this section, we present a self-service fit assessment tool used to determine the workload's suitability for migration to a container. The tool consists of a utility called mfit, a standalone Linux CLI tool used to drive the assessment process along with dedicated Linux and Windows data-collection scripts that are invoked either automatically by mfit or manually, depending on the scenario.

The fit assessment tool generates a report presenting pre-VM assessment results including both a score for the VM's suitability for migration to a container and recommendations on resolving various obstacles. Table 15.1 provides a summary of possible fit scores.

Table 15.1 Fit scores produced by the fit assessment tool

Fit score	Description
Score 0	Excellent fit
Score 1	Good fit with some findings that might require attention
Score 2	Requires minimal effort before migrating

Table 15.1 Fit scores produced by the fit assessment tool *(continued)*

Fit score	Description
Score 3	Requires moderate effort before migrating
Score 4	Requires major effort before migrating
Score 5	No fit
Score 6	Insufficient data collected to assess the VM

FIT ASSESSMENT PROCESS

The fit assessment process consists of three distinct phases: discovery, assessment, and reporting. Each of the phases is detailed next:

- *Discovery*—Gather data about the VMs and store it in a local lightweight database for use in the next phases (located in the ~/.mfit folder by default). The two types of data discovery methods follow:
  - (Optional) *VM/inventory-level discovery*—Use the mfit tool to pull inventory and configuration about VMs in one or more vCenters using the vSphere API. Future versions of the fit assessment tool will support pulling inventory from public clouds such as GCP, AWS, and Azure. This method is optional, and fit assessment can be performed without it, albeit somewhat less thoroughly.
  - *Guest-level data collection*—Consists of running a data-collection script inside the VM to be assessed. The fit assessment tool provides a Bash script for Linux VMs and a PowerShell script for Windows VMs. Each script gathers data about the OS configuration and about running services, processes, installed packages, and so on and produces a single archive file to be imported into the database by the mfit tool and used later in the assessment phase. The process of running the collection script and importing the data can be either manual or automated, using the mfit tool in the following scenarios:
    - *Linux only*—Run collection script and collect results via SSH.
    - *Linux and Windows on vSphere*—Run collection script and collect results using the vSphere API.
- *Assessment*—Use the mfit tool to analyze the collected data and apply a set of fit assessment rules[10] for each VM assessed.
- *Reporting*—Use the mfit tool to produce a report to present the assessment outcomes in either CSV, HTML, or JSON format. The latter can then be displayed in Google's cloud console (http://mng.bz/ydVq).

Now that you know how the tool will discover and report the workloads, we can move on to how to use the tool so you can start your migration journey.

---

[10] For a list of fit assessment rules see http://mng.bz/v1VM.

BASIC TOOL USAGE INSTRUCTIONS

A basic overview for using the fit assessment tool follows. Full documentation is available at http://mng.bz/41YV.

Note that appending `--help` to each `mfit` command will show detailed command usage, including all possible flags and subcommands.

Installation

At the time of writing, you can download the `mfit` tool (version 1.9) on your workstation used for driving the fit assessment with the following commands:

```
wget https://anthos-migrate-release.storage.googleapis.com/v1.9.0/linux/amd64/mfit
chmod +x mfit
```

Inventory discovery

Run the following command to perform discovery of all VMs in a vCenter:

```
./mfit discover vsphere -u <vcenter username> --url <https://vcenter-host-
    name-or-ip>
```

> **NOTE** If your Virtual Center is using a certificate that is not trusted by the machine you are running `mfit` on, you can add the `-i` option to ignore SSL errors.

You will be prompted to enter the vCenter password, and once executed, you will see a summary of the discovery process:

```
Running preflight checks...
[✓] DB Readable
[✓] DB Writable
[✓] Available Disk Space
[✓] Supported VC version

[+] Found 27 VMs
Collecting data...
27 / 27 [-------------------------------------------------------------] 100.00% 13 p/s
```

You may be wondering what actually happened because the output is limited from the discovery process, telling you only that the prechecks have passed and the tool discovered 27 virtual machines. This is just the initial collection step, and once everything is collected, you can assess and create a report of the VMs using the `mfit` tool, which we will cover after the manual collection process is explained.

Manual guest-level data collection

At the time of writing, you can download the Linux collection script on the VM that you want to evaluate for migration using these commands:

```
wget https://anthos-migrate-release.storage.googleapis.com/v1.9.0/linux/
    amd64/mfit-linux-collect.sh
chmod +x mfit-linux-collect.sh
```

Run the collection script like this:

```
sudo ./mfit-linux-collect.sh
```

The script will generate a TAR file named m4a-collect-<MACHINE NAME>-<TIMESTAMP>.tar in the current directory.

For Windows users, at the time of writing, you can download the Windows collection script on the VM that you want to evaluate for migration from the following URL: http://mng.bz/X5E6.

Run the collection script as follows:

```
powershell -ExecutionPolicy ByPass -File .\mfit-windows-collect.ps1
```

The script will generate a TAR or ZIP file (depending on OS version) named m4a-collect-<MACHINE NAME>-<TIMESTAMP>.tar/zip in the current directory.

Import the collected data file

After running the collection script on the assessed VM, download it to the workstation where mfit was installed by any means. Then, import it into mfit's local database:

```
./mfit discover import m4a-collect-<MACHINE NAME>-<TIMESTAMP>.tar/zip
```

Automatic guest-level data collection

mfit contains the guest-collection script embedded in it and can automatically run it and retrieve the results in the following scenarios.

VMware tools

If the assessed VM is running on vSphere and has VMware tools installed, mfit can use vSphere APIs to automate the execution of the collection script (the one suited for the VM's OS type) and the retrieval of the results. To run guest-level collection via VMware tools, run the following command:

```
./mfit discover vsphere guest -u <vcenter username> --url <https://vcenter-host-name-or-ip> --vm-user <vm username> <vm MoRef id or name>
```

You will be prompted to enter both the vCenter and VM/OS passwords.

SSH

If the Linux machine running mfit has SSH access to the assessed VM, mfit can use that to automate the execution of the collection script and the retrieval of the results. To run guest-level collection via SSH using the SSH key of the current local user (located in ~/.ssh), run the following command:

```
./mfit discover ssh <vm-ip-or-hostname>
```

To run guest-level collection via SSH with additional authentication options, run the following command:

```
./mfit discover ssh -i </path/to/ssh_private_key> -u <remote-username> <vm-ip-or-hostname>
```

For additional options for running guest-level collection via SSH, consult the official documentation or run `./mfit discover ssh -help`.

Assessment

To examine the discovered VMs and collected data, run the following command:

```
./mfit discover ls
```

To perform assessment on this data, run the following command:

```
./mfit assess
```

This will create an assessment result and store it in `mfit`'s local database for use when generating reports.

Report generation

Once assessment has been performed, we are ready to generate a report. To generate a standalone HTML report, run the following command:

```
./mfit report --format html > REPORT_NAME.html
```

To generate a JSON report, run the following command:

```
./mfit report --format json >  REPORT_NAME.json
```

The report can then be displayed on Google's cloud console: http://mng.bz/Q8zj.

In this section, we discussed the fit assessment tool used to determine a workload's suitability for migration to a container. Once the assessment is made and the workloads suitable for migration are chosen, we can start the migration process itself. That's the topic of the next section.

15.4.2 *Basic migration example*

In this basic example, we will use the CLI to set up a Compute Engine virtual machine on GCE and then use M4A to migrate the VM to a GKE cluster. Note that we need to create another Kubernetes "processing cluster" used with the intent of driving the migration process itself. The processing cluster will do the work of pulling the application from the VM and generating all the artifacts as containers. Let's start.

First, we create a source VM. In this basic example, the VM will host an Apache web server. The VM can be created with the following command:

```
gcloud compute instances create http-server-demo --machine-type=n1-standard-1
--subnet=default --scopes="cloud-platform" --tags=http-server,https-server
--image=ubuntu-minimal-1604-xenial-v20200702  --image-project=ubuntu-os-cloud
--boot-disk-size=10GB --boot-disk-type=pd-standard
```

Then, let's make sure that the VM is accessible from internet with the next command:

```
gcloud compute firewall-rules create default-allow-http --direction=INGRESS -
-priority=1000 --network=default --action=ALLOW --rules=tcp:80 --source-
ranges=0.0.0.0/0 --target-tags=http-server
```

Now we can now log in to the VM just configured using the GUI (see figure 15.4) and install Apache:

```
sudo apt-get update && sudo apt-get install apache2 -y
```

| ⊘ | us- | 1 |
| migration-processing | central1-c | |

Figure 15.4 Connecting the migration cluster

Now we have a source virtual machine with an Apache web server running. The next step is to create the Kubernetes processing cluster:

```
gcloud container clusters create migration-processing --machine-type n1-
standard-4   --image-type ubuntu --num-nodes 1 --enable-stackdriver-
kubernetes
```

Next, let's make sure that we give the processing cluster the correct processing rights. We need to create a specific service account for M4A, add a policy binding with `storage.admin` rights, create a JSON key to access the processing cluster, and get the credentials for the processing cluster. We can do this with the following four commands. Note that `named-tome-295414` is the name of my project and you should change it to match yours:

```
gcloud iam service-accounts create m4a-install
gcloud projects add-iam-policy-binding named-tome-295414
    --member="serviceAccount:m4a-install@named-tome-
    295414.iam.gserviceaccount.com"  --role="roles/storage.admin"
gcloud iam service-accounts keys create m4a-install.json   --iam-account=m4a-
    install@named-tome-295414.iam.gserviceaccount.com   --project=named-
    tome-295414
gcloud container clusters get-credentials migration-processing
```

Once we have the credentials, we can log in to the processing cluster and install M4A. Let's do that with the following command. Note that `m4a-install.json` is the JSON key we have just created:

```
migctl setup install --json-key=m4a-install.json
```

We can use `migctl` to check whether the deployment is successful:

```
migctl doctor
[✓] Deployment
```

After that, we can set up the source for migration, together with a specific service account, `m4a-ce-src`, the `compute.viewer` and `compute.storageAdmin` policy bindings required during the migration process, and the creation of a JSON key `m4a-ce-src.json`:

```
gcloud iam service-accounts create m4a-ce-src
gcloud projects add-iam-policy-binding named-tome-295414
    --member="serviceAccount:m4a-ce-src@named-tome-
    295414.iam.gserviceaccount.com"   --role="roles/compute.viewer"
gcloud projects add-iam-policy-binding named-tome-295414
    --member="serviceAccount:m4a-ce-src@named-tome-
    295414.iam.gserviceaccount.com"   --role="roles/compute.storageAdmin"
gcloud iam service-accounts keys create m4a-ce-src.json   --iam-account=m4a-
    ce-src@named-tome-295414.iam.gserviceaccount.com   --project=named-tome-
    295414
```

Once we have created the credentials for the source, we can proceed to set up the source with the following command. Note that ce stands for Google Compute Engine (GCE):

```
migctl source create ce http-source --project named-tome-295414 --json-
    key=m4a-ce-src.json
```

After creating a migration source, we can now create a migration plan to containerize our VM:

```
migctl migration create my-migration --source http-source   --vm-id http-
    server-demo --intent Image
```

If you want to look at the migration plan (e.g., to modify it), you can use the following command:

```
migctl migration get my-migration
```

You can then start the actual migration:

```
migctl migration generate-artifacts my-migration
```

As result, you should see something like this:

```
running validation checks on the Migration...
migration.anthos-migrate.cloud.google.com/my-migration created
```

Once the migration starts, you can check the progress with the following command. Note that the flag -v gives a verbose dump of the status, which is useful if something goes wrong:

```
migctl migration status my-migration
```

When the migration is concluded, you will see something similar to the output shown here:

```
NAME           CURRENT-OPERATION      PROGRESS   STEP          STATUS      AGE
my-migration   GenerateMigrationPlan  [2/2]      CreatePvcs    Completed   11m23s
```

The next step is to get the generated artifacts:

```
migctl migration get-artifacts my-migration
```

Once the generation has completed, you should see something like this:

```
Downloaded artifacts for Migration my-migration. The artifacts are located in
    /home/a_gulli.
```

To access the migrated workload, we need to expose the Pods using a Service. Modifying the generated deployment_spec.yaml to add a Service of type `LoadBalancer` will enable us to reach the workload on port 80:

```
apiVersion: v1
kind: Service
metadata:
 name: hello-service
spec:
 selector:
   app: http-server-demo
 ports:
   - protocol: TCP
     port: 80
     targetPort: 80
 type: LoadBalancer
```

We can now deploy the artifacts on our Kubernetes cluster like this:

```
kubectl apply -f deployment_spec.yaml

deployment.apps/app-source-vm created
service/app-source-vm created
service/my-service created
```

It might be useful to check that everything went well:

```
kubectl get service
```

As a result, you should see something like this:

```
NAME            TYPE           CLUSTER-IP      EXTERNAL-IP    PORT(S)        AGE
app-source-vm   ClusterIP      None            <none>         <none>         44s
kubernetes      ClusterIP      10.63.240.1     <none>         443/TCP        41m
my-service      LoadBalancer   10.63.243.209   35.232.24.49   80:32417/TCP   43s
```

In this case, the external IP address is 35.232.24.49. Now we can open a browser and check that everything is OK (see figure 15.5).

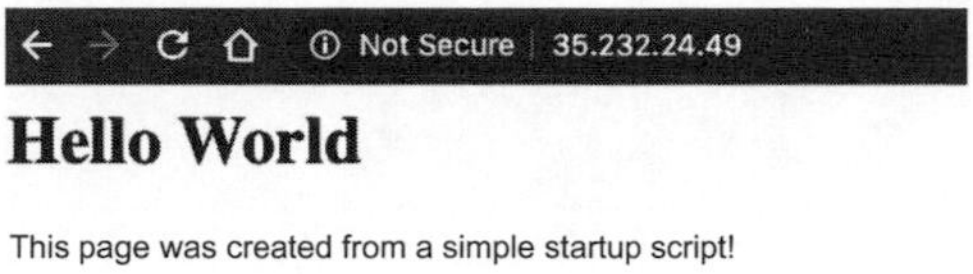

Hello World

This page was created from a simple startup script!

Figure 15.5   Accessing the web server migrated from VM to containers

Congratulations! You have successfully migrated a virtual machine running on GCE into a container running on GKE using the CLI. If you want to see another example of basic migration, we suggest you consider the hands-on lab, "Migrate to Containers: Qwik Start," available at http://mng.bz/X5jp.

Now that you know how to execute a migration using the CLI, we will move on to the next section where we will use the Cloud console UI to perform a migration.

15.4.3   Google Cloud console UI migration example

In this section, we use M4A to migrate an application running as a virtual machine on Google Compute Engine to GKE. When using the console UI, Google Cloud clusters are the only supported environment, not Anthos on AWS or VMware. The GKE processing clusters can be in the cloud or on-prem. The migration will be run through the graphical user interface (GUI) available via the Google Cloud console. Note that the migration process is consistent between the CLI and the GUI.

A GKE cluster will be used as a "processing cluster" to control the migration. The artifacts generated during the process will be stored on Google Cloud Storage (GCS), and the final container images are pushed to Google Container Registry. Under the hood, this is identical to the CLI-driven migration.

The first step is to access Anthos Migrate from the console (see figure 15.6) at http://mng.bz/Mlpn.

For the sake of simplicity, we will deploy a VM from Marketplace with a Tomcat server preinstalled. Then, we will migrate Tomcat from the VM to a container.

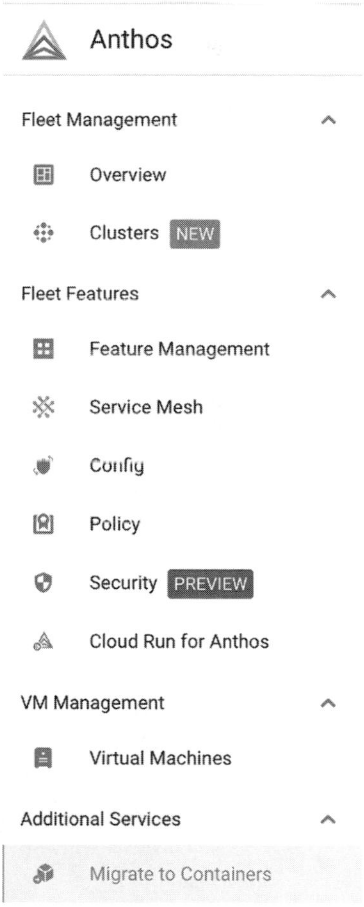

Figure 15.6   Accessing Anthos Migrate to containers

Let's start by accessing the Google Click to Deploy repository with Tomcat (see figure 15.7). The URL is https://console.cloud.google.com/ marketplace/details/click-to-deploy-images/tomcat.

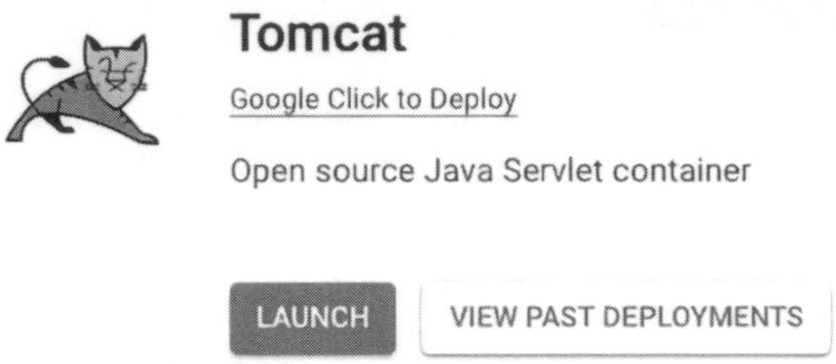

Tomcat

Google Click to Deploy

Open source Java Servlet container

LAUNCH   VIEW PAST DEPLOYMENTS

Figure 15.7   Deploying a Tomcat application to VMs

Then, let's select the zone where we want to deploy (see figure 15.8).

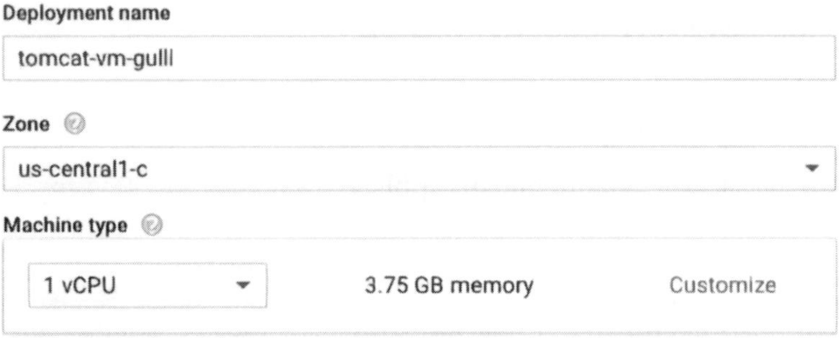

Deployment name

tomcat-vm-gulli

Zone ⃝

us-central1-c ▾

Machine type ⃝

| 1 vCPU ▾ | 3.75 GB memory | Customize |

Figure 15.8   Deployed Tomcat application

Once the VM with the Tomcat server is deployed, you can access the website from an external IP, as shown in figure 15.9.

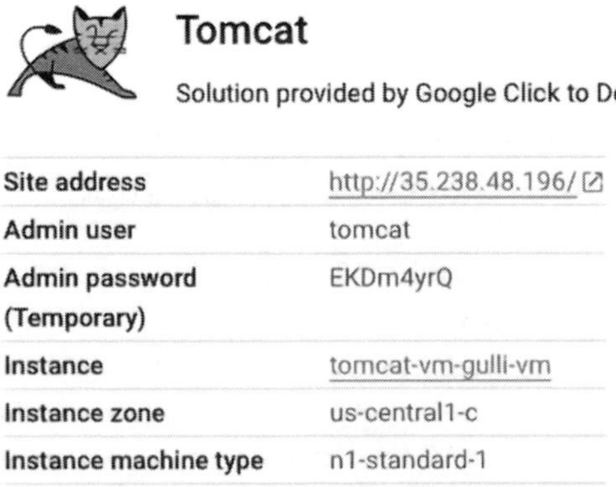

Tomcat

Solution provided by Google Click to Deploy

Site address	http://35.238.48.196/ ↗
Admin user	tomcat
Admin password (Temporary)	EKDm4yrQ
Instance	tomcat-vm-gulli-vm
Instance zone	us-central1-c
Instance machine type	n1-standard-1

Figure 15.9   Tomcat solution deployed with Google Click to Deploy

In this deployment, the IP address is http://35.238.48.196/, so if you access the website, you should see the output shown in figure 15.10.

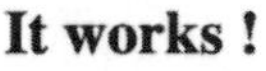

It works !   **Figure 15.10**   **Accessing Tomcat with a web browser**

The next step is to start the proper migration process. First, create a "processing cluster," a cluster that will be used to control the migration of our source VM. You can perform this task by accessing the Migrate to Containers menu on Anthos and selecting the Add Processing Cluster option (see figure 15.11).

⊞ ADD PROCESSING CLUSTER   **Figure 15.11**   **Starting the migration process**

It is convenient to follow the suggestion provided in the GUI and create a new cluster dedicated to processing (see figure 15.12).

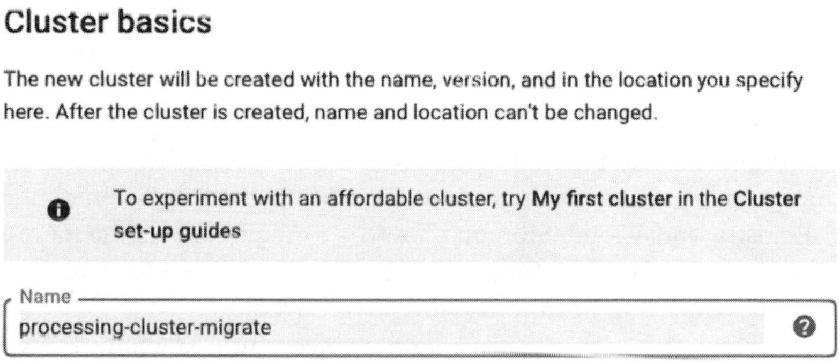

Cluster basics

The new cluster will be created with the name, version, and in the location you specify here. After the cluster is created, name and location can't be changed.

> ⓘ   To experiment with an affordable cluster, try **My first cluster** in the **Cluster set-up guides**

Name
processing-cluster-migrate   ❓

Figure 15.12   **Choosing a name for the processing cluster**

Once the cluster is ready, you should be able to see it via the Google Cloud console in the GKE section (see figure 15.13).

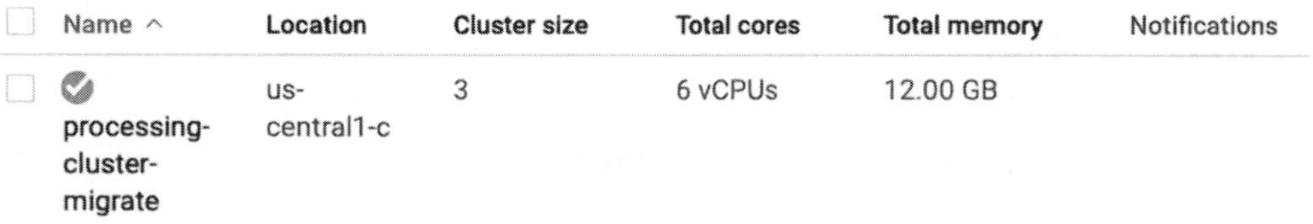

	Name ∧	Location	Cluster size	Total cores	Total memory	Notifications
☑ ✅	processing-cluster-migrate	us-central1-c	3	6 vCPUs	12.00 GB	

Figure 15.13   **The processing cluster is ready for use.**

Then, you can select the cluster (see figure 15.14) and select whether the target is Linux or Windows.

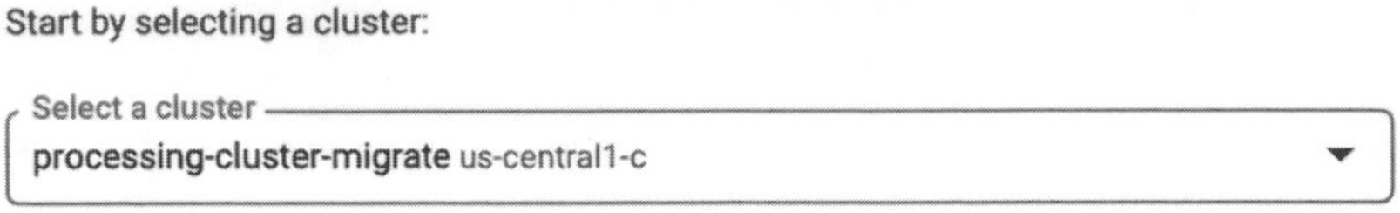

Start by selecting a cluster:

Select a cluster
processing-cluster-migrate us-central1-c   ▼

Figure 15.14   Selecting the processing cluster

At this point, we need to make sure that the processing cluster has the proper processing rights. To this extent, the GUI suggests running a number of commands in the cloud shell. You just need to click Run in Cloud Shell, as shown in figure 15.15.

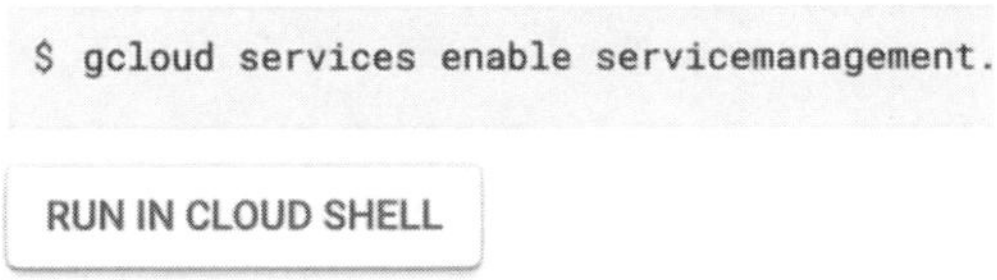

```
$ gcloud services enable servicemanagement.
```

RUN IN CLOUD SHELL

Figure 15.15   Using the UI to run the setup required by M4A

Let's see the required steps in detail. First, we need to enable the Google Cloud APIs. Then, we need to create a service account for storing the migration artifacts in the Container Registry and Cloud Storage. Then, we need to add the permissions to access the Container Registry and Cloud Storage. Finally, we need to create and export a new key to a file required by M4A to use the service account.

Once these steps are done, we can migrate to containers. Again, the GUI makes this step very intuitive. The last step is to check with `migctl doctor` that the deployment status is correct (see figure 15.16).

[✓] Deployment   **Figure 15.16   Correct deployment of M4A**

Once the processing cluster is configured, select a migration source from where the VM will be pulled (see figure 15.17).

➕ ADD SOURCE   **Figure 15.17   Adding a migration source**

Currently, you can pull from GCE (see figure 15.18). (You can also use Migrate for Compute Engine [http://mng.bz/eJav] to import local vSphere environments, AWS, and Azure to GCE.)

② Define source name and type

Define a name for the new source.

Name *

migrate-vm-tomcat-gulli|

Select the source environment from which you want to migrate workloads.

Compute Engine   ▼

Learn how to define other source types (**VMWare**, **AWS** and **Azure**) supported currently through the tool's CLI. Learn more

Figure 15.18   Adding a migration source

Once you have chosen a name, you can select the project in which the source VMs are placed (see figure 15.19).

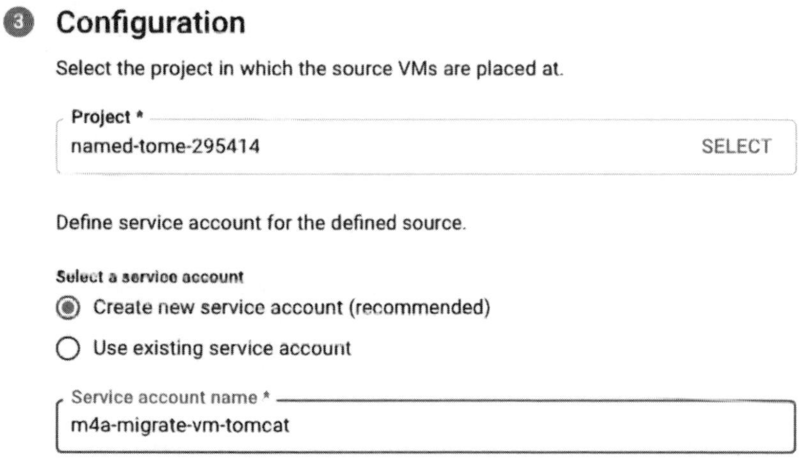

③ Configuration

Select the project in which the source VMs are placed at.

Project *

named-tome-295414   SELECT

Define service account for the defined source.

Select a service account

⦿ Create new service account (recommended)

○ Use existing service account

Service account name *

m4a-migrate-vm-tomcat

Figure 15.19   Selecting the project in which the source VMs are placed

Now that the processing cluster and the migration source have been created, we can start the migration (see figure 15. 20).

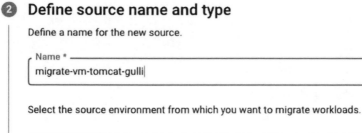 START MIGRATION   **Figure 15.20   Starting a migration process**

The migration requires a name, a source, a VM OS type, the VM ID, and the migration intent. Let's specify these via the GUI, as shown in figure 15.21.

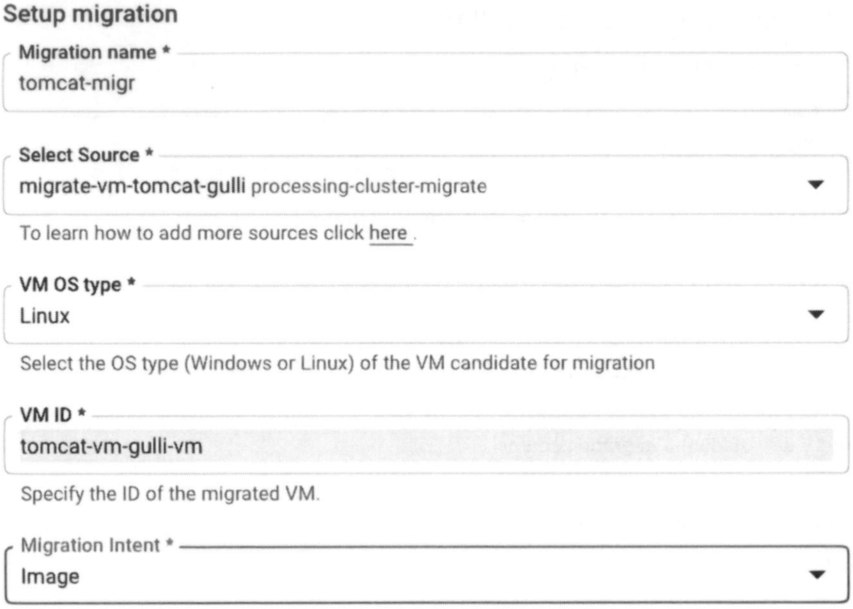

Setup migration

Migration name *

tomcat-migr

Select Source *

migrate-vm-tomcat-gulli processing-cluster-migrate   ▼

To learn how to add more sources click here .

VM OS type *

Linux   ▼

Select the OS type (Windows or Linux) of the VM candidate for migration

VM ID *

tomcat-vm-gulli-vm

Specify the ID of the migrated VM.

Migration Intent *

Image   ▼

Figure 15.21   **Specifying the migration name, the migration source, the VM OS type, the VM ID, and the migration intent.**

Then, M4A will start generating the migration plan (see figure 15.22).

Migration name ↑	VM ID	Status
tomcat-migr	tomcat-v...	———— Generating migration plan

Figure 15.22   **Generating the migration plan**

During the migration, we can check the progress with the following command, which will produce a detailed debug log:

```
migctl migration status my-migration -v
```

Once the migration plan is generated (see figure 15.23), you can inspect the results with the GUI.

Migration name ↑	VM ID	Status
tomcat-migr	tomcat-v...	✔ Migration plan generated

Figure 15.23   **An overview of the migration plan generated by M4A**

In particular, the Options menu allows you to edit the generated migration plan, as shown in figure 15.24.

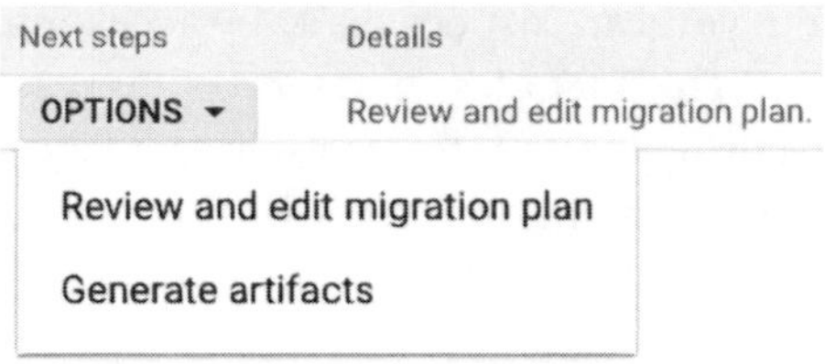

Next steps   Details

OPTIONS ▾   Review and edit migration plan.

Review and edit migration plan

Generate artifacts

Figure 15.24   Reviewing and editing the generated migration plan

Let's look at what has been generated by editing the migration plan, as shown in figure 15.25.

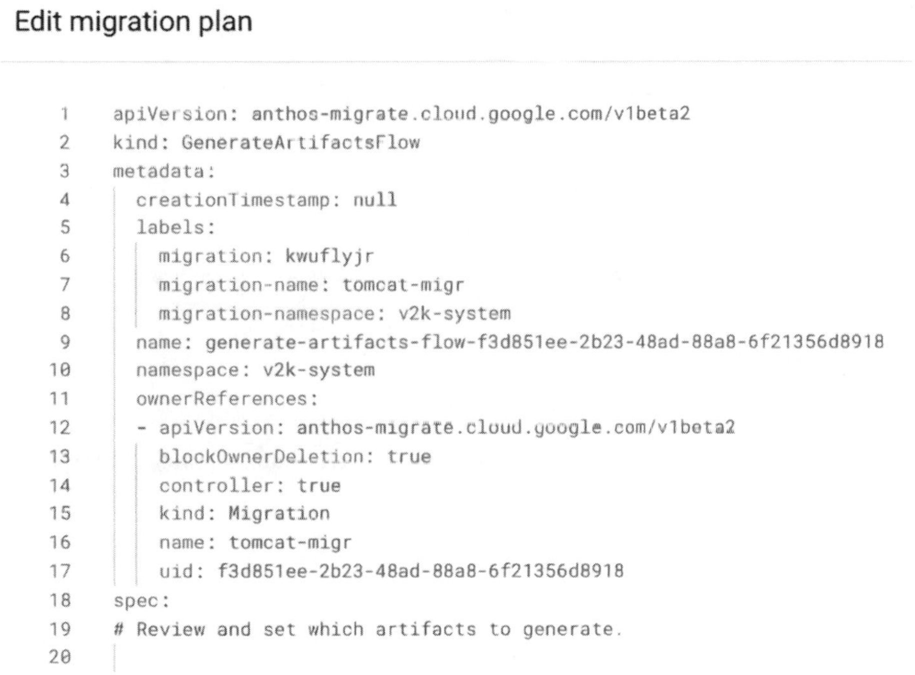

Edit migration plan

```
 1   apiVersion: anthos-migrate.cloud.google.com/v1beta2
 2   kind: GenerateArtifactsFlow
 3   metadata:
 4     creationTimestamp: null
 5     labels:
 6       migration: kwuflyjr
 7       migration-name: tomcat-migr
 8       migration-namespace: v2k-system
 9     name: generate-artifacts-flow-f3d851ee-2b23-48ad-88a8-6f21356d8918
10     namespace: v2k-system
11     ownerReferences:
12     - apiVersion: anthos-migrate.cloud.google.com/v1beta2
13       blockOwnerDeletion: true
14       controller: true
15       kind: Migration
16       name: tomcat-migr
17       uid: f3d851ee-2b23-48ad-88a8-6f21356d8918
18   spec:
19   # Review and set which artifacts to generate.
20
```

Figure 15.25   Editing the generated migration plan

Normally, you don't need to change the migration plan. However, being able to is useful if you either need to strip out unneeded VM components or need to add some additional configuration. After checking and, if necessary, editing the migration plan, you can start generating the artifacts (see figure 15.26).

SAVE AND GENERATE ARTIFACTS   SAVE

Figure 15.26   Generating artifacts with the edited migration plan

Once the migration plans are generated, you can inspect them by accessing the Artifacts tab from the Google Cloud console. This includes the Dockerfile, the container image for deployment (that can be directly deployed), the container image base layer (the nonrunnable image layers), the Deployment spec YAML, the migration plan YAML, and the artifact links YAML (see figure 15.27).

STATUS   ARTIFACTS

Dockerfile ↗

Container image for deployment ↗

Container image base layer ↗

Deployment spec YAML ↗

Migration plan YAML ↗

Artifact links YAML ↗ ❓

Figure 15.27   Generated migration artifacts

The generated artifacts are stored in GCS with separate buckets for base and image layers (see figure 15.28).

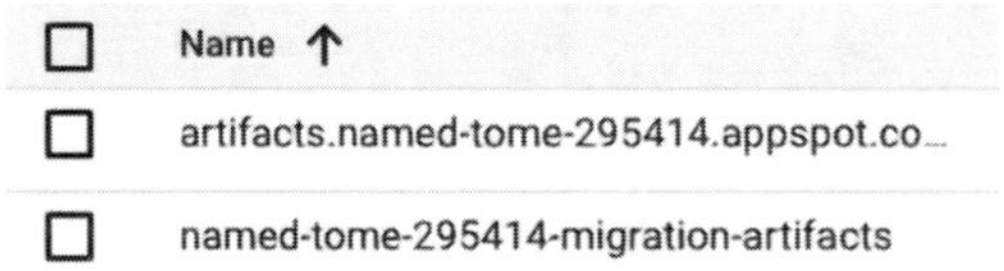

☐ Name ↑

☐ artifacts.named-tome-295414.appspot.co...

☐ named-tome-295414-migration-artifacts

Figure 15.28   Artifacts stored in GCS

Let's look now at the system image with the Dockerfile, the Deployment spec, the manifest and the migration YAML (see figure 15.29).

	Name	Size	Type
☐	Dockerfile	700 B	text/plain; charset=utf-8
☐	deployment_spec	1.7 KB	text/plain; charset=utf-8
☐	manifest.yaml	735 B	text/plain; charset=utf-8
☐	migration.yaml	3.1 KB	text/plain; charset=utf-8

Figure 15.29   Dockerfile, Deployment spec, manifest, and migration files

In addition, images generated for migration are automatically pushed to the Google
Container Registry, and you can browse them via the console, as shown in figure 15.30.

Name ^	Hostname
🗄 tomcat-vm-gulli-vm	gcr.io
🗄 tomcat-vm-gulli-vm-non-runnable-base	gcr.io

Figure 15.30   Images generated for migration and pushed to the GCR

All the generated artifacts can be downloaded via the CLI as follows:

```
migctl migration get-artifacts my-migration
```

These artifacts include the following:

- *deployment_spec.yaml*—Configures your workload
- *Dockerfile*—Used to build the image for your migrated VM
- *migration.yaml*—A copy of the migration plan

AN OVERVIEW OF DOCKERFILE

In this section, we take a deep look at the Dockerfile generated by M4A. You can edit
the file to customize your image, for instance, either for installing new packages or for
installing an upgraded version of the M4A runtime. The file contains the original container repository for runtime, the image containing data captured from the source
VM, and the initial entry point. A typical M4A Dockerfile follows:

```
# Please refer to the documentation:
# https://cloud.google.com/migrate/anthos/docs/dockerfile-reference

FROM anthos-migrate.gcr.io/v2k-run-embedded:v1.5.0 as migrate-for-anthos-
    runtime

# Image containing data captured from the source VM
FROM gcr.io/named-tome-295414/tomcat-vm-gulli-vm-non-runnable-base:11-13-
    2020--15-0-39 as source-content

# If you want to update parts of the image, add your commands here.
# For example:
# RUN apt-get update
# RUN apt-get install -y \
#    package1=version \
#    package2=version \
#    package3=version
# RUN yum update
# RUN wget http://github.com
```

```
COPY --from=migrate-for-anthos-runtime //

# Migrate for Anthos image includes entrypoint
ENTRYPOINT [ "/.v2k.go" ]
```

We will see more details on the M4A-generated Dockerfile later in this chapter when we discuss the postmigration integration with CI/CD pipelines. In the next section, we will discuss the details of the deployment_spec.yaml file.

AN OVERVIEW OF DEPLOYMENT_SPEC.YAML

In this section, we will discuss the deployment_spec.yaml generated by M4A. First, let's define some terminology we will use later:

- *Stateless*—An application is stateless when the server does not store any state about the client session. In other words, there is no stored knowledge of or reference to past transactions.

- *Stateful*—An application is stateful when the server stores data about the client session. In other words, the current transaction may be affected by what happened during previous transactions. For this reason, a stateful application needs to use the same servers each time a request from a user is processed.

With this context in mind, let's consider deployment_spec.yaml. This file will be different according to the intent flag selected in the UI, as described next:

- *Intent: Image*—The YAML defines a stateless application with identical Pods[11] managed as a service. Different parts of the YAML follow:
  - *Deployment*—The set of identical Pods deployed from the image generated from your migrated VM. They are stored in GCR.
  - *Service*—Groups Pods in your deployment into a single resource accessible from a stable IP address. By default, a single cluster internal IP is reachable only from within the cluster with no load balancing. The Kubernetes endpoints controller will modify the DNS configuration to return records (addresses) that point to the Pods, which are labeled with "<app>": "<app-name>"where the name of the app is inferred from the migctl migration create my-migration command. Note that Pods will be visible only within the cluster by default, so, it might be appropriate to expose Pods outside of your cluster. We will see an example later in the chapter.
  - *Logging configuration*—Configures logging to Cloud Logging by listing many of the most common log files.
- *Intent: ImageAndData*—The YAML defines a stateful application with different Pods associated with persistent volumes. Different parts of the YAML follow:
  - *StatefulSet*—The set of Pods deployed from the image generated from your migrated VM. They are stored in GCR.
  - *Service*—Similar to the Service defined in the Image section.

---

[11] A Pod encapsulates one or more applications and is the smallest unit of execution in Kubernetes.

- *PersistentVolume*—Used to manage the durable storage.
- *PersistentVolumeClaim*—Represents a request for and claim to the `Persistent-Volume` resource (such as specific size and access mode).
- *Logging configuration*—Similar to what was defined for stateless.
  - *Intent: Data*—Different parts of the YAML follow:
    - *PersistentVolume*—Similar to what was defined for stateful.
    - *PersistentVolumeClaim*—Similar to what was defined for stateful.

A typical M4A deployment_spec.yaml is shown in the next listing.

Listing 15.1 The deployment_spec.yaml generated by M4A

```
# Stateless application specification
# The Deployment creates a single replicated Pod, indicated by the 'replicas'
    field
apiVersion: apps/v1
kind: Deployment
metadata:
  creationTimestamp: null
  labels:
    app. tomcat-vm-gulli-vm
    migrate-for-anthos-optimization: "true"
    migrate-for-anthos-version: v1.5.0
  name: tomcat-vm-gulli-vm
spec:
  replicas: 1
  selector:
    matchLabels:
      app: tomcat-vm-gulli-vm
      migrate-for-anthos-optimization: "true"
      migrate-for-anthos-version: v1.5.0
  strategy: {}
  template:
    metadata:
      creationTimestamp: null
      labels:
        app: tomcat-vm-gulli-vm
        migrate-for-anthos-optimization: "true"
        migrate-for-anthos-version: v1.5.0
    spec:
      containers:
      - image: gcr.io/named-tome-295414/tomcat-vm-gulli-vm:11-13-2020--15-0-39
        name: tomcat-vm-gulli-vm
        readinessProbe:
          exec:
            command:
            - /code/ready.sh
        resources: {}
        securityContext:
          privileged: true
        volumeMounts:
        - mountPath: /sys/fs/cgroup
          name: cgroups
```

```
        volumes:
          - hostPath:
              path: /sys/fs/cgroup
              type: Directory
            name: cgroups
status: {}


---
# Headless Service specification -
# No load-balancing, and a single cluster internal IP, only reachable from
      within the cluster
# The Kubernetes endpoints controller will modify the DNS configuration to
      return records (addresses) that point to the Pods, which are labeled with
      "app": "tomcat-vm-gulli-vm"
apiVersion: v1
kind: Service
metadata:
  creationTimestamp: null
  name: tomcat-vm-gulli-vm
spec:
  clusterIP: None
  selector:
    app: tomcat-vm-gulli-vm
  type: ClusterIP
status:
  loadBalancer: {}


---
```

DEPLOYING THE CONTAINER GENERATED BY M4A

In this section, the steps needed to deploy the container generated by M4A are discussed. Deploying the deployment_spec.yaml is very easy:

```
migctl setup install --runtime
kubectl apply -f deployment_spec.yaml
```

As a result, you should see something like this:

```
deployment.apps/tomcat-vm-gulli-vm created
service/tomcat-vm-gulli-vm created
```

If you want, you can check the status of the deployed Pods:

```
kubectl get pods
```

You should see something like this:

```
NAME                                    READY   STATUS    RESTARTS   AGE
tomcat-vm-gulli-vm-66b44696f-ttgq6      1/1     Running   0          21s
```

By default, the container is deployed with no load balancing and a single-cluster internal IP, which is reachable only from within the cluster. The Kubernetes endpoints controller will modify the DNS configuration to return addresses that point to the Pods, which are labeled with `"app": "tomcat-vm-gulli-vm"`. Of course, you can change the deployment and add a Service of type `LoadBalancer`. Let's do that by adding the following to the deployment spec:

```
apiVersion: v1
kind: Service
metadata:
  name: hello-service
spec:
  selector:
    app: tomcat-vm-gulli-vm
  ports:
    - protocol: TCP
      port: 80
      targetPort: 80
  type: LoadBalancer
```

Then, let's check that the Service is indeed accessible:

```
kubectl get service hello-service
NAME            TYPE           CLUSTER-IP     EXTERNAL-IP      PORT(S)        AGE
hello-service   LoadBalancer   10.88.10.207   34.67.239.170    80:32033/TCP   76s
```

Figure 15.31 shows what happens when we try to access the Service from the internet.

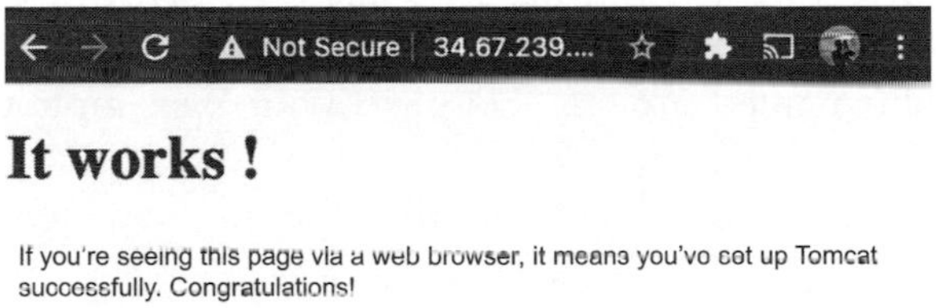

It works !

If you're seeing this page via a web browser, it means you've set up Tomcat successfully. Congratulations!

Figure 15.31 Accessing the Tomcat container after migration with M4A

Congratulations! You now have a routable container holding the full Tomcat installation previously available in a VM! The migration happened automatically, with no need to either recompile or access the original source code.

Before concluding, here's a hint about the GUI: if you need to edit multiple files, it might be convenient to use the built-in editor, which is based on Eclipse. The editor is a quick and easy way to review and change all the files generated by M4A (see figure 15.32).

One note before concluding: in addition to Google Container Registry and Google Cloud Storage for data repositories, M4A version 1.6 and higher supports additional repositories including ECR, S3, and Docker registries. In the next section, we are going to talk about Windows migration.

```
                                                     ≣ migration.yaml ×
EXPLORER: A_GULLI      Ↄ ⧉ ⋯
                                            1    apiVersion: anthos-migrate.cloud.google.com/v1beta2
  ≣ deployment_spec.yaml                     2    kind: GenerateArtifactsFlow
  📄 deployment_spec.yaml.safe               3    metadata:
  📄 deployment_spec.yaml.save               4      creationTimestamp: null
  ⚓ Dockerfile                               5      labels:
  ≣ m4a-ce-src.json                          6        migration: bysjvrqt
  ≣ m4a-install.json                         7        migration-name: my-migration
  ≣ migration.yaml                           8        migration-namespace: v2k-system
  🖩 README-cloudshell.txt                    9      name: generate-artifacts-flow-e21fcb1f-7d6b-4aef-99f6-7
  ≣ sa.json                                 10      namespace: v2k-system
                                           11      ownerReferences:
                                           12      - apiVersion: anthos-migrate.cloud.google.com/v1beta2
```

Figure 15.32   The built-in editor used to manipulate migration configuration

15.4.4 *Windows migration*

In this section, we discuss how to migrate Windows VMs to GKE. Please note that Windows migration supports Compute Engine as a source. However, as discussed earlier, it is possible to migrate a Windows VM from other sources into Compute Engine using Migrate for Compute Engine (sometime referred as Migrate to Virtual Machines; see http://mng.bz/pdj8). The resulting VM can be then migrated to GKE. Unsurprisingly, Windows migration is similar to that for Linux. Indeed, behind the scenes, M4A uses a unified M4A CLI utility named migctl. Let's see a quick example using the CLI interface.

First, similarly to Linux, you can use migctl with the following statement for adding a migration source:

```
migctl source create ce my-ce-src --project my-project --json-key=m4a-ce-src.json
```

Remember that my-ce-src is the name of the source, my-project is the name of the project, and m4a-ce-src.json is the name of the JSON key file obtained after creating a service account for using Compute Engine as a migration source. Then you can create a migration with the following command

```
migctl migration create my-migration --source my-ce-src --vm-id my-id --
    intent Image -workload-type=WindowsIIS
```

where my-migration is the name of the migration and vm-id is the name of the Compute Engine instance, as shown in the Google Cloud console. The migration plan just created can be retrieved with the following command:

```
migctl migration get my-migration
```

If needed, you can customize the migration plan by editing the file my-migration.yaml. When editing is completed, you can then upload the edited migration plan with the following command:

```
migctl migration update my-migration
```

The next step is to execute the migration and generate artifacts:

```
migctl migration generate-artifacts my-migration
```

During the migration, you can monitor the status:

```
migctl migration list
```

When the migration concludes you can access the artifacts:

```
migctl migration get-artifacts my-migration
```

As a results, you should see something like this:

```
Artifacts are accessible through 'gsutil cp gs://PATH/artifacts.zip ./'
```

Hence you can get the artifacts with the following command:

```
gsutil cp gs://PATH/artifacts.zip ./
```

The next step is to use the artifacts to build a Docker image. We can use Windows PowerShell to expand the artifacts.zip:

```
Expand-Archive .\artifacts.zip
```

Then log in to the Container Registry:

```
docker login gcr.io
```

The next step is to build the container using the next code snippet:

```
docker build -t gcr.io/myproject/myimagename:v1.0.0 .\artifacts\
docker push gcr.io/myproject/myimagename:v1.0.0
```

When you generate artifacts for Windows workloads, the artifacts are copied into a Cloud Storage bucket as an intermediate location that you can download. This file contains a Dockerfile, the deployment_spec.yaml file, and several directories from the source, which you then use to build the Windows container. Once the build is completed, the container image will be placed in the Container Registry, and the image can be deployed to a GKE cluster. Note that the Google Cloud console for Anthos has included Windows workload support since M4A v1.5. The experience is identical to the one already discussed for Linux. If you want to see another example of Windows migration, consider the hands-on lab "Migrate for Anthos: Windows" available at http://mng.bz/yd7y.

15.4.5 *Migration from other clouds*

As of November 2021, migration from other clouds is based on a two-step approach. First, virtual machines are migrated (technically, they are converted into GCE instances). Then, the migrated virtual machines are containerized.

M4A uses the product Migrate for Compute Engine (M4CE) (sometime referred as Migrate to Virtual Machines; https://cloud.google.com/migrate/compute-engine) to stream virtual machines located on other clouds or on-prem, moving them onto GCE instances. Migrate for Compute Engine can be installed via the marketplace (http://mng.bz/Mlao) and allows the migration of thousands of applications across multiple data centers and clouds from source platforms such as VMware, Microsoft Azure, and Amazon EC2.

To use M4CE, you need to set up a site-to-site VPN connection and firewall rules to enable communication between the VPC in which the manager is positioned and the VPC of the source VM on the other cloud. The interested reader may find the online firewall documentation at https://cloud.google.com/vpc/docs/firewalls useful. Dynamic routing based on the BGP protocol (http://mng.bz/zmVB) can be set up via GCP Cloud Router (http://mng.bz/0ygN) working on either Cloud VPN (http://mng.bz/aMro) or dedicated high-speed Cloud Interconnect (http://mng.bz/Klgj). Cloud Interconnect extends your on-prem network to Google's network through a highly available, low-latency connection.

In addition, thousands of virtual machines can be migrated in batches by aggregating them in waves according to their logical role. M4CE allows us to define runbooks to decide which VM should be migrated and in what order. A simulated testing phase can be planned before the effective migration. The main components of M4CE follow:

- *A migration manager*—Used to orchestrate migration. The manager runs on a separate Google Compute Engine VM and offers a migration console to manage and monitor all the system components. Note that the manager might require specific permissions to handle specific actions, such as turning on and off a VM. These permissions can be defined with policies.

- *A Cloud Extension*—Used to handle storage migrating from the source platform. An extension is a conduit for VM storage between the migration source and destination. These extensions run on separate Compute Engine VMs and serve data to migrated workloads during the migration process itself. Note that extensions work with a dual-node active/passive configuration for high availability; each node serves workloads and, at the same time, provides backup for the other node.

Different components are then deployed on source platforms, as described here:

- *On vSphere*—A backend component serves runtime data from VMware to extensions on Google Cloud. Data is then used by the VMs on Compute Engine. In addition, a vCenter plug-in connects vSphere to the migration manager and orchestrates the migration on vCenter.
- *On Amazon EC2 and Azure*—An importer is deployed at runtime and serves runtime data from the source to extensions on Google Cloud. Data is then used by the VMs on Compute Engine.

Since Migrate 1.9, you can also deploy containers to GKE Autopilot clusters and Cloud Run, but that topic is outside the subject of this book.

In this section, we have briefly introduced M4CE, which M4A uses to move VMs between clouds and on-prem. Migration can happen in minutes, while data migrates transparently in the background. The interested reader can learn more online at http://mng.bz/GRXv. In addition, more helpful information on how to migrate an EC2 instance from AWS to Compute Engine on Google Cloud is available at http://mng .bz/gJ2x. The next section is about several Google best practices adopted for M4A.

15.5   *Advanced topic: M4A best practices*

In this section, we discuss some best practices for M4A. The idea is to provide guidance on real-time scenarios frequently encountered by customers. This section is rather advanced and assumes that you are very familiar with Kubernetes environments. Different details of Kubernetes are discussed in detail. Let's start with the following:

- *VM hostnames*—One convenient pattern is to transform VM hostnames into Kubernetes service names (see http://mng.bz/WAQa). Note that service names are a set of Pod endpoints grouped into a single resource. So, retaining this naming convention helps with consistency.
- *Multiple apps/services per VM*—If multiple applications or services exist per VM, it might be convenient to define a Kubernetes Service for each of them. Again, this naming convention helps with consistency.
- *Host file customizations*—If your VMs use specific customization on the host file for DNS resolution, then it is recommended to use the Kubernetes Pod spec `hostAliases` (http://mng.bz/81qz). Adding entries to a Pod's /etc/hosts file provides a Pod-level override of hostname resolution. Moreover, it helps to replicate multiple application environments, such as production, staging, and testing.
- *Multi-VM stacks*—If you have a multi-VM-stacks environment, then it might be convenient to place codependent Pods in the same Kubernetes namespace and use short DNS names. In addition, you should use Kubernetes' NetworkPolicy to restrict access between frontend and backend Pods. This organization would help keep your environment organized, safer, and more effective.

- *Referring to external services*—If your applications use external services, it is worth considering using the Kubernetes ExternalName Service without a selector (http://mng.bz/Elqd), a best practice in Kubernetes to abstract external backends.

- *NFS file share*—Currently, M4A does not automatically migrate NFS mounts. Therefore, you need to manually define NFS persistent volume directives and add them to the generated Pod YAML. The interested reader can find more information on mounting external volumes online (http://mng.bz/Nmqn).

- *Unneeded services*—Migration is a consolidation moment. Therefore, it is appropriate to double-check all the services running on your virtual machine and disable those that are not needed on containers. Migrate for Anthos will automatically disable unnecessary hardware or environment-specific services and a predefined set of additional services running on VMs. See a detailed list of different services automatically disabled at http://mng.bz/DZqR.

- *Environmental variables*—If your application requires an environment variable, it is a good practice to move definitions to the Kubernetes Pod YAML, ensuring you follow the best practice of having all your infrastructure as code.

- *Scripts using Cloud instance metadata*—If your scripts look up metadata, it is worth replacing this lookup with either Kubernetes ConfigMap (http://mng .bz/lJl2) or, again, using the env variables defined in your Kubernetes Pod YAML definition.

- *Application logs*—You can have logs generated by workload containers migrated with M4A and written to Cloud Logging. By default, M4A considers entries written to stdout of init, the parent of all Linux processes, and contents from /var/log/syslog. Adopting this strategy will enhance the level of automation in your environment and the observability of your applications.

- *GKE Ingress controller*—If you migrate to GKE, it might be convenient to use GKE network ingress control for controlling the network traffic accessing workloads. Doing so will eliminate the need for changing your application with additional routing rules, VPNs, filters, or VLANs. For instance, if you migrate a three-tiered application, you might want to split it into multiple containers. The frontend service is accessed via a GKE Google load balancer (http://mng.bz/Blq1) for load scalability. In addition, you might want to define network policies for enforcing access to the application service only by the frontend Pods and not from the external world. Similarly, you might want to define policies to access the database layer from the application layer only. These choices would increase the security of your environment.

- *Linux-specific runlevel 3*—In a Linux environment, certain services are configured to start by default only at runlevel 5. Currently, M4A reaches runlevel 3 only. VMs migrated into GKE with M4A will be booted in the container at Linux runlevel 3. Consequently, certain services should be configured to start automatically at runlevel 3. These might include X11, XDM, and the GUI used for VNC.

In this advanced section, we have discussed several best practices that you can adopt for fine-tuning environments migrated with M4A. In the next section, we will discuss how to upgrade images postmigration.

15.6   Postmigration integration with CI/CD pipelines

Artifacts generated with M4A can be used for Day 2 operations, such as software updates, configuration changes, security patches, and additional operations with files. You can easily integrate these artifacts with a CI/CD typical pipeline consisting of source, build, test, and deploy (see figure 15.33).

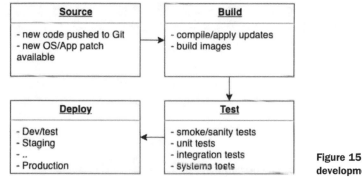

Figure 15.33   Typical CI/CD development phases

Artifacts are generated with multistage builds so they can be incrementally maintained without incurring the risk of inflating the generated container image. Figure 15.34 shows an example of integration of M4A with CI/CD pipelines.

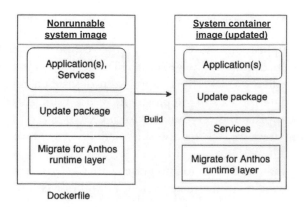

Figure 15.34   Integration of M4A with CI/CD pipelines

A typical Docker artifact is composed of two parts (see figure 15.35). The first part is the M4A runtime, and the second part is the nonrunnable base representing the capture system image layer from the migrated VM.

```
# Please refer to the documentation:
# https://cloud.google.com/migrate/anthos/docs/dockerfile-reference

FROM anthos-migrate.gcr.io/v2k-run-embedded:v1.4.0 as migrate-for-anthos-runtime

# Image containing data captured from the source VM
FROM gcr.io/myproject/myworkload-non-runnable-base:v1.0.0 as source-content

# If you want to update parts of the image, add your commands here.
# For example:
# RUN apt-get update
# RUN apt-get install -y \
#               package1=version \
#               package2=version \
#               package3=version
# RUN yum update
# RUN wget http://github.com


COPY --from=migrate-for-anthos-runtime / /

# Migrate for Anthos image includes entrypoint
ENTRYPOINT [ "/.v2k.go" ]
```

Figure 15.35   A typical Dockerfile generated by M4A, useful for CI/CD pipelines

If you need to update the M4A runtime, you can simply replace the first FROM directive as appropriate from the Dockerfile. For instance, suppose that you need to support M4A 1.8.1. You can achieve with the following new directive, which replaces the current one:

```
FROM anthos-migrate.gcr.io/v2k-run-embedded:v1.8.1 as migrate-for-anthos-runtime
```

If you need to update your application, you can change the second Docker FROM directive. In detail, you typically download the generated Dockerfile from your container registry (such as GCS), edit the Dockerfile to apply your desired changes, build a new layered image, and update the existing deployment with a rolling update. As discussed, this image-layered approach is very suitable for a CI/CD-based (see chapter 12) deployment environment where DevOps and site reliability engineering (SRE) methodologies are the key.

In this section, we have discussed how to integrate with CI/CD pipelines for increasing your organizational agility. In the next section, we will discuss how to integrate with service meshes.

15.7   Postmigration integration with ASM

Earlier in this chapter, we discussed the benefits of using a service mesh—transparent gains in terms of communication, policy management, observability, and agility. The key observation is that the adoption of Anthos Service Mesh (see chapter 4) is another step toward the adoption of SRE and DevOps methodologies.

For instance, ASM makes it possible to check the service status together with key metrics for our applications such as error, latency, and request rates; visualize the topology; check the estimated cost; and define service-level indicators (see figure 15.36).

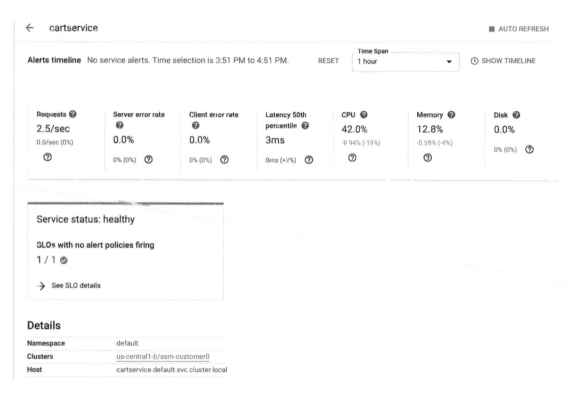

Figure 15.36   Using ASM for inspecting an application after migration

Once again, it is important to point out that these gains are free with no need to change any code in your migrated application. Once it is containerized, your application becomes a first-class cloud native application, which can be managed with modern cloud native methodologies and significant cost savings. You can arguably add your legacy VM into the mesh by using `WorkloadEntry`. The point is more that you gain all the benefits of being on Kubernetes (portability, scalability, etc.), as well as the Service Mesh encapsulating all the services within a cluster, without having to extend beyond the cluster perimeter.

Summary

- Moving to cloud-based applications offers the benefit of having a modern container-based environment using infrastructure in a more efficient way than traditional virtual machines. Gains are in terms of reduced costs, improved portability, scalability, resiliency, simplified developer experience, and reduced time to market.
- You can use Migrate for Anthos to have a fully automated transformation, with no need for the original source code.
- The best workload candidates for migration include stateless web frontend, multi-VM, multitiered stacks, business logic middleware, medium- to large-sized databases, and low duty-cycle and bursty workloads. We have reviewed the components that make up the Migrate for Anthos architecture together with real-world migration scenarios.
- We have learned some common best practices for migration using Migrate for Anthos including postmigration integration with CI/CD pipelines and with Anthos Service Mesh.

Breaking the monolith 16

Phil Taylor

This chapter covers

- Modernizing legacy applications
- Using Anthos for modernization
- Benefits of Anthos for microservices
- Real-world examples
- Antipatterns to avoid

Developing and supporting applications at scale in today's markets is harder than ever before. With the rapid acceleration of business markets, applications rapidly evolve from early-stage prototypes to large-scale applications. With traditional deployment methodologies and processes, we can evolve our architectures and organically find and fix problems as the application scales. Because of the speed at which teams need to move today to keep up with business demands, our architecture and deployment processes need to be agile and scalable from day 1. Thankfully, recent innovations in containers and container platforms like Anthos coupled with modern development patterns, such as microservice architectures, help us easily build and deploy applications, without compromising on efficiency, performance, or quality.

16.1   *Modernizing legacy applications*

Although these new patterns and tools are great for greenfield development projects, it can be frustrating and sometimes overwhelming to support our legacy applications. Many teams face the challenge of keeping the airplane flying while rebuilding it mid-flight. It can be tempting to put all your eggs in one basket and focus only on rebuilding your application using modern, software architecture patterns and containers. We have seen several teams take this approach and fail. The teams who have the most success see the journey as a series of incremental improvements to the original design.

We recommend the following approach when thinking about how to move from monolithic legacy design to modern architecture design:

- Modernize the legacy application development and deployment process.
- Consider language and/or framework upgrades or replacements that may improve the development and deployment life cycle. For example, if we have a Java WebSphere application, we may consider moving this to an Apache Tomcat web server framework if the application is not heavily tied into the features of WebSphere.
- Modernize to containers where you can use Migrate for Anthos to rapidly move your application's operating environment from VMs to containers. This will help make incremental improvements to the operations of your application that should give your team time to focus on modernization efforts.
- Adding a continuous integration pipeline for building and unit-testing your application can help teams identify and fix problems faster. In turn, this will provide them a quick feedback loop that will give them the confidence they need to start modernizing the application.
- Adding a continuous deployment pipeline that deploys your application to a lower environment and performs automated integration or user acceptance testing will further increase the productivity of the team.
- Adding end-to-end observability and instrumentation is key at this phase. We can no longer rely on logging into a dedicated virtual machine to view logs or debug our application. We need the ability to monitor and investigate incidents that may be occurring across a large set of nodes in our operating environment.
- Using a managed container operating environment like GKE or Anthos here will allow your teams to focus on software and deployment innovations rather than operating the container environment.

Next, you will want to modernize the legacy application itself, not just the development and deployment process. This will create agility, velocity, and efficiency for the development teams and infrastructure. Breaking the application into smaller domains and decoupling its capabilities into individual services with well-known contracts will create additional efficiencies. For example, you will be able to build and test a single business domain service in isolation, allowing for rapid iteration of capabilities. Standard contracts between services will create a well-defined boundary to determine when you are introducing breaking changes that may affect other dependent services. You will have two options: incrementally extract and rewrite capabilities or rewrite the entire application. Most of the time, this choice will depend on the business's goals and appetite for investment. We will cover the first option briefly here because it is the most common approach we see customers adopting.

You have ways to peel off capabilities on the edge and rewrite them to be cloud native. We would like to say it's always so easy in real life. A lot of teams start with common services like authentication and authorization or logging. This approach will allow your teams to take smaller bites of the apple to start moving your application architecture into a modern microservices design.

At this point, you might be asking yourself, why not just use Migrate for Anthos on the legacy application and be done with it?. The answer depends on your particular use case and the life of the application. That approach may be well suited for an application that is scheduled to sunset or be replaced. For applications that will be around longer, you will want to eventually rewrite them to take advantage of modern architecture patterns like microservices and serverless architecture. The many advantages to the aforementioned architectures are highlighted here:

- Development advantages
  - Smaller teams focus on a single business problem domain.
  - Modern techniques for development and testing of code support the 100% autonomous build, test, and deployment of services. Although it is possible to achieve 100% test coverage and automated deployments with legacy applications, the amount of effort required is significantly greater than starting with a design that supports it up front.
  - Decoupled services allow us to choose the technology stack that is best suited for the business capabilities the team is building.
  - Different teams can manage different microservices. This approach is often used to create a service per team where the team needs to understand only the business domain that applies to the service they're developing. Consider a service that contains payment and taxation logic. In this scenario, the developer needs to understand concepts like payment transactions and gateways, PCI compliance, and federal or local tax rules. By splitting the service domain boundary between payments and taxes, we can reduce the domain knowledge required by the developers supporting each service. With a microservices approach, the payment team no longer needs to understand the intricacies of federal or local tax rules; they simply need to understand the API contact for adding the appropriate taxes to a given transaction.
- Operational advantages
  - *Increased reliability/high availability*—Each application service is compiled and deployed separately by design. This reduces the blast radius of service outages to a single microservice.

- *Portability*—Containers create mobility, allowing us to run a service where it makes sense, on-prem or in a cloud provider. Although this can be accomplished with VMs, container platforms have made it easier to deploy and schedule the workloads in other environments or automatically move workloads to better operating nodes with zero downtime.
- *Lower operating costs*—Containers provide a higher density than VMs, yielding additional savings compared to VMs or physical environments.
- *Elasticity of demand for individual services*—With a microservice design, we can automatically scale up services to meet demand and scale them back during idle times for cost efficiency. This is also possible with VM-based designs, but teams traditionally scale the entire VM due to lack of understanding of how to scale an individual service running within the VM.
- *Automated deployment pipelines*—Using a container-based solution allows us to more easily automate end-to-end operations.
- *Self-healing*—By moving services that require high availability into the container platform, we can more easily set up automations to handle common failure and recovery tasks. Kubernetes provides liveness and readiness checks as well as rescheduling capabilities natively, which make this a simple task in most cases.

16.2   *Using Anthos for modernization*

Anthos provides a complete solution to run our containerized applications or legacy applications we want to migrate to containers. Anthos can help us modernize in place, move our workloads to the cloud, and enable hybrid application strategies more easily with capabilities for keeping clusters consistent between cloud and on-prem environments and advanced service mesh networking. See figure 16.1 for an overview of the Anthos components described here:

- Anthos Config Management provides an easy way to centrally manage configuration as code.
- Anthos Service Mesh provides a way for us to specify loosely coupled service dependencies, establish secure communication channels between services, and instrument a centralized observability system.
- Anthos GKE provides a reliable and consistent runtime environment for our Kubernetes-based workloads on-prem or in public cloud environments.
- Cloud Logging and Cloud Monitoring provide centralized tooling for monitoring, auditing, and troubleshooting clusters and workloads.

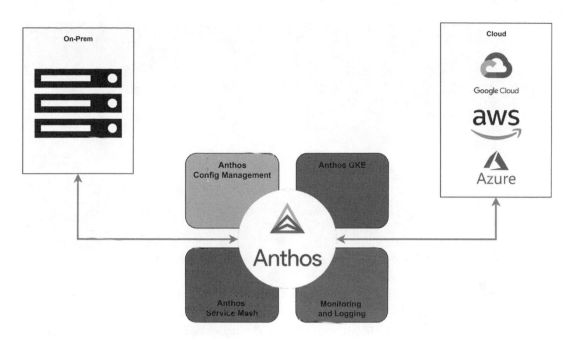

Figure 16.1 Overview of Anthos components

16.2.1 *Approach to modernization*

As we discussed in the introduction, a couple of ways to modernize your applications exist, and the path you choose may be different, depending on the specific application and business needs. Some applications or components in your application may not be great candidates for containerization. Some factors that may affect your decision to containerize your application or a component of your application follow:

- *Using GCE*—If the application is business critical and poses too high of a risk, you may consider migrating this application to Google Compute Engine (GCE) VMs before proceeding with containerization. By moving the application to GCE first, you mitigate the risk of having to learn new operational patterns to support the application. This can give your team the time they need to learn Kubernetes and Anthos applied to less critical workloads first.
- *Licensing constraints*—For example, your application may depend on a software application that does not allow containerization.
- *Operational support*—The team that supports your application is not ready to take on the new tool chain required to support a containerized application.
- *Other factors*—These include regulatory compliance requirements, performance when interacting with other applications, and existing hardware investments.

Consider figure 16.2, which visualizes the high-level flow of modernizing a Java application.

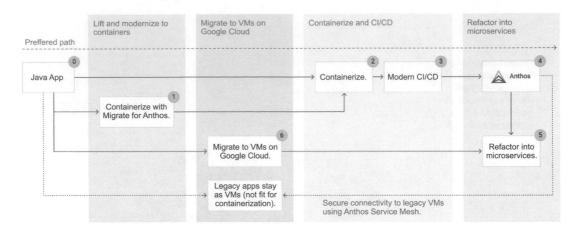

Figure 16.2   Modernizing a Java application

The approach would be the same regardless of the technology stack you originally used to build your application. Also keep in mind that this is a simple example—your application may consist of multiple application components or services, which all need to interact to create the end-to-end application user experience. Based on the criteria listed earlier, you will need to decide which application components you will replatform into containers and which ones you will keep as VMs. Then you can work through the modernization plan as illustrated. The following outline adds a little more clarity to each step:

- *Step 0*—Identify the target application or component to be modernized.
- *Step 1*—If the application is suitable, we will use Anthos Migrate (chapter 15) to containerize the target application.
- *Step 2*—If the application is too complex, we will manually containerize the application. We will go into more detail on this approach in the next section.
- *Step 3*—Update your existing CI/CD pipeline, or build a new one that will build, test, and deploy the application to Anthos.
- *Step 4*—Operate your application using Anthos to manage configuration, security, and connectivity to legacy applications.
- *Step 5*—Refactor your application into a microservices architecture.
- *Step 6*—Move legacy applications not currently suited for containers to Compute Engine, then modernize them by refactoring each application into microservices, using modern open source frameworks designed for cloud native applications.
- Legacy applications not in scope for the modernization plan will remain in their current form and will likely remain in a legacy data center. We will use Anthos Service Mesh for securing connections to these workloads, such as ERP systems and core mainframe applications.

Figure 16.3 illustrates a three-tiered Java application, aka monolithic. In some cases, the legacy app will use a commercial Java application server (e.g., WebSphere, Web-Logic). If you have analyzed the application source and it is not taking advantage of proprietary features of the commercial application server, now would be a good time to move to an open source application server (Apache Tomcat, JBOSS) and eliminate unnecessary licensing costs. After all, you will be rebuilding the application deployment anyway, and public container images are available as starting points for either of the open source application servers mentioned. If your team is considering a redesign or rewrite, you may also want to consider moving to modern Java frameworks within your application, like Spring Boot (https://spring.io/projects/spring-boot). If you go down this path, you may also consider using the Spring Cloud GCP (https://spring.io/projects/spring-cloud-gcp) project, which will accelerate your migration and provide libraries for interacting with common GCP services like Pub/Sub, Cloud Spanner, and Cloud Storage. If you are looking to avoid getting locked in to a specific vendor, you may consider abstracting the aforementioned services by using interface design to abstract away the cloud provider–specific implementations.

**Traditional three-tiered
Java App**

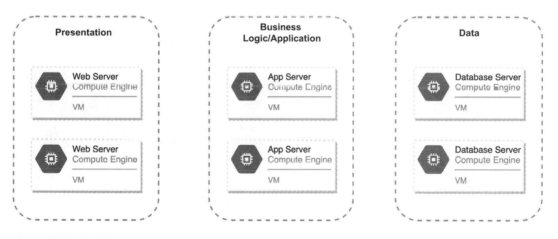

Figure 16.3   Traditional three-tiered Java application

Once you have figured out which applications or application components are best suited for containerization, you can follow the next steps.

CONTAINERIZE YOUR APPLICATION
The first step in the journey is getting your application running inside a container. If you're containerizing an ASP.NET application, you will have two approaches to consider: port to .NET Core or use Windows classic Kubernetes nodes. The approach you choose will depend on how easily you can port the application for ASP.NET to .NET Core and

how long the application will be supported. In general, we recommend porting the application to .NET Core, which will run on Linux, thus simplifying your Anthos clusters. Additionally, as with Java applications, it might potentially require a major rewrite.

In this chapter, we will focus on the steps required to replatform a typical enterprise Java application to containers running on Anthos. A couple of tools are available for Java developers to make the process of building a container image for an application easier, which plug into an existing build workflow (see figure 16.4). If your team is not comfortable writing container image descriptors, you may consider using tools such as the following:

- *Jib* (https://github.com/GoogleContainerTools/jib)—Integrates with Maven and doesn't require a Docker daemon on the build machine. Developers follow a typical build process, and Jib builds and outputs an optimized container image for your application. The optimized container image splits dependencies from classes, making it fast and efficient on future builds. Only the layers that have changed will be rebuilt.
- *Google Cloud buildpacks* (http://mng.bz/dJKo)—Buildpacks are designed to abstract the container image–building process, so the developer can follow a normal build process. Based on the CNCF v3 specification, these buildpacks output container images following best practices designed to run on GCP container services: Anthos, Cloud Run, or GKE.

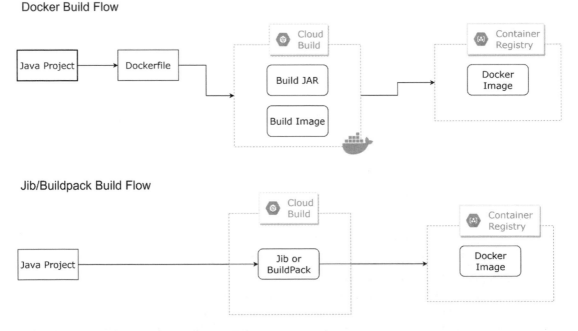

Figure 16.4   Docker build vs. Jib/buildpack flow

Once you have chosen your path and containerized your application, it's time to connect it to a CI/CD build pipeline for faster deployment iterations. At this point, you have containerized the monolith. Later in this chapter, we will discuss how to refactor it into microservices.

BUILD AND DEPLOY YOUR APPLICATION USING MODERN CI/CD

Next, we want to build a CI/CD pipeline to manage our new build process and deploy our application. This will create more efficiencies in our development process by eliminating manual tasks in favor of automation, thus allowing us to build, validate, and ship code faster. As we refactor to microservices, we decouple our application services into independently deployed components, which increases the overall complexity to deploy and manage our modern application. Without well-defined and complete CI/CD pipelines and an automated approach to address quality control and deployments, we see teams slow down rather than speed up.

Figure 16.5 depicts the necessary stages and flow for building a CI/CD pipeline to build and deploy a Kubernetes application.

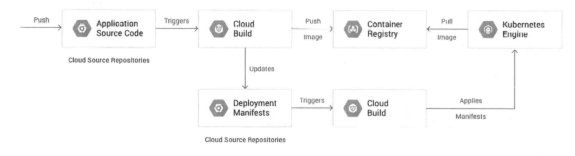

Figure 16.5   Example CI/CD pipeline for a Kubernetes application

OPERATING YOUR APPLICATION ON ANTHOS

At this point, you can use Anthos as a consistent Kubernetes operating environment to reduce your operational overhead while increasing development cycle velocity. Refer to chapter 5 for more information on operating your application. Moving your applications into containers and adding CI/CD pipelines should give your operators and developers more cycles to focus on modernizing additional applications or move on to a deeper modernization (refactoring into microservices) of an application you already have running on Anthos.

REFACTORING YOUR APPLICATION INTO MICROSERVICES

What we have learned since the invention of public cloud platforms is that one architecture stands above all others for cloud native applications: microservices. The microservices architecture was pioneered by companies like Google and has since been adopted by mainstream companies performing in the elite DevOps space (see http://mng.bz/rd4J). This chapter is not intended to be the holy grail of building microservice applications—plenty of good books on the topic are out there. We will take the time to highlight the architecture and key advantages to this approach, though. As illustrated in figure 16.6, with a monolithic architecture, we couple all of the service code into a single compiled application, which creates a hard coupling between the technical components and the teams building them. It also means that when that application is running in a single process, known side effects exist: an application crash in one component may take out the entire app, and scaling the application means scaling all components, which leads to waste in our computing environment.

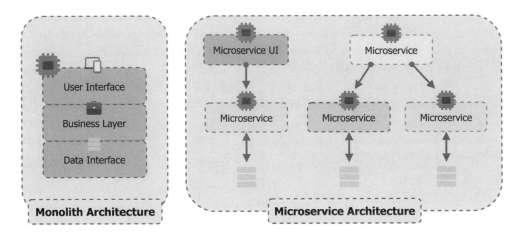

Figure 16.6   Monolith vs. microservice architecture

Most teams use domain-driven design (see http://mng.bz/Vp4y) in the design and creation of their microservices. With a microservice architecture, we decouple the services responsible for separate business domains into their own isolated services. This allows us to decouple the teams responsible for developing each service, reducing the domain expertise required. We standardize interactions between services by using industry best practices for protocols and data payloads, which provides the following technical and development benefits as outcomes to a microservices-based architecture:

- We decompose an app into a set of smaller services that are easier to understand.
- They are faster to develop and easier to maintain because we limited the breadth of domain knowledge required.
- They can be developed independently by a team focused on that service, increasing overall product development velocity.
- They are deployed and scaled independently; we're scaling services, not servers.
- They make it easy to enable continuous deployment on complex applications because we can limit our test boundaries to a single service during service development iterations.

The business benefits follow:

- We gain increased deployment frequency, resulting in reduced time to market for new features and patches. We can iterate development and add new capabilities to a single service with little or no effect to other application services.
- We get better infrastructure utilization because we scale services, not servers. Because we have more cleanly defined application service boundaries, we can deploy services individually and scale only the ones we need to scale. In the past, it was common for operations teams to scale an entire server or VM because scaling an individual service was a complex task, and they didn't understand the application well enough to split it up.
- We achieve faster mean time to recovery for security patches. Because microservices are mainly deployed using containers, we simply patch the code and redeploy the application using a Kubernetes rolling update with zero downtime. In the past, we would have attempted to patch the VM and do an in-place upgrade of the application. Most operations teams would agree this led to more downtime than was typically planned.
- We experience reduced deployment failure or rollback. Because we have isolated the service boundaries, the scope of our deployments is also reduced. Combining this with automated testing and deployment of the application, our success rate increases significantly.

You can take two approaches when choosing to refactor your application into a microservices architecture: first, spin up a team focused on rewriting the entire application using a greenfield approach. This approach will be less disruptive to your production application, but it will add more risk to the overall project because you need the entire application to be rewritten before you can realize the benefits. The second approach is to apply the strangler fig pattern (http://mng.bz/xdgd) to slowly iterate away the design of the legacy application and refactor it into microservices.

We recommend using the strangler fig pattern because it reduces the risk in adopting the new design patterns and overall refactoring of the application into a microservices architecture. This method may add a little more work to the overall project because we need to extract the logic and work it back into the existing application. It allows us to incrementally improve our application architecture, providing more and more value each time we create a new production release, which reduces the amount of risk and starts to provide value more quickly to the business.

Many teams struggle with the simple question, where do we start? The answer will be different for each application. However, the pattern is generally the same: look for features that support the application and are easy to decouple. For example, a centralized authentication and authorization service is usually a good choice.

Consider using the framework Google recommends (http://mng.bz/Alqo) for evaluating which feature to move first. A summary of the framework follows:

- Business process
- Design and development
- Operations
- People and teams

Business process

You should evaluate and consider the effects that moving the feature will have on the business users. Developers and operations teams need to learn a lot of new concepts to successfully modernize an application. Early in your modernization process you should avoid moving business-critical systems or features.

Design and development

Next, you should evaluate the complexity of the feature, its dependencies, and the amount of refactoring required to move it. Consider the following factors:

- Data usage, number of schemas (isolated or shared), and size
- Dependencies on other features
- Other features that depend on this feature
- Connectivity requirements
- Design elements that may create complexity in refactoring or have no clear solution

Operations

While evaluating which features to move first, you should consider the following:

- Service-level agreements with the business
- Maintenance windows and tolerance for downtime

Consider focusing on features that are more lenient on downtime and don't have critical business SLAs requiring high availability.

People and teams

In the early stage, it is preferable to focus on teams that are in support of modernization and have well-defined processes. If possible, avoid teams that are holding out or where processes are available only through tribal knowledge.

OPTIMIZE YOUR ON-PREM LEGACY APPLICATIONS USING ANTHOS SERVICE MESH

Most people taking this approach to modernize their application will end up with some components or dependencies still running on VMs. We can use Anthos Service Mesh (ASM) to add observability and security capabilities in managing these workloads, consistent with our Kubernetes workloads. The benefits ASM provides to VMs are listed here (and see figure 16.7):

- Use the same declarative policy and security management framework as containers running on Anthos.

- No code changes required; once the VM registers with Anthos, it is treated like a service running in GKE.
- Take advantage of the same observability you get from your container workloads in a single dashboard; metrics appear just like a service running in GKE.

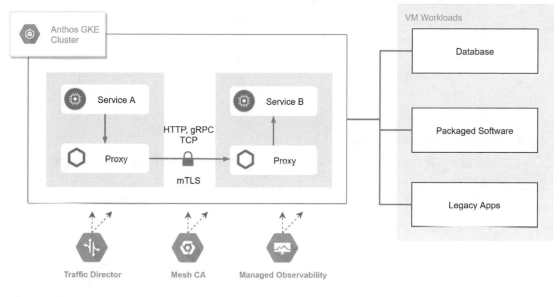

Figure 16.7 Integrating VMs with Anthos Service Mesh

16.3 *Benefits of Anthos for microservices*

The goal of a microservice architecture is to decouple the business service logic into individual, self-contained services to provide acceleration of development and optimization of performance. The drawback is that you are creating complexity in the configuration, deployment, and maintenance operations of your application. The packages that you need to reinstall due to updates in the common software introduce a pain in the neck every time you have to redo and update lots of different environments. Anthos solves the most common problems associated with supporting these types of applications:

- *Consistency*—A consistent runtime environment across multiple public cloud and on-prem data centers.
- *Automation*—A key to success with microservices is your ability to automate the deployment of your entire application. Anthos provides configuration as code to enable this capability. You can apply configuration and security policies and even deploy your application components using ACM.
- *Dependency management and security*—Increased complexity in decoupled services is more easily managed using a service mesh. Instead of embedding physical

service-to-service dependencies in our applications, a popular pattern in microservices-based solutions is to embed logical references that are resolved by the service mesh. ASM provides this capability as well as the ability to inject security policy, enforce mutual TLS, and bridge traditional VMs into your application as though they were other Kubernetes-based services.

- *Observability*—Understanding your application's performance is more difficult once you have broken it into microservices. Instead of monitoring one Java process with a sophisticated tool, you will need to monitor lots of services for performance and understand when one is degraded or broken. Anthos Service Mesh provides the ability to visualize and inspect your application performance as well as set service-level objectives (SLOs) so you can be alerted or have automated processes remediate service performance.

16.4   *Real-world examples*

Lots of real-world examples exist where we need to run compute workloads close to the user (aka running on the edge). These are great use cases for Anthos, which provides the ability to apply configuration and security policies as code. Two easy-to-identify use cases are retail and manufacturing.

Imagine you are a large cruise line. You have developed a new user experience using many of the concepts we have described in this book. Your team has built a new microservices-based architecture with web and mobile application user experiences. This new digital experience is used to provide lots of shipboard capabilities to your customers, like activity planning, meal ordering, events, announcements, and concierge services. The problem you keep having is a lack of consistency in the fleet. You are running into problems keeping the hardware and software updated on each ship, leading to an inconsistent user experience, outages, and many more problems. The effort to update is a time-consuming human effort to apply patches and upgrade software. So, even though your development team took a modern approach, you are struggling to operate this complex solution. You need Anthos. Although it won't eliminate the process of updating hardware or core networking changes, it will handle everything else, lessening the gap between manual and automated processes and reducing your overhead to operate the solution. Anthos will provide you with the following capabilities to get a handle on your environments and avoid configuration and deployment problems:

- *Anthos GKE*—Provides a managed Kubernetes distribution that ensures you are running the same runtime platform on each environment.
- *Anthos Service Mesh*—Provides security and observability capabilities to ensure your container environment and workloads are secure and your developers can easily find problems by using SLOs.
- *Anthos Configuration Management*—Provides a centralized policy-as-code approach to core cluster configuration, security policies, and application deployment consistency.

Now imagine that your team has built the solution with Anthos at the center of operations. Your team has designed each cluster and documented your core cluster configuration and security policies as code using Anthos Config Management. To bring a new shipboard data center online, it's as simple as racking and stacking the gear, getting the hardware on the network, installing Anthos, and then registering the cluster with the control plane and ACM. Then ACM will bootstrap the cluster with the right configuration and security policies.

16.5   *Antipatterns to avoid*

We have discovered several antipatterns over the years while helping teams modernize their applications into a microservice architecture:

- *Tempting big bang approaches*—Many teams decide to scrap what they have and start over, rewriting the entire application all at once into a microservice architecture. In our experience, this tends to lead to a waterfall approach, with significantly longer efforts and overrun budgets before the business can realize the benefits. A better approach is to peel the onion, one layer at a time, as we have mentioned earlier in the chapter. This fits better into a lean or agile approach to modernizing the application and starts to provide benefits much faster.

- *Ignoring architecture design principles of microservices* (http://mng.bz/ZoMR)—To correctly create microservices, we isolate all functionality within a new service. This typically means moving the interface logic, the business logic, and the data schemas required for stateful services. Many teams stumble here and leave the data schemas in a shared data store. This can be tempting when teams don't understand the services boundaries well or don't understand how to solve downstream capabilities like analytics or reporting. In a mature microservice-based solution, all components must be isolated and independently versioned and deployed.

- *Data-driven migration* (http://mng.bz/Rl6Z)—Given the first antipattern we discussed, it becomes tempting to focus heavily on the data and attempt to use the data boundaries as service boundaries. This is typically a mistake in legacy systems and generally results in migration thrashing (lots of migration iterations to get it right). Instead, consider an intermediary step where you focus on logic first and data second. This will allow you to get the business service boundaries correct and better understand how to split out the data.

- *Decoupling capabilities not code* (http://mng.bz/2adg)—Developers and technical managers take ownership of the code written, which is why they are tempted to extract and reuse existing code when refactoring the monolithic code base into microservices, when, in reality, a high cost and low value results from this approach. Most organizations and teams will benefit from a rewrite of the code. This allows them to revisit the business process, potentially optimize legacy processes, and improve the code base in the process (add unit tests, standardize on new languages, etc.). In some cases, it makes sense to reuse existing code—a good example would be to extract a complex algorithm that is not well understood or documented. In this situation, it would be safer to extract and reuse the code and then modernize at a later stage, once the team understands what it is doing and can safely rewrite.

Summary

- Modernizing legacy applications doesn't always have to start with a complete rewrite or refactor. Moving the application into containers can help reduce operational burden and give your team time to innovate on the next version of the app.
- While modernizing your application, look for opportunities to reduce technical debt, like migrating your web server framework or updating core libraries.
- Other ways to reduce technical debt include removing code for bootstrapping TLS security or observing and relying on Anthos for these capabilities at the platform level.
- Consider new design patterns like microservices if you will be rewriting or refactoring your application.
- Avoid taking a big bang approach—give preference to incremental improvements to the application.
- Use Anthos for consistent runtimes, automation, dependency management, security, and observability to ensure development teams have a consistent set of capabilities to rely on in their operating environments.

Compute environment
running on bare metal

Giovanni Galloro

This chapter covers

- An introduction to Anthos on bare metal
- Deployment options
- Networking architecture
- Storage architecture
- Installing and configuring Anthos on bare metal

The original release of Anthos required you to deploy your clusters on a vSphere infrastructure and didn't offer the option to deploy on a different hypervisor or to physical servers. For the initial release, this made sense because vSphere is used by numerous enterprises, and it allowed businesses to use their existing infrastructure and skill sets. As the use cases for containers and Kubernetes grew, however, it became clear that organizations wanted, and needed, more flexible deployment options.

To address these additional use cases, Google expanded Anthos to include a bare metal deployment model. One point to highlight is that you do not have to deploy Anthos on bare metal to actual physical servers. The bare metal model allows you to deploy to any supported operating system, whether a physical server or virtual machine, or even VMs running on Hyper-V or KVM.

You can think of the bare metal option as a "bring your own Linux" deployment model. Rather than having an appliance to deploy your nodes, like the vSphere deployment model, you need to provide ready-to-use servers before you can deploy Anthos on bare metal. Now let's introduce you to Anthos on bare metal.

17.1   Introduction to Anthos on bare metal

As described in previous chapters, Anthos is a platform designed for multiple deployment environments, as summarized in figure 17.1.

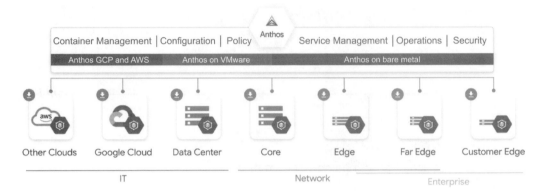

Figure 17.1   Anthos deployment environments

Anthos on bare metal is a deployment option to run Anthos on physical servers, deployed on an operating system provided by the customer. It ships with built-in networking, life cycle management, diagnostics, health checks, logging, and monitoring. Additionally, it supports CentOS, Red Hat Enterprise Linux (RHEL), and Ubuntu, all validated by Google. With Anthos on bare metal, you can use an organization's standard hardware and operating system images, taking advantage of existing investments, which are automatically checked and validated against Anthos infrastructure requirements.

17.1.1   Comparing Anthos on-prem deployment options

Now that you have options to deploy Anthos on-prem, how do you decide which is the best for your organization? Both options have their own advantages and disadvantages, and to decide which deployment is best for you, you'll need to consider your personal requirements. In table 17.1, we have provided an overview of some advantages and disadvantages of each option.

Table 17.1 Advantages and disadvantages of Anthos on VMware and Anthos on bare metal

Anthos on VMware	Anthos on bare metal
Runs on VMware Best for organizations who want <ul><li>vSphere as a corporate standard</li><li>Hardware shared across multiple teams or clusters (Dev/Test)</li><li>Integrated OS life cycle management</li><li>Self-healing/autoscaling for clusters</li></ul>	Runs on bare-metal or on-prem IaaS Best for organizations who want <ul><li>Reduced cost and complexity (due to elimination of the vSphere license)</li><li>Low-latency workloads (telco and high-performance computing)</li><li>To unlock new use cases for edge computing with simplified software stack</li><li>To run closer to the hardware for better performance</li></ul>
Deployment advantages	
<ul><li>Easier to deploy multiple clusters</li><li>Provided node appliance requires little maintenance</li><li>Includes two vSphere storage providers for persistent disks</li><li>Node autohealing</li><li>Easy to scale cluster nodes up or out</li></ul>	<ul><li>Can be deployed to any supported Linux node, on-prem, or in a CSP</li><li>No workload scheduling conflicts</li><li>Expanded GPU compatibility</li><li>Allows node customizations to meet an organization's requirements</li><li>Better node performance</li><li>Uses existing corporate standards (e.g., logging and monitoring standards)</li></ul>
Deployment disadvantages	
<ul><li>Requires additional VMware licensing.</li><li>Customization of node appliance not supported.</li><li>Limited GPU supported through pass-through.</li><li>Requires additional training for either the VM teams or the Kubernetes support teams.</li><li>The vSphere scheduler and Kubernetes scheduler are not aware of each other.</li><li>Storage DRS can break your cluster.</li></ul>	<ul><li>Requires planning to right-size nodes to avoid wasted resources</li><li>Does not include a storage provisioner other than local host storage</li><li>Difficult to scale in most enterprises</li><li>No node autohealing</li><li>Managing and updating nodes underlying the OS</li></ul>

17.2 Anthos bare metal architecture

Whereas Anthos on VMware cluster nodes are deployed from preconfigured VM images provided by Google, Anthos on bare metal relies on customers to provide a supported operating system version that they manage and patch themselves. As you can see in figure 17.2, the operating system can be installed directly on a physical server or on a VM running on any virtualization platform (KVM, OpenStack) that supports one of the Linux distributions compatible with Anthos on bare metal.

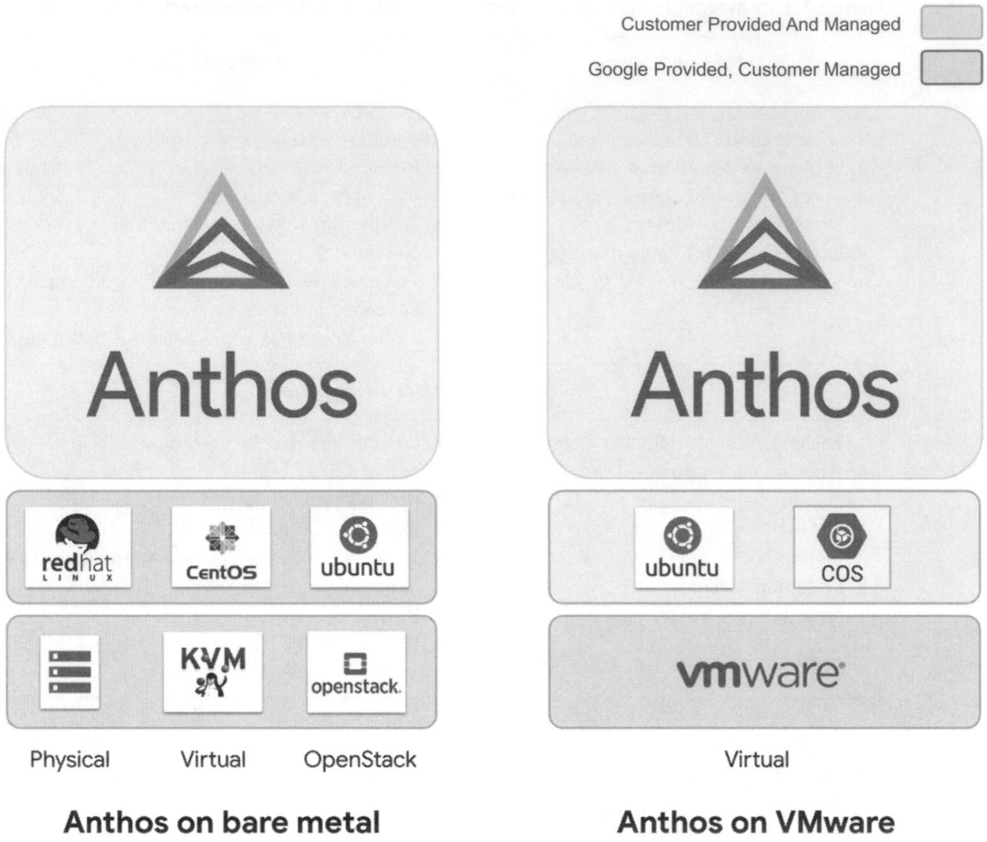

Figure 17.2   Anthos on-prem deployment options, shared responsibility model

17.2.1 *Cluster architecture*

In this section, we will discuss the architecture of a bare metal cluster. Much of the architecture you know from the Anthos on VMware deployment is the same for bare metal; however, the bare metal option includes a few architecture differences from the VMware model.

CLUSTER ROLES

An Anthos bare metal installation has the following two kinds of clusters:

- *User cluster*—Where applications are deployed, it includes control plane nodes and worker nodes where containerized application instances run.
- *Admin cluster*—A cluster that manages one or more user clusters. It is used to install, update, upgrade, and delete user clusters through an Anthos on bare metal–specific operator configured through two custom resources: `Cluster` and `NodePool`.

An admin cluster includes only control plane nodes, where the components used to manage the installation run. It also hosts some security-sensitive data, including SSH keys to access nodes' OS and GCP service account keys. Unlike Anthos on VMware, user cluster control plane nodes are decoupled from the admin cluster.

HIGH AVAILABILITY

You can run the user or admin cluster control plane in high-availability (HA) mode, so a control plane node failure does not affect cluster operations. This mode requires three or more control plane nodes. If high availability is not required, you can run a single control plane node in each cluster, but this method should be used only for nonproduction workloads.

Along with the control plane, you need to consider high availability for the worker nodes as well. For applications with high availability, you'll need a minimum of two worker nodes. As with the control plane, you should never run production workloads without HA for the worker nodes.

DEPLOYMENT MODELS

This is where you will start to see the differences between how Anthos deploys between VMware and bare metal. Anthos on bare metal provides a few different deployment models, offering flexibility to meet different organization requirements.

Standalone cluster deployment

In a standalone cluster deployment model, shown in figure 17.3, a single cluster serves both as the admin cluster and the user cluster. Because this model doesn't require a separate admin cluster, you save three nodes in an HA setup. This situation can be helpful in scenarios where each cluster is managed independently or for a single cluster where each deployment location is required, for example, an edge use case or for an isolated network.

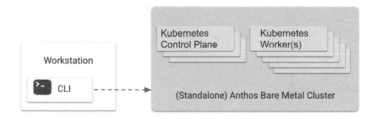

Figure 17.3   Standalone cluster deployment

From a security perspective, you need to consider that user workloads will run on the same cluster as the control plane. You will need to carefully consider securing your cluster to protect information like the node SSH keys and GCP service account keys. Implementing RBAC policies, OPA policies, network policies, and proper auditing will help to secure the cluster.

To provide more flexibility for these types of deployments, starting with Anthos version 1.8, Google reduced the minimum number of supported nodes per cluster from two to one and introduced, for standalone clusters, the new edge profile, which further reduces the hardware requirements.

Multicluster deployment

This is the same deployment model that Anthos on VMware uses. In a multicluster deployment model, shown in figure 17.4, you have a single admin cluster managing multiple user clusters. This model is useful if you need to centrally manage a fleet of clusters deployed in the same data center.

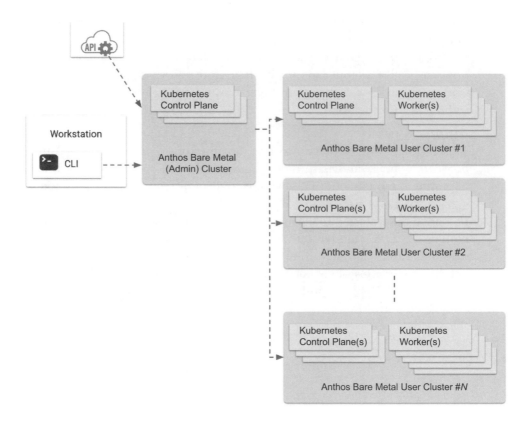

Figure 17.4   Multicluster deployment

Hybrid cluster deployment

The hybrid cluster deployment model, shown in figure 17.5, is similar to the multi-cluster deployment with one difference: you can use the admin cluster to run user workloads along with the standard worker nodes.

As you can see, Anthos on bare metal added greater deployment flexibility compared to the VMware deployment model. The added flexibility doesn't stop there, though. In the next subsection, we will discuss the updates to the networking architecture.

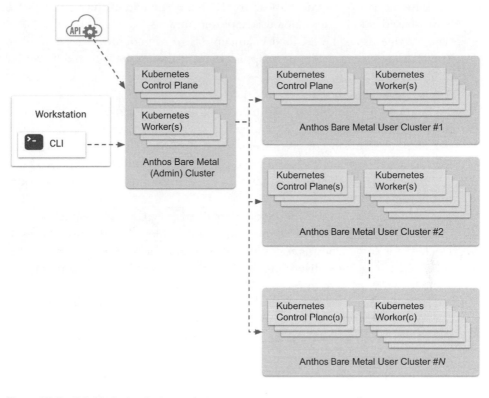

Figure 17.5 Hybrid cluster deployment

NETWORKING ARCHITECTURE

It makes sense that the networking architecture for the bare metal option would differ from the VMware model's. In the VMware deployment, you can use an external load balancer, or you can use the bundled load balancer, Seesaw. If you use the Seesaw option, Anthos deploys a preconfigured virtual machine, or machines in HA mode, to your VMware environment.

In the bare metal deployment, Google doesn't supply any appliances or VM images for any component. Don't worry, though—Google has this covered using other components like HAProxy and MetalLB.

Load balancing

Anthos on bare metal requires layer-4 (L4) load balancing to expose the control plane endpoint, ingress endpoint, and applications, using the `LoadBalancer` type Service. The load balancer's responsibility is to route and balance the traffic to the appropriate nodes.

Whichever cluster deployment model you choose, Anthos on bare metal can provide the needed load-balancing capabilities through a bundled L4 load balancer (bundled load balancer mode) or, alternatively, you can use an external load-balancing solution provided and configured by the customer (manual load balancer mode).

Whichever option you choose for L4 load balancing, during the installation an Envoy-based Istio Ingress gateway is deployed, and it's exposed through a `LoadBalancer` type Service using the L4 load balancer. This Envoy deployment is used to provide application proxy capabilities to applications, exposing them through standard Kubernetes ingress objects.

Bundled load balancer mode

To begin with, let's discuss load balancing for the control plane. If you choose bundled load balancing, Anthos on bare metal deploys L4 load balancers during cluster installation, removing the requirement of providing an external load balancer. The load balancers can run on a dedicated pool of worker nodes, or they can be located on the same nodes as the control plane. In either case, the load balancer nodes must be in the same subnet.

Starting with Anthos 1.9, Google changed how L4 load balancers are deployed. Previously, the HAProxy container image was deployed to the node(s) as a standard Docker (i.e., not Kubernetes controlled) container as a systemd Service. Starting with version 1.9, the Keepalived and HAProxy containers have been updated to run as static Kubernetes Pods on the load balancer nodes.

HAProxy is used only for load-balancing the control plane. To provide L4 to the data plane, Anthos deploys a popular, open source solution called MetalLB, which services requests in the cluster for any service that is deployed using the `LoadBalancer` type.

To recap the bundled load balancer components:

- *Control plane load balancing*—The control plane virtual IP address (VIP), routing traffic to the Kubernetes API server running on control plane nodes, is exposed through an HAProxy load balancer running as a Kubernetes Pod on the load balancer nodes, together with a containerized Keepalived service that manages HAProxy high availability.
- *Data plane load balancing*—The `LoadBalancer` type Service objects created for the applications and the Istio Ingress gateway deployed with Anthos on bare metal are exposed through an Anthos-managed MetalLB deployment running on the load balancer nodes. IP addresses for `LoadBalancer` type Services can be automatically assigned from a predefined pool and are part of the same subnet where load balancer nodes are deployed.

Both control plane load-balancing components (HAProxy and Keepalived) and data plane load-balancing components (MetalLB) run together on designated nodes (cluster control plane nodes or dedicated load balancer worker nodes).

Figure 17.6 shows an architecture example of a user cluster deployed in a single subnet with bundled load balancers running on control plane nodes. Figure 17.7 shows an architecture example of an user cluster deployed in a single subnet with bundled load balancers running on dedicated worker nodes.

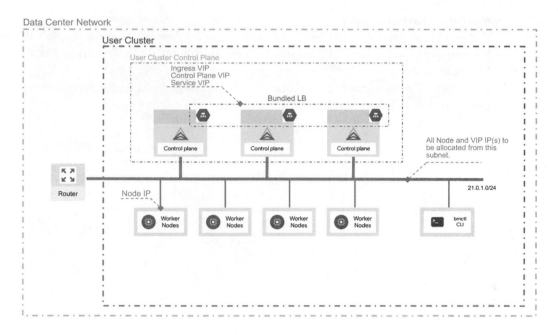

Figure 17.6 Load balancers running on control plane nodes

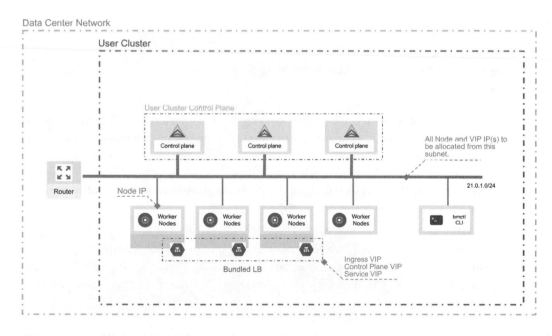

Figure 17.7 Load balancers running on dedicated worker nodes

Manual load balancer mode

If you choose manual load balancer mode, the Anthos installation doesn't deploy the bundled load balancers, and you are responsible for deploying an external load-balancing solution.

Figure 17.8 shows an example of a user cluster deployed in a single subnet with an external load balancer configured in manual load balancer mode.

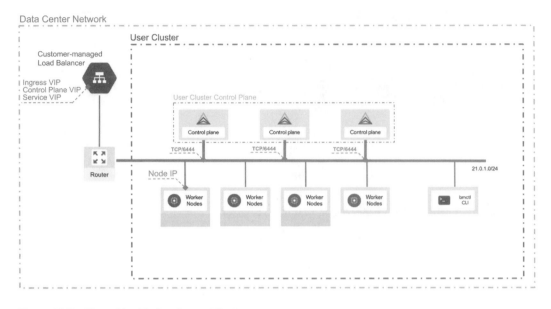

Figure 17.8   Manual load-balancing architecture

Internal cluster networking

Anthos on bare metal deploys an overlay network based on GENEVE tunnels that requires layer-3 (L3) connectivity between the nodes in the cluster, except for load balancer nodes that are required to be in the same layer-2 (L2) domain.

Similar to how Anthos on VMware works, Pod IP addressing works in island mode, which means IP addresses assigned to Pods are accessible only from the same cluster, and Pod CIDR ranges can be reused across clusters.

STORAGE ARCHITECTURE

The main approach to provide persistent storage for workloads running on Anthos on bare metal is through a Container Storage Interface driver from an Anthos-ready storage partner. You can find a list of partners and validated storage solutions at http://mng.bz/1MdX.

Anthos on bare metal also bundles the `sig-storage-local-static-provisioner`, which provides mount points on each node and creates a local persistent volume (PV) for each mount point. Because of its limitations, you should use local PVs only for nonproduction environments or specific advanced use cases.

OBSERVABILITY

You can use Google Cloud operations to collect logs and monitoring metrics for Anthos on bare metal, just like in other Anthos deployment environments. By default, system components logs are sent to Cloud Logging and system components metrics are sent to Cloud Monitoring. Cloud operations can also collect application logs and metrics (using Google Managed Service for Prometheus) by enabling it in the cluster configuration.

As an alternative to Cloud operations, you can use other solutions if preferred, such as Prometheus/Grafana, Elastic Stack, Sysdig, Datadog, or Splunk.

IDENTITY INTEGRATION

Anthos on bare metal can integrate, through the Anthos Identity Service authentication proxy, with any identity provider that supports OpenID Connect (OIDC) or LDAP to manage user and group authentication to clusters using existing user identities and credentials. If you already use or want to use Google IDs to log in to your Anthos clusters instead of an OIDC or LDAP provider, is it recommended you use the Connect gateway for authentication.

With this integration, you can manage access to an Anthos on bare metal cluster by using standard procedures in your organization for creating, enabling, and disabling accounts. You can employ Kubernetes RBAC to bind specific roles to users and groups defined in the identity provider to authorize them to perform specific actions on specific resources.

17.3 *Installation and configuration overview*

In this section, we will provide an overview of the requirements to deploy a cluster. Understanding the requirements is an important step before attempting to deploy a cluster, which we will discuss in the next section.

Google has made deploying Anthos on bare metal an easy process. Like the VMware deployment, you configure the cluster options in a configuration file and perform the deployment using a single binary executable called bmctl.

Anthos requires you to meet requirements for both software and hardware. Most organizations easily meet the requirements, but you should always verify that your infrastructure meets all requirements before deploying.

17.3.1 *Operating systems and software requirements*

As described in the introduction and architecture sections, Anthos on bare metal is installed on servers provided and configured by the customer. Servers can be physical or virtual, as long as they have one of the supported operating systems, configured to meet the Anthos requirements. Servers to be used as Anthos on bare metal nodes need to have one of the following operating systems:

- CentOS 8.2/8.3/8.4/8.5
- Red Hat Enterprise Linux (RHEL) 8.2/8.3/8.4/8.5/8.6
- Ubuntu 18.04 and 20.04

Each supported version requires a slightly different configuration. If you are using RHEL or CentOS, the firewalld service must be configured to allow traffic to TCP and UDP ports—these will be covered in the internal connectivity requirements in section 17.3.4. On these operating systems, if SELinux is enabled in enforcing mode, a policy for container isolation and security is configured during the Anthos on bare metal setup. If you are running the nodes on Ubuntu, you must disable the Uncomplicated Firewall service.

Time is very important for a cluster. To ensure that all nodes have their clocks in sync, all servers need to have an NTP service configured and enabled. Finally, because the installation establishes an SSH connection to the nodes, you'll need an SSH key pair to access each node with root privileges.

17.3.2 *Hardware capacity requirements*

Anthos on bare metal will work on any hardware compatible with one of the supported operating systems. The number of nodes required for an installation depends on the chosen deployment and load-balancing model, as described earlier. The number of worker nodes required will depend on the capacity requirements of the applications that the cluster(s) will host.

Table 17.2 describes the minimum and recommended hardware requirements for each node, whatever its role, using the default profile, excluding the applications capacity requirements that should be added.

Table 17.2   Hardware requirements for Anthos on bare metal

Resource	Minimum	Recommended
CPUs/vCPUs	4 core	8 core
RAM	16 GiB	32 GiB
Storage	128 GiB	256 GiB

Table 17.3 describes the hardware requirements for the edge profile introduced in Anthos on bare metal version 1.8.

Table 17.3   Hardware requirements for the edge profile

Resource	Minimum	Recommended
CPUs/vCPUs	2 core	4 core
RAM	Ubuntu: 4 GB CentOS/RHEL: 6 GiB	Ubuntu: 8 GB CentOS/RHEL: 12 GiB
Storage	128 GiB	256 GiB

17.3.3 Admin workstation

Besides the nodes, it's suggested to have an additional workstation to run the installation tool. This workstation must have the same Linux operating system running on cluster nodes with Docker 19.03 or higher configured to be managed by nonroot users. In addition to Docker, the machine must have the following:

- gcloud with anthos-auth and kubectl installed.
- More than 50 GB of free disk space.
- L3 connectivity to all cluster node machines.
- Access to all cluster node machines through SSH via private keys with password-less root access. Access can be either direct or through sudo.
- Access to the control plane VIP.

17.3.4 Networking requirements

Anthos has different requirements for external versus internal network connectivity.

EXTERNAL CONNECTIVITY REQUIREMENTS

All Anthos on bare metal nodes will need outbound HTTPS connectivity to the internet to do the following:

- Register to the GCP console and be managed from there through GKE Connect
- Send metrics and logs to Cloud operation endpoints
- Pull images from the Google Container Registry

This connectivity can use the public internet, an HTTP proxy, or a private connection like Google Cloud VPN or Dedicated Interconnect.

INTERNAL CONNECTIVITY REQUIREMENTS

This section will detail the internal networking requirements for your cluster. Each component of the cluster has different requirements, and tables 17.4–17.7 list the specific connectivity ports used for cluster node traffic.

Table 17.4 Control plane nodes

Protocol	Direction	Port range	Purpose	Used by
UDP	Inbound	6081	GENEVE encapsulation	Self
TCP	Inbound	22	Provisioning and updates of admin cluster nodes	Admin workstation
TCP	Inbound	6444	Kubernetes API server	All
TCP	Inbound	2379–2380	etcd server client API	kube-apiserver and etcd
TCP	Inbound	10250	kubelet API	Self and control plane
TCP	Inbound	10251	kube-scheduler	Self
TCP	Inbound	10252	kube-controller-manager	Self

Table 17.4   Control plane nodes *(continued)*

Protocol	Direction	Port range	Purpose	Used by
TCP	Inbound	10256	Node health check	All
TCP	Both	4240	CNI health check	All

Table 17.5   Worker nodes

Protocol	Direction	Port range	Purpose	Used by
TCP	Inbound	22	Provisioning and updates of user cluster nodes	Admin cluster nodes
UDP	Inbound	6081	GENEVE encapsulation	Self
TCP	Inbound	10250	kubelet API	Self and control plane
TCP	Inbound	10256	Node health check	All
TCP	Inbound	30000–32767	NodePort services	Self
TCP	Both	4240	CNI health check	All

Table 17.6   Load balancer nodes

Protocol	Direction	Port range	Purpose	Used by
TCP	Inbound	22	Provisioning and updates of user cluster nodes	Admin cluster nodes
UDP	Inbound	6081	GENEVE encapsulation	Self
TCP	Inbound	443	Cluster management	All
TCP	Both	4240	CNI health check	All
TCP	Inbound	7946	Metal LB health check	Load balancer nodes
TCP	Inbound	10256	Node health check	All
UDP	Inbound	7946	Metal LB health check	Load balancer nodes

Table 17.7   Multicluster port requirements

Protocol	Direction	Port range	Purpose	Used by
TCP	Inbound	22	Provisioning and updates of cluster nodes	All nodes
TCP	Inbound	443	Kubernetes API server for added cluster	Control plane and load balancer nodes

With the networking requirements covered, let's move on to the additional requirements for configuring the cluster load balancer.

LOAD-BALANCING REQUIREMENTS

Before installing Anthos on bare metal, you need to choose an architecture for load balancing (manual versus bundled) and, in the case of bundled, decide whether your load balancers will be installed on control plane nodes or dedicated worker nodes. Whatever solution you choose, the following VIP addresses must be reserved:

- *One VIP for the control plane for each cluster*—If you're using the bundled load balancer, this will be automatically created based on the configuration you defined during installation. If you're using a manual load balancer, this needs to be manually associated with a backend server group containing all the IP addresses of the cluster's control plane nodes. The backend port the control plane listens on is 6444.

- *One VIP for the Ingress service for each user cluster*—If you're using the bundled load balancer, this will be automatically created based on the configuration defined during installation. If you're using a manual load balancer, this needs to be manually configured with the same IP address assigned to the `istio-ingress` Service created in the `gke-system` namespace in the cluster and associated with a backend server group containing the IP addresses of the cluster nodes. The backend port would be the NodePort of the `istio-ingress` Service. If you want to use the Ingress gateway both for HTTP and HTTPS traffic, it's possible that you have to configure one VIP (and backend pool) for each port.

- *One VIP for each* `LoadBalancer` *type Service created in the cluster*—If you're using the bundled load balancer, these will be automatically assigned based on the pool defined during installation. If you're using a manual load balancer, it needs to be manually configured with the same IP address assigned to the Service object and associated with a backend server group containing all the IP addresses of the cluster worker nodes. The backend port would be the NodePort of the Service object.

If the cluster deployment will use the bundled load balancer, the following items must be configured:

- The load-balancing nodes need to be in the same L2 network, whereas other connections, including worker nodes, require only L3 connectivity.
- All VIPs must be in the load balancer machine subnet and fully routable.
- The gateway of the load balancer subnet must listen to gratuitous ARP messages and forward ARP packets to the load balancer nodes.

Moving on, the next section will cover the Google Cloud Platform requirements.

17.3.5 *Google Cloud Platform requirements*

The Anthos on bare metal installation has a few GCP project requirements, including required APIs, service accounts, and required roles.

REQUIRED GCP APIS

For a successful deployment, the project to which the cluster will be connected must have several APIs enabled. You can do this manually, or you can enable them automatically as an option when you execute the deployment using bmctl. The following APIs must be enabled in the GCP project used for installation:

- anthos.googleapis.com
- anthosaudit.googleapis.com
- anthosgke.googleapis.com
- cloudresourcemanager.googleapis.com
- container.googleapis.com
- gkeconnect.googleapis.com
- gkehub.googleapis.com
- iam.googleapis.com
- serviceusage.googleapis.com
- stackdriver.googleapis.com
- monitoring.googleapis.com
- logging.googleapis.com
- opsconfigmonitoring.googleapis.com

If any of the APIs is not enabled before you run the deployment, the preflight check will catch the missing API and stop the deployment from continuing.

REQUIRED SERVICE ACCOUNTS AND ROLES

Another requirement before deploying Anthos on bare metal is to create the required service account(s) and required roles. Although you can use a single account with all the roles, it is considered a bad security practice. Your organization will have its own security requirements, but it is advised that you create all the accounts as distinct service accounts.

You can elect to create the service accounts manually, or you can create them during the installation, using a parameter of the bmctl installation tool. Anthos on bare metal needs the following Google Cloud service accounts with the roles specified:

- A service account Container Registry (gcr.io) with no special role
- A service account used to register the cluster to the GCP console with the GKE hub admin IAM role
- A service account used to maintain a connection between the cluster and Google Cloud with the GKE Connect Agent IAM role
- A service account used to send logs and metrics to Google Cloud's operations suite with the following IAM roles:
  - Logs writer
  - Monitoring metric writer

– Stackdriver resource metadata writer
– Monitoring dashboard configuration editor
– Ops config monitoring resource metadata writer

If you want to enable these APIs and create the needed GCP service accounts during installation using the bmctl tool, the account used for installation must have either the project owner/editor role or, at least, the following roles assigned:

- Service account admin
- Service account key admin
- Project IAM admin
- Compute viewer
- Service usage admin

Finally, we will cover one more requirement that Anthos will use for cluster metrics.

CLOUD METRIC REQUIREMENTS
To send metrics to Google Cloud's operations suite, in addition to the service accounts listed in the previous section, you must create a Cloud Monitoring workspace within the GCP project.

17.4   Creating clusters

After all the requirements have been satisfied, you can proceed with the cluster creation. The following sections assume that all the installation tasks are performed from a machine that satisfies the requirements stated in section 17.3.3.

17.4.1   Creating an admin, hybrid, or standalone cluster

As we have detailed, you can deploy Anthos on bare metal using a few different cluster models, including separate admin/user clusters, hybrid clusters, or standalone clusters. In this section, we will discuss the process of deploying each model.

SUMMARY OF INSTALLATION FLOW
You install the first cluster in a specific deployment environment, regardless of the selected model, using the bmctl tool. Additional user clusters in the same environment can be created by applying an Anthos on bare metal user cluster configuration file, which is similar to the first cluster configuration, with a few minor changes. The high-level steps to create the first cluster follow:

1 Download the bmctl tool.
2 Use bmctl to create a cluster config template file.
3 Modify the config file with desired settings.
4 Run bmctl to create the cluster.

Figure 17.9 shows the flow for the first cluster creation with bmctl.

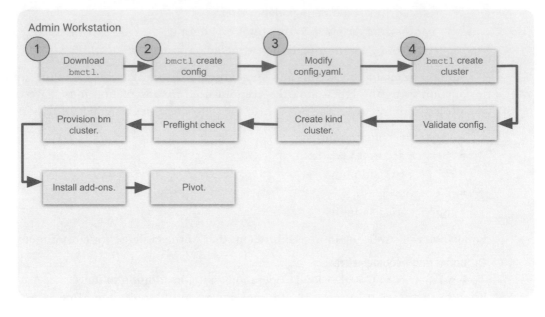

Figure 17.9   Cluster creation flow using bmctl

The initial four steps are initiated by the user, and when you perform step 4, the `bmctl create cluster` command, the following steps are executed:

- *Validate Config*—The cluster configuration file is checked to verify that specs are well formed, no IP address overlap occurs, service account keys are available, and the cluster has not been already registered in GCP console.
- *Create kind cluster*—As part of the setup, bmctl initially creates a temporary kind (Kubernetes in Docker) cluster on the admin workstation in which some of the resources needed for the admin cluster, such as cluster and NodePool objects or Secrets containing static site generator and service account keys, are created from the configuration file specs.
- *Preflight check*—Checks are performed on cluster machines and network requirements, such as OS version and configuration, filesystem available space, and reachability of GCP API endpoints.
- *Provision bare metal cluster*—Binaries are copied to target nodes, and installation is executed, including node initialization and join.
- *Install add-ons*—Add-on components like GKE Connect Agent, logging and monitoring components, bare metal operator, and MetalLB are installed.
- *Pivot*—The process of moving bare metal resources from the kind cluster to the provisioned cluster. Kubernetes resources will be deleted from the kind cluster afterward.

Finally, let's dive into creating a cluster!

LOGGING IN TO GCP AND DOWNLOADING THE BMCTL TOOL

Remember that Google supplies a tool to deploy Anthos on bare metal called bmctl. On the workstation that you will use to deploy the cluster, download the bmctl tool by following the steps here (for our example, we will assume the working directory is ~/baremetal):

1 Log in with gcloud, using `gcloud auth application-default login`, as a user that has the roles described in the "Installing account role requirements" subsection of the Installation requirements section.

2 Download the bmctl tool from the URL or storage bucket you will find in the documentation, shown here:

```
gsutil cp gs://anthos-baremetal-release/bmctl/<VERSION>/linux-amd64/bmctl
bmctl)
```

3 Make bmctl executable:

```
chmod a+x bmctl
```

Now that we have the bmctl executable, we can move on to creating the cluster configuration.

CREATING THE CLUSTER CONFIGURATION

To deploy a cluster, we need to have a cluster configuration file that contains all the parameters and options for the deployment. The bmctl tool can create a new configuration file for us by using the `create config` option:

```
bmctl create config -c CLUSTER_NAME --project-id=CLOUD_PROJECT_ID
```

where CLUSTER_NAME is the name you want to give to the cluster and CLOUD_PROJECT _ID is the project ID of the project you want to use with Anthos on bare metal.

If you haven't already enabled the required APIs, you can add the `--enable-apis` option to the previous command to enable them, and if you haven't created the required service accounts yet, you can add the option `--create-service-accounts` to have them created along with the needed roles.

POPULATING THE CLUSTER CONFIGURATION FILE

Before creating the cluster, we need to properly prepare the configuration file created by bmctl. The file is saved by default in a folder named with the cluster name inside a folder named bmctl-workspace. In this section, we will explain the options in the configuration file.

SSH private key

This is the SSH private key that will be used to connect to the nodes during the cluster deployment. Add to the `sshPrivateKeyPath:` spec the full path to access an SSH private key authorized to access all the target nodes as root, for example:

```
sshPrivateKeyPath: /root/.ssh/anthoskey
```

GCP service account keys

If you manually created the GCP service accounts before running bmctl, you need to populate the related fields with the full paths to service account keys as in the next example. If you used the bmctl --create-service-accounts parameter, they will be already populated:

```
gkeConnectAgentServiceAccountKeyPath: /root/bmctl-workspace/.sa-keys/anthos-
    demos-anthos-baremetal-connect.json
gkeConnectRegisterServiceAccountKeyPath: /root/bmctl-workspace/.sa-
    keys/anthos-demos-anthos-baremetal-register.json
cloudOperationsServiceAccountKeyPath: /root/bmctl-workspace/.sa-keys/anthos-
    demos-anthos-baremetal-cloud-ops.json
gcrKeyPath: /root/bmctl-workspace/.sa-keys/anthos-demos-anthos-baremetal-
    gcr.json
```

Cluster type

Depending on the chosen cluster deployment model, set the type spec value in the Cluster custom resource accordingly, choosing between admin, hybrid, or standalone as in the following example:

```
---
apiVersion: baremetal.cluster.gke.io/v1
kind: Cluster
metadata:
 name: admin-cluster
 namespace: cluster-admin-cluster
spec:
 type: hybrid
```

Control plane configuration

Depending on the chosen control plane architecture, add the IP address of the target control plane node in the nodePoolSpec: specification in the controlPlane: section. An example follows with an HA architecture based on three control plane nodes. Remember, if you want to enable a highly available control plane, you need to supply at least three IP addresses:

```
controlPlane:
  nodePoolSpec:
    nodes:
    # Control plane node pools. Typically, this is either a single machine
    # or three machines if using a high availability deployment.
    - address: 172.16.0.3
    - address: 172.16.0.4
    - address: 172.16.0.5
```

Pod and Services CIDR blocks

The clusterNetwork: section includes the CIDR ranges assigned to Pods and Kubernetes Service objects inside the cluster; these ranges are visible only inside the cluster and are never used externally. Change the defaults only if there is any overlap with existing services on your network that any running Pod in the cluster could need to contact.

Load balancer configuration

You need to populate the `loadBalancer:` section based on the chosen load balancer mode (bundled or manual) and the desired configuration options for that mode. A description of the various specifications follows:

- `mode`—The load balancer mode; you need to choose between `bundled` or `manual`.
- `ports.controlPlaneLBPort`—The port on which the load balancer serves the Kubernetes API server.
- `vips.controlPlaneVIP`—The VIP assigned to the Kubernetes API server on the cluster.
- `vips.ingressVIP`—The VIP assigned to the layer-7 (L7) Istio Ingress gateway on the cluster; this must be part of the address pool defined later. This VIP is needed only if the cluster is hybrid, standalone, or user; it's not needed on the admin cluster and can stay commented out.
- `addressPools`—The pool used by the data plane load balancer to assign VIPs to the Ingress gateway and `LoadBalancer` type Kubernetes Service objects; it must include the Ingress VIP defined earlier, but it's not needed on the admin cluster and can stay commented out.
- `nodePoolSpec`—Lists the address of the nodes in which you want to deploy the bundled load balancers. It needs to be used only if you want to specify dedicated worker nodes for bundled load balancers. If left commented out, the load balancers will be deployed on control plane nodes.

Remember that if the bundled load balancer is being deployed, all the VIPs (control plane and address pools, including the Ingress gateway) must be in the same subnet of the load balancer nodes. The following code shows a configuration for a hybrid cluster with bundled load balancers deployed on two dedicated worker nodes with the IP addresses 172.16.0.7 and 172.16.0.7:

```
# Load balancer configuration
  loadBalancer:
    mode: bundled
    ports:
      controlPlaneLBPort: 443
    vips:
      controlPlaneVIP: 172.16.0.16
      ingressVIP: 172.16.0.17
    addressPools:
    - name: pool1
      addresses:
      - 172.16.0.17-172.16.0.26
    nodePoolSpec:
     nodes:
     - address: 172.16.0.7
     - address: 172.16.0.8
```

Proxy configuration

If nodes need to pass through an HTTP proxy to connect to the internet, populate the proxy: section with the needed information:

- url—The URL that the proxy server is accessible on in the format http:// username:password@fqdn:port
- noProxy—A list of IPs, hostnames, or domains that should not be proxied

The following example configures an entry for a proxy server accessible at http:// 172.16.0.101:3128 with no authentication needed and a noProxy entry for the 172.16.0.0/16 range, which tells the system to exclude sending IPs in that range to the proxy server:

```
proxy:
  noProxy: // specifies a list of IPs, hostnames, and domains that should
    skip the proxy.
  - 172.16.0.0/16
  url: http://172.16.0.101:3128 // address of the proxy server.
```

Cloud operations for logging and monitoring

To configure the options for logging and monitoring, you need to add the projectID and location, described next, in the clusterOperations: section:

- projectID—The project ID of the project in which you want to host metrics and logs.
- location—A Google Cloud region where you want to store logs and metrics. It's a good idea to choose a region that is near your on-prem data center.

By default, Cloud operations collect only logs and metrics from workloads in the admin cluster and for user clusters and workloads in system namespaces such as kube-system, gke-system, gke-connect, istio-system, and config-management-system. System components logs and metrics are used also by Google support to troubleshoot problems in case of support cases. In addition to the metrics for system namespaces, Cloud operations also collect metrics on resource usage on nodes from all the Pods.

You can also configure Cloud operations to collect application logs and use Managed Service for Prometheus to collect application metrics. You can enable both capabilities after installation by modifying the stackdriver custom resources, as in other Anthos deployment options.

Storage configuration

The storage: section includes the configuration for the local volume provisioner (LVP) that you can use to provide persistent volumes using mount points on local nodes. Using local persistent volumes binds the Pod to a specific disk and node. If that disk or node becomes unavailable, then the Pod also becomes unavailable. Due to this, workloads using local PVs need to be resilient to this kind of failure. Therefore, using local persistent volumes generally fits proof of concept or advanced use cases where data persistence is not critical or data is replicated to other volumes and is recoverable in case of node or disk unavailability.

The three types of storage classes for local PVs in an Anthos on bare metal cluster follow:

- *LVP node mounts*—This storage class creates a local PV for each mounted disk in a specified directory. Each PV maps to a disk with a capacity equal to the underlying disk capacity. The total number of local PVs created in the cluster is the number of disks mounted under the path across all nodes.
- *LVP share*—This storage class creates a local PV backed by subdirectories in a local, shared filesystem on every node in the cluster. These subdirectories are automatically created during cluster creation. Workloads using this storage class will share capacity and input/output operations per second because the PVs are backed by the same shared filesystem.
- *Anthos system*—This storage class creates preconfigured local PVs during cluster creation that are used by Anthos system Pods. Do not change or delete this storage class, and do not use this storage class for stateful apps.

The `lvpNodeMounts:` section contains the parameters described here to configure the LVP node mounts:

- `path`—Local node directory path under which the disk to be used as local persistent volumes are mounted.
- `storageClassName`—The `StorageClass` with which PVs will be created. The `StorageClass` is created during cluster creation.

The `lvpShare:` section contains the following parameters to configure the LVP share:

- `path`—The local node directory path under which subdirectories will be created on each host. A local PV will be created for each subdirectory.
- `storageClassName`—The `StorageClass` with which PVs will be created. The `StorageClass` is created during cluster creation.
- `numPVUnderSharedPath`—The number of subdirectories to create under `path`. The total number of LVPs that share persistent volumes in the cluster would be this number multiplied by the number of nodes.

The example configuration that follows uses the default parameters for a hybrid cluster:

```
storage:
  lvpNodeMounts:
    path: /mnt/localpv-disk
    storageClassName: local-disks
  lvpShare:
    path: /mnt/localpv-share
    storageClassName: local-shared
    numPVUnderSharedPath: 5
```

Authentication

As mentioned earlier, Anthos on bare metal uses the Anthos Identity Service authentication proxy to integrate with existing identity providers through OpenID Connect

(OIDC) or LDAP. Anthos Identity Service allows users to authenticate using existing corporate credentials both through the GCP console and kubectl (in that case, the gcloud CLI is used to authenticate and create a kubeconfig file containing the ID token to be used by kubectl).

The `authentication:` section in the cluster configuration file can be used to configure authentication during cluster creation. It is also possible to configure authentication after cluster creation using the `ClientConfig` object or fleet-level Anthos Identity Service.

The following example configuration sets the parameters for OIDC authentication during cluster creation:

```
authentication:
  oidc:
    issuerURL: "https://infra.example.dev/adfs"
    clientID: "be654652-2c45-49ff-9d7c-3663cee9ba51"
    clientSecret: "clientSecret"
    kubectlRedirectURL: "http://localhost:44320/callback"
    username: "unique_name"
    usernamePrefix: "oidc:"
    group: "groups"
    groupPrefix: "oidc:"
    scopes: "allatclaims"
    extraParams: "resource=token-groups-claim"
    deployCloudConsoleProxy: true
    certificateAuthorityData: base64EncodedCACertificate
    proxy: http://10.194.2.140:3128
```

The example shown next uses LDAP:

```
authentication:
  - name: ldap
    ldap:
      connectionType: ldaps
      group:
        baseDN: ou=Groups,dc=onpremidp,dc=example,dc=net
        filter: (objectClass=*)
        identifierAttribute: dn
      host: ldap.google.com:636
      user:
        baseDN: ou=Users,dc=onpremidp,dc=example,dc=net
        filter: (objectClass=*)
        identifierAttribute: uid
        loginAttribute: uid
      serviceAccountSecret:
        name: google-ldap-client-secret
        namespace: anthos-identity-service
        type: tls
```

Node pools for worker nodes

If the first cluster in an installation is a hybrid or standalone cluster intended to host user workloads, you will need to configure the worker nodes NodePool resource in the cluster config file, providing the IP addresses of the target worker nodes. An example using three worker nodes in a node pool follows:

```
# Node pools for worker nodes
apiVersion: baremetal.cluster.gke.io/v1
kind: NodePool
metadata:
 name: node-pool-1
 namespace: cluster-hybrid-cluster
spec:
 clusterName: hybrid-cluster
 nodes:
 - address: 172.16.0.8
 - address: 172.16.0.9
 - address: 172.16.0.10
```

> **NOTE**   If the cluster is an admin cluster, this section is not needed.

CREATING THE CLUSTER

Now that we have a fully populated configuration file, we can deploy the cluster using the bmctl create cluster option as follows:

```
bmctl create cluster -c CLUSTER_NAME
```

Replace CLUSTER_NAME with the name of the cluster you defined when you created the cluster configuration file. This process will take some time, and once the cluster has been successfully created, you will be able to connect to it by using the generated kubeconfig file.

CONNECTING TO THE CLUSTER

After cluster creation is completed, you can use the kubeconfig file created by the installation tool inside the bmctl-workspace/CLUSTER NAME folder to connect to it using kubectl.

You can also connect from the GCP console using a bearer token. Many kinds of bearer tokens are supported. The easiest method is to create a Kubernetes Service Account in the cluster and use its bearer token to log in.

If you configured the cluster for identity integration with an identity provider, you can authorize existing users and groups to perform specific actions on specific resources creating RoleBindings or ClusterRoleBindings to assign them to roles that have the desired permissions. After you have created the needed bindings, you can log in to the cluster from the GCP console by selecting the option Authenticate with Identity Provider Configured for the Cluster.

To authenticate to the cluster to perform actions through kubectl, you need to perform the following steps after you created the needed RoleBindings and/or ClusterRoleBindings:

1   *Create and distribute the authentication configuration file.* You need to create an authentication configuration file that will be distributed to the clients that

would need to access the cluster with kubectl. This file contains the OIDC configuration needed from the gcloud CLI to initiate the authentication and token request from the client.

Execute the following command from the admin workstation or any machine that has access to the kubeconfig file created by the installation:

```
gcloud anthos create-login-config --kubeconfig CLUSTER_KUBECONFIG
```

Replace CLUSTER_KUBECONFIG with the kubeconfig file created by the installation. If the command completes successfully, the authentication configuration file, named kubectl-anthos-config.yaml, is created in the current directory. This kubeconfig file provides admin access to the cluster and should be provided only to people who need to access the cluster with kubectl for administrative tasks. Most organizations should secure this file using existing security standards that are part of a "break-glass" process.

2 *Authenticate with the cluster.* The client machine used to access the cluster needs to have kubectl and the gcloud CLI, including the anthos-auth component. From the client machine, execute the following command to obtain an ID token from the OIDC provider and configure the local kubeconfig accordingly to successfully authenticate with the cluster:

```
gcloud anthos auth login \
 --cluster CLUSTER_NAME \
 --user USER_NAME \
 --login-config AUTH_CONFIG_FILE_PATH \
 --login-config-cert CA_CERT_PEM_FILE \
 --kubeconfig CLUSTER_KUBECONFIG
```

The login options are described here:

- CLUSTER_NAME—Optional. This is the name of the cluster as you want it to be defined in the target kubeconfig file. If this flag is omitted, you are prompted to choose from the clusters that are specified in your authentication configuration file.
- USER_NAME—Optional. This is the username to use in the kubeconfig file; if omitted, it defaults to CLUSTER_NAME-anthos-default-user.
- AUTH_CONFIG_FILE_PATH—Specifies the path of the authentication configuration file.
- CA_CERT_PEM_FILE—Specifies the path to a PEM certificate file from your CA, which is needed if the authentication configuration file is stored on an HTTPS server.
- CLUSTER_KUBECONFIG—The target kubeconfig file where the OIDC ID token is written; if omitted, it defaults to the kubectl default location.

The command will open the browser on the OIDC provider consent login page where you need to insert credentials. Your kubeconfig file now contains an ID token that your kubectl commands will use to authenticate with the Kubernetes API server on your cluster.

17.4.2 *Creating a user cluster*

Once you've created an admin or hybrid cluster, you can add user clusters to it. You do this by applying a new config file that contains only the `Cluster` and `NodePool` custom resource manifests for the new cluster. The high-level steps to create the first cluster follow:

1 Use bmctl to create a cluster config template file.
2 Modify the config file with the desired settings.
3 Apply the config file with bmctl.

These tasks are a subset of what you already did to create the first cluster. In the next section, we will detail the configuration file to deploy the user cluster.

CREATING THE CLUSTER CONFIGURATION

As you did for first cluster creation, launch the following command to create the cluster config file

```
bmctl create config -c CLUSTER_NAME
```

where `CLUSTER_NAME` is the name you want to give to the user cluster.

POPULATING THE CLUSTER CONFIGURATION FILE

As you did for the first cluster creation, you need to prepare the configuration file created by the `create config` command. The file is saved by default in a folder named with the cluster name inside a folder named bmctl-workspace.

For many of the sections of the config file, the same instructions already given for first cluster creation apply to the user cluster, too, so follow the instructions given in the "Populating the cluster configuration file" in section 17.4.1.

> **NOTE** It's important to ensure the IP addresses used in the control plane and load balancer sections and NodePool resources don't overlap with the ones you already used for the first cluster.

In the next section, you will find the tasks that are specific for a user cluster.

Removing the credentials section

The user cluster will use the credentials provided during admin/hybrid cluster creation, so we do not need to supply the credentials for GCP. Because these are not required, we need to delete the lines from the file, such as the section containing pointers to keys:

```
gcrKeyPath: <path to GCR service account key>
sshPrivateKeyPath: <path to SSH private key, used for node access>
gkeConnectAgentServiceAccountKeyPath: <path to Connect agent service account
    key>
```

```
gkeConnectRegisterServiceAccountKeyPath: <path to Hub registration service
    account key>
cloudOperationsServiceAccountKeyPath: <path to Cloud Operations service
    account key>
```

Cluster type
Set the type spec value in the Cluster to user:

```
---
apiVersion: baremetal.cluster.gke.io/v1
kind: Cluster
metadata:
 name: user-cluster
 namespace: cluster-user-cluster
spec:
 # Cluster type. This can be:
 type: user
```

LOAD BALANCER CONFIG
Next, you need to supply the configuration for the user cluster load balancer as follows. The IP addresses used here cannot overlap with those assigned to the first cluster's load balancing:

```
# Sample user cluster config for load balancer and address pools
loadBalancer:
    vips:
      controlPlaneVIP: 10.200.0.71
      ingressVIP: 10.200.0.72
    addressPools:
    - name: pool1
      addresses:
      - 10.200.0.72-10.200.0.90
```

CREATING THE CLUSTER
After you complete the cluster configuration file, you can create the first cluster with the following command:

```
bmctl create cluster -c CLUSTER_NAME --kubeconfig ADMIN_KUBECONFIG
```

Once the user cluster deployment is completed, you can use the kubeconfig that is generated to connect to the new cluster.

CONNECTING TO THE CLUSTER
After cluster creation, you can get the kubeconfig to connect to it using kubectl from the Secret created in the user cluster namespace by the installation process. An example command to extract the kubeconfig follows:

```
kubectl --kubeconfig ADMIN_KUBECONFIG get secret USER_CLUSTER_NAME-kubeconfig
-n USER_CLUSTER_NAMESPACE -o 'jsonpath={.data.value}' | base64 -d > bmctl-
workspace/user-cluster/USER_CLUSTER_NAME-kubeconfig
```

You can also connect from the GCP console using a bearer token, or, if you configured the cluster for identity integration, users can authenticate with the cluster from the GCP console and gcloud CLI following the steps described in "Connecting to the cluster" in section 17.4.1.

17.5   Upgrading clusters

When a new version of Anthos on bare metal is released, you can upgrade your clusters. In nonstandalone cluster installations, you need to upgrade the admin/hybrid cluster first, and then the user clusters.

17.5.1   Upgrading an admin, standalone, or hybrid cluster

The steps to perform an upgrade to an admin, standalone, or hybrid cluster follow:

1 Modify the cluster config file used during cluster creation to change the Anthos on bare metal cluster version from the existing one to the one you want to upgrade to. See the following example configuration for an upgrade to version 1.13:

```
apiVersion: baremetal.cluster.gke.io/v1
kind: Cluster
metadata:
 name: admin-cluster
 namespace: cluster-admin-cluster
spec:
 type: hybrid
 # Anthos cluster version.
 anthosBareMetalVersion: 1.13.0
```

2 Download the desired version of the bmctl tool (the version to which you want to upgrade the cluster):

```
gs://anthos-baremetal-release/bmctl/<VERSION>/linux-amd64/bmctl
```

3 Execute the following command to upgrade the cluster

```
bmctl upgrade cluster -c CLUSTER_NAME --kubeconfig ADMIN_KUBECONFIG
```

where CLUSTER_NAME is the name of the cluster and ADMIN_KUBECONFIG is the kubeconfig file created by the installation.

17.5.2   Upgrading a user cluster

After you have upgraded the admin or hybrid cluster, you can upgrade the user cluster(s) with the following steps:

1 As done for the admin/hybrid cluster config file, modify the user cluster config file to change the Anthos on bare metal cluster version from the existing one to the one you want to upgrade to.

2   Execute the following command to upgrade the cluster version

```
bmctl upgrade cluster -c CLUSTER_NAME --kubeconfig ADMIN_KUBECONFIG
```

where CLUSTER_NAME is the user cluster name to be upgraded and ADMIN_
KUBECONFIG is the kubeconfig file created by the installation of the first admin/
hybrid cluster.

Summary

- Anthos on bare metal allows an organization to deploy Anthos on non-VMware platforms, including bare metal or alternate hypervisors.
- Different deployment options are provided when using the bare metal installation, including admin/user, hybrid, and standalone clusters.
- Anthos on bare metal includes multiple choices for load balancing, including using an external load balancer, known as manual mode, or the included option, known as bundled mode. Bundled mode will deploy an HAProxy solution for the control plane and MetalLB for workloads.
- The default storage option provided by the bare metal installation is limited to local host storage and should be used only for development clusters.
- Installing Anthos on bare metal provides an easy deployment and upgrade process, using a few self-documented configuration files that are deployed using a single executable, bmctl.

index

RELATED MANNING TITLES

Kubernetes in Action, Second Edition
by Marko Lukša

ISBN 9781617297618
1017 pages (estimated), $69.99
Summer 2023 (estimated)

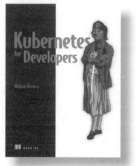

Kubernetes for Developers
by William Denniss

ISBN 9781617297175
265 pages (estimated), $59.99
Summer 2023 (estimated)

Microservices Patterns
by Chris Richardson

ISBN 9781617294549
520 pages, $49.99
October 2018

Cloud Native Patterns
by Cornelia Davis

ISBN 9781617294297
400 pages, $49.99
May 2019

For ordering information, go to www.manning.com